CANON LAW

Libero Gerosa

Continuum
London New York

First published in North America and the United Kingdom 2002 by

The Continuum International Publishing Group Inc
370 Lexington Avenue, New York, NY 10017

The Continuum International Publishing Group Ltd
The Tower Building, 11 York Road, London SE1 7NX

First published in Continental Europe 2002 by
LIT VERLAG Münster – Hamburg – Berlin – London
Grevener Str. 179   D-48159 Münster

Originally published as *Das Recht der Kirche*
© 1996 by Bonifatius GmbH Druck – Buch – Verlag, Paderborn

English translation and English language edition © 2002 by LIT VERLAG

Printed in Germany

Library of Congress Cataloging-in-Publication Data

Gerosa, Libero.
Canon law / Libero Gerosa
     p. cm.
   Includes bibliographical references and index.
   ISBN: 0-8264-1390-0 (hardcover) - - ISBN 0-8264-1391-9 (pbk.)
   1. Canon law. I. Title. KBU2215.G47   2002
   262.9–dc21

2002002077

CONTENTS

PREFACE

Notwithstanding its central position as one of the main theological subjects (Art. 51 no.16 of the Ordinationes de la Sapientia Christiana) Canon Law continues to be a discipline whose themes and problems hardly disturb theologians. In addition to this, since the Vatican Council II there has been a reductionist understanding, very widespread among believers, and even among the cultivators of the theological and pastoral sciences, as if it were a positivistic, sociological and merely external dimension of the life of the Church. Behind this we come across the unsubstantiated impression of an irredeemable hiatus between the experience of the law on the one hand and the experience of the faith in the Church of today on the other. The key conciliar concept of the *communio ecclesiarum* implies nevertheless a structural and human reality in which is embodied with its unifying force, a theological dimension, namely, the grace conceded by means of the word and sacrament guaranteed by the apostolic succession, for which Canon Law is not only founded anthropologically and sociologically but also theologically.

The basic thinking that inspires the present manual is rightly the conviction that the whole of Canon Law, as much as an internal structure of the ecclesiastical community as well as in the sense of a science with its own epistemology and methodology, conforms and clarifies starting from the original elements of the Church just as the author understands them: word, sacrament, apostolic succession and charism. With this conception it also agrees with von Balthasar according to whom Canon Law as *communio* has in the Church the function of guaranteeing that she is and continues to be a community in love: A Community in that love whose origin is Jesus Christ and which is given to mankind by the Holy Spirit. On this basis the author succeeds in offering us a global and consistently theological interpretation of Canon Law, realising in this a function which has scarcely been covered by any of the other manuals in use. The systematic starting point chosen for this book already sharply distinguishes it from the other compendiums and commentaries that have appeared in recent years, indicating in its own external structure this integral theological reading of Canon Law as a living and actual vision of the reality of the Church.

In this work, which intends to be an aid for students, we reflect also on the growing connection of the author with the interdisciplinary work in the character and manner of thinking of AMATECA. The constant dealing with experts of other theological disciplines and of very different cultural origins indicates that Canon Law can also show the way that *"the unity of the entire theological lesson emerges clearly from the internal roots of each theme, in a way that all the subjects are directed towards an intensive knowledge of the knowledge of Christ"* (Sapientia Christiana 67,2). Behind all of this it is not difficult to guess that this is actuating the conviction of J. Ratzinger that within the framework of theology there is need of a constant *ablatio*, that is to say, an elimination of the antiquated and the superfluous so that the "nobiles forma", that is to say, the really essential, emerges. Only thus can we once again make fruitful and keep alive the relationship between an experience of the faith and an experience of ecclesial law. Due to this, this manual could be very useful and profitable.

Antonio Maria Ruoco Varela
Cardinal Archbishop of Madrid

INTRODUCTION

The principle that inspired this book is the following: Canon Law can be explained starting from three fundamental elements of the Church: Word, Sacrament and Charism. It was my teacher, Eugenio Corecco, who had the fruitful insight of this principle, at one and the same time epistemological and pedagogic. Together we then envisaged, and subsequently projected, the editing of a manual which would represent the finished exposition and the systematic application of this principle. The pastoral obligations, as Bishop of Lugano, of my teacher and friend, then the testing time of his illness, borne with a serene dignity, and virtually transformed into a new lesson in humanity, unfortunately prevented Eugenio Corecco from devoting himself in any way to the development in detail of this work. It fell to me to give form and content to the chapters we had conceived for this manual. I succeeded in bringing this to completion before Monsignor Corecco died. He was ascribed with me as co-author of the Italian edition of this work which seemed to me both a gesture of just recognition and of sincere affection in his regard, as if to seal with a last sign such a long tradition of thinking and working together.

In agreement with the scientific direction of AMATECA, it is in my name only that I now publish this work in different languages, because in reality I am effectively the author. This detracts nothing from the debt that I never cease to acknowledge to myself towards Eugenio Corecco for all that he taught me, from the university chair as in life.

In the preparation of the German edition, which has every reason to be considered as the principal, I have profited from the assistance of a number of collaborators, who I again thank very warmly here. I finally owe particular thanks to Dominik Burghardt (Paderborn) and especially to James G Nicol (Glasgow), who in different ways have collaborated in the editing of this English edition.

Lugano, 1 September 2000
Libero Gerosa

ABBREVIATIONS

Besides the usual in the scientific field and those more familiar to the study of Canon Law, the following abbreviations have also been used:

Actas in CIDC = *La Norma en el Derecho Canonico.* Actas del *III* Congreso Internacional de Derecho Canonico, Pamplona 1979.

Actes IV CIDC = *Les droits fondamentaux du chrétien dans l'Église et dans la Société.* Actes du IV Congrès Internacional de Droit Canonique, a cura di E. Corecco, Herzog-A. Scola, Fribourg-Freiburg i. Br.-Milano 1981.

Actes V CIDC = *Le nouveau Code de Droit Canonique.* Actes du V Congres International de Droit Canonique, a cura di M. Theriault-J. Thorn, Ottawa 1986.

Akten VI IKKR = *Das Konsoziative Element in der Kirche.* Akten des VI. Internationalen Kongresses für kanonisches Recht, a cura di W Aymans-K. Th. Geringer-H. Schmitz, St. Ottilien 1989.

Actes VII CIDC = *La synodalité: la participation au gouvernement dans l'Eglise.* Actes du VIIe Congres International de Droit Canonique (Paris 21-28 septembre 1990), 2 Voll., Paris 1992.

Aymans-Mörsdorf = W. Aymans-K. Mörsdorf, *Kanonisches Recht. Lehrbuch aufgrund des Codex Iuris Canonici,* Begründet von KanR I E. Eichmann, fortgeführt von K. Mörsdorf, neubearbeitet von W. Aymans, Bd. I: Einleitende Grundfragen und Allgemeine Normen, Paderborn-München-Wien-Zürich 1991.

Communio = Strumento internazionale per un lavoro teologico: Communio, Milano 1972 ss.; dal 1993 Rivista Internazionale di Teologia e Cultura: Communio.

EDD = *Enciclopedia del diritto,* diretta da C. Mortati-F Santoro Passarelli, Milano 1958 ss.

EV = *Enchiridion Vaticanum.* Testi ufficiali e versione italiana. Vol. I: Documenti ufficiali del Concilio Vaticano II (1962-1965), 11. a Ed., Bologna 1979; Voll. II ss.: Documenti ufficiali della Santa Sede, 10.a Ed., Bologna 1976 ss.

HdbkathKR = *Handbuch des katholischen Kirchenrechts,* a cura di J. Listl-H. Müller-H. Schmitz, Regensburg 1983.

LKD = *Lexikon der katholischen Dogmatik,* a cura di W Beinert, Freiburg-Basel-Wien 1987.

MK = *Münsterischer Kommentar zum Codex Iuris Canonici unter besonderer Berücksichtigung der Rechtslage in Deutschland, Österreich und Schweiz,* hrsg. von K. Lüdicke, Loseblattsammlung Essen, Stand vom November 1993.

Mörsdorf, Lb = K. Mörsdorf, *Lehrbuch des Kirchenrechts auf Grund des Codex Iuris Canonici,* 11.a Ed., München-Paderborn-Wien 1964-1979.

NDDC = *Nuovo Dizionario di Diritto Canonico,* a cura di C. C. Salvador-V De Paolis-G. Ghirlanda, Cinisello Balsamo (Milano) 1993.

Periodica = Periodica de re morali canonica liturgica, Roma 1905 ss.; dal 1991 Periodica de re canonica.

Caution: The notes are numbered starting from 1 in every individual chapter thus the abbreviation op. cit. refers to works already quoted in the same chapter.

First Chapter: The Theological Foundation of Canon Law

1. The Experience of Law in the Ecclesial Communion

However liberating belonging to the ecclesial community can be, the normal reaction of the faithful before Canon Law is somewhat similar to that of the citizen before the law of the State. Even in the Church the perception of the juridical is not univocal and presents, at least under its phenomenological profile, not a few analogies with the common and ambivalent experience of the law of every human society.

1.1 The Ambivalence of the Experience of Law

The common phenomenological experience of law is characterised, substantially, by two diverse and contrasting perceptions.

Indeed, on the one hand the law is perceived by the citizen and mankind in general as an external reality, like a human expression of a heteronomous will power, which limits the freedom and autonomy of the person. The law is seen as the concrete manifestation of the compulsory force of an organised power system or downrightly as the expression of the free will of the strongest.

Consequently the law appears as a manipulatable reality, determined by ideology and whoever holds the reins of power, as well as a non-unitarian totality of heterogeneous and often antinomous norms.

On the other hand, the same law reveals itself to mankind as the indispensable instrument that guarantees, precisely through the imposition of determined limits on individual liberty, order and peace for common civil life. In this latter viewpoint the law manifests itself to mankind as a social factor of prime importance that permits the individual and the collective to plan their civil future with confidence. The law is therefore perceived as a balancing element and as the human expression of a superior justice that transcends individual interests.

The overlapping of the two perceptions, the former negative and the latter positive, explains why the phenomenological experience of the law can be defined as paradoxical.

The situation of the *christifidelis* faced with Canon Law is for some somewhat similar and therefore also paradoxical.

In the Church too the experience of ecclesial law reveals itself above all as negative: the confession of faith in Christ, mankind's Redeemer, which forms a strong spur to personal liberty, is limited in its concrete manifestations by canonical norm; so too divine law, which finds in prophesy and charism two particular expressions, can historically affirm all its binding force only through the interpretation and positivisation of human law. On the other hand, less immediate is the positive experience of Canon Law as a totality of norms that guarantee the permanence of the identity of the Church and the unity of the symbol of the faith, inseparable from the action of the Holy Spirit, through the protection of the substantial truth of the Sacrament and the Word of God.

Canon Law guarantees the objectivity and the truth of the ecclesial experience because, through the protection of the irrepressible value of fidelity in the communion for the self-realisation of the Church, it teaches the individual faithful to overcome the temptation of individualism and the particular Churches to overcome the parallel temptation of particularism. This given fact, which forms the essence of the positivity of Canon Law, is not however immediately grasped and recognised as such by the faithful.

In this way the pre-eminence, at least on the phenomenological-existential level, of the negative aspects of the paradoxical experience of Canon Law has often been the enticement, from the beginning of the Church up until today, for many spiritualistic movements. Exasperating the tension between *caritas* and *ius*, as well as the tensions between contingent and transcendent, between particular and universal, between historical and eschatological, and finally between institutional and charismatic, these spiritualisms substantially anticipated the conflicts and then exploded with the protestant Reformation and crystallised in the antithesis established by Luther on the soteriological level between law and gospel, a contrast that has re-emerged in the post-Council period in the Catholic field under the form of a cautionary dichotomy between Canon Law and Sacrament, as well as between juridical and pastoral structures.

1.2 THE INFLUENCE OF ECCLESIOLOGICAL SPIRITUALISM AND JURIDICAL POSITIVISM ON THE CONCEPT OF ECCLESIAL LAW

The contrast between law and gospel which has its origins in the irremediable ecclesiological dualism between *ecclesia abscondita* or *spiritualis* and *ecclesia universalis* or *visibilis* prevents protestant theology from recognising in Canon Law – retaining nevertheless a human element from which the ecclesial reality cannot completely prescind – any salvational value.

On the contrary, Luther having expelled Canon Law from the content of the faith due to having denied every link between the juridical element of the Church and her dogma, the problematic which opens itself up around this dimension of the Christian experience ends up flowing, through the rediscovery of the proper origins and proper ecclesial knowledge stirred up by the romanticism in German Protestantism, in the radical negation of Rudolph Sohm: "The fragility of human faith believed it was able to guarantee the permanence of the Church of Christ by human means, with columns and wooden beams of a human juridical order ... Canon Law has shown itself above all as an attack on the spiritual essence of the Church ... The nature of the Church is spiritual, the nature of the law is worldly. The nature of Canon Law stands in contradiction to the nature of the Church" [1]. On the same track, but much later, even in the Catholic field the law of the Church would be characterised in an analogous way. In fact, even before he chose the evangelical Church, Joseph Klein defines Canon Law as an "external reality" in the Church in contrast to the liturgy. [2]. As such this constitutes a threat to the liberty of the faith.

In the protestant camp, the reaction to such a radical challenge is immediate. First of all Karl Barth, inverting the Lutheran formula of "law and gospel", seeks to re-introduce the law, whether secular or canonical, in the content of the faith as an element proposed and judged by Revelation. The attempt however proved to be unsatisfactory because of his aversion to natural law and philosophy, which prevented Barth from marrying, as in medieval culture, divine law with human and natural law. In fact, the latter remained a purely human reality, compared with which divine law is totally transcendent. Even the most recent attempts, for example those of Eric Wolf and Hans Dombois (which will be dealt with later!) did not resolve the problem. In fact, for them divine law constitutes only a human idea (in the platonic sense of the term), which is structured with the help of external biblical indications (*biblische Weisung*) of calvinist origins, and therefore these are simply limited in pont of fact to displacing the dualism of Luther from the ecclesiological level to the juridical, leaving it however unaltered in substance. The ultimate reason lies in the fact that these attempts, although exhibiting the great merit of confronting the problem from a decidedly theological point of view, are all indebted – albeit according to different times and means – to a double error in method. Today, as

---

[1] R. Sohm, *Kirchenrecht, I Die geschichtlichen Grundlagen,* Leipzig 1892 (2. Aufl. 1923, Neudruck: Darmstadt 1970), p. 700.

[2] cf. J. Klein, *Skandalon. Um das Wesen des Katholizismus,* Tübingen 1958, p. 194 and p. 119.

it was yesterday for Sohm, this double methodological oversight is the result of an ecclesiological spiritualism and juridical positivism. [3]

The ecclesiological spiritualism, which conceives of the Church essentially as the exclusive work of the Holy Spirit, hinders these attempts at a theology of Canon Law from reaching a convincing conclusion because they are inexorably kept enclosed in a protestant vision of divine law. The latter, from Luther until the present, is understood " ... in a so spiritualised sense that it cannot see how it can be binding for the historical church. Protestant theology does not manage to establish a binding connection between the church and the Christian but only a direct connection between God and the consciousness of man." [4] In effect Canon Law, already in the vision of Luther which recognises a soteriological sense to the *ius divinum* of the *ecclesia spiritualis,* in its function as an ordering principle of the *ecclesia visibilis* remains inexorably human law, and as such incapable of binding the conscience of the Christian: this is required only for reasons dictated by the sociological necessity of regulating the communitarian life of Christians, as if they were simple citizens and not living members of the mystical body which is the Church.

Juridical positivism, for which there is no law other than that which is univocally conceived by the juridical experience of the State, for its part hinders these same attempts to free it, on the scientific level, from the monist conception of the law and therefore to vindicate not only in abstract the autonomy of the Church before the State, but to concretise it in an autonomy of Canon Law in comparison with that of the State. Without the conviction of the fact that Canon Law is not assimilable to the secular law but is instead a law *sui generis,* some theoretical attempt to restore a theological legitimacy to Canon Law is destined to leave the fundamental question without a convincing reponse: does the Church, by the internal requirements of her theological being and her mission of salvation, really and necessarily have need of Canon Law?

1.3 THE NEED FOR A CRITICAL DIALOGUE WITH THE PHILOSOPHY OF LAW

The double error in method revealed in the preceding section is certainly not exclusive to protestant theology. Even in the Catholic tradition – characterised by a deep unity between the *analogia fidei* and the *analogia entis* [5] – there

---

[3]   It is the agreed opinion of A. Ruoco Varela-E. Corecco, *Sacramento e diritto: antinomia nella Chiesa,* Milano 1971, p. 16

[4]   E. Corecco, *Teologia del diritto canonico, in: Nuovo Dizionario di teologia,* a cura di G. Barbaglio-S. Dianich, Alba 1976, pp. 1711-1753, here p. 1753.

[5]   The above as for St Thomas Aquinas the former contains the latter as its fundamental element cf. H.U. von Balthasar, *Karl Barth,* Einsiedeln 1976, p. 273; on the importance of this characteristic for clarifying the relationship between theology and philosophy, cf. G. Söhngen, *La sapienza della teologia sulla via della scienza,* in: My Sal, Vol. II, pp. 511-599.

were made, and sometimes even today are made – great concessions whether to theological spiritualism, or to juridical positivism. Indeed, although Catholic Canonism has never ceased to affirm itself as an autonomous science with regard to the law of the state, it has never succeeded in giving a precise theological definition for its proper *objectum formale quod.* If the modern canonist, like the medieval one, still defines Canon Law with the category of *iustum* or *objectum virtutis iustitiae,* even in the general theories of the XIX and XX century, developed in the more authoritative canonical schools (from that of the *Ius Publicum Ecclesiasticum* to the modern *Scuola laica italiana* and the *School of Navarra)* the natural-law principle of *ubi societas ibi ius* always re-emerges, even if under many different guises. The latter, given its philosophical roots is incapable of mediating a specific theological understanding of ecclesial law on its own. On the other hand, precisely because the faith does not threaten either reason or philosophy as much as defends them from the absolutist pretext of gnosis, [6] the theology of Canon Law cannot forget the philosophy of law. The one has need of the other and vice versa. This means that Canon Law as a science must resort to the multiplicity of the *usus philosophiae* in theology without however considering it as its *domina* in its attempt to legitimise the existence of law in the Church. A similar weakness worsens further where, under the influence anti-juridical climate of the immediate post-Council period, it was considered possible to resolve the question by simply substituting philosophy with sociology. In this case it ends up inevitably by reducing Canon Law to only an extrinsic element because it is postulated in such an exclusive way from a need for finality or for societal or ecclesial convenience.

If one wishes to avoid either every natural-law type of solution, or to reduce the law of the Church to a simple regulation or highway code for pastoral action [7], it is necessary that the theology of Canon Law avoids splitting the mystery of the Church into an internal element of a theological nature and an external one of a juridcal nature to regain, also with the help of philosophy, the complex unitareity, structural and ethical, of the ecclesial reality. In critical dialogue with the philosophy of law, the theology of Canon Law must demonstrate that the juridical dimension – in as much as it is juridical – is already present in the structural elements upon which Christ wished to establish his Church; or else, that the juridical precept is already contained in the structural elements of the plan of Salvation without losing anything of its juridical character for this.

---

[6] Cf. J. Ratzinger, *Wesen und Auftrag der Theologie. Versuche zu ihrer Ortsbestimmung im Disput der Gegenwart,* Einsiedeln-Freiburg 1993, p. 25.

[7] On the theological-pastoral nature of Canon Law, cf. L. Gerosa, *Diritto ecclesiale e pastorale,* Torino 1991, especially pp. 3-8.

In other words the theological nature and the juridical character of Canon Law are inseparable one from the other. If the former establishes the inalienable specificity of the law of the Church (expressed for example in the role of custom in the production of juridical norms or of canonical equity in the realisation of justice), the latter permits the understanding that in every expression of the particular attributes of such a law there persists elements (for example the order between human relations in a community or the interaction between liberty and ties that bind) common to every notion of law.

The dialogue between theology of Canon Law and the philosophy of law allows the canonist to more easily avoid on one hand the so-called danger of juridicisation of the faith and the Church, and on the other that of the evanescent theologisation of canonical norms.[8] The authentic overcoming of the antinomy between sacrament and law does not exclude but creates new possibilities for reciprocal relations between Canon Law and other forms of law. Francesco Suarez (1548-1617) sensed this when, in another cultural context, he genially synthesised the unitary origin of the law in the formula *ius divinum, sive naturale sive positivum*, restated in the CIC/1917 in the first paragraph of can. 27. According to this formula "human civil law has as its ascendent natural divine law, while Canon Law finds its immediate source of derivation in positive divine law. By virtue of the ontological dependence of human civil law on natural law, St. Thomas affirmed that the human legislator can bind his subjects not only externally, but also in conscience. From the specific ontological dependence of Canon Law on the *ius divinum positivum*, knowable only by faith, the *doctor eximius* concludes that the ecclesiastical legislator also has the power to absolutely demand from his own subjects the fulfilment of solely internal human acts. With this affirmation, Suarez has drawn all the possible conclusions for the case for the interiorisation of law, given by biblical Tradition, and emitted in a clear way already in the ninth and tenth commandments of the Decalogue"[9].

---

[8] Cf. P. Krämer, *Theologische Grundlagen des Kirchlichen Rechts nach dem CIC 1983*, in: AfkKR 153 (1984), pp. 384-398; G. Luf, *Rechtsphilosophische Grundlagen des Kirchenrechts*, in: HdbkathKR, pp. 24-32.

[9] E. Corecco, *Il valore della norma disciplinare in rapporto alla salvezza nella tradizione occidentale*, in: *Incontro fra canoni d'Oriente e d'Occidente. Atti del Congresso Internazionale*, a cura di R. Coppola, Bari 1994, Vol. 2, pp. 275-292, here pp. 285-286.

2. PRINCIPAL ATTEMPTS AT A THEOLOGICAL FOUNDATION FOR CANON LAW

2.1 THE OPEN PERSPECTIVE OF PROTESTANT JURIDICAL SCIENCE

In the protestant camp the problem of a theology of ecclesial law became acute immediately after the Second World War, when in Germany it was a question of finding a juridical collection of Churches within the new political-constitutional relationships. The principal attempts however are to be attributed not to theologians but to jurists, among who should be mentioned Johannes Heckel, Erik Wolf and Hans Dombois. Their reply to the question concerning the existence and the function of a law of the Church can be schematically summarised thus.

In the attempt to overcome the blind-alley in which the programme of "Justification and Law" of Karl Barth ended up, where the substitution of the *analogia entis* with the *analogia fidei* brought natural law to a ruthless end, these authors grasped -albeit with different levels of worth- the methodological importance of posing the problem of the existence of Canon Law contemporaneously with that of the existence and function of the Church. The law of the Church as a theological problem does not surface after the birth of the Church, but already exists before the Church and with the Church, because such a law is ultimately a postulate and necessity for the whole process of the history of salvation. As such the law of the Church is an autonomous reality and different from every form of human law and constitutes the formal limit of Canon Law which, in its material content, remains even so purely human.

What is not clear is by dint of which theological principle this law of the Church as divine law claims the right and proper existence of ecclesial law, i.e. the Canon Law of a particular Church. Indeed, on the one hand the law of the Church as divine law is so radically spiritualised as to render it practically impossible to recognise simultaneously a concrete and real juridical effectiveness, and on the other the law of the Church as the Canon Law of a particular Church is conceived in such a human way as to radically call into question, notwithstanding its qualification as ecclesial, the existence of its connection – albeit solely extrinsic – with the Church *abscondita* and with divine law. It remains nevertheless more than legitimate to ask if the normative content of the "spiritual law of charity" of Heckel, of the "biblical indications" of Wolf or of the "law of grace" of Dombois still correspond to the traditional idea of law. [10] On the other hand divine law being totally transcendent in compari-

---

[10] For a full analysis of the rich contribution of protestant theology to the theological foundation of the Canon Law of the Church, cf. E. Corecco, *Theologie des Kirchenrechts: Methodologische Ansätze,* Trier 1980, pp. 59-79; A. Ruoco Varela, *Evangelische Kirchenrecht-*

son with ecclesial law once again it becomes impossible to establish some sort of binding juridical relationship between the Church and the Christian, which also has a positive significance for the relationship between God and the conscience of man. Without recapturing the fundamental elements of the Catholic doctrine on the relationship between nature and the supernatural [11], even such Church-Christian relationships and their juridical dimensions remain obscured and in consequence the function of Canon Law will inevitably always be solely negative, because it expresses an existence exclusively justified by the sinful nature of mankind.

Conscious of this difficulty, Catholic theology has conceived its first response to the problem of the theological foundations of Canon Law, posed by protestant jurists in the period after the Second World War, also within the fuller thematic of justification, crystallised by Luther in his binominal law and gospel and by the Catholic tradition it its binominal law and grace. Only in the second round did it succeed in opening new methodological ways to the study of canon law as a whole.

2.2 CANON LAW AND ITS JUSTIFICATION IN CATHOLIC THEOLOGY

A) GRACE AS THE FOUNDATION FOR CANON LAW (SÖHNGEN)

The work *Gesetz und Evangelium* (Freiburg-München 1957) by Gottlieb Söhngen represents one of the rare and more successful attempts to analyse the theme of law and gospel from the Catholic point of view. According to the German theologian the conjunction "and" does not mean "and also", because not only for protestant theology but also for the Catholic the nature of the two words of the two-part name is not identical. "The essence of the law lies in its imperative character, while that of the gospel and of grace lies in God's participation in the heart of man. For that reason an *analogia nominum* does not exist by which it can be said that the law is also gospel and that the gospel is also law, but only an *analogia relationis* (Barth), established by the fact that the imperative of the new law – which is not just law by dint of its being law – has grace and charity as its foundation". [12] The innovation of the new law – already underlined by the formula of St. Thomas Aquinas: *Lex nova est ipsa gratia* (*S. Th.* I-II, q. 106, a. 1) – is such that it is not possible to establish a different analogy than that of the relationship between this and the ancient law of Moses. While the latter was only *extrinsecus posita*, the *nova lex evangelii is*

---

    stheologie heute. Möglichkeiten und Grenzen eines Dialogs, in: AfkKR 140 (1970), pp. 106-136.
[11] The inexhaustible richness of this tradition is masterfully illustrated by: H. De Lubac, *Le Mystère du Surnaturel,* Paris 1965.
[12] E. Corecco, *Teologia del diritto canonico,* op. cit., p. 1736.

lex data [13], as the fullness of charity. The existence of Canon Law cannot therefore be justified – as Luther did – in the same way as the Mosaic Law, that is solely as an obstacle or limit against human concupiscence. Canon Law is not justified only by sin but belongs in a positive way to the human experience, in the sign of grace. It is the latter that also contains the law and not vice versa, because in the same way with which the pedagogic power of dogma does not bring about salvation so too it is not from the formal imperative power of the juridical norms of the Church that salvation comes [14]. Nevertheless, as the medieval canonists have already underlined when they dared to identify *aequitas canonica* with God Himself, they always defer – even if it is with different degrees of intensity – to the principles contained in Revelation and thus ultimately in the Gospel. In this sense Canon Law neither leads to salvation, nor communicates grace, but is by its nature at the service of this meta-juridical reality, in which it finds its ultimate proper foundation.

B) ESCHATOLOGY AS A CONSTITUTIVE ELEMENT OF THE JURIDICAL
   CHARACTER OF THE CHURCH (RAHNER)

That divine law is present in Canon Law not only as the formal horizon, from which parenetical indications come, but also as an ontological substratum is further developed in the theology of Karl Rahner even if the latter has never directly or with any depth tackled the problem of law in the Church. In particular the ontological connection between divine law and Canon Law is highlighted by Rahner in his theological reflections on ecclesiastical office or ministry [15]. And not without reason, because even if the latter is not the most suitable starting point for developing a theology of Canon Law it certainly occupies a key place in Catholic Canon Law studies.

Without ministry even the Church, and with her the definitive and eschatological presence of Christ in the world and in history, would cease to exist. Ministry in the Church, unlike that of the Old Testament, is ultimately definitive, because it is given so that the Christian and the non-Christian can ascertain where the Church makes itself real. In its function of manifesting the eschatological presence of the Church ecclesial ministry finds its theological root, and with this claims Canon Law as its necessary expression. Indeed, the eschato-

---

[13]   G. Söhngen, *Gesetz und Evangelium*, in: LThK, Vol.4, coll. 831-835, here col. 833.

[14]   Cf. G. Söhngen, *Grundfragen einer Rechtstheologie*, München 1962, p. 28.

[15]   Cf. especially the two chapters *"Die ekklesiologische Grundlegung der Pastoraltheologie"* (pp. 117-215) and *"Die Disziplin der Kirche"* (pp. 333-343) of the: *Handbuch der Pastoraltheologie. Praktische Theologie der Kirche in ihrer Gegenwart*, hrsg. von F.X. Arnold-K. Rahner-V. Schurr-L.M. Weber, Vol. I, Freiburg-Basel-Wien 1964; cf. also: K. Rahner, *Der theologische Ansatzpunkt für die Bestimmung des Wesens des Amtpriestertums*, in: Idem, *Schriften zur Theologie*, Vol. IX, Einsiedeln-Zürich-Köln 1972 (2. Aufl.), pp. 366-372; Idem, *Kirche und Sakramente*, Freiburg-Basel-Wien 1960, pp. 85-95.

logical dimension of the Church must show to the world – in conformity with the principle of the Incarnation – its eschatological or definitive nature for salvation. The unique forms of human institution that can show this communitarian definitive nature and this human-historical irrevocability are ministry, in its function of responsibility, and the law as the binding expression of ministry. Canon Law can thus be considered – still according to Karl Rahner – as the imperative outcome of that which is indicative and constitutes the essence of the Church [16]. In this perspective this possesses simultaneously a character of service and a specific or particular relativity.

For what theological reason the New Testament ministry necessarily had need of a juridical form is not explained by Rahner if not through recourse to the societal structure of the Church, which being a community of salvation (*Heilsgesellschaft*) necessarily possesses a juridical structure [17]. But this presupposes as the major premise of the syllogism, with which the existence of ecclesial law justifies itself, the axiom *ubi societas ibi est ius,* which has a natural-law origin and as such is ultimately incapable of theologically founding Canon Law.

c) CANON LAW AS A FUNCTION OF THE CONCEPT OF CHURCH (BARION)

If for the protestant jurist Rudolph Sohm faith and law diverge radically, for the Catholic canonist Hans Barion the same realities converge to the extent of coinciding on at least two levels: first of all in the possibility of the faith assuming a juridical form without sacrificing its essence and in second place in the fact that the Church is not divided into two realities independent of each other, because the so-called Church of the law is nothing if not the legitimate realisation of the Church of Christ.

The first point of convergence is illustrated by Hans Barion through his analysis of the structure of a dogma: the latter is an assertion of faith communicated in juridical form and therefore, under the formal profile, it is a juridical norm (*Rechtssatz*) that prescribes in a binding juridical manner a content of faith. The latter, such as it is, represents an element of divine law, which in its becoming formalised in dogma contributes to juridically defining the Church. In this sense "Faith determines the concept of Church and the latter determines Canon Law" [18].

The second point of convergence between faith and law is the logical consequence of the principle affirmed many times by Hans Barion, that "Canon Law is a function of the concept of Church" [19]. In point of fact, such a prin-

---

[16] Cf. *Handbuch der Pastoraltheologie, op.* cit., pp. 136-137 and p. 336.
[17] Cf. ibid., p. 334.
[18] H. Barion, *Rudolph Sohm und die Grundlegung des Kirchenrechts,* Tübingen 1931, p.26.
[19] Ibid., p. 13.

ciple does not mean that ecclesial law is an arbitrarily chosen function of the concept of Church, rather that this represents a necessary element of the invariable structure of the Church, rooted in the divine arrangement of the Church of Christ and having the function of guaranteeing that the Church itself remains faithful to its divine origin. This function of Canon Law is strictly bound to the hierarchical constitution of the Church, because – as the German canonist loves to repeat – the hierarchy is founded on divine law and in its turn produces Canon Law. The latter, in as much as it is divine law, is founded in Revelation, in as much as it is ecclesial law, it is founded in the hierarchy; both elements taken together constitute the Church, which as such is a Church of law. The Canon Law in force is therefore nothing other than a development – albeit mediated by the hierarchy – of the foundation of the Church on the part of Christ [20].

There are two methodological weaknesses at the base of this attempt to theologically establish the existence of Canon Law: on the one hand the exclusively formal consideration of two complex and vital realities like the faith and the Church; and on the other the appeal to the foundational will of Christ, who wanted his Church also with a juridical structure [21]. Both of these methodological weaknesses are strictly bound to a conception of Church as *societas inaequalis,* substantially irreconcilable with the ecclesiology of the Vatican Council II.

2.3 THE NEW METHODOLOGICAL WAYS OF CANON LAW

If one casts an eye over the canonical production of the second half of the last century up until the promulgation of the Pio-Benedictine Code of 1917 it can easily be established that even the great canonists instead of bowing before the problem of the theological justification for Canon Law found themselves heading by preference towards a systematic study of the sources and to a lesser degree towards the development in detail of a general theory of Canon Law. The great historical-systematic works of Hinschius, Wernz, Scherer and Sägmüller represent the most important outcome of this work. The study of Canon Law after the first codification was on the contrary generally exhausted in an exegetical-manualist analysis of the norms of the code, for the most part in-

---

[20] H. Barion, *Sacra Hierarchia. Die Führungsordnung der Katholischen Kirche*, in: *Tymbos für W. Ahlmann*, Berlin 1951, pp. 18-45, here p. 18.

[21] For a fuller critique cf. P. Krämer, *Theologische Grundlegung des Kirchlichen Rechts. Die rechtstheologische Auseinandersetzung zwischen H. Barion und J. Klein im Licht des II. Vatikanischen Konzils*, Trier 1977, pp. 47-62; H.J. Pottmeyer, *Konzil oder CIC/1917? Die Konzilskritik des Kanonisten Hans Barion*, in: *Ministerium Iustitiae*. Festschrift für H. Heinemann, hrsg. von A. Gabriels-H.J.F. Reinhardt, Essen 1985, pp. 51-65.

different either to the need for their theological foundation or to the need to define the proper method of scientific work.

For all this time, and in some sectors of the study of Canon Law up until the eve of the Vatican Council II, from the methodological point of view the only point of reference – as we will see better later – was the Roman school of *Ius publicum ecclesiasticum*. It was in fact the latter that applied to the Church for the first time in a systematic way the natural-law category of extraction of *societas perfecta*, thanks to which a human institution can be said to possess all the juridic means to autonimously reach its proper aim. If the apologetic power of a similar cultural to defend the liberty of the Church before the self-affirmation of the liberal State, as a unique sovereign society, is undeniable, its weakness in the order of the theological foundation of a juridical structure for the Church is equally easily intuitable. In the last analysis the only theological reason that justifies the equation *Ecclesiam esse societam perfectam* is an act of the will of Christ understood nominalistically: it is because Christ wanted it this way that the Church is a juridically perfect society.

In the conciliar and pre-conciliar period, whether through the lessening of the apologetic necessity or even under the influence of the debate between protestants and Catholics on the theological foundation of Canon Law, various authors and schools of Canon Law abandoned the philosophical horizon and voluntarist orientation of the IPE method to begin to anticipate new method-ological means. In the second half of the last century only one exception is recorded: that of the canonical system of the law historian and canonist George Phillips (1804-1872).

A) THE BIBLICAL CATEGORY OF "REGNUM CHRISTI" (PHILLIPS)

George Phillips places the equation *Ecclesia esse Regnum Christi* at the base of his canonical system [22]. Although on the level of method a certain parallelism between this thesis and that of the central dominant doctrine of the IPE is un-deniable, the argumentative line of the German canonist (Church=Kingdom of Christ=juridical-constitutional structure) certainly presents a great advantage in the arrangement of the theological foundation of Canon Law: the axis upon which his whole system turns, that is to say the notion of the Kingdom of God, is a concept of biblical and not philosophical extraction.

On the conviction that Canon Law is a reality totally determined by the notion of Church and that the latter was founded by Christ as the Kingdom of God on earth, the German canonist bases first of all the juridic nature of the

---

[22]   This is immediately deduced from the introduction (pp.13-14) of the first volume of his famous *Kirchenrecht*: G. Phillips, *Kirchenrecht, Voll.* 1-4, Regensburg 1845-1851. The con-stitutional elements are developed in the first part (pp. 1-287) of the II volume, central to which is the question of the unity of ecclesiastical power (pp. 126-148).

constitution of the Church: there is not in fact a kingdom that does not have a monarchical and juridical constitution, therefore the Church, which is the kingdom founded by Christ, also has its monarchical constitution and its law. In second place the same category of *Regnum Christi* permits a better illustration and understanding of the unity and indivisibility of ecclesiastical power. Every power is conferred by God through the primacy, therefore not only is it not possible to radically divide or separate the *Ordo* from the *Iurisdictio,* but Canon Law in as much as it is law is founded in this unity.

Even if in Catholic theology they have talked for a long time of a monarchic episcopate it is clear enough that there is a logical leap both in the claim to be able to deduce a monarchic structure of the Church from the theological reality of the Kingdom of God, and in the affirmation that this same is of a juridic nature [23]. Moreover to identify the Church with the Kingdom of God is theologically incorrect and does not correspond to the ecclesiological doctrine of the Vatican Council II. Notwithstanding these serious limits, under the methodological profile, Phillips' work without doubt constitutes an important advance, not so much because he placed a biblical category at the centre of his canonical thinking, as much as for having identified - albeit starting from only a partial aspect of the person of Christ – in Christology itself the *locus theologicus* most appropriate to theologically establishing Canon Law.

B) THE CONCEPT OF "PRIMARY JURIDICAL ORDERING" (ITALIAN LAY CANONICAL SCHOOL)

Among the first and more important attempts, after the promulgation of the CIC/1917, to develop a methodology different from the dominant one of the IPE that of the Italian Lay School of Canon Law must surely be numbered, even if this itself never totally abandoned either the category of *societas perfecta,* or the juridical-apologetic application of claiming an autonomy for Canon Law compared with that of the State. The scientific output of this school indeed clearly distances itself from the manualism of the first half of this century, in which the concentration on the analaytical study of the Pio-Benedictine Code impeded the giving of time and space to questions relative to the theological and philosophical foundation of the law of the Church.

There are two historical-cultural factors which have driven the school of Italian lay canonists to concern themselves with the methodological renewal of their own discipline: first of all, in order to safeguard the teaching of their own proper material at the chairs of ecclesiastical law of the state faculties of jurisprudence, the need to demonstrate the scientific nature of the study of Canon Law as a juridical science became ever more acute; and in second place

---

[23]   Cf. A. Ruoco Varela-E. Corecco, *Sacramento e diritto: antinomia nella Chiesa?, op. cit., p. 38.*

the dominant positivistic attitude at these faculties necessarily demanded the accomplishment of an effort towards the foundation of Canon Law starting from the canonical system itself, without evidently having to assume on the theoretical level the pure doctrine of law, expounded by Kelsen. Starting from these historical-cultural factors the scientific foundation for Canon Law of the Lay Italian canonical school developed around two central themes; that of the juridical character or juridic-ness of Canon Law and that of the juridical quality of canonical science [24].

The proof of the juridicality of Canon Law is scientifically developed in detail starting from the concept of primary juridical ordering, apparently not derived from any previous philosophical presupposition, but in fact the fruit of nineteenth century juridical positivism. The juridical quality of the study of Canon Law is deduced from the logical-juridical examination of the canonical norms, which demonstrate the intrinsic juridical unity of such an arrangement. The theoretical ability and scientific rigour with which the lay Italian canonists developed in detail these two themes lessens however when it comes to the question of giving an account of the specific nature of Canon Law in comparison to that of the State. Here not only are they obliged to establish the epistemological incapacity of their method of scientific work, but to refer the problem of the theological foundation of Canon Law back to theology, declaring it to be simply of a para-juridical nature, because it is all directed by the category of the *salus animarum* as the ultimate purpose of canonical ordering itself [25]. This serious epistemological limit of the Italian lay canonical school cannot be overcome not even by the successive substitution of the *salus animarum* category with that of the *bonum commune ecclesiae,* because such a concept is not so much of theological origin as socio-philosophical. In the knowledge of this, at the end of the Sixties another school of lay canonists – that of Navarra - sought to overcome this epistemological limit of the lay Italian school while at the same time preserving the enormous technical-juridical baggage through its redevelopment in detail starting from a new ecclesiological and pastoral inspiration.

---

[24] For a critical review of the different contributions of the Italian Lay study of Canon Law, cf. for example: P. Fedele, *Il problema dello studio dell'insegnamento del diritto canonico e il diritto ecclesiastico in Italia,* in: Archivio di Diritto ecclesiastico 1 (1939), pp. 50-74; A. Ruoco-Varela, *Allgemeine Rechtslehre oder Theologie des kanonischen Rechts? Erwägungen zum heutigen Stand einer theologischen Grundlegung des kanonischen Rechts,* in: AfkKR 138 (1969) pp. 95-113.

[25] Cf. E. Corecco, *Teologia del diritto canonico,* op. cit., p. 1741 and above all A. De La Hera, *Introduccion a la ciencia del derecho canonico,* Madrid 1967, pp. 223-248.

c) THE ECCLESIOLOGICAL CATEGORY OF "THE PEOPLE OF GOD" (SCHOOL OF NAVARRA)

The *School of Navarra*, objectively more homogeneous than the so-called Italian lay canonists [26], is characterised by a double theoretical comparison: that with the Vatican Coucil II's proposal to study Canon Law in the light of the mystery of the Church (OT 16,4) and that with the systematic application to Canon Law of the concept of primary juridical ordering, developed in detail by Italian lay canonists.

By virtue of the former comparison the School of Navarra rediscovers the dimensions of sociality and justice in the Church and thus the possibility of claiming for the study of Canon Law the task of *sub specie fidei* reflecting on the juridical structure of the mystery of the Church; by virtue of the latter comparison a further development of the reflection of the juridicality of Canon Law is possible for the same school.

In the first comparison the central category is that of the People of God, applied by *Lumen Gentium* to the organically and communitarianly structured Church. The juridical dimension of the Church is not therefore a superstructure or a simple convenience, but a necessity without which the Church itself would not be comprehensible, just as it was founded by Jesus Christ. In other words, Canon Law is the principal of a social order the Founder wanted for his Church; one is not possible without the other and vice versa, because there is contemporaneity between the juridical order and ecclesial society. In this way it accepts the hypothesis that the "foundational will of Christ is the fundamental norm of juridical production in the Church and of the juridicality of each of its norms, without being an extraneous norm to Canon Law, because Divine Law is Law in the Church in so much as it conforms with it, constituting and informing it as a juridical society or, if you will, as a juridical ordering" [27]. And here the latter theoretical comparison adopted by the School of Navarra emerges. Before examining the latter, of a purely technical nature, we cannot however avoid observing that the theological infrastructure assured by the School of Navarra to Canon Law on the one hand is ultimately – and not without some parallelism with modern protestant doctrine – guilty of volontarism, and on the other hand remains simply a formal limit inside which canonical study must move so as not to overstep the mark in technical-juridical solutions irreconcilable with the ecclesiology of Vatican Council II.

---

[26] It is not infrequent, even among the four principal representatives of the School (P. Lombardia, J. Hervada, P.J. Viladrich, A. De La Hera), the explicit replacement of one or other author. For a comparative review of their principle theses, cf. C.R.M. Redaelli, Il *concetto di diritto della Chiesa nella riflessione canonistica tra Concilio e Codice*, Milano 1991, pp. 163-224.

[27] Cf. A. De La Hera, *Introduccion a la ciencia del derecho canonico*, op. cit., p. 217.

In the latter comparison, on the other hand, the School of Navarra welcomes from the Italian lay canonists – in a critical way and capable of seeking out new solutions – the themes of the primary ordering and the juridicality of Canon Law. The concept of ordering is applied to the juridical structure of the Church in the knowledge that the canonical ordering is not the totality of the structure of the Church, but only the general effect of its juridical factors considered in their intrinsic connection with the non-juridical factors which together with the former constitute the People of God. In this sense the canonical ordering is nothing other than that of the Church considered *sub ratione iuris*; in other words this represents the juridical concept of the Church in which nonetheless the fundamental element is not constituted by the norms but by juridical relationships. The unity of this juridical ordering is not then sought in the uniqueness of the source – divine law with its positivising norms – but in the unity of the social body that these regulate. In this way the School of Navarra seeks to overcome both the limits of traditional canonical study which, exclusively concentrated on the norms, does not manage to give a full account of the unity of the ecclesial juridical structure, and those of the Italian lay canonists which through a particular positivisation of divine law risks undervaluing the constitutional and foundational role in relation to the Church itself. Notwithstanding this, precisely on this level, the dependence of the School of Navarra on secular juridical science makes itself more evident, as is also shown by the fact that the founder of the movement – Pedro Lombardia – could indicate the development in detail of the fundamental rights of the Christian as the central problem of the constitutional law of the Church because ultimately Canon Law itself in its entirety is nothing other if not the principle of social order demanded by the tensions existing even in the life of the Church [28]. The use of a Monist concept of law is evident and in fact, under the epistemological profile, the School of Navarra conceives of Canon Law not as a theological but a juridical science, even if its object is a law characterisable as *ius sacrum*.

D) CANON LAW AS THE METAPHYSICAL CONSEQUENCE OF THE PRINCIPLE OF INCARNATION (BERTRAMS)

During his long years of teaching at the Pontifical Gregorian University, the German Jesuit Wilhelm Bertrams developed in detail a canonical system, already profoundly unitarian on the eve of the Vatican Council II, in which the logical development of Canon Law as a science necessarily postulates an ontological foundation for Canon Law itself. For this reason the starting point chosen by him to justify the existence of law in the Church is different and more clearly theological than that of the Italian lay school. The central thesis

---

[28] Cf. P. Lombardia, *Escritos de Derecho Canonico*, Voll. 1-3, Pamplona 1973-1974, especially: Vol. 2, pp. 457-477; Vol. 3, pp. 121-133 and pp. 471-501.

of this new system is the following: the Church, in so far as it is a continuation of the Incarnation of Jesus Christ, is a human society raised to the supernatural sphere [29].

If the central idea of elevation of this thesis was known for some time to the Catholic canonical tradition, under the methodological-systematical profile, this is developed in a new way by Bertrams starting from the so-called principle of the Incarnation. According to this principle in the Church too, as in every other human society, the internal metaphysical structure cannot actuate itself without the mediation of an external socio-juridical structure. In other words, just as the soul cannot manifest itself to man without the mediation of the body, so the supernatural element of the Church cannot be historically sought out without the mediation of an external ecclesial structure.

Ultimately by virtue of this same principle of the Incarnation Bertrams attributes in a rigorous way the *munus sanctificandi* to the power of orders and that of *docendi* and *regendi* to the power of jurisdiction. In doing so on the one hand he forgets that the teaching as much as the governing are bound in the Church to the Sacrament of Orders, and on the other that this same sanctifying is not separated from the exercise of the *potestas iurisdictionis*. The risk of falling once again into the dualism between sacramental order and socio-juridical order remains unchanged when all is said and done, notwithstanding the notable efforts made to establish ontologically the juridical structure of the Church [30]. With respect to this ontological foundation it is more necessary to observe what follows.

The distinction between the internal and external structure of a society, as a conceptual tool for overcoming the contrast between society and community, is a fundamental principle of the socio-philosophical theory of Gustav Grundlach, which Bertrams applies to the Church to establish the existence of its law. In this perspective, the juridical structure of the Church is indeed imposed by the fact, universally recognised in the heart of philosophical anthroplogy, that the internal structure of man necessarily tends to express itself on the external level in social forms, as confirmed by the classical axiom *In foro externo nihil est quod non apparet* [31].

---

[29]   This thesis is developed above all in the following writings: W. Bertrams: *Die Eigennatur des Kirchenrechts,* in: Gregorianum 27 (1946) pp. 527-566; Idem, *Grundlegung und Grenzen des kanonischen Rechts,* in Gregorianum 29 (1948), pp. 588-593; Idem, *Vom Ethos des Kirchenrechts,* in: W. Bertrams, *Quaestiones fundamentales iuris canonici,* Roma 1969, pp. 47-60.

[30]   It is the clear opinion of K. Mörsdorf, *Schriften zum kanonischen Recht,* hrsg. von W. Aymans-K.Th. Geringer-H.Schmitz, Paderborn 1989, p. 214.

[31]   Cf. W. Bertrams, *De natura iuridica fori interni Ecclesiae,* in: PerRMCL 40 (1951), pp. 307-340.

These socio-external forms, anthropologically established, do not simply constitute the formal condition for the exercise of law – for Bertrams already postulated ontologically from the internal structure of the plan for salvation and hence of the Church – but create law itself, giving it a real content. In fact, according to the Gregorian canonist, the fundamental rights – rooted in baptism – do not only become suspended in their exercise, but absolutely do not exist whenever the faithful place themselves outwith the external juridical ordering of the Church [32].

Beyond the fact that the arguments proposed by Bertrams to establish an otological link between the Church and law are, when all is said and done, of a philosophical and not theological nature, his system easily lays itself open to extrinsical interpretations. In order to avoid this danger, in the same line of thought as other authors, in particular Alfons Stickler and Hans Heimerl [33], they have tried to place in the mystery of the Incarnation of the Son of God itself the ultimate root of the social character of the Church. For Stickler Jesus Christ, becoming incarnate, assumed human nature in all its dimensions, including the socio-communitarian which is realised also juridically in the Church. For Heimerl the juridical character of the Church is posited by the fact that the Church, insofar as it is an historical moment applicable to salvation, continues to mediate soteriogically the intervention of Christ by virtue also of its normative imperativness. Both do not seem however to notice that their theological foundation for Canon Law stops at the threshold of juridicality, because if it is true that the mystery of the incarnation posits the visibility of the Church and its unity as "one complex reality, made from a double element, human and divine" (LG 8,1), it has not yet been said in an explicit way if and why such visibility necessarily posits its juridicality [34].

E) CANON LAW AS A SOCIOLOGICAL NECESSITY (HUIZING)

The thought of the Dutch author Peter Huizing on the bases and nature of law in the Church cannot be understood outside of the programme of de-theologisation of Canon Law and de-juridicisation of theology, launched by a certain stream of post-conciliar canonists from the platform of the interna-

---

[32]   Cf. W. Bertrams, *Die Eigennatur des Kirchenrechts,* op. cit., pp. 536-547.

[33]   Cf. A.M. Stickler, *Das Mysterium der Kirche im Kirchenrecht,* in *Das Mysterium der Kirche in der Sicht der theologischen Disziplinen,* hrsg. von C. Holböck-Th. Sartory, Salzburg 1962, Vol. II, pp. 571-647; H. Heimerl, *Aspecto cristologico del Derecho Canonico,* in: Ius Can 6 (1966), pp. 25-51; *Das Kirchenrecht in neuen Kirchenbild,* in: *Ecclesia et Ius.* Festgabe für A. Scheuermann zum 60. Geburtstag, a cura di K. Siepen-J. Weitzel-P.Wirth, München-Paderborn-Wien 1968, pp. 1-24.

[34]   Agreeing with this opinion E. Corecco, *Teologia del diritto canonico, op.* cit. p. 1742 and A. Rouco-Varela, *Allgemeine Rechtslehre oder Theologie des kanonischen Rechts,* op. cit. p. 111.

tional review *Concilium*[35]. The principal objectives of this programme are the immediate reform of the Code of Canon Law and the pastoral updating of all the laws of the Church, from which one cannot expect a deepened thouroughly articulate theoretical contribution. For the most part the contributions of the various authors are very heterogeneous and directed towards very different practical aims. Nevertheless it is not difficult to trace in them some common denominators in the order of their conception of Canon Law and their reason for being.

The most salient tracts of the effort to de-theologise Canon Law, common to different authors of this post-conciliar stream of Canon Law study, can be summarised thus.

Canon Law, insofar as it is a science, is diverse and relative in reference to theology, and insofar as it is ecclesial order, it is on the other hand relative to the sacraments. This relativity of Canon Law renders it particularly changeable and adaptable to the ecclesial demands of the time. Precisely due to this, Canon Law has a distinct character of service and an eminently pastoral function in the ordering of the mission of the Church. This pastoral and of service function cannot be effective if the normative content of canonical law is not accepted by everybody in the Church[36].

The decisive importance of this acceptance in order to establish the binding character of a juridical norm in the Church reveals the foundation of Canon Law itself: just like any other society, the Church also "cannot do without obligatory rules, recognised and observed by all the interested parties", because "any community claiming to subsist without a binding order, ends up committing suicide"[37]. Arguing in this way, however, it appears clear that the ultimate reason for the existence of Canon Law is solely a sociological type of requirement and consequently such law is a purely external regulation, positive and human, incapable of intrinsically and structurally determining ecclesial life. For the latter the juridical norms only have a significance of ethical or organising rules, because the binding force of canonical norm is not derived from its metaphysical-theological foundation, but from its capacity to smooth out the possible conflicts between individual conscience and belonging to the Church, between charism and institution.

---

[35] Cf. N. Edelby-J. Jimenez, *Kirchenrecht und Theologie* (Vorwort), in: Concilium 1 (1965), pp. 625-626.

[36] Cf. P. Huizing, *Reform des kirchlichen Rechts*, in: Concilium 1 (1965), pp. 670-685, especially p. 676; Idem, *L'ordinamento della Chiesa*, in: MySal, vol. 8, pp. 193-228, here especially p. 212, pp. 213-215 and pp. 219-227; Idem, *Teologia pastorale dell ordinamento canonico*, in: Gregorianum 51 (1970), pp. 113-128.

[37] Cf. P. Huizing, *Teologia pastorale*, op. cit., p. 119 and Idem, *L'ordinamento della Chiesa*, op. cit. p.195.

F) WORD AND SACRAMENT AS FUNDAMENTAL ELEMENTS OF THE JURIDI-
   CAL STRUCTURE OF THE CHURCH (MÖRSDORF)

Even before the Vatican Council II [38], and especially by virtue of his decision to compete in depth – even at a distance of more than fifty years – with the radical criticism of Canon Law by Sohm, Klaus Mörsdorf (1909-1989) perceived with extreme lucidity that in order to succeed in furnishing the theological proof for the existence of an ecclesial juridical order, the study of Canon Law must avoid every ecclesiological spiritualism or extrinsicism as well as every natural-law type solution. This must demonstrate that the juridical dimension is already present in the structrual elements upon which Christ wished to establish his Church; or, that the juridical precept is already contained in the structural elements of the plan for Salvation. As he affirms in the introduction to the first volume of his by now famous manual: "The juridical structure of the Church is founded in its divine origin in the Man-God and in the holy sovereignty exercised by Him in this" [39].

Starting precisely from this conviction, which with Canon Law brings into play the very understanding of the mystery of the Church, Klaus Mörsdorf reascends the heights of the numerous attempts – valid even if not totally convincing – to establish christologically the existence of Canon Law, and succeeds in attaching it firmly to theology. The ecclesiological bridge thrown up by Mörsdorf between the mystery of the Incarnation – as the determining principle of the structure of the Church – and the juridical ecclesial ordering rests on two piers: Word and Sacrament.

The latter are both primary constitutive elements and not derived from the Church. Indeed, as the canonist from Munich explicitly affirms: "Word and Sacrament are two elements, different but reciprocally bound, of the construction of the visible Church" [40].

Both – in as much as word and sign – are also then contemporaneously primordial forms of human communication and because they have an ontological structure are capable of expressing a juridically binding precept.

In point of fact, in any human and not just biblical cultural tradition, through word and sign relevant juridical facts are always brought into being. Assuming these to communicate to man his salvation, Christ has conferred

---

[38]   In fact, in chronological order, the principal essays by Klaus Mörsdorf on this argument are all before or contemporary with the Council: *Zur Grundlegung des Rechts der Kirche*, in MthZ 3 (1952), pp. 329-348; *Altkanonisches "Sakramentsrecht"? Eine Auseinandersetzung mit den Anschauungen Rudolf Sohms über die inneren Grundlagen des Decretum Gratiani*, in: Studia Gratiana (1953), pp. 485-502; *Kirchenrecht*, in LThK, Vol. VI (1961), pp. 245-250; *Wort und Sakrament als Bauelemente der Kirchenverfassung*, in: AfkKR 134 (1965), pp. 72-79.

[39]   K. Mörsdorf, Lb, Vol. I, p. 13.

[40]   K. Mörsdorf, *Zur Grundlegung des Rechtes der Kirche,* op. cit. p. 330.

upon them a supernatural value and a soteriological incidence, able to bind the faithful not only morally but also juridically. "The word becomes *kerygma* and the symbol a *sacramental* sign of the presence of God" [41]. Becoming Incarnate, Jesus Christ has given to the Word and to the Sacrament a definitive value for human existence, because he has impressed upon them "a generative and conservative force of community" [42].

This force, intrinsic and binding, makes the Word of Christ an essential element of the construction of the visible Church, an element that has its own juridical dimension. The latter is not established however upon the capacity of the Word to be understood by the listener, but on the formal motive that comes from the fact that the one who utters it is the Son of God himself: *locutio Dei attestans*. In other words: "The Church's proclamation of the Word has a juridical character because it acts upon the mandate of the Lord. The Lord posed the request of God in a way that the one who is called is bound to obedience not only by dint of the intrinsic reasonableness of the Word, but also for the formal reason that the proclaimer of the Word is the Son of God. He demands recognition with his explicit appeal to the fact of being the one sent by the Father. When the Pharisees confronted him, affirming that his witness was not true because He was witnessing to himself, the Lord objected starting from the rule of the Law of Israel according to which the witness of two men has the value of proof, and thus refers to the Father who sent him as the second witness" [43]. Understood this way, the juridical character of this dimension of exigency (*Geltungsangspruch*) of the Word of God is beyond doubt. Christ takes it from his own mission received from the Father which permitted him to awaken in his listeners the impression of being in the presence of one who was capable of speaking ... *sicut potestatem habens* (Mt 7,29). The Apostles, on the other hand, took it from the fact of having been personally chosen by Christ as juridically constituted representatives with full powers (*rechtliche Bevollmächtigung*). Consequently even the Word of the bishops requires obedience and possesses a juridical character for the following reason, that it is proclaimed in the name of and on behalf of Christ. The same force, intrinsic and binding, is possessed by the sacramental sign. Indeed Klaus Mörsdorf gathers and develops the juridical dimension of the Sacrament in his analogy with the juridical symbol (*Rechtssymbole*). As much the sacrament as the symbol are the sensible signs that efficaciously produce an invisible reality.

The symbol produces invisible reality because, whether in the universal cultural tradition (but above all in the east) or in the biblical tradition, it has al-

---

[41]   E. Corecco, *Teologia del diritto canonico,* op. cit. p. 1744.
[42]   K. Mörsdorf, Lb, Vol. I, p. 14.
[43]   Ibid., p. 14.

ways been seen as a form of human communication having an invisible effect but socially recognised as a source of rights and duties and therefore as a juridically binding fact [44]. Belonging to this juridical symbolism, for example, is the act of deed of sale in German law, according to which the material availability of the goods is necessary for the title to the relative property rights. Many elements of this juridical symbolism have remained in the Church, especially in its liturgy. It is enough to think of the laying on of hands in the administration of the sacrament of Holy Orders, the origin of which in the eastern juridical culture is evident.

The sacrament, on the other hand, produces also an invisible reality which is a source of rights and duties, and is therefore juridically relevant, but does it not by virtue of a recognition on the part of the human society, to which tradition such juridical symbolism belongs, but thanks to the fact that the ultimate subject who fulfils such a sign is Christ himself, who instituting it has impressed upon it its proper significance and proper efficacy.

Focusing on the strict relationship that exists between juridical symbol and sacrament, the canonist from Munich reattempts at the same time to establish the juridicality of the sacramental order of the Church and its specificity, insofar as it is *ius sacrum*, in comparison with state law. On the contrary, precisely because Word and Sacrament bind not by virtue of their subjectively conceived content, but by the fact that the ultimate subject who proclaims and celebrates them is Christ, both possess a formal juridical character which confers on Canon Law a binding force greater than that of the law of the state, because it is more deeply rooted in the normative of the *ius divinum positivum*.

This does not naturally mean that for Klaus Mörsdorf all of Canon Law in its entirety should be considered as *ius divinum*. Indeed, however much God puts into effect through Word and Sacrament, it is simultaneously a gift (*Gabe*) – the salvific efficacy of which depends on its acceptance in faith on the part of man – and a duty (*Aufgabe*), which is fulfilled in the free and personal decision of the latter. In the juridical structure of the Church it is therefore possible – analogously to what happens in the sacrament, where we distinguish the external sign from the internal effect of grace caused by the former – to distinguish a constitutive order, based on the Church as a sacramental sign of salvation ultimately independent of the will of man, and an operative order, in which what is established in the former can find its development fruitful and efficacious thanks to the free adherence of man [45]. Both orders are distinct but

---

[44] The capacity of the symbol to sustain responsibility and solidarity, fundamental values of the juridical culture, is spotlighted also by the most recent analysis of the symbolic experience developed by the science of religions, philosophy and anthropology; cf. for example J. Vidal, *Sacro, simbolo, creativit,* Milano 1992, p. 34 and pp. 82-85.

[45] Cf. K. Mörsdorf, Lb. Vol. I, pp 16-21 and especially p. 17.

not separable, because they are nothing other than two facets of the same reality: the Church which, as Vatican Council II teaches, is *una realitas complexa* (LG 8,1).

Once again it appears clear that for Mörsdorf the specificity of Canon Law is totally directed by the sacramental nature of the Church. For this reason he cannot conceive of canonical science other than as " a theological discipline with a juridical method" [46]. Is this legitimate? If the recognition goes to Mörsdorf for the enormous merit of having identified a precise *locus theologicus* for Canon Law and of having developed a secure and convincing theological foundation, on the other hand – precisely because the method of every science must be defined by its object – one cannot but wonder if it is effectively possible to apply the juridical method to a theological reality. It is only in the light of the teaching of the Vatican Council II on the Church as *communio* that the disciples of Mörsdorf have been able to formulate a reply to this question too. In point of fact, it is the concept of *communio* that best defines the form of social aggregation generated first of all by Word and Sacrament, but also by the aggregative power of charism. And therefore only after having identified in the realisation of the *communio* the specific *telos* of the law of the Church, different from the ultimate purpose of the juridical ordering of the state, will it be possible for the *Münchener Schule*, founded by Mörsdorf himself, to clarify its own methodology and epistemology with greater precision and security.

3. SYSTEMATIC DEVELOPMENTS OF THE THEOLOGICAL FOUNDATIONS OF CANON LAW IN THE LIGHT OF THE VATICAN COUNCIL II

The rapid review of the principal attempts at a theological foundation for Canon Law, developed in detail in the Catholic field, has clearly demonstrated both that Canon Law is understood as a reality that is not extrinsic but belongs to the essence of the Church itself, and that this has no connection with the mystery of the latter and its salvific function. Now, as the Vatican Council II teaches, the nature of this mystery is sacramental (LG 1), by which this – in all of its aspects and therefore also in the juridical – is knowable ultimately only through faith.

This does not mean attributing to Canon law a salvific value similar to that of the Word of God and the Sacraments, but rather to explain how the Church has need of this law to be itself, to perdure in time and space as a sacrament of salvation for all mankind. Before showing how at the base of conciliar ecclesiology Canon Law is nothing if not the implicit structural dimension of the

---

[46] Ibid., p. 36.

ecclesial communion, it is however necessary to propaedeutically signpost the principles which legitimise the existence of a similar law.

3.1 PRINCIPLES FOR THE LEGITIMISATION OF AN ECCLESIAL LAW

It is to the credit of Peter Krämer for having pointed out and developed the propaedeutical importance of these principles for understanding correctly the teaching of the *Münchener Schule* on the ontological, epistemological and methodological constitution of Canon Law [47]. There are three principles for the legitimisation of a theologically established Canon Law: *ecclesial community, religious freedom* and *the bond of faith*.

A) ECCLESIAL COMMUNITY

It would be a wasted effort to search in the Bible for an explicit teaching on the meaning of law for the People of God. Still, as often happens for other themes not dealt with *expressis verbis* by Holy Scripture, in its totality it throws a clarifying light on the theological significance of such an idea, also because in biblical terminology the Event itself can be a Word [48].

Although the legalistic overlapping of the rabbis often obfuscated the essential character of the Hebraic law, it is not difficult to uncover how in the writings of the Old Testament the salvific will of God towards man was normally described with juridical expressions [49]. Rather, it is unanimously accepted that "the most precious contibution given by Old Testament juricical thought is that of having presented God as the immediate and personal source of law" [50]. If on the one hand this immediacy of the divine origin of law has ended up by unilaterally emphasising the volontaristic character, up to the point of identifying the practice of the law with obedience to the will of God, on the other hand it does not mean that the Old Testament wanted to reduce the relationship between God and man to a juridical rapport. The juridical character of the divine will, witnessed to by the Old Testament discourses on law, simply wishes to show that in this there is no arbitrary or abusive element, but rather precisely in this the dignity of the human person is established. It is man that God has placed at the centre of creation and of his plan for salvation, through

---

[47]   The most important writings dedicated to this theme by the canonist from Eichstätt are: P. Krämer, *Theologische Grundlegung des kirchlichen Rechts,* op. cit.; Idem, *Wort-Sakrament-Charisma,* Stuttgart-Berlin-Köln 1992, pp. 23-27.

[48]   Cf. for example J Ratzinger, *Schriftauslegung in Widerstreit. Zur Frage nach Grundlagen und Weg der Exegese heute,* in: *Schriftauslegung im Widerstreit,* hrsg. von J. Ratzinger. Freiburg-Basel-Wien 1989, pp. 15-44, here p. 39.

[49]   Cf. for example Ex 20,2-17; Dt 17, 14-20; Jer 1,17 and 30,18; Lev 20,2-5; Prov 1,3. For an overview of the biblical concept of law, cf.: A. Stiegler, *Der kirchliche Rechtsbegriff. Elemente und Phasen einer Erkenntnisgeschichte,* München 1958, pp. 31-70.

[50]   E. Corecco, *Diritto,* in: *Dizionario Teologico Interdisciplinare,* Vol. I, Torino 1977, pp. 112-133, here p. 120.

which man is not without rights before God, because in reality he has " in his heart a law inscribed by God: his dignity lies in observing this law" (GS 16)

In the writings of the New Testament the Hebraic law is confirmed in part (Mt 7,12), in part made relative in its function (Gal 3,24-25), always and in every case completed and deepened in its meaning (Mt 5,17), thanks above all to the underlining of love or communion as the ultimate criterion which must guide the relationship of man with God and with his peers [51]. In particular in the New Covenant liberty and ordering (community) are two eschatological realities and as such relative each to the other: "The *Eschaton* makes itself historical and social at the same time as ordered liberty and as free ordering" [52]. In other words the ordering of the community, in so far as it is rooted in the *ius divinum*, is at the service of liberty and the latter is the very dynamism of juridical ordering.

From these biblical data on the theological significance of law it is possible to deduce a first principle of legitimisation of a theologically founded ecclesial law: an ecclesial law is legitimate only if it refers to the ecclesial community and if it highlights the elements that constitute it as a salvific community established by Jesus Christ; the same law is not legitimate if it claims to determine in a juridically binding way the immediate relationship of man with God, as if it were possible to capture such a relationship in juridical norms [53].

B) RELIGIOUS LIBERTY

The Augustinian axiom *credere non potest homo, nisi volens* [54] has received a solemn confirmation in the conciliar declaration on religious freedom: "One of the key truths in Catholic teaching, a truth that is contained in the Word of God and constantly preached by the Fathers, is that man's response to God by faith ought to be free, and that therefore nobody is to be forced to embrace the faith against his will. The act of faith is of its very nature a free act. Man, redeemed by Christ the Saviour and called through Jesus Christ to be an adopted son of God, cannot give his adherence to God when he reveals himself unless, drawn by the Father, he submits to God with a faith that is reasonable and free. It is therefore fully in accordance with the nature of faith that in religious matters every form of coercion by men should be excluded. Consequently the principle of religious liberty contributes in no small way to the development

---

[51] Cf. Mt 12,28-34 and IJn 4,7; for an analysis of the meaning of love in the New Testament, cf. C. Spicq, Art. in: *Lexique théologique du Nouveau Testament*, Fribourg 1991 pp. 18-23.

[52] H. Schürmann, *Die neubundliche Begründung von Ordnung und Recht in der Kirche*, in: Idem, *Studien zur neutestamentlichen Ethik*, Stuttgart 1990, pp. 247-268, here p. 264.

[53] Cf. P. Krämer, *Kirchenrecht*, op. cit., Vol. I, p. 24.

[54] Cf. PL 43,315 (*Contra litteras Petiliani*). From then, under different forms, it has always been present in the canonical tradition, cf. CIC/1917 can. 1351: *Ad amplexandam fidem catholicam nemo invitus cogatur.*

of a situation in which men can without hindrance be invited to the Christian faith, embrace it of their own free will and give it practical expression in every sphere of their lives. " (DH 10)

With this the fathers of the Council wanted above all to affirm the right to religious liberty in every civil society, a right rooted in the dignity of the human person and conforming to Christian revelation. Such a right cannot however be limited to the free acceptance of the faith, as can be deduced from the context dedicated to the missions in which the Pio-Benedictine Code inserted it. The right to religious liberty is referred back to the exercise of the faith in its globality: not only is the act of faith free but also its way of guiding the life of man [55]. Indeed, the fathers of the Council once again affirm, "Man's dignity therefore requires him to act out of conscious and free choice, as moved and drawn in a personal way from within, and not by blind impulses in himself or by mere external constraint. " (GS 17).

From this clear teaching of the Vatican Council II can be deduced a second principle of legitimisation of a theologically founded ecclesial law: an ecclesial law is legitimate only in the measure in which it respects the right to religious liberty; the same ecclesial law is not legitimate whenever it harms or abolishes the right to religious liberty [56].

c) THE BOND OF FAITH

The exegetical and semantic researches upon the Greek words $\varepsilon\lambda\varepsilon\upsilon\theta\varepsilon\rho\iota\alpha$ (freedom) and $\pi\alpha\rho\rho\eta\sigma\iota\alpha$ (openness) as apt to explain the notion of liberty have fully demonstrated that, precisely because of its juridical value, liberty is a concept that leads to being rather than doing [57]. Liberty, full belonging, sonship (Gal 4,5) and possession of rights are synonymous in theological language. For this reason in the Church it is not possible to speak of liberty quite apart from the bond of faith. The ecclesial ordering of liberty is wholly finalised in order to render it possible that Word and Sacrament connect the participation of divine being in the faith in an authentic and integral way [58]. In this ordering to the principle of liberty and personal responsibility in the act of faith corresponds the obligation to "seek the truth", to "adhere to the known truth" and to "direct their whole lives in accordance with the demands of truth" (DH 2,2).

---

[55]   Cf. H. Schmitz, *Tendenzen nachkonziliarer Gesetzgebung,* Trier 1979, p. 31.

[56]   Cf. P. Krämer, *Kirchenrecht,* op. cit. Vol. I p. 25.

[57]   Cf. above all: D. Nestle, *Eleutheria. Studium zum Wesen der Freiheit bei den Griechen und in Neuen Testament. Teil I Die Griechen,* Tübingen 1967; H. Schlier, $\pi\alpha\rho\rho\eta\sigma\iota\alpha$, in: ThWNT, Vol. V, coll. 869-884.

[58]   Cf. J. Ratzinger, *Freiheit und Bindung in der Kirche,* in: Actes IV CIDC, pp. 37-52, especially pp. 47-51.

Both the formal expression or definitive proclamation of the truth of the faith, contained in the *depositum fidei* of the Catholic Church, and the obligation to give to these *credenda* one's own personal assent have a normative value and are of a juridical nature. This does not mean however that the faith, an act of liberty par excellence, in the Church which is a community of faith, should be considered as a rigid juridical reality. It is not by chance that the Fathers of the Council speak of progress in the "understanding of the faith" (GS 62,2) and in the grasping of "sacred tradition" (DV 8,2), as well as a "hierarchy of truth" (UR 11,3). Such a process is profoundly dynamic because it is guided by the Holy Spirit, through two gifts, of a charismatic nature, made by the Church: that of infallibility (LG 25,3) and that of the *sensus fidei* (LG 12,1).

From all this is derived a third principle of legitimisation of a theologically founded ecclesial law: an ecclesial law is legitimate if it is useful contemporaneously for the realisation of an integral transmission of the truth of faith and a free and living adhesion to this: such a law is illegitimate on the other hand if it claims to make real the protection of the faith with a rigid normative and is so abstract as to repudiate the role of the opportune free decision in the faith [59].

Community, liberty and bond legitimise the existence of an ecclesial law because every notion of law is referred to these. To have illustrated the applicability of these principles to the Church does not mean however the need for Canon Law has yet been demonstrated. In order to do this there has to be a closer analysis of the concept of Church bearing in mind, as Antonio Ruoco Varela – a disciple of Klaus Mörsdorf – suggests, that dealing with a mystery one's proper attention cannot be concentrated only on a particular aspect – as for example that of the People of God or of the Mystical Body of Christ – but there is a need to proceed progressively bearing in mind all the essential connections from which this is constituted [60]. It will be necessary then for each of these connections, however briefly, to estimate the specific theological significance in the process of forming the juridical-ecclesial order, which finds in the *communio* its ultimate end.

3.2 SOURCES OF THE JURIDICAL STRUCTURE OF THE CHURCH AS "COMMUNION"

The Vatican Council II posited as its principal task that of reiterating to the world how the Church sees itself and conceives its mission among men. To

---

[59] Cf. P. Krämer, *Kirchenrecht*, op. cit., p. 27.

[60] A. Ruoco-Varela, *Le statut ontologique et epistemologique du droit canonique. Notes pour une théologie du droit canonique*, in: RSPhTh 57 (1973), pp. 203-227.

fulfil this task the council Fathers started from a "sacramental" [61] vision of the ecclesial mystery: "the Church in Christ is in the nature of sacrament – a sign and instrument, that is - of communion with God and of unity among all men" (LG 1). In this vision there is already implicitly present that of the Church as *communio cum Deo et hominibus* which becomes the central and fundamental idea of the documents of the Council and makes of the ecclesiology of communion the "foundation for the ordering of the Church and above all for a correct relationship between unity and plurality in the Church" [62].

Precisely because it is central and fundamental the concept of κοινωνια is apt to summarise and manifest all the theological and juridical meanings of the different images with which the Vatican Council II describes the mystery of the Church. Rather, given that the latter *vivit iure divino,* to study the sources starting from those from which the Church juridically structures itself as *communio,* means clarifying the relationships between ecclesial communion and Canon Law and therefore subsequently deepening the discourse on the theological foundations of the latter.

A) THE PRINCIPAL ELEMENTS OF THE CONCILIAR NOTION OF THE CHURCH AND THEIR SIGNIFICANCE FOR CANON LAW

At the end of the second chapter of the dogmatic Constitution *Lumen Gentium* in only one phrase the conciliar Fathers synthesise the biblical images used by them to describe the mystery of the Church: "Thus the Church prays and likewise labours so that into the People of God, the Mystical Body of Christ, and the Temple of the Holy Spirit, may pass the fullness of the whole world, and that in Christ, the head of all things, all honour and glory may be rendered to the Creator, the Father of the universe" (LG 17). The trinitarian perspective of this declaration of the mystery of the Church does nothing other than accentuate the complementary character and reciprocal integration of the three biblical images used: People of God, Mystical Body of Christ and Temple of the Holy Spirit [63].

With the rediscovery of the biblical image of People of God, the Fathers of the Council – above all in LG 9 – intended to witness to three fundamental characteristics of the Church: its being constituted not by a human decision, but by a choice or election by God (LG 6, 3 and 4); its character of community, because God leads mankind to salvation not individually but gathering them together in his people (LG 4,2); its dynamic orientation, in as much as it is a

---

[61]   Cf. LG 9,3; 48,2; AG 1,1 and the study by O. Semmelroth, *La Chiesa come sacramento di salvezza,* in: MySal, Vol. 7, pp. 377-437.

[62]   Cf. Synodus Episcoporum, Relatio finalis. *Ecclesia sub verbo Dei mysteria Christi celebrans pro salute mundi,* Città del Vaticano 1985, II C, La Chiesa come comunione, n. 1.

[63]   Cf. Aymans-Mörsdorf, KanR I, p. 21.

People journeying between what God has already accomplished for the salvation of man and what has not yet been revealed (LG 5,2; 8,4). Consequently it is not difficult to grasp the aspects of a juridical nature in the reciprocal relationships existing between all those who belong to the Church as the People of God: the joint responsibility of all for the mission of the Church (LG 31,1); their equality in dignity and in action (LG 32,3); their rights and duties in the building up of the Church (LG 37,1).

The simultaneous application of the Pauline image of the Mystical Body of Christ allowed the Fathers of the Council to be immediately on their guard against any possible unilateral interpretations: the People of God exists solely as the Mystical Body of Christ (LG 7,3 and 4), because only in Jesus Christ does the history of salvation find its fulfilment and its radically new form. As such the Church is a sacramental reality, and therefore at the same time visible and invisible, of the intimate union with God and with other men (LG 1). Under the canonical profile this means at least two things: first of all the socialness and visibility of the Church are of a sacramental nature, and therefore not qualifiable by secular parameters, as Robert Bellarmine – in reaction to the protestant reformation – did by alternatively comparing the visibility of the Church to that of the Venetian Republic; in second place the ecclesial community is hierarchically structured, because the diversity of offices depend on the variety of gifts lavished by the Holy Spirit and "among these gifts the primacy belongs to the grace of the Apostles to whose authority the Spirit subjects even those who are endowed with charisms" (LG 7,3)

Finally in numerous passages – as for example in LG 4,1; SC 2; AG 7,2 and PO 1 – the Church is defined by the Fathers of the Council as the "Temple of the Holy Spirit", because if "Christ is the Head" of this "Mystical Body", the function that the Holy Spirit fulfils in this same body is comparable to "that which the principle of life, the soul, fulfils in the human body" (LG 7,7). This means that the Holy Spirit instructs and directs the Church "with varied hierarchic and charismatic gifts" (LG 4,1), through which even the faithful upon whom the latter have been lavished have the right and the duty to exercise them for the good of the whole ecclesial communion (AA 3,3), for the building up of the Church as a reality of communion.

With this latter notion the Council Fathers summarise and sythesise all the different aspects of the mystery of the Church, illustrated with the recapturing of the newly analysed biblical images. Indeed, notwithstanding the polyvalent use of the New Testament term κοινωνια, whose principal significance is that of "common possession of a good" [64] or " participation in a common interest"

---

[64]   J Hamer, *L'Église est une communion*, Paris 1962, p. 176. For a canonical analysis of this conciliar notion, cf. O. Saier, *Communio in der Lehre des Zweiten Vatikanischen Konzils*.

it is easy to distinguish two fundamental accepted meanings of the conciliar notion of *communio;* the former generically designs human communitary relationships (*communio inter personas* or *communio fraterna*); the latter indicates the sacramental reality and therefore qualitatively different from ecclesial relationships, both at the level of ecclesiology and that of theological anthropology.

The canonical significances of this latter accepted meaning of the conciliar notion of *communio* are different. Before reviewing them it is however indispensible to illustrate how Word, Sacrament and Charism concur within the juridical structurisation of this *una realitas complexa* (LG 8, 1), which is the Church as communion, because all three constitute the primary sources.

B) WORD AND SACRAMENT IN THE BUILDING UP OF THE ECCLESIAL COMMUNION

The systematic and substantial priority restored by Klaus Mörsdorf, even before the Vatican Council II, to Word and Sacrament in order to build up the Church in its juridical aspects as well is reinforced both by the rediscovery of the structural reciprocity between these two originating instruments of the ecclesial communication of salvation, and by the registration of the complementarity between the eschatological and pneumatological root of the operative unity between Word and Sacrament in the building up of the Church as a *communio.*

Indeed, after the Vatican Council II, on the one hand the Word-Sacrament connection is defined within a fantail of positions that go from that of Otto Semmelroth, according to whom the Word is to be understood as a quasi-sacrament, to that of Karl Rahner, according to whom the Sacrament is to be considered as "the highest form of the expressed Word"[65]. In any case one fact is considered central by all: Word and Sacrament are two different but reciprically ordered entities and thus must be considered as two principles, strictly associated and dependent on each other, of the one process – Christological and pneumatological – of the formation of the Church as the place of salvation for man[66]. On the other hand at the very heart of this perspective it becomes even clearer that if the Christological origin of Word and Sacrament – as fully demonstrated by Klaus Mörsdorf – stamps a binding juridical force on the common symbolic communicative character, the making explicit of the juridical value of the latter does not however suppress the intrinsic dynamism proper

---

Eine rechtsbegriffliche Untersuchung, München 1973, especially pp. 1-24.

[65] In this regard cf. the brief but precise article by G. Koch, *Wort und Sakrament, in LKD, pp. 559-560* which reprises the essentials of his earlier work: *Wort und Sakrament als Wirkweisen der Kirche.* in G. Koch u.a. *Gegenwärtig in Wort und Sakrament,* Freiburg 1976, pp. 48-83.

[66] Cf. W. Kasper, *Wort und Sakrament,* in: W. Kasper, *Glaube und Geschichte,* Mainz 1970, pp. 285-310.

to every communicative sign. A confirmation can be found in the not yet sufficiently explored spiritual or pneumatological dimension of the unity between Word and Sacrament. This dimension was at least intuited as the inevitable complement of the Christological origin of the unity between Word and Sacrament by Söhngen where, in a very suggestive way, he affirms: "The Sacrament is completed by the Word with the fullness of a more efficacious spirituality and the Word completed by the Sacrament with the fullness of a more spiritual efficacy" [67]. However the same author does not say unfortunately if this efficacious spirituality of the Word and this spiritual efficacy of the Sacrament have a relevant ecclesiology specific and different from that possessed by the Christological dimension of the same unity between Word and Sacrament. To understand deep down the juridical significance of both it is however necessary to analyse, albeit briefly, the pneumatological dimension of the Word and the Sacrament not least their respective openness to Charism.

As has already been seen, far from considering Canon Law as uniquely based on the Sacrament, Klaus Mörsdorf recaptures and illustrates above all the juridical dimension of the Word, totally disregarded on the other hand by the lutheran author Rudolph Sohm. For the canonist from Munich the juridical character of the Word of Jesus Christ derives from his own mission received from the Father, which permits him to awaken in his listeners the impression of being in the presence of someone capable of speaking "... sicut potestatem habens" (Mt 7,29). The Apostles, on the other hand, derived it from the fact of having been personally chosen by Christ as juridically constituted representatives with full powers (*rechtliche Bevollmächtigung*). Consequently the Word of the bishops requires obedience and posseses a juridical character for the following reason, that this is pronounced in the name and on behalf of the Lord [68]. In the ecclesiology of the Vatican Council II it becomes clear however that a double link binds this Word: the *missio* or formal mission (*formale Sendung*) received from Christ through the Apostles and their successors, as well as the *nexus communionis* (can.749 §2), in the professing, protecting and proclaiming the *veritatem revelatam*. This apostolic service to the Word of God, which is realised *Spiritu Sancto assistente* (can. 747 §1) therefore concerns the whole of the Church. The guardian of this *munus* is the ecclesial *communio* in as much as and because this is structured as interactive reciprocity between the apostolic magisterium and the *sensus fidei* of all the faithful [69]. This means that, pre-

---

[67] "Vom Wort wird das Sakrament mit der Fülle mächtiger Geistigkeit und vom Sakrament wird das Wort mit der Fülle geistlicher Wirksamkeit erfüllt" (G.Söhngen, *Symbol und Wirklichkeit im Kultmysterium*, Bonn 1937, p. 18).

[68] Cf. K. Mörsdorf, *Kirchenrecht. III. Theologische Grundlegung*, in: HthG, Vol. II (München 1970), pp. 484-485, here p. 484.

[69] Cf. W. Aymans, *Begriff, Aufgabe und Träger des Lehramts*, in: HdbkathKR, pp. 533-540.

cisely where the *munus docendi* expresses more clearly its juridical character it also manifests its own pneumatological dimension. The ultimate reason for this concommitance is probably to be found in the analogy often underlined by Catholic exegesis between charismatic Word and apostolic Word[70]. In the light of such an analogy the right to obedience (*der Anspruch auf Glaubensgehorsam*) of the Word, God and the Church, seems like the derivation of an event, the revelation of the truth, which is a dialogical-personal event (*ein personal-dialogisches Geschehen*) and as such not detachable from the experience of the *communio* of sacramental origin[71]. Consequently the objectivisation of the faith in this truth, realised through the formal expression and defininitive proclamation of the so-called *depositum fidei* on the part of the ecclesiastical authority, is thus a limitation of a juridical nature but this is wholly ordered to efficaciously realising the *personalem ed actuosam adhaesionem fidei* (GS 7,3). And the latter is a grace and as such is in a strict relationship of affinity with the charism.

Analogously also the juridic dimension of the Sacrament in the light of the communion of the Vatican Council II appears as if strictly connected with the pneumatological, if the point of view is taken that the two most important recapturings of conciliar sacramental theology: the ecclesiological rediscovery of the communitarian dimension of the sacraments and the anthropological conviction of their being signs capable of generating a new solidarity. Both concur to render more understandable and convincing Klaus Mörsdorf's intuition that, as has already been seen, it grasps and develops the juridical dimension of the Sacrament in his analogy with the juridical symbol (*Rechtssymbole*). In fact, putting into focus the strict affinity existing between juridical symbol and sacrament, the canonist from Munich succeeds at the same time in establishing the juridicality of the sacramental order of the Church and its specificity, insofar as *ius sacrum,* in comparison with state law. This specificity is not however exclusively reducible to the fact that within any people a symbol is juridically binding only in the measure that it is recognised as such by the traditional culture of the people itself, while the sacramental sign is juridically binding for the People of God only because it is instituted by Christ, that is the definitive possibility of salvation offered by God to man. Also the social or communitarian reality generated by the juridic symbol and that generated by the sacrament are different, that is ruled and ordered by different principles, because the solidarity born of the celebration of the sacraments is not purely human or natural. This is the *communio fidelium* in which the salvation

---

[70]   Cf. H. Schlier, *Wort. II. Biblisch*, in: HthG, Bd. IV (München 1970), pp. 417-439 and in particular pp. 436-438.

[71]   Cf. P. Krämer, *Theologische Grundlegung des Kirchlichen Rechts,* op. cit., p.125.

brought by Christ and communicated to mankind by the sacraments is actu-
ated as "the concrete realisation of that which the Church is as such and in its
totality" [72]. And the Church – as the Vatican Council II teaches – is not a human society like the others, rather it forms *unam realitatem complexam, quae
humano et divino coalescit elemento* (LG 8,1). Consequently, precisely by dint
of this reciprocal immanence between the Church and sacraments, the latter
reflect the specificity of the ecclesial community also as juridical acts and vice
versa. This means that there is no caesura between the juridical dimension of
the Church and that of the sacraments, even where this should be less evident,
as it should be in the case of Baptism, foundation of every right and duty of the
faithful, or in the case of the Eucharist, *fons et culmen* of all of ecclesial life,
to the point that the Church itself can be substantially defined as a *communio
eucharistica.* [73]

The proof that the pneumatological dimension of the Word and Sacrament
does not limit but expands and reinforces their capacity to produce juridical
relationships within the Church as a *communio* opens the way to both the recapturing of the constitutional ecclesiological role of the charism, and to the
discovery of its juridical dimension. In the first place, at the level of decisive
Canon Law, is the fact that the conciliar lesson on charisms testifies to how the
ministry is not the springboard for all of the questions of a constitutional order;
secondly of greater importance on the other hand is the comparison with the
consuetudo canonica, always considered a source of law in the Church.

c) THE ECCLESIOLOGICAL-CONSTITUTIONAL ROLE OF *Charisma*

The Vatican Council II makes sober use, when all is said and done, of the terms
Charisma and *Charismaticus* [74]. Paradoxically however such sobriety does not
put the charisms into the shade, but ends up by witnessing in a major way both
to the specific nature of charisms in relation to the other gifts of the Holy Spirit,
and their decisive ecclesiological role.

From a close reading of LG 12,2, in which the New Testament sense of
charism is fully diffuse, it becomes clear that the Fathers of the Vatican Council II wanted to put into focus its specific nature through five assertions: a)

---

[72]   J. Ratzinger, *Theologische Prinzipienlehre. Bausteine zur Fundamentaltheologie*, München
1982, p.50.

[73]   R. Ahlers, *Communio Eucharistica – Communio Ecclesiastica. Zur wechselseitigen Imma-
nenz von Eucharistie und Kirche, in: Das Bleibende im Wandel. Theologische Beiträge zum
Schisma von Marcel Lefebvre*, hrsg. von R. Ahlers-P. Krämer, Paderborn 1990, p. 87-103.

[74]   The term *Charisma* occurs eleven times (LG 12,2; 25,3; 30; 50,1; DV 8,2; AA 3,3-4; 30,6;
AG 23,1; 28,1; PO 4,2; 9,3), while the derived adjective *Charismaticus* only three times
(LG 4,1; 7,3; AG 4); for a detailed analysis of these texts cf. G. Rambaldi, *Uso e significato
di "Charisma" nel Vaticano II. Analisi e confronto di due passi conciliari sui carismi*, in:
Gregorianum 66 (1975), pp. 141-162.

charisms are "special graces" (*gratias speciales*), b) dispensed liberally by the Spirit "among the faithful of every order", c) with which "they are rendered apt and ready" (*aptos et promptos*) to assume the different functions in the service of a "greater expansion of the Church": d) these same charisms are distinguished into "extraordinary" and "more simple or more widely diffused", e) but all indiscriminately subordinate to the "judgement of the authority of the Church" as much as it regards their genuinity and, given that such ensues, they cannot be extinguished.

In LG 4,1 it is affirmed: "He (the Holy Spirit) guiding the Church in the way of all truth (cf. Jn 16,13) and unifying her in communion and in the works of ministry, he bestows upon her varied hierarchic and charismatic gifts ... ". In this text it is underlined how the mysterious unity of the ecclesial communion is realised by the Holy Spirit through two different types of gifts connected simultaneously and constantly to the Church: the hierarchic and the charismatic. The same with dogmatic truth if on the one hand it hinders the contrasting of the charism to the ministry and thus of unilaterally reducing the Church to a charismatic community, on the other hand it also hinders reducing equally unilaterally the mystery of the Church to a pyramidical structure concentrated on the hierarchy. Both the hierarchical gifts, and the charismatic come from the same Spirit of Christ and can, even if according to different modalities, be considered both as structures or functions *ex institutione divina* (LG 22,1 and LG 32,1)

Finally in reading AA 3,3-4 the canonist is immediately struck by the importance given by the conciliar Fathers to the "right and duty of all believers" to exercise their charisms received from the Holy Spirit. Without minimally prejudicing the canonical importance of such an assertion one cannot however avoid observing that such a "right and duty" is a necessary implication of the general principle of constitutional order affirmed by LG 12,2 according to which charisms can be given to every category of the faithful. In the passage from the Decree on the Apostolate of the Laity, more even than in that of the Dogmatic Constitution on the Church, the authenticity of such an interpretation is confirmed by the explicit summons to the right to follow one's proper charism, which is exercised "in communion with his brothers in Christ and with his pastors especially" (AA 3,4).

From these three conciliar texts the lines of demarcation between which it is possible to specify the ecclesiological-constitutional role of Charism can equally be deduced: 1. Charism is a special grace, different from Word and Sacrament, but equally structurally orientated to the building up of the ecclesial *communio*; 2. in as much as such, Charism is not reducable to either a personal talent, or to a gift of the Spirit dispensed indiscriminately through baptism;

3. its relationship of complementarity with ministry on the one hand shows that Charism belongs to the Constitution of the Church and on the other hand unmasks the falsity of the opposition, of a romantic-protestant origin, between Charism and Institution. Starting from these principles, and in particular the last, it is easier to understand why in contemporary dogmatic theology it is by now a fact acquired with certainty that in the Church the Constitution is a category or entity greater than the Institution. For example, the theologian Hans Urs von Balthasar, in full syntony with a long dogmatic tradition, arrives at defining the ecclesial Institution as a sort of "kenotische Verfassung", that is as a kenotic reduction of the mystery of the Church, ideal for hindering – through the logic of ecclesial obedience which guarantees the persistence of the *Memoria Christi* – a privatisation of the ecclesial experience [75].

To fully measure the canonical importance of this Balthasarian definition of the ecclesial Institution it is however important to realise that the equation between Institution and sacrament is of a false order, because every sacrament and therefore also baptism, which confers the common priesthood and the *sensus fidei,* is an institutional element in the Church. Nevertheless, the ecclesial Institution is not reducible to the ministerial priesthood. To this also belongs the common priesthood which, together with the *sensus fidei,* constitutes the foundation of the particpation of all the faithful in the mission of the Church in the world. An indisputable proof of this is the fact that the sacrament of baptism, forever considered a *ianua sacramentorum,* constitutes the criterion of differentiation between the constitutional quality of Christian religion – proper to many sects exclusively founded on the faith in Christ through the Word – and the constitutional quality of ecclesiality which, being such as it is, requires at least the sacramental depth of baptism [76]. And precisely in baptism flowers paradigmaticly the juridical value of all the sacraments and consequently also of the Word, which, while not always being proclaimed in concomitance with the celebration of the Sacraments, has however always, at least in the words of the synthetic and definatory form of every sacrament, the function of producing the soteriological and socio-juridical effect of the symbolic sacramental sign.

The conception of baptism as a carrier element, not only of the ecclesial Constitution but also of the Institution, permits the easy measurement of how the relationship faithful-Church is not identical, nor homologous with that of citizen-State. In fact, in the Church as a reality of communion, contrary to what happens in the modern State, every inter-ecclesial relationship is not realised

---

[75] Cf. *Pneuma und Institution. Skizzen zur Theologie,* Vol. IV, Einsiedeln 1974, pp. 129-130 and pp. 229-233.

[76] Cf. E Corecco, *Battesimo* in: *Digesto delle Discipline pubblicistiche,* curato da R. Sacri ed altri, Vol. II (1987), pp. 213-216.

according to a person-institution dialectic, but rather as a relationship between Institution and Institution, that is between person and person. And the reason is the following: while in the State offices are characterised by a sort of hypostasisation, in the Church her ministers do not exist in the guise of self-standing realities, that is as institutional abstractions in relation to the sacraments. These exist as ontological components of baptised people and eventually as people ordained with the sacrament of Orders [77].

For this reason, if by institution is meant the stable and constitutive structures of a social reality, agreement is needed that this structure is conferred on the Church by the Sacrament and the Word, which interpenetrate each other in turn, giving an origin among other things to that central figure of a canonical subject which is the *Christifideles,* liable and immanent in all three states of ecclesial life and therefore in the persons of the laity, priests and religious. The Church as Institution does not however simply coincide with the organisation of public powers, that is authority. The ecclesial Institution always verifies itself around the two poles of Baptism and Holy Orders, converging with the other sacraments in the Eucharist, in which the principle structure of the Constitution of the Church likewise manifests itself. Indeed in the Eucharist the whole Church is represented, because this sacrament is in the meantime the *fons et origo* as well as the *culmen* of the whole life of the Church, as Vatican II affirms (SC 10). In this therefore comes the fulfilment of the process of integration between Institution and Constitution begun in baptism, as the *initium et exordium* of all the grades of ecclesial communion.

From what has been expounded up to here the following conclusions can be drawn, valid for both dogmatic theology and for Canon Law: in the Church, the Institution substantially consists in the juridico-structural developments historically assumed by both the common priesthood and the ministerial priesthood; the Constitution, on the other hand, is not a rigid quantity (*starre Grösse*), because together with Word and Sacrament it must reckon with its third primary element: Charism [78]. This includes however all those elements which are structurally necessary for the very existence of the Church, for the individualisation of its identity as a subject, even juridical. This conclusion can be easily understood in its juridical consequences if the canonist does not forget that both the aspects of the ecclesial reality, that is to say the Constitution and the

---

[77]   For a compared study of the two notions of Institution and Constitution in state and in canonical law, cf. L. Gerosa, *Carisma e diritto nella Chiesa. Riflessioni canonistiche sul "carisma originario"dei nuovi movimenti ecclesiali,* Milano 1989, pp. 108-179.

[78]   The fact that the Constitution of the Church is not a rigid quantity is demonstrated by the fact that it is not guaranteed by a supreme tribunal, but simply by the help of the Holy Spirit, promised by Christ; cf. K. Mörsdorf, *Kirchenverfassung. I. Katholische K.,* in: LThK, Vol. VI (Freiburg im Br. 1961), coll. 274-277, here coll. 274-275.

Institution, are subject to the constant intervention of the Holy Spirit whose *opus proprium* is the construction of the *communio,* in which man can fully rediscover his freedom [79]. Precisely because of this double pneumatological influence of the *communio* the canonist is faced with an equal preoccupation with two different and opposite convictions: " ... whether it is the position which denies and undervalues the ecclesial function of Canon Law for underlining the importance of charisms, or that which extols the juridical element, because the one as much as the other ... seem unilateral. Both coincide, conclusively, in conceiving the law of the Church as something which has sense only in the light of the institutional fact and in seeing the charismatic dynamism as something which, for its vitality, remains at the margins of law" [80]

In this correct perspective, juridical is not therefore synonomous with institutional, and the two categories of Institution and Constitution have a different significance in the Church from that which they assume in the juridical ordering of the modern State.

If one reflects then on the fact that not even the modern state constitutions appear so exhaustive as the juridical liberal tradition would seem to claim – in any case there exist fundamental rights (as for example the right to life) which while having a constitutional character are not positively formalised in the institutional documents – it becomes clear how, in order to better define Institution and Constitution in the Church, it is necessary for the canonist to separate himself from the constant referral to the models of the state. In fact, unlike the modern State, the Church does not only not possess a formal Constitution but its material Constitution contains a structuring element which does not permit the identification of the Constitution with the Institution. This structuring element is Charism which, being given by the Holy Spirit to the Church to build up the communion through the realisation of the fruitful equilibrium of the institutional bipolarity (clergy and laity) which characterises it, develops a pivotal ecclesiological role between Institution and Constitution; a role which reveals all of its constituent force in relation to the construction of the *communio.* Recalling the Institution to the absolute priority of the Spirit and relativising the power of any element or organ of the hierarchical Constitution of the Church, in order that none of these becomes absolutely self-sufficient, Charism enlivens the Institution itself and helps it to overcome the difficulty of the competitiveness proper to every form of power, which in the Church is

---

[79] Cf. J. Ratzinger, *Der Heilige Geist als "communio". Zum Verhältnis von Pneumatologie und Spiritualität bei Augustinus,* in: C. Heitmann-H. Mühlen (Hrsg.), *Erfahrung und Theologie des Heiligen Geistes,* München 1974, pp. 223-238.

[80] P. Lombardia, *Carismi e Chiesa istituzionale,* in: *Studi in onore di Pietro Agostino d'Avack,* Vol. II, Milano 1976, pp. 957-988, here p. 965.

always translated into a pre-eminence of the hierarchy over the laity or of the laity over the hierarchy.

Under the juridical profile this particular ecclesiological role of Charism certainly has its specific weight, measurable through its capacity to be – at least in its most completed form, or in the so-called "originating charism" or "charism of foundation" – with the Word and Sacrament, a source of the juridically binding relationships of communion.

d) CHARISM, PERSON AND COMMUNITY

The analysis of the associative phenomenon generated by an *originating* or *of foundation* charism [81] permits the identification of its four fundamental characteristics in arranging the ecclesial communion: 1. the capacity of the charism to enable the participation in a particular form of following Christ, in which the believer is given the possibility of living the ecclesial mystery in its totality and universality; 2. the capacity of the charism to pastorally interpret the *communio fidelium* in an experience of fraternity, having as its pivot *auctoritas*; 3. the capacity of the charism to open the believer – through this fraternity – to the *communio ecclesiarum* and the mission; 4. the capacity to render operative the unity between common priesthood and ministerial priesthood, putting in relief the reciprocal arrangement of the juridical dimension and the pneumatological dimension of Word and Sacrament.

All four characteristics, while not placing themselves at the same level as the ontological effects of Baptism, are clearly to be considered as structuring elements or expressive of the structuring force of the originating charism. Within the associative phenomenon generated by the latter, such elements are not simple rules of custom, but possess a binding character, which develops an essential role in determining the nature and purpose of the group or ecclesial movement. Is this binding character of a juridical nature? To respond to the question it is necessary to establish a paragon between charism and *consuetudo*, which in its turn is a type of communitarian charism [82] and therefore a form of direct participation by the People of God in the *aedificatio Ecclesiae*. On the juridical level this means that custom is a type of the sources of law species.

As such *consuetudo* represents both an instrument of juridical knowledge, and a typical way of producing the right different from the law. On the latter consideration the doctrine is conflicting. What is under discussion is not so much the fact that *consuetudo* is a suitable method for producing rules of

---

[81]   For a similar analysis, cf. L. Gerosa, *Carisma e diritto nella Chiesa*, op. cit., pp. 79-90.

[82]   Cf. R. Bertolino, *Sensus fidei et coutume dans le droit de l'Église*, in: Freiburger Zeitschrift für Philosophie und Theologie 33 (1986), pp. 227-243; L. Gerosa, *Carisma e diritto nella Chiesa*, op. cit., pp. 180-203.

conduct, rather than as much as to know if such rules are really of a juridic nature.

Evidently the solution given to the problem is strictly bound to the notion of law within which it operates, and therefore to the much laboured *quaestio* of the definition of Canon Law. Among the many replies the most convincing, at least in the realm of general theory, seems therefore that which, to resolve the problem of the specific difference between the so-called rules of custom and the customary norms, proposes a criterion of a general order, distinguishing between extrinsic rules (not necessary for the existence of particular groups) and incidental rules on the very structure, the nature and the finality of such groups or associations. While the former are nothing other than rules of custom, the latter are juridical norms, technically named *consuetudo* [83]

Applying such a criterion to the ecclesial reality it appears clear how only the rules of conduct which express in a concrete way the structuring force of the originating charism, at the base of the given movement and of the given association, are of a juridical nature. As such these document in an unequivocal way the capacity of a charism to be a source of law, both in the strict sense of a procedure for the formation of a juridical norm, and in the wider sense of an instrument of juridical knowledge. If such rules are structuring within the associative phenomenon generated by the originating charism, they are so because, by their nature, they have a deep incidence on the level of the concrete realisation of the ecclesial *communio* as such. In other words, their juridical value is manifested also in their capacity to interact with the whole juridical system to which they belong, showing forth their specific nature.

Dealing here with the canonical system, the structuring elements of charism must interact with the other elements of the *communio* as the formal principle of the whole juridical ordering of the Church. And in point of fact, through these structured elements, a charism shows all of its own creative force of law, because, thanks to these, it joins the institutional or the communitarian with the personal, the ecclesial or the object with the subject, according to the logic of the reciprocal immanence characterising the *communio* at its every level, structural and anthropological.

This structuring force of a charism manifests its juridical value especially in the interaction between *persona* and *communio*, typical of the ecclesial experience. In other words the rules of conduct generated by the originating charism are of a juridical nature because they permit the faithful who participate in the reality of ecclesial communion generated by such a charism

---

[83]   It is the solution which Norberto Bobbio developed in his youthful work on "custom as a normative fact" very far from his recent Kelsian positions, and reprised in: N. Bobbio, *Consuetudine,* in: EDD, Vol. IX (Milano 1961), pp. 426-443.

to overcome the dialectic between person and community, rediscovering the structural relationality of his *persona* as an ontological determination of human existence, expanded and made manifest by the sacrament of baptism, according to the scholastic principle: *Gratia non destruit, sed supponit et perficit naturam*. Now precisely by dint of this, its structural relationality, the person has become the central notion of the so-called juridical experience. And consequently if it is true, as the enormous canonical literature in favour shows [84], that Canon Law cannot ignore the notion of person thus understood, it is just as true that the canonist can be helped to clarify the problems connected with this by paying attention to the role of charism in the overcoming of the dialectic between person and community, thanks above all to its capacity to provoke a conspiracy of relationships in which the *bonum privatum* and the *bonum publicum* are reciprocally immanent and therefore totally ordered to the *bonum communionis Ecclesiarum*.

All of this means that, as the history of the Church fully and in many ways documents, Charism as a primary element of the ecclesial Constitution has its juridical dimension, with a proper binding force, and – as such – is a source of juridical production in a broad sense. Precisely because of this it can challenge and provoke the ecclesial Institution both when it is given to the faithful who exercise the ministerial priesthood, as when it is given to the faithful who only exercise the common priesthood, whether they are men or women. And in both cases its provocation demonstrates its proper authenticity and its proper capacity to construct a Church through the realisation of an effective interaction between the personal and communitarian aspects of the Christian experience, where the freedom of the spirit always joins together with ecclesial obedience in the truth of faith. Without such interaction and without an adequate distinction of its juridical elements from those merely moral, the *communio Ecclesiae* slides inevitably either towards clerical authoritarianism or towards democratic subjectivism.

3.3 CONCLUSION: *communio Ecclesiae* AND CANON LAW

In the ecclesiology of communion of the Vatican Council II visible ecclesial structure and spiritual community are not two quantities or different unities, but form the Church as "one complex reality which comes together from a human and a divine element" (LG 8,1). In place of the expression *unam realitatem complexam* the conciliar Fathers, in full syntony with their idea of the Church, could of course also have used here the biblical-patristic term of *communio*, making it even clearer that in the Church law and communion are not two op-

---

[84]   One consults for example the two following works: S. Cotta, *Persona. I. Filosofia del diritto* and C. Mirabelli, *Persona fisica. d) Diritto canonico,* in: EDD, Vol. XXIII (Milano 1983), pp. 159-169 and pp. 230-234.

posites, but rather contemporary and inseparable elements of its constitutional structure [85]. There are three sources of the latter – as was fully illustrated in the preceding section: Word, Sacrament and Charism, even if the latter is always and only at the service of the first two. This means that in the Church institutional and juridical are not synonymous, even if all that is juridical is at the service of the ecclesial communion. In fact, as Eugenio Corecco rightly observes, the *communio* is " ... the specific modality with which, within the ecclesial community, they become juridically bound both as intersubjective relationships and as those existing on a more structural level between the particular Churches and the universal. The reality of the *communio* has however a binding force which overcomes the tendentially only mystical limits of the eastern *Sobornost*" [86].

The truth of this assertion is underlined with clarity in no.2 of the *Nota explicativa praevia* of *Lumen Gentium*, where it is specified how the key concept for the whole of conciliar ecclesiology was going to be understood: with the term *communio* "a certain vague effect is not what is intended, but an organic reality, which requires a juridical form and at the same time is animated by charity" [87]. It is a question therefore of a reality with a clear juridical-constitutional value, able to be sythesised in the principle of the so-called *communio Ecclesiae et Ecclesiarum,* even if the expression recurs only once more (AG 19,3) in the conciliar texts. This principle – as will be seen in a detailed way in the last chapter of the manual – finds its *locus theoligicus* in LG 23,1, where the Fathers of the Council define the relationship between the universal Church and the particular Churches: ... *in quibus et ex quibus una et unica ecclesia catholica exsistit* [88]. In the Catholic accepted meaning of the word communion means however two things of great importance not only for the constitutional law of the Church but also for the whole of Canon Law: on the structural level (that is to say of the *communio Ecclesiarum*) there is in force in the Church a reciprocal imminence between the universal and the particular; on the anthropological level (that is to say of the *communio fidelium*) there is registered an analogous reciprocal immanence between the mystical body of the Church and the Christian faithful. The metaphysical and juridical identity of the latter is given by the fact "that by dint of baptism man has been structurally rooted, and not just in the ethical profile, in Christ. The Christian

---

[85] Cf. P. Krämer, *Kirchenrecht I*, op. cit., p. 30.

[86] *Teologia del diritto canonico*, op. cit., p. 1714.

[87] For a full commentary on this fundamental conciliar clarification cf. J. Ratzinger, *Erläuternde Vorbemerkung,* in: LThK-Vat II, Vol. I, pp. 350-359, especially p. 353.

[88] For a study of the constitutional significance of this formula, cf. W. Aymans, *Die Communio Ecclesiarum als Gestaltgesetz der einen Kirche,* in: AfkKR 139 (1970), pp. 69-90, here p. 85.

represents Christ because the whole of Christ with his Mystical Body is present in him. The Christian cannot therefore be conceived as an individual entity opposed to the collective, but as a subject to whom the whole of the community of Christians is mysteriously, but really, immanent"[89].

In conclusion, in the light of the ecclesiology of communion developed in detail by the Vatican Council II it becomes clear that the ultimate end of Canon Law is not simply to guarantee the *bonum commune Ecclesiae,* but rather that of realising the *communio Ecclesiae.* After the Vatican Council II it is no longer possible to apply in a mechanical and uncritical way the scholastic definition of law as *objectum virtutis iustitiae* to Canon Law[90]. In fact it is clear by now that in the Church the law is not simply defined by the fundamentally binding character of the human *iustitia legalis* (both commutative and distributive), but rather starting from a superior form of justice, the ecclesial communion is an icon of love and justice inscribed in the trinitarian mystery: "My judgement is just, because my aim is to do not my own will, but the will of him who sent me." (Jn 5,30). Given that ecclesial sociability is not born from a natural dynamism but from grace (Word, Sacrament, Charism), the *communio* represents the structural reality in which grace is embodied with its ultimately binding force. Consequently in the Church the notion of the object of the virtue of justice is not defined, but the object of the *communio Ecclesiae et Ecclesiarum*[91]. In other words ecclesial communion *in omnibus institutionis canonicis applicetur et hoc modo totum ordinem canonicum informet*[92]. This represents therefor the ontological statute of the law of the Church and as such the formal principle of Canon Law[93]. This means that on the one hand every element of the juridical system of the Church is directed by this principle, on the other hand that the very epistemological and methodological statute of canonical science – as will be seen in the next chapter in section five – cannot prescind from this given fact.

A similar conception of Canon Law overcomes in a single blow every formal discussion that aims to contrast or separate the form from the content of the Church in the various theological disciplines, because in theology the content is the interior form that directs, that is it gives form and unites its every

---

[89]   E. Corecco, *I diritti fondamentali del cristiano nella Chiesa e nella Società. Aspetti metodologici della questione,* in: Actes IV CIDC, pp. 1207-1234, here p. 1224.

[90]   Cf. Thomas Aquinas, *S. Th. II-II,* q. 57, a. 1.

[91]   This is the conclusion of E. Corecco, *Theologie des Kirchenrechts,* in: HdbkathKR, pp.12-24, here p.23.

[92]   H. Müller, *Utrum "communio" sit principium formale-canonicum novae codificationis Iuris Canonici Ecclesiae Latinae?,* in: Periodica 74 (1985), pp. 85-108, here p. 107.

[93]   Cf. E. Corecco, *Teologia del diritto canonico,* op. cit., p. 1752.

single external element or exterior form [94], so that in this it can do no other than be for us full concordance between form and content.

FUNDAMENTAL BIBLIOGRAPHY

Aymans W., *Die Communio Ecclesiarum als Gestaltgesetz der einen Kirche,* in: AfkKR 139 (1970), pp. 69-90.

Bertolino R., *Sensus fidei et coutume dans le droit de l'Église,* in: Freiburger Zeitschrift für Philosophie und Theologie 33 (1986), pp. 227-243.

Corecco E., *Teologia del diritto canonico, in: Nuovo Dizionario di teologia,* a cura di G. Barbaglio-S. Dianich, Alba 1976, pp. 1711-1753.

Corecco E., *Theological justifications of the latin canon law,* in: *Le nouveau Code de Droit Canonique I. Actes du Ve Congres Internationale de Droit Cononique tenu à l'Université St. Paul d'Ottawa (19–25 aout 1984),* Ottawa 1986, pp. 69-96.

Gerosa L., *Carisma e diritto nella Chiesa. Riflessioni canonistiche sul "carisma originario" dei nuovi movimenti ecclesiali,* Milano 1989.

Krämer P., *Theologische Grundlegung des Kirchlichen Rechts. Die rechtstheologische Auseinandersetzung zwischen H. Barion und J. Klein im Licht des II. Vatikanischen Konzils,* Trier 1977.

Mörsdorf K., *Schriften zum kanonischen Recht,* hrsg. von W. Aymans-K.Th. Geringer-H.Schmitz, Paderborn 1989.

Ruoco Varela A., *Evangelische Kirchenrechtstheologie heute. Möglichkeiten und Grenzen eines Dialogs,* in: AfkKR 140 (1970), pp. 106-136.

Saier O., *Communio in der Lehre des Zweiten Vatikanischen Konzils. Eine rechtsbegriffliche Untersuchung,* München 1973.

---

[94] Cf. H.U. von Balthasar, *Herrlichkeit. Eine theologische Ästhetik,* Bd. II/Teil 1, Einsiedeln 1962 p.20.

Second Chapter: Sources, Methods and Instruments of Canon Law

Canon Law insofar as it is a *law* of the *Church* has always been part of the destiny of one or the other. The study of its sources, its method and its instruments is the environment in which one is greatly faced with the real contents that these concepts of *law* and *Church* come bit by bit to assume in the history and life of the People of God. Such a study cannot therefore be separated from what was said in the first chapter on the theological foundation of Canon Law, of which it somewhat represents a necessary corollary.

1. Sources and formation of Canon Law

1.1 The sources of Canon Law

In the law of the Church two types of source are distinguishable: the internal or material, which produce law even without the intervention of the ecclesiastical legislator, and the external or formal which are single laws or canonical norms. The former are strictly bound to the problem of the unity of Canon Law, the latter to the long process of codification of ecclesiastical laws.

a) Material sources and unity of Canon Law

In the preceding chapter we saw that the ultimate purpose of the juridical structure of the Church is the realisation of the *communio* and that Canon Law participates in this way in the sacramental nature of the whole of the ecclesial mystery. The originating nucleus of the juridical structure of the new People of God is therefore established in positive divine law (*ius divinum positivum*) itself. This affirmation does not obfuscate, but rather puts in a true light the fact that in the communitarian structure of the Church natural divine law (*ius divinum naturale*) also develops its own role, even if only secondary or subsidiary, because if the Scholastics teach that *gratia non tollit sed perficit naturam* the Vatican Council II affirms in big letters that the "Church ... is at once the sign and safeguard of the transcendental dimension of the human person" (GS 76,2). Both forms of divine law mentioned concur, together with purely human elements (*ius humanum* or *ius mere ecclesiasticum*), in the formation of ecclesial law. If the normative significance of the three single elements of this classical distinction, arising once more from Francisco Suarez, is different depending on their closeness or not to the centre of the mystery of the Church, the fact that the whole of Canon Law in its totality participates in such a mystery witnesses to its originating particular attributes in comparison with state law.

The so-called *ius canonicum*, in all of its articulated development, always has its ultimate material source in divine law from which it derives not only its existence but also its juridicality. Consequently it is a mistake to consider either the totality of the canonical norms of positive divine law as absolutely invariable, or the totality of the canonical norms of law *mere ecclesiasticum* as reformable at whim. While the former totality can be defined as a revealed law knowable through Tradition or made visible by the latter, the latter while not being an immediate concretisation of the biblical information is however strictly bound to the historical-normative concretisation of divine law whether positive or natural[1]. The classical distinction between *ius divinum* and *ius mere ecclesiasticum* is to be simply understood as the attempt to adopt a first fundamental distinction between the material contents of Canon Law, in order to determine with greater precision the juridically binding force of every single norm. Other criteria for distinction, however secondary in comparison with this, are traceable in the collections of ecclesiastical law and above all in the canonical codifications of this century.

B) THE PRINCIPAL COLLECTIONS OF ECCLESIASTICAL LAWS

Right from the beginning in order to favour the forming and persistence of a juridical certainty in the Church, as well as a correct application of the single norms, the need was felt to compile collections containing the various laws and decrees promulgated by the ecclesiastical authority. In the first six centuries these collections (for example the *Collectio Romana* or the *Versio Isidoriana*) were compiled applying a simple chronological criterion; from the sixth century on a sytematic criterion was also introduced, for example in the famous *Collectio Dionysio-Hadriana* sent as a gift in 774 by Pope Hadrian I to Charlemagne. A little later, especially with Hincmar of Rhiems (806-882) and Ivo of Chartres (1040-1116), there was an attempt to unify the material of these collections, and to introduce rules for the adaptation of the ecclesiastical laws to the needs of the time[2]. This first attempt to systematically harmonise ecclesiastical laws, in order to avoid contradictions in their application, reached its apex in the *Concordia discordantium canonum* published in Bologna by the monk Gratian around 1140. This work, very quickly called simply the *Decretum*, not only signaled the beginning of the definitive establishment of Canon Law as an autonomous discipline but would act as the model for successive collections of ecclesiastical laws, above all of the Decretals (*Summae Decretalium*). The latter, together with the Decretum, would then be reunited in the course of the tridentine reform in a *Corpus Iuris Canonici*, whose *Editio Romana of* 1582 was already hinted at by Pope Gregory XIII in the Bull *Cum pro munere of* 1 July 1580 as the approved collection for teaching and juridical praxis. We are not yet dealing with an authentic code, exclusive and binding, but with approval the *Corpus Iuris Canonici* becomes, together with the collection of Pontifical Bulls (like the monumental one known under the name of *Magnum Bullarium Romanum*), the collection of the more important ecclesiastical laws and therefore the principal source of the Canon Law in force before 1917. This comprises: Gratian's Decree, the Decretals of Gregory IX (*Liber Extra*), the *Liber Sextus of* Boniface VIII, the

---

[1]   Cf. A. Aymans-Mörsdorf, KanR I, pp. 32-37.
[2]   For a rapid historical examination of the development of these rules of interpretation, cf. G. May-A. Egler, *Einführung in die kirchenrechtliche Methode,* Regensburg 1986, pp. 43-45.

Clementine of Clement V and finally the two private collections called *Extravagantes Joannes XXII* and *Extravagantes communes*[3]

1.2 THE MODERN CANONICAL CODIFICATIONS

A) THE 1917 CODE

Notwithstanding the undoubted progress established by the publication of the *Corpus Iuris Canonici* as an approved collection, already at the Vatican Council I (1869-1870) it was underlined by a number of parties how the consultation of the same turned out less than easy especially because of its fullness and the different juridical value of its individual parts. The difficulties in distinguishing the Canon Law effectively in force are further multiplied by a double given fact: on the one hand the *Corpus* together with the laws also collects the provisions emanating from individual cases, from which only the *probati auctores* are in a positon to extract the general juridical norm; on the other hand the *Corpus* itself neither collects all the sources, nor abrogates those that through time have become obsolete. Consequently it can be understood how, towards the end of the XIX Century, the need for a complete and unitary systemisation of the sources of Canon Law, in order to facilitate the knowledge of the laws in force and their correct application, had begun to make itself felt, by this time acutely. The demand was greatly highlighted by the fact that in the state field an analogous need had already for some time been gone into, a little on all sides, in the compilation of modern codes, especially under the rationalising impetus of the Enlightenment, but also to favour political interests and the centralisers of the absolute States[4].

Faced with this deficient and contradictory hotch-potch of sources, the cause of a grave uncertainty in the law of the Church, in the preparatory meetings of the Vatican Council I, not a few of the bishops considered the situation as intolerable and therefore considered indispensable a *reformatio iuris*. "If some limited themselves to asking for a revision of the *Corpus* or a new collection, others identified the remedy in the drawing up of a modern type code, that is which presents the characteristics of authenticity, brevity, clarity, systematism, and completeness; that is to say a text, promulgated by the supreme authority, which exposes in brief and accessible forms to everyone the whole of the legislation in force, subdividing it rationally into titles, chapters and articles according to the order of the various subjects"[5]. The wish to include the codification of the whole of Canon Law among the themes to be dealt with in the ecumanical assizes however came up against a dilatory and negative attitude from the officials of the Roman Curia and above all from the special congregation instituted by Pius IX for the examination of the postulates to be put before the conciliar fathers. These uncertainties and contradictions, not to mention the prospect of a great bank of work to be got through in a short space of time and in concomitance

---

[3]   The best edition of the *Corpus Iuris Canonici* is that of E. Friedberg, Leipzig 1879/81 (Reprinted Graz 1955). On the long and complex process of formation of the *Corpus*, cf. L. Muselli, *Storia del diritto canonico. Introduzione alla storia del diritto e delle istituzioni ecclesiali*, Torino 1992, pp. 49-51 and pp. 57-58.

[4]   Cf. G. Fasso, *Storia della filosofia del diritto*, vol. III: *Ottocento e Novecento*, Bologna 1970, pp. 11-30.

[5]   G. Feliciani, *Le basi del diritto canonico*, Bologna 1979, p. 14.

with more urgent political problems, suggested the transformation of the wish into an *umile domanda* addressed to the Pontiff Pius IX then decided to put in reserve the idea of a global restructuring of ecclesiastical legislation and to act later on his own and by sections, beginning with the penal where the confusion was so great as to render almost impossible the protection of the rights of the accused and canonical discipline itself ultimately inapplicable[6].

In reality even this first initiative – limited to the penal field – is not a true *Codex* but rather a new collection which regroups, simplifies and consolidates the pre-existing ecclesiastical normative. This demonstrates that the road to be covered to reach the drawing up of a true and proper Code of Canon Law, capable of systematically and unitarianly ordering the whole law of the Church, was still a long way off. It would be Pius X, the Pope who came from the practice of the *cura animarum*, with the MP *Arduum sane munus* of 19 March 1904 who would make known the project for the codification of Canon Law and its master lines.

Notwithstanding the real difficulty of drawing up *in unum* all the ecclesiastical laws effectively in force, and in spite of the differences surrounding the inconveniences which could give room to a codification in the modern sense[7], under the direction of Cardinal Pietro Gasparri the huge work was finally brought to an end at Pentecost 1917, the day on which Benedict XV promulgated the *Codex Iuris Canonici*, which entered into force however a year later, on 19 May 1918.

This first Code of the Church is composed of 2414 canons, arranged in five books: the Ist book *Normae Generales* (cans. 1-86), besides some introductory clarifications and regulations on the computation of time, contains norms relative to law and custom as sources of Canon Law as well as norms relative to rescripts, privileges and dispensations; the IInd book is entitled *De Personis* (cans. 87-725) and arranged into three distinct parts (*De clericis, De religiosis, De laicis*) is the substance of the so-called constitutional law of the Church; in the IIIrd book *De rebus* (cans. 726-1551) norms of different types are gathered, in particular those relating to the Sacraments (cans. 731-1143), to the Magisterium (cans. 1322-1408) and to ecclesiastical patrimonial law (cans. 1409-1551); the IVth book *De processibus* (cans. 1552-2194) contains the norms relating to the canonical judiciary process, both ordinary and extraordinary; in the Vth and last book (cans. 2195-2414) the penal law of the Church is dealt with. To the five books, in appendices, there follow some pontifical constitutions, among which the principal regards the election of the Pontiff.

Under the juridical profile, the Code of 1917 represents an authentic collection, that is to say approved and promulgated by the Pontiff as supreme legislator, and unique, in the sense that all of its dispositions, old and new as may be, came to be

---

[6]   On the significance of the limits of the Constitution *Apostolica Sedis* (1869) of Pius IX, cf. L. Gerosa, *La scomunica è una pena? Saggio per una fondazione teologica del diritto penale canonico*, Fribourg (CH) 1984, pp. 149-156.

[7]   If some authors favourable to a canonical codification published absolutely private works of codification (for example De Luise, Colomiatti, Pillet, Pezzani), others maintained on the other hand that the codification risked making Canon Law rigid, through its extremely elastic nature and free from any formalism: cf. F. Ruffini, *La codificazione del diritto ecclesiastico*, in: *Scritti giuridici minore*, chosen and ordered by M. Falco-A.C. Jemolo-F. Ruffini, Milano 1936, I, pp. 59-97.

considered as emanating with the same importance and therefore with the same obligatory character. The aim of the codification of substituting the multiplicity of sources with an *unicus fons* of Canon Law was not however fully reached. Indeed, on the one hand the Code does not abrogate the agreements of the Holy See with the various nations (can. 3), leaves intact acquired rights (can. 4), tolerates particular customs and laws contrary to its dispositions (cans. 5 and 6); on the other hand the Code itself, except where it reproduces norms of divine law or disposes otherwise in an explicit way, does not apply itself to the Eastern Catholic Churches (can. 1) Moreover, after its promulgation, numerous ecclesiastical laws were enacted which modified or integrated it [8].

If the linguistic form of this first Code of the Church is for the most part clear, simple and concise, its juridical terminology leaves room for insidious uncertainties. "Principles promising a purification of juridical language, fulfilled in individual parts of the code, are most times annulled in their efficacy by the fact that in other parts, and not infrequently precisely in the individual parts in question, more antiquated terms are used. Almost all the technical terms are used now with one meaning, now another; on the other hand several expressions are often to be found for one and the same thing" [9]. Moreover, if with legal definitions the CIC of 1917 tries to impress a greater clarity on canonical laws, the ecclesiastical legislator himself does not always adhere to his own definitions. In the interpretation of the text of the code one must nevertheless renounce all formalism and always consider the spirit and the sense of the law. In doubtful cases it is necessary to have recourse to an authentic interpretation of the code, guaranteed by an apposite cardinalatial commission, instituted by Benedict XV with the MP *Cum iuris canonici* of 15 September 1917. Its interpretations have the force of law and are published from time to time in the *Acta Apostolica Sedis* [10].

Notwithstanding these limits the Pio-Benedictine canonical codification represents a progress so notable in ecclesiatical legislative technology as to provoke a generally very positive first acceptance for the Code of the Church. Gradually this almost unanimous positive appreciation was replaced by diverse critisms. Among these the most important were concerned with the methodological attitude of the Code, its systematic and its tendency to a rigid centralisation.

Regarding the methodological attitude of the Pio-Benedictine Code that the legislator applies, a notable separation between history and the law in force cannot be denied. Indeed, the CIC of 1917 does not just formally abolish all the preceding collections, but also by inserting into its substance a large part of the preceding Canon Law introduces a good 854 canons without any reference to the preceding sources [11].

---

[8]   Cf. X. Ochoa, *Leges Ecclesiae post CIC editae (1917-1985)*, Voll. I-VI, Roma 1966-1987.

[9]   K. Mörsdorf, *Codice di diritto canonico (CIC)*, in: SacrM, Vol. II here coll. 458. From the same author comes the most complete analysis of the terminology of the Pio-Benedictine Code: K. Mörsdorf, *Die Rechtssprache des Codex Iuris Canonici. Eine kritische Untersuchung*, Paderborn 1937 (Unveränderter Nachdruck 1967).

[10] The text of the quoted MP can be found in: AAS 9 (1917). pp. 483-484.

[11] Cf. P. Gasparri-I. Seredi, *Codicis Iuris Canonici Fontes*, Vol. IX (Roma 1939), Tabella AI, pp. 7-164. Cf. also G. Feliciani, *Le basi del diritto canonico*, *op*. cit. p. 20.

The sytematic of the CIC/1917 is still strictly bound to the classical tripartition *Personae-res-actiones* of Roman Law [12]. This appears today to be little adapted to express the connection between the canonical normative and the ecclesial mystery. For example, by now for some time it has been perceived as untenable the fact that the juridical norms relative to the sacraments are entered in *De rebus*. Moreover, if it is a mistake to consider the CIC of 1917 simply as the juridical projection of a political plan of centralisation of powers intended to suffocate every legitimate ecclesial pluralism, neither is it possible to deny the validity of the double critical opinion of Ulrich Stutz [13]. For the protestant canonist, the CIC of 1917 is on the one hand so strongly influenced by the Vatican Council I as to be able to be designated as Vatican Canon Law (*Vatikanisches Kirchenrecht*), and on the other, applying to the Church the socio-philosophical concept of *societas perfecta,* it ends up by reducing constitutional law to the organisation of public ecclesiatical powers and therefore Canon Law itself to a law almost exclusively for the clergy (*ein fast ausnahmsloses Geistlichkeitsrecht*). Nevertheless, the values of the Pio-Benedictine canonical codification are such, that only after more than forty years its updating was beginning to be thought of seriously, that is from when Pope John XXIII on the 15 January 1959 announced the forthcoming celebration of a Roman diocesan synod and of an ecumenical council [14].

B) THE 1983 CODE (CIC)

Exactly 24 years after this announcement, on the 25 January 1983 Pope John Paul II promulgated the new Code of Canon Law for the Latin Catholic Church. In the meantime the Church had celebrated its twentieth ecumenical council by whose teaching the new reform of Canon Law is necessarily inspired. The secretary general of the Vatican Council II himself, Cardinal Pericle Felice, was later called upon to preside over the *Pontificia Commissio Codici Iuris Canonici Recognoscendo*, instituted on 23 March 1963 and initially composed only of cardinals. Pope Paul VI widened and completed it with experts and consultors coming from all over the world in order to guarantee the fullest consultation possible [15].

---

[12]   The re-division of the material was introduced into Canon Law by Giovanni Paolo Lancelotti (1522-1590), a jurist from Perugia, who conceived of his systematic of his compendium of Canon Law (*De personis, de rebus, de iudiciis, de criminibus et poenis*) on the basis of the work of codification of the Emperor Justinian (527-564); cf. G. May-A. Egler, *Einführung in die kirchenrechtliche Methode,* op. cit., pp. 67-68.

[13]   Cf. U. Stutz, *Der Geist des Codex Iuris Canonici,* Stuttgart 1918, pp. 127-156 and pp. 83-89. As a result of this opinion, cf. also: W. Aymans, *Die Quellen des kanonischen Rechts in der Kodifikation von 1917,* in: IusCan 15 (1975), pp. 79-95, and especially p. 87, and P. Ciprotti, Codex Iuris Canonici, in: EDD, Vol. VII (Milano 1960), coll. 236-241, here col. 239. On the important stimulus given to scientific activity by the first commentators, like the protestant Stutz, Jewish Fallo and the Catholic Vidal, Eichmann, Del Giudice, cf. L. Muselli, *Storia del diritto canonico, op. cit., pp. 85-91.*

[14]   Cf. AAS 51 (1959), pp. 65-69.

[15]   The list of members is to be found in: Communicationes 1 (1969), pp.7-13 and that of the consultors in: Communicationes 1 (1969) pp. 15-28; in the successive issues of the same review the Commission communicated from time to time the various changes. The principles which had to guide the work of the commission were published in: Communicationes 1 (1969), pp. 86-100. For a critical analysis of these directing principles, cf. H.

The work of the Pontifical Commission unfolded in four great stages: a first (1965-1977), dedicated to the working out in detail of the single projects (*Schemata*) on the basis of the *Principia quae Codis Iuris Canonici recognitionem dirigant* fixed by the Synod of Bishops of 1967; a second (1972-1980), in which various *organa consulta-tiva* (that is Bishops' Conferences, Congregations of the Roman Curia, Universities and Religious Orders) were able to examine the schemas and draw up their critical observations; a third (1980-1982), expressed in various moments: an evaluation of the criticism and proposals for amendments, revision of the Schema CIC 1980, collection of the results and publication of the *Schema Novissimum* (1982); a fourth and last phase of work (1982-1983), constituted of the final rereading of the text of the Code on the part of the Pope together with a small group of experts and the immediate preparations for its promulgation.

In every one of these stages the Pontifical Commission found itself faced with three different complete sets of norms and teachings with juridical significance: the Code of 1917, the Vatican Council II, and the post-conciliar legislation. The comparison with the norms of the old Code is dictated by the obvious necessity of guaranteeing continuity in the juridical tradition of the Church. The comparison with the conciliar teaching, and in particular with its ecclesiology, is what permits this canonical tradition itself to stay alive and to develop itself in the light of the new self-knowledge of the Church, whose most significant elements were highlighted by John Paul II in the CA *Sacra Disciplinae Leges*, that is to say: the category of *People of God* for the definition of the constitutional structure of the Church, that of *service* for understanding the function of hierarchy, that of *communio* for establishing the participation of all of the faithful in the mission of the Church and of the exercise of the *tria munera Christi*, as well as the juridical positioning of the *Christifideles* and in particular the laity [16]. The comparison with the third and final totality of norms indicated finally to the Pontifical Commission the way to follow in order to translate the dogmatic teachings and pastoral indications of the Council into juridical language. This task was not however easy, because the post-conciliar canonical normative, often introduced *ad interim* or *ad experimentum* [17], was not seldom presented without the formal character of a law and it is again contradictory both in its terminology, and in its applicability [18]. For this reason, immediately after the promulgation of the CIC Pope John Paul II instituted on the 2 January 1984 a *Pontificia Commissio Codici Iuris Canonici Authenticae Interpretando* (PCI), transformed into the *Pontifical Council for the Interpretation of Legislative Texts by* the CA *Pastor Bonus* of the 28 June 1988 on the reform of the Roman Curia [19].

Schmitz, *Reform des kirchlichen Gesetzbuches CIC 1963-1978, 15 Jahre Päpstliche CIC-Reformkommission,* Trier 1979.

[16] Cf. AAS 75 (1983), Pars II, p. XII.

[17] Cf. for example the MP *Ecclesiae Sanctae* published by Pope Paul VI on 6 August 1966 and containing the norms for the application of the conciliar decrees; the text is to be found in: AAS 58 (1966) pp. 758-787.

[18] In this regard cf. H. Schmitz, *Der Codex Iuris Canonici von 1983,* in: HdbkathKR, pp. 33-57 especially pp. 37-38.

[19] Cf. AAS 76 (1984), p. 342 and pp. 433-434; AAS 80 (1988), pp. 841-934.

The result of this great and long work of reform can be briefly described: the new Code of the Latin Church is shorter than the Pio-Benedictine and collects together 1752 canons ditributed in seven books. In the first book (cans. 1-203) the general norms applicable as a matter of principle in all the sectors of Canon Law are codified; the second book (cans. 204-746) under the title *De Populo Dei* gathers together the bulk of the canonical norms inherent to the constitutional structure of the Catholic Church of the Latin Rite; the third book, *De Ecclesiae munera docendi* (cans. 747-833), and the fouth, *De Ecclesiae munera sanctificandi* (cans. 834-1253), present the juridical regulation of the two principal actions of the Church: the proclamation of the Word of God and the celebration of the Sacraments; the fifth book (cans. 1254-1310) regulates the administration of the goods of the Church and the sixth (cans. 1311-1399) the application of canonical sanctions. The *Codex Iuris Canonici* then closes with a seventh book *De processibus* (cans. 1400-1752) on canonical procedures, excluding those relating to the causes of beatification and canonisation. In addition other important sections of the canonical normative, as for example that regarding the Roman Curia, are not contained in the new Code of Canon Law. On the contrary, the latter makes full use of the deferment of customs and particular laws by means of which it is structurally open to later developments.

Under the profile of the juridical systematic, the new Code has therefore learned the conciliar lesson on the Church as *communio,* above all in its central books (II-III-IV), where for the first time Word and Sacrament appear as the supporting elements of the ecclesial structure [20]. But also under the material profile, as we shall see better later on, the CIC of 1983 presents in comparison with that of 1917 two innovations so important as to justify, at least in part and *post factum,* its realisation notwithstanding the resistance of those who, during the work of reform, had maintained the need for the Church too to opt for a decodification of its laws [21]. The first innovation consists in the fact that the new codification of ecclesiastical laws is no longer guided in the first instance by the search for a rational formulation and systematisation of canonical norms, as much as that of developing them according to their connections with the contents of the faith. The second innnovation is found in the change of identity of the principal subject of the entire ecclesial juridical structure: no longer the cleric but the *Christifidelis*, that is the faithful, as a primordial subordinate figure to that of the layman, priest and religious.

C) THE CODE FOR THE EASTERN CATHOLIC CHURCHES (CCEO)

In 1917 Pope Benedict XV not only promulgated the Code of Canon Law for the Latin Church, but instituted the *Sacred Congregation for the Eastern Churches* [22]. In this way he offers a determining contribution to the realisation of the project for a codification of the Canon Law for the Eastern Catholic Churches. Floated at various

---

[20]   For a detailed evaluation of the systematic of the new Code, cf. H. Schmitz, *De ordinatione systematica novi Codicis Iuris Canonici recogniti,* in: Periodica 68 (1979), pp. 171-200.

[21]   On the problems posed by the fact of proceeding to a new codification of the laws of the Church, cf. E. Corecco, *Presupposti culturali ed ecclesiologici del nuovo Codex,* in: *Il nuovo Codice di Diritto Canonico. Aspetti fondamentali della codificazione postconciliare, edited by* S. Ferrari, Bologna 1983, pp. 37-68.

[22]   Cf. MP *Dei providentis*, in: AAS 9 (1917), pp. 529-533.

times during Vatican Council I[23] this project began to be realised however only under the Pontificate of Pius XI, who in 1929, after having consulted the bishops of Eastern Rite, entrusted the preparatory work to a first *Commissione cardinalizia per gli studi preparatori della Codificatione orientale,* presided over by Cardinal Pietro Gasparri, then substituted in 1939 by a *Pontificia Commissione per la redazione del Codice di diritto canonico orientale*, presided over first by Cardinal Sincero and then by Cardinal Massimi[24]. The latter commission[25], with the help of experts, succeeded in 1943 in publishing a first outline of a code for all of Eastern law, then submitted to a full consultation and finally rewritten and printed again in 1945 as the *Codex Iuris Canonici Orientalis.* Divided into 24 titles, this code was newly revised, amended many times and finally in the month of January 1948 presented to Pope Pius XII, who however decided to promulgate it in stages: on the 22 February 1949, with the Apostolic Letter *Crebrae allatae sunt*[26], he promulgated the canons on the Sacrament of Marriage; on 6 January 1950, with the Apostolic Letter *Sollecitudinem nostrum*[27], he promulgated the canons relating to processes; on 9 February 1952, in the Apostolic Letter *Postquam apostolicis litteris*[28], he promulgated the canons on religious, on the temporal goods of the Church and on the meaning of the words; finally on 2 June 1957, with the Apostolic Letter *Cleri sanctitati*[29], he promulgated the canons on the Eastern Rites and on Persons. Of the 2666 canons contained in the schema of 1945, only three fifths were therefore promulgated, while the others remained in the archives of the Congregation[30]. In fact, right from the indiction of the Vatican Council II it appears clear to all that even the very difficult codification of Eastern Canon Law, advanced by Pius XI, must by this time seek to marry fidelity to the Eastern tradition with the theological principles and the pastoral orientation of the great ecumenical gathering.

Some of these orientations turned out to be decisive for the very conception of the process of the codification of Eastern Canon Law. It is enough to think that before the Vatican Council II it was usual to speak, even in official documents, of the *Eastern Church* in the singular[31]. The ecclesiological renewal adopted by the Vatican Council II has on the other hand allowed the rediscovery, together with the value of diversity in the unity of the Church as communion, also the importance and the richness of the different rites, which characterise the theological, spiritual and disciplinary identity

---

[23]   Cf. J.D. Mansi, *Sacrorum conciliorum nova et amplissima collectio,* Vol. 49, pp. 200 and 1012; Vol. 50, pp. 515 and 516.

[24]   On the difficulties starting this work cf. L. Muselli, *Storia del diritto canonico,* op. cit., pp. 111-115.

[25]   Cf. AAS 21 (1929), pp. 669 and AAS 27 (1935), pp. 306-308.

[26]   Cf. AAS 41 (1949), pp. 89-119.

[27]   Cf. AAS 42 (1950), pp. 5-120.

[28]   Cf. AAS 44 (1952), pp. 65-150.

[29]   Cf. AAS 49 (1957), pp. 433-600.

[30]   The texts of the canons not promulgated, exactly 1095, were later collected and published by I. Zuzek in numbers from 1976-1979 of the review *Nuntia*, containing the acts of the *Pontificia Commissione per la revisione del Codice di diritto canonico orientale*, instituted in 1972 by Pope Paul VI (Cf. Nuntia 1, 1973, p. 2) substituting the previous commission.

[31]   In this regard, cf. R. Metz, *Le nouveau code du droit canonique des églises orientales catholiques,* in: Revue de droit canonique 42 (1992), pp. 99-117 and especially pp. 99-100.

of the individual particular Churches: "Among them there is such a wonderful bond of union that this variety in the Universal Church, so far from diminishing its unity, rather serves to emphasise it. For the Catholic Church wishes the traditions of each particular Church or rite to remain whole and entire … " (OE 2). Such a principle holds in a wholly special way for the *sui iuris* Churches or eastern rites, distributed in the following way:

TRADITIONS	CHURCHES	STATUS	ADHERENTS
I. Alexandrian	1. Coptic	Patr.	152.584
	2. Ethiopean	Metr.	118.550
II. Antiochian	3. Syriac	Patr.	100.245
	4. Maronite	Patr.	2.176.152
	5. Syro-Malankar	Metr.	281.868
III. Armenian	6. Armenian	Patr.	142.853
IV. Chaldean	7. Chaldean	Patr.	469.764
	8. Syro-Malabar	Metr.	2.987.050
V. Constantinopolitan	9. Bielorussian	(-)	?
(Byzantine)	10. Bulgarian		15.000
	11. Greek		2.350
	12. Hungarian		272.000
	13. Italo-Albanian		61.404
	14. Melchite	Patr.	1.024.410
	15. Rumanian	Metr.(1948)	1.562.979
	16. Ruthenian	Metr.	261.628 + 461.555
	17. Slovakian		391.060
	18. Ukranian Arc.	Maj.	4.194.900
	19. Yugoslavian		48.768
	20. Alabanian	(-)	?
	21. Russian	(-)	?

After the Vatican Council II there was no longer the sense of speaking of the Eastern Churches in the singular. Alongside the Orthodox Churches, with their around 150 million faithful, the 21 Eastern Catholic Churches in full communion with Rome are grouped into five distinct liturgical-disciplinary traditions: Alexandrian, Antiochean, Armenian, Chaldean and Constantinopolitan. These primary traditions or rites, so named because (except for the Armenian) they are matrices for other distinct rites, contain – according to the Annuario Pontificio 1992 – around 15 million faithful [32].

The new grasp of knowledge of the multiplicity of Eastern Catholic Churches, instigated by the Vatican Council II, cannot but influence and orientate the method of proceeding to the canonical codification of Eastern law. The latter is normally classified in the pre-conciliar manuals of Canon Law as a particular law (special or per-

---

[32] Schema and data are taken from: G. Nedungatt, *Presentazione del CCEO*, in: EV, Vol. XII (Bologna 1992), pp. 889-903. The author here rightly notes that the expression *Chiese orientali* while being more correct has however an historical and not geographical acceptance, because these churches born in the eastern part of the Roman Empire, are now present all over the world. On the historical movements of these churches, cf. G. Bedouelle, *La storia della Chiesa,* Milano 1993, pp. 163-186.

sonal), that is relative or derivative and therefore placed on a lower level in comparison with the norms of the CIC, considered as common law. In the light of conciliar teaching, on the other hand, Eastern law enjoys an equal dignity with the Latin. For that reason the *Pontifical Commission for the Revision of the Eastern Code of Canon Law*, instituted by Pope Paul VI on the 10 June 1972, considered Eastern law right from the beginning as complementary to the Latin, because both are part of a whole, as recalled in the image of the lungs used later on by Pope John Paul II in the act of promulgation of the *Codex Canonum Ecclesiarum Orientalium*[33].

The *Code of Canons of the Eastern Church* in the same degree as the *Code of Canon Law* is all encompassing. The reason however is different because the CCEO contains only the norms that are common to all of the 21 Eastern Apostolic Churches. "Differently from the CIC, which is the code of a single Church, the Latin Church, the CCEO is not the code of the Eastern Church (in the singular), rather the common code for the twenty-one Eastern Churches"[34]. This being the arrangement, it is obvious that the CCEO defers very often to the particular law of each of these churches and makes a much fuller use than the CIC of the expression *lex particularis* (around 180 times). In this way, as the definitive denomination of the Code also indirectly indicates, the CCEO places itself in the tradition of the Eastern canonical collections and reflects the high consideration and veneration in which are held the *Sacri canones,* approved by the first seven ecumenical councils and common to all the Eastern Churches[35].

To get a better grip on this tradition of the ancient canonical collections of Eastern law, the CCEO divides the material into titles and not into books. After the 6 preliminary canons in the CCEO are to be found therefore the following thirty titles: 1. The Christian faithful and their rights and duties (cans. 7-26); 2. *Sui Iuris* Churches and rites (cans. 27-41); 3. The supreme authority of the Church (cans. 42-54); 4. Patriarchal Churches (cans. 55-150); 5. Major archiepiscopal Churches (cans. 151-154); 6. Metropolitan Churches and all the other *sui iuris* Churches (cans. 155-176); 7. Eparchs and Bishops (cans. 177-310); 8. Exarchates and Exarchs (cans. 311-321); 9. Assemblies of the hierarchies of various *sui iuris* Churches (c. 322) 10. The clergy (cans. 323-398); 11. The laity (cans. 399-409); 12. Monks and all other religious and members of the other institutes of consecrated life (cans. 410-572); 13. Associations of the Christian faithful (cans. 573-583); 14. The evangelisation of peoples (cans. 584-594); 15. The ecclesiastical magisterium (cans. 595-666); 16. Divine worship and especially the Sacraments (cans. 667-895); 17. Baptised non-Catholics who come into full communion with the Catholic Church (cans. 896-901); 18. Ecumenism, that is the promotion of Christian Unity (cans. 902-908); 19. Persons and juridical acts (cans. 909-935); 20. Offices (cans. 936-978); 21. The power of government (cans. 979-995); 22. Recourse against administrative decrees (cans. 996-1006); 23. The temporal goods

---

[33]   Cf. the CA *Sacri canones* of 18 October 1990, in: AAS 82 (1990), pp. 1033-1044, here p. 1037.

[34]   G. Nedungatt, *Presentazione del CCEO,* op. cit., p. 890.

[35]   Cf. E. Eid, *Discorso di presentazione del "Codice dei canoni delle Chiese orientali" al Sinodo dei Vescovi (25.X.1990),* in: Nuntia 31 (1990), pp. 24-34, here p. 29. For a view of the totality of the enormous work of collecting the sources of eastern law, on the eve of its codification, cf. L. Glinka, *Resoconto sulla pubblicazione delle fonti della codificazione orientale,* in: Nuntia 10 (1980), pp. 119-128.

of the Church (cans. 1007-1054); 24. Judgements in general (cans. 1055-1184); 25. Contentious judgements (cans. 1185-1356); 26. Some special processes (cans. 1357-1400); 27. Penal sanctions in the Church (cans. 1401-1487); 29. Law, customs and administrative acts (cans. 1488-1539); 30. Prescription and the computation of time (cans. 1540-1546).

As can easily be noted these titles are presented according to an order of substantial priority, from which the strict and deep link existing between the sacramental structure of the Church and the juridical comes to be witnessed in some way. Even the Mission (Title 14) and Ecumenism (Title 18) find notable space: in the CIC missionary activity is included among the Church's duty of teaching and only one canon is dedicated to ecumenism (can. 755). In general one gets the impression that less abstraction in the systematic has favoured a greater simplification, or at least a clearer transparency, in the Eastern canonical discipline in respect to the theological contents of its own tradition. Even under the material profile some particular emphases can be noted: for example a more theological and biblical vision of marriage as a covenant (can 776), a greater balance between personal power and collegial power, a special appreciation of religious, but also of theologians (can. 606). Starting from these particular emphases it is legitimate to ask if the CCEO does not constitute a catholic alternative to the CIC[36].

Certainly in the light of conciliar teaching on plurality in unity, precisely the diversity of emphases offered by the canonical codification of Eastern law confirms the actuality of the words of Leo XIII, quoted by John Paul II, that "perhaps there is nothing so wonderful for illustrating the note of catholicity in the Church of God"[37].

2. THE STUDY OF CANON LAW AS SCIENCE

Among the various theological disciplines the study of Canon Law is the first to be emancipated as an autonomous science. Its separation from dogmatic theology is commonly placed in the middle of the twelfth century, at the time that is of the *Decretum Gratiani*. This does not subtract from the fact that in the process of formation of the study of Canon Law as a science it is possible to distinguish at least four great stages of development: the epoch of Canon Law pre-Gratian (or *ius vetum*), the time of the classical study of Canon Law (or of the *ius novum*), the long period of post-tridentine Canon Law defined, up until the promulgation of the *Codex* of 1917, as *ius novissimum* and the birth – above all thanks to the Vatican Council II – of the contemporary study of Canon Law[38].

---

36   This is the conclusive opinion of C.G. Fürst, *Katholisch ist nicht gleich lateinisch: Der gemeinsame Kirchenrechtskodex für die katholischen Ostkirchen,* in: Herder Korrespondenz 45 (1991), pp. 136-140.

37   CA *Sacri canones,* op. cit., p. 1036 (EV, 12, 413)

38   The analysis of the methodological development of theology in its different models (cf. Vagaggini, *Teologia,* in: *Nuovo Dizionario di Teologia,* edited by G. Barbaglio and S. Danich, Alba 1977, pp. 1597-1711) is the base on which E. Corecco (cf. *Considerazioni sul problema dei diritti fondamentali del cristiano nella Chiesa e nella Società. Aspetti metodologici della questione,* in: Actes IV CIDC, pp. 1207-1234, especially pp. 1208-1213) proposes this periodicisation of the formation of the study of Canon Law as a science, even if with some

The first of these stages of development is characterised by a fragmentary legislative production, often deprived of universal recognition. The canonical norms of the first centuries "tend to resolve the concrete problems of the Church without the pretext of being the expression of an organic system, conceptually developed in detail. They undergo, without great complexities, inflections imposed by Roman law or Germanic law, according to different moments and different geographical situations. In the early Middle Ages they were often transformed into *capitulari*, but in their original function, the canonical norms only had the pretext of operatively translating, in the concrete life of ecclesial discipline, the theological image that the Church has of the mystery of the Incarnation and the ascetic experience of the Christian"[39]. Given these objective limits in its first phase of development Canon Law finds itself once more incapable of generating a theoretical and systematic reflection. The last stage of its development represents on the other hand a change of direction so radical at the level of the epistemological and methodological statute of Canon Law, as to merit being dealt with separately[40]. In order to understand the way in which the study of Canon Law has achieved the dignity of a science it is enough then to pause briefly on the two central stages of its formation: the so-called classical study of Canon Law and the school of the *Ius Publicum Ecclesiasticum*.

2.1 THE PRINCIPAL STAGES IN THE FORMATION OF THE STUDY OF CANON LAW

A) THE CLASSICAL STUDY OF CANON LAW

The time of the classical study of Canon Law embraces around two hundred years, from 1142 – the probable date of the publication of the *Decretum Gratiani* – to 1348, the year of the death of the greatest decretalist Johannes Andrea. In this period were laid down the bases and the principal orientations for the scientific work of canonists, by this time autonomous even if parallel with those of dogmatic theologians. In fact the Decretal belongs quite rightfully to the new theology developing itself in the XII Century in the environment of the urban, cathedral or conventual schools, and then called for this reason *scholastic*. Brought to a conclusion immediately after the Lateran Council II (1139), the Decretal was composed by Gratian with the intention of offering a systematic compendium containing all the essentials of the numerous collections of ecclesiastical laws that had appeared up until then. Analogously to what had been done for dogmatic theology by Peter Lombard, the *Magister Sententiarum* who sought to follow a complex and systematic vision of the truth of the faith through an intense rational reflection, Gratian – applying the dialectic method of the *ratio* to the totality of canonical laws – tries to overcome the presumed contradictions of the different *auctoritates*, discussing in a critical and balanced way the value of the texts in order to then extract logical and binding conclusions. Doing so he creates the foundations

---

reservation, cf. L. Muselli, *Storia del diritto canonico*, op. cit., pp. 8-9.

[39] E. Corecco, *Considerazioni sul problema dei diritti fondamentali del cristiano*, op. cit. p. 1210.

[40] Cf. 2.3 of the first chapter and especially 2.2 of the second chapter of this manual.

for a new science, distinct from dogmatic theology even if in reciprocal contact with this [41].

This autonomy permits to the disciples of Gratian a stricter comparison with the methodology of the jurists or the scholars of Canon Law, flourishing in Bologna in that epoch. In consequence of this the conceptual elaboration of Canon Law detaches itself even more from that of the anthropological-metaphysical founded on the scholastic *ratio* theory to base itself on the reasoning and on the syllogism of practical reason typical of Roman law. The *ius canonicum* becomes therefore the general science of law and Canon Law a common law which indiscriminately orders as much the ecclesial juridical relations as the secular. In the context of Christianity it is clear that "it is not the content that diversifies the two sciences, but their legislative source. Canon Law appears consequently as a branch of a universal juridical ordering, which starting from one and the same formal notion of law – that developed in detail by Scholastic philosophy – is capable of giving a response to any problem of material, ecclesial and secular justice" [42].

This strict scientific symbiosis between secular law and Canon Law for a long time impeded the study of Canon Law from reaching a deep knowledge of the mystery of the Church and consequently of understanding the ecclesial specificity of Canon Law. This incapacity is made worse in the modern era, at a time in which the confessional divisions and the clear separation between faith and reason favour the calling to attention of the cultural and scientific supremacy of the *ius publicum civile*, which in the XVIII and XIX Centuries became the principal instrument with which the Enlightenment and liberal State imposed the exclusivity of its own territorial-juridical sovereignty in all the sectors of life. The reaction of Catholic canonists to this challenge gives origin to a new school of the study of Canon Law, the object of the study of the next section.

Here it should be once more remembered that within the classical study of Canon Law it is necessary to distinguish between *Decretists* and *Decretalists*. The former explain and interpret the work of Gratian in their university lectures. They develop his comments (*dicta*) in a particular way, which from simple *glossae interlineares* or *glossae marginales* become often even more well articulated commentaries, autonomously published as *apparatus glossarum* or simply *Glossae*. The latter, through the application of the systematic-analytical method, transform themselves later into true and proper *Summae*. If among the most noted decretists certainly to be pointed out are Rolando Bandinelli (1100-1181), Stefano di Tournai (1128-1203), Sicardo di Cremona (1160-1205), Laurentius Hispanus (author of the *Glossa palatina* of 1214), and finally Johannes Zemecke (1170-1246), called Johannes Teutonicus and author of the *Glossa ordinaria,* which occupies a prime position in the teaching of the classical study of Canon Law and above all in the juridical practice of the time, under the profile method one cannot forget the work of the canonist from Pavia, Bernardo Balbi,

---

[41] On the origin and method of the classical study of Canon Law, cf. G. May-A. Egler, *Einführung in die kirchenrechtliche Methode,* op. cit., pp. 46-60; A.M. Landgraf, *Diritto canonico e teologia nel secolo XII,* in: StG 1 (1953), pp. 371-413.

[42] E. Corecco, *Considerazioni sul problema dei diritti fondamentali del cristiano,* op. cit, p. 1211. Cf. also A. Ruoco Varela, *Le statut ontologique et épistémologique du droit canonique. Notes pour une théologie du Droit canonique,* RSPhTh 57 (1973), pp. 206-208.

who died as Bishop of his city in 1213. In fact in his *Summa Decretalium* the material is divided into five books: *Iudex* (ecclesiastical jurisdiction), *Iudicium* (procedure), *Clerus* (persons), *Connubia* (marriage) and *Crimen* (crimes and punishments). This distinction then became classic and, apart from some exceptions, after its reception into the Decretals of Gregory IX methodologically it guided the treatment of Canon Law almost up to the threshold of the first codification[43].

This is valid in a wholly particular way for the decretalists, dedicated to the interpretation of the *Quinque Compilationes antiquae*, among whom are remembered above all Bernardo da Pavia (died in 1213) and Riccardo di Lacy, called *Anglicus* and who died in 1237. Among the youngest decretalists, who studied above all the Decretals published after the *Liber extra*, to be pointed out on the other hand are Sinibaldo dei Fieschi, who became Pope under the name of Innocent IV (1243-1254); Enrico da Susa (1200-1271), called *Hostiensis* and author of the *Summa aurea*, so called because of the sovereign way it deals with both Roman and Canon Law; and finally the already quoted Giovanni d'Andrea (1270-1348), the last great representative of the classical study of Canon Law, who due to his great scientific production later merited the title of *Fons et tuba iuris*.

The high scientific level, reached by the classical study of Canon Law, could not however be maintained for long and from the second half of the XIV Century up to beyond half of the XVI Century canonical science also participated in the general levelling out known by all of the theological disciplines of this period. New types of canonical literature were born; that of the *Responsa* or *Consilia*, containing a series of juridical responses to practical questions, and that of the penitential summas (*summa de casibus* or *summa confessarum*). The character of practical compendium of these summas for use by confessors ended up by favouring an ever-deeper mixture between moral theology and Canon Law. Even after the Council of Trent it was necessary to wait for some time before seeing the study of Canon Law reaching its new *epocha aurea*, that of the neoclassical study of Canon Law, whose legacy was later assumed by the already quoted school of *Ius Publicum Ecclesiasticum*.

B) THE *Ius Publicum Ecclesiasticum* (IPE)

The *Ius Publicum Ecclesiasticum* was born as confessional law and its primary task, analogous to that of positive theology, is of an apologetic nature. The institutional visibility of the Catholic Church and its rights of citizenship as a *societas perfecta* become the points of reference of a true and proper cultural battle on the one hand against protestantism and on the other against the absolutist and secularised state. Under the chronological profile it is with the school of Würzburg that the theme of Church as *societas* definitively takes the upper hand over every other constitutional type problematic. This methodological *novum* is in fact introduced on the stimulus of the Catholic reaction to the theses of the protestant Samuel von Pufendorf (1632-1694), which considered the Church as a *societas aequalis,* that is as some sort of private association subject to the jurisdiction of the State, a unique true *societas inaequalis* having the *summa potestas* and its own *imperium constitutivum*[44].

---

[43]   In this regard, cf. L. Muselli, *Storia del diritto canonico*, op. cit., pp. 44-45.

[44]   On the role of detonator played by the thesis of Pufendorf cf.: J. Listl, *Kirche und Staat in der neueren katholischen Kirchenrechtswissenschaft*, Berlin 1978, pp. 67-82.

The doctors of the University of Würzburg responded defining the Church as a *Republica Sacra*, independent, distinct from the State and not reducible to a simple *societas arbitraria*, that is founded on a free contract stipulated by its members. On the contrary, by dint of its having been constituted by Christ, the community of believers is a *societas necessaria* and as such, while not having a territory, possesses a true *summum imperium*, that is to say all the powers necessary for the achievement of its proper purpose: the eternal salvation of its members.

Fifty years later the Roman school revived this new doctrine, specifying it on the systematic and scripturalistic level. In 1862 it would at last be possible to publish in Rome the famous hundred *Theses ex Iure Publico Ecclesiastico*, thanks to which the new discipline, by now autonomous also on the university level, could be presented in the raiment of the official address of the Holy See[45].

Among the compilers of this Roman *Thesarium* there is Cardinal Giovanni Soglia (1779-1856), author of the very famous *Institutiones Iuris Publici Ecclesiastici*, published for the first time in Loreto in 1842 with the explicit intention of being *veluti pars dogmatica Iuris Canonici*.

Taking up again the same categories introduced by Pufendorf, Soglia shows *ex sacra litteris* that the Church is a *Status* or a *societas inaequalis*, in which power is conceded not *toti Ecclesiae*, but to Peter, and therefore to the Apostles and their successors. Such power is a true and proper *summum atque indipendens imperium* and thus includes all the moments of power, even the coercitive, because *sine iure coercendi, nihil efficax est potestas*[46].

It is however under the Pontificate of Leo XIII (1878-1903) that the assertion *Ecclesia est societas perfecta* acquires the depth of a true and proper doctrine, above all thanks to the efforts of another cardinal of the Curia: Felice Cavagnis (1841-1906). The latter, called to the chair of *Ius Publicum Ecclesiasticum* at the Roman Seminary, with his *Institutiones Iuris Publici Ecclesiastici*, succeeded in becoming detached from the polemic tone of Soglia and impressing on all the treatment of a more rigorous, more didactic and doctrinally richer methodological focus.

The starting point for this general theory of Canon Law is to be sought in the definition, normally exposed in a first chapter, of a juridically perfect society. The right to a similar society is perfect and independent in the measure in which *in suo ordine* it possesses *omnia media necessaria et proportionata* to attain its societary end.[47]

The second step consists in showing that the Church possesses this same juridical perfection being founded by Jesus Christ as a society *inaequalis*, visible and external, juridical and supreme. Precisely by dint of these societary characteristics of the Church, its law posseses (*ex voluntate Fundatoris*) all of the instruments *suo fini proportionata*, that is necessary for the realisation of the purpose for which it exists. Such

---

[45] For a study of the origin and historical development of the IPE as an autonomous discipline of Canon Law refer to: E. Fogliasso, *Il Ius Publicum Ecclesiasticum e il Concilio Ecumenico Vaticano II*, Torino 1968, pp. 3-61.

[46] Cf. G. Soglia, *Insitutiones Iuris Publici Publici Ecclesiastici*, Loreto 1842, Pars Secunda Lib II. paragraph 34, p. 259.

[47] Cf. F. Cavagnis, *Institutiones Iuris Publici Ecclesiastici*, Roma 1906 (Editio quarta), vol. I, p. 57.

a positing of the *argumentatio* remains substantially the same in all of the successive *Institutuiones* or *Summae* produced by the new discipline of the IPE[48].

The particular attention given by the more qualified representatives of the IPE to the biblical foundation of the socio-juridical dimension of the Church confirms the impression of a methodological basic defect. In reality it is evident that it deals only with the attempts to want to find confirmed in Sacred Scripture the principal bases of the philosophy of the State to be able to apply them to the Church, making use in the argumentation of a philosophical-secular preconception of law, extraneous to the so-called hierarchological passages of the New Testament and the specific nature of the ecclesial reality[49].

The verification of the insufficiency of a similar methodological positing of the problem is neither difficult, nor hindered by the great influence long exercised by the doctrine of the IPE. In point of fact, at the very core of the debates between the various schools of the IPE, there have sometimes been witnessed the congenital limits to the theory of the *societas perfecta* and in particular the danger of considering the Church in its societary aspect, almost as if it were a simple society of natural law[50].

A further confirmation of this inadequacy lies in the fact that the category of *societas perfecta,* at the basis of the doctrine of the IPE, is of natural law extraction and as such incapable of justifying the existence of Canon Law without referring once again to the Roman adage *ubi societas, ibi ius.*

Two facts finally demonstrate, even if only indirectly, how it is impossible to apply to the Church, in a rigorous way, the category of a juridically perfect society.

First of all the Pio-Benedictine Code itself, while showing on distinct occasions a clear dependence on the doctrine of the IPE, avoids explicitly qualifying the Church as a *societas perfecta*[51], even where affirming its fully autonomy before the State.

In second place, the Vatican Council II during the work of preparing for the Dogmatic Constitution on the Church refused to include in the definitive text a systematic chapter on Church-State relations, in which the ecclesial reality would come to be considered in its aspect of a juridically perfect society[52].

---

[48]   For verification it is enough to consult: A. Ottaviani, *Institutiones Iuris Publici Ecclesiastici,* Città del Vaticano 1959, Vol I, nn. 164-170; or J. Ferrante, *Summa Iuris Constitutionalis Ecclesiae,* Roma 1964, n. 59.

[49]   Agreeing with this opinion: E. Corecco, *Teologia del diritto canonico,* op. cit., p. 1740; A. De La Hera, *Introducciòn a la ciencia del derecho canonico,* Madrid 1967, pp. 38-52; cf. also A. De La Hera-Ch. Munier, *Le droit publique ecclésiastique à travers ses définitions,* in: RDC 14 (1964), pp. 32-63.

[50]   For such a proposition is is enough to point out the opinion of one of the most noted canonists and moralists of this century, the Jesuit Arthur Vermeersch (1858-1939): "On raisonne trop sur l'Église, comme si elle était une société de droit naturel. Il y a là un abus ou une méprise qu'il importe de signaler" (Idem, *La tolérance,* Lourain 1912, p. 96).

[51]   The fact that in the CIC/1917 they don't use this *terminus technicus* for various authors is indicative of its inadequacy; cf. Mörsdorf, Lb, Vol. I, p. 42; U. Stutz, *Der Geist des CIC,* op. cit., pp. 109-126.

[52]   The text of this project for a chapter, entitled *De relationibus inter Ecclesiam et Statum,* is to be found in: G. Alberigo-F. Magistretti, *CD "Lumen Gentium". Synopsis historica,* Bologna 1975, pp. 307-308.

Both proofs, and in particular the latter, far from signifying an abandonment on the part of the Magisterium of the fundamental principles that regulate the relations between Church and State, whose clarification is certainly due in great part to the school of the IPE, witness rather how the category of *societas perfecta* cannot, on the dogmatic level, be considered in the same measure as the other images, like those of *Corpus Christi, Populum Dei* or *Sacramentum Mundi* used by *Lumen Gentium*. It is not by chance that the second book of the new Code is entitled precisely *De Populo Dei*, almost wishing to witness to the special root of Canon Law which, in contrast to the secular, is not generated by the dynamism spontaneous to human society, but – as was fully seen in the first chapter – by that specific to the nature of the Church, whose social nature is a fruit of grace and therefore knowable only through the faith.

Precisely because of its intrinsic ecclesiological fragility the doctrine of the IPE did not find, unlike the classical medieval study of Canon Law, an organic legislative transfer, but simply an operative application on the level of concordats[53]. Certainly the CIC of 1917 has assumed not a few elements of it, "but in substance it has codified classical Canon Law, reformed in its contents, more than in its basic attitude, by the Council of Trent"[54]. The later study of Canon Law has on the other hand progressively and deeply changed its epistemological and methodological parameters, above all thanks to the working out in detail of a theology of Canon Law. The latter, even in the light of the Vatican Council II and of the Pontifical magisterium[55], appears as a particular discipline of ecclesiology. Does it derive from this necessarily that also that part of the study of Canon Law, which does not directly concern itself with the theological foundation of Canon Law, so much as the systematic working out in detail of its material contents, belongs to theology as a science? With this question is posed the problem, all now debated, of the method of canonical science.

2.2 THE METHOD OF THE STUDY OF CANON LAW

In the previous sections on the sources of Canon Law and the principal stages of the study of Canon Law we already have a way of seeing how this discipline has progressively acquired its scientific autonomy. It is above all thanks to Gratian that it has been possible to discover in the totality of religious science a specific moment intrinsically bound but nevertheless dintinguishable from the other aspects of theology[56]. The systematic grouping and the analytical study of the ecclesial sources of a juridical character have produced already then some differentiation on the level of work

---

[53] Not only in some concordats, like the Spanish one of 1953 (Article 2) is the character of juridically perfect society of the Catholic Church explicitly recognised, but also the Vatican Council II, while opting for a new proposal deriving from the affirmation of the fundamental right of freedom of religion, retains by this time definitively acquired, on the level of relations of Church and State, many principles developed by the IPE.

[54] E. Corecco, *Considerazioni sul problema dei diritti fondamentali del cristiano*, op. cit., p. 1112.

[55] Cf. OT 16,4; Paul VI, *Discorso ai partecipanti al II Congresso Internazionale di Diritto Canonico*, in: Atti del II Congresso Internazionale di Diritto Canonico (Milano 10-16 September 1973) Milano 1975, pp. 579-588.

[56] Cf. R. Dreier, *Methodenprobleme des Kirchenrechts*, in: ZevKR 23 (1978), pp. 343-367, here p. 348.

method, but to such a differentiation there was however not connected either "a substantial separation from theology"[57], or a setting up of the theme of questions on the nature of the discipline and of the method of the study of Canon Law, that emerged much later under the influence of the modern and contemporaneous organisation of the science and theory of the science[58]. The deepened reflection on these questions appears then as "one of the more urgent tasks"[59] within the effort of methodologial of renewal of all of post conciliar theology.

Klaus Mörsdorf is certainly the first to define the study of Canon Law as a theological science and to recall with systematic rigour to the memories of his colleagues the theological character of Canon Law, which he likes to call with the appellative of *ius sacrum*[60]. Even before him there was no lack of those who claimed that the *sentire cum Ecclesia* is an irrenounceable condition for a deep knowledge of Canon Law. It is enough to think that from 1936 Vincenzo del Giudice, with a healthy dash of humourism, observed that "to believe to be able to study the law prescinding from theological concepts, which are at the base and form the sap of the institutions, is an illusion comparable to that of those who propose the study of physiology with corpses or botany with herbaria"[61]. However it is only starting from the spur of the founder of the school for the study of Canon Law of Munich that in the immediate post-Council period there opened up a true and proper debate on the epistemological and methodological constitution of Canon Law as a science.

A) THE DEBATE ON THE SCIENTIFIC METHOD IN POST-CONCILIAR STUDY OF
   CANON LAW

After the Vatican Council II the flourishing of a full theological pluralism did not impede the tracking of a certain unanimity in the recognising in Canon Law its own particularity which distinguishes it without doubt from the secular. On the if and how this particularity influences the scientific method of this discipline the disagreement is on the other hand complete. The fantail of the different positions can be spread out around three principal ribs or branches – one central and two extremes – to which, albeit a little forcedly, it is possible to reconduct all the other folds representing the more toned down opinions. This results in the following interpartive schema:
– the study of Canon Law is a juridical discipline with a juridical method (C.G.
   Fuerst, J. Hervada)

---

[57] W. Aymans, *Die wissenschaftliche Methode der Kanonistik*, in: *Fides et Ius*. Festschrift für G. May zum 65. Geburtstag, hrsg. von W. Aymans-A. Egler-J. Listl, Regensburg 1991, pp. 59-74 (tr. it.: *Osservazioni critiche sul metodo della canonistica*, in: *Scienza giuridica e diritto canonico*, edited by R. Bertolino, Torino 1991, pp. 97-119, here p. 101).

[58] On the problematic in general, cf. W. Stegmüller, *Probleme und Resultate der Wissenschaftstheorie und Analytischen Philosophie*, 4 Voll., Berlin 1969-1984; on the repercussions for the study of Canon Law cf. W. Aymans, *Osservazioni critiche sul metodo della canonistica*, op. cit., p. 102.

[59] W. Kasper, *Per un rinnovamento del metodo teologico*, Brescia 1969, p. 15.

[60] His writings in favour are gathered in the first section of K. Mörsdorf, *Schriften zum Kanonischen Recht*, hrsg. von W. Aymans-K.J. Geringer-H. Schmitz, Paderborn 1989, pp. 3-67; the last article of the series (*Kanonisches Recht als theologische Disziplin*) is published also in: Seminarium 15 (1975), pp. 802-821 and AfkKR 145 (1976), pp. 45-58.

[61] V. Del Giudice, *Istituzioni di Diritto Canonico*, Milano 1936, p. 6.

- the study of Canon Law is a theological discipline with a juridical method (K. Mörsdorf, W. Aymans)
- the study of Canon Law is a theological discipline with a theological method (E. Corecco)

To the central position of Klaus Mörsdorf, which opened the debate on the theoretical level and then was specified and completed by his disciple Winfried Aymans [62], it is possible to reconduct also in some way the attempts of those who, following a just desire to not wish to accentuate the contrasts between the different schools of the study of Canon Law, sought – albeit with less theoretical force than the canonist from Munich – to integrate between them the different methods creating the hybrid formula: "the study of Canon Law is a theological and juridical discipline with a theological and juridical method" [63].

The two extreme positions, on the other hand, are the reactions of some, perhaps exaggeratedly unilateral, to the evident dichotomy present in the formula of Klaus Mörsdorf. Both appear coherent because in this "the method corresponds to the nature of the discipline" [64], but at the same time they show a certain unilaterality because from the respective formulations a clear connection with theology and respectively with law does not result. In particular, those who define Canon Law as "a juridical science with a juridical method" on the one hand end up inevitably by placing "the fundamental theological questions outside the study of Canon Law, where they are pre-clarified, in order to be then assumed simply by the study of Canon Law", on the other hand they seem to let it be understood in order to conceive again and in any way "the connection with theology as exterior only" [65]. The risk of relapsing into a radical antinomy between law and sacrament is evident above all in the light of the teaching of the Vatican Council II. In order to avoid this risk, and with the knowledge that in the Church the constituent theological elements necessarily also lead to a juridical normative, Eugenio Corecco has coined the formula: "The study of Canon Law is a theological discipline with a theological method" [66].

---

[62] Not only in the already quoted article on the method of study of Canon Law (cf. footnote 57), but also in the manual: Aymans-Mörsdorf, KanR I, pp. 67-71.

[63] Cf. for example G. May-A. Egler, *Einführung in die kirchenrechtliche Methode,* Regensburg 1986, esp. pp. 17-22. Towards the same conception propose also H. Heimerl-H. Pree, *Kirchenrecht-Allgemeine Normen und Eherecht,* Wien-New York 1983, pp. 20-22; S. Berlingò, *Giustizia e carità nell'economia della Chiesa. Contributi per una teoria generale del diritto canonico,* Torino 1991, pp.16-22.

[64] W. Aymans, *Osservazioni critiche sul metodo della canonistica,* op. cit., p. 99.

[65] Ibid., p. 99.

[66] His principal contribution on the question of the method of the study of Canon Law remains the collection of writings: *Theologie des Kirchenrechts. Methodologische Ansätze,* Trier 1980 (for the formula in question cf. p. 98): however two preceding stages should not be forgotten, nor the libretto: A. Ruoco Varela-E. Corecco, *Sacramento e diritto: antinomia nella Chiesa ? Riflessioni per una teologia del diritto canonico,* Milano 1971 (esp. pp. 43-48 and pp. 64-66) and the interventions in the discussion at the International Congress of Pamplona, in: Actas III CIDC, vol. 1, pp. 1189-1190 and pp.1232-1238 and in particular for the formula on method, p. 1234.

One cannot deny that even this last extreme formula, such as it is, runs various risks of being misunderstood. On the one hand its conciseness seems not to take in the scientific complexity of Canon Law and does not respond to the question as to what is the role of the phenomenon of *law* in this discipline; on the other hand it risks provoking a reaction of rejection in those who fear that with this the very concept of canonical juridicalness can be dissolved. In fact however, if it is taken not as a definitory formula but as an orientating criterion, then this appears to be in a position to indicate the road to overcoming not only the dichotomy of the formula of Mörsdorf, but also the much more serious divarication – really not only of Kelsen, but of the whole of the nineteenth century juridical culture[67] – between what can be defined as a conceptual mathematics and the juridical experience. Thus as Corecco conceived and proposed it, this formula signifies first of all that, in the study of Canon Law, the scientific method is not something heterogeneous composed of different elements and lumped together only exteriorly among themselves, but a unitary and specific way of thinking and practicing law in the Church[68]. In second place, as in all the other theological disciplines also in Canon Law, the journey towards the truth (*méthodos*) ultimately speaking cannot be other than the truth itself and consequently also in this discipline it is necessary to understand that "the problems of method are always really problems of content"[69]. *Communio* being – as has already previously been seen – the so-called *obiectum quod* of Canon Law, a synthetic category that takes in in itself all the others such as the People of God and Mystical Body, the cognoscitive instrument or *obiectum quo* capable of grasping the intrinsic essence of it cannot be anything other than the faith[70].

To characterise in this manner the scientific method of the study of Canon Law does not mean in any way to diminish its own specificity within theology. On the contrary, within the post-conciliar theological pluralism, characterised by an excess of compartmentalisation, this means positing the indispensible premises in order to save correctly the specific identity of the study of Canon Law in relation to the other theological disciplines, whose autonomy is never absolute, because the originality of theology as science imposes a relationship of reciprocal integration among all of its individual components[71]. This also means that, in spite of the general principle ac-

---

[67] In this regard, cf. F. Viola, *Ermeneutica e diritto. Mutamenti nei paradigmi tradizionali della scienza giuridica*, in: *La controversia ermeneutica*, edited by G. Nicolaci, Milano 1989, pp. 61-81, in particular pp. 62-64.

[68] This conception of scientific method, developed in detail by E. Corecco (cf. *Intervento*, in: Actas III CIDC, pp. 1196-1197) as an alternative to the models of the enlightenment culture in which is exasperated the primacy of science against all other types of knowledge such as experience, finds significant comparisons also in contemporary juridical science, cf. K. Larenz, *Methodenlehre der Rechtswissenschraft*, Berlin-Heidelberg-New York 1991 (6. ed.), pp. 234-249.

[69] Cf. W. Kasper, *Per un rinnovamento del metodo teologico*, op. cit. p. 17.

[70] Cf. E. Corecco, *Intervento*, in: Actas III CIDC, pp 1235-1236.

[71] In this regard, cf. H.U. von Balthasar, *Einfaltungen. Auf wegen christlichen Einigung*, Einsiedeln-Trier 1987, pp. 63-68.

cording to which theology is never reducible to its method[72] also being valid for the study of Canon Law as a science, the role of the canonist can be schematically defined in the following way: he is on the one hand distinguished from the jurist, because he is a theologian who operates in the light of the *fides qua* and the *fides quae creditur*, on the other hand he distinguishes himself from the dogmatist or from any other theologian, because the material object of his knowledge is not the Christian mystery in its globality, but simply in its juridical-institutional implications, these being of divine law or human law[73]. If in the development of this fundamental role, certainly of interest also for the other theologians, the individual Christian remains free to "dedicate himself preferably, according to his own inclination, to questions and sectors which require to a greater degree a juridical thought or a theological thought"[74], the modalities of his scientific approach to the questions he chooses are not subject to his discretion, but imposed by such contents. In other words, the question of method always reproposes with urgency the question surrounding the fundamental elements of a definition of canonical law. And it is precisely at this level that Eugenio Corecco develops in detail a hypothesis of work in whose track his formula on method also becomes more understandable: the *lex canonica* is above all an *ordinatio fidei*[75].

B) THE WAY TOWARDS A NEW DEFINITION OF CANON LAW

The Vatican Council II having explicitly underlined that in the exposition of Canon Law one ought to keep "in mind the mystery of the Church" (OT 16,4), not only is it licit to but rightful to consider it as a "theological reality", which "participates in the normativity proper to the Word and Sacrament" and which for that reason cannot be considered simply as a "social or sociological superstructure of the mystery of the Church, like modern law could be in relation to ethics, or like Canon Law could so be, in the protestant traditional conception, in relation to the invisible Church, considered as the one true Church"[76]. This ecclesiological connection is not the context or the horizon of Canon Law, rather the theological element that reforms the scientific method from within. Consequently in the Catholic study of Canon Law, every other type of approach "which were to leave out of consideration or were to use with purely extrinsic criteria the theological contents, of themselves immanent to the juridical-canonical contents, is destined to fail"[77]. Deeply convinced that this was the only way to lead Canon Law out of the profound crisis into which it was heading in the immediate post-Conciliar period, during the international congress of Canon Law, held in Pamplona in October 1976, Eugenio Corecco perceived the necessity, by now in-

---

[72]   The observation is by K. Rahner, *Überlegungen zur Methode der Theologie*, in: *Schriften zur Theologie*, Bd. IX, Einsiedeln-Zürich-Köln 1972, pp. 79-126, here p. 94.

[73]   Cf. E. Corecco, *Considerazioni sul problema dei diritti fondamentali del Cristiano nella Chiesa e nella Società. Aspetti metodologici della questione*, in: Actes IV CIDC, pp. 1207-1234, here p. 1215.

[74]   W. Aymans, *Osservazioni critiche sul metodo della canonistica*, op. cit., p. 117.

[75]   On the genesis and meaning of this hypothesis of work, cf. L. Gerosa, *"Lex canonica" als "ordinatio fidei". Einleitende Erwägungen zum kanonischen Recht*, hrsg. von L. Gerosa-L. Müller, Paderborn 1994, pp. IX-XXIII.

[76]   E. Corecco, *Valore dell'atto "contra legem"*, in: Actas III CIDC, pp. 839-875.

[77]   Ibid., p. 843.

evitable, to place under discussion the *definitio classica* of canonical law, formulated by Saint Thomas Aquinas: the *lex canonica*, by the same standard as every other type of law, is an *ordinatio rationis ad bonum commune ab eo qui curam habet communitatis promulgata*[78].

Already other canonists had highlighted some defects of the definition worked out in detail by Aquinas, as for example the lack of clarity concerning the *legis auctor,* the *subiectum* or the *forma* of the *lex canonica*[79]. It is however the first time that, in the Catholic field[80], there also entered into the discussion the principal element of this definition, that is to say the ordering of the reason or *ordinatio rationis*[81]. This is only possible starting from the evidence that the passage from the cultural realm of Christianity to that of modernity has produced a change so radical in the juridical science, as to change the role both of the civil law, progressively reduced to state law, and that of the *lex canonica*, definitively stripped of its meaning of common law and binding by now only the Catholic faithful.

The culture of Christianity, within which Saint Thomas has developed in detail a definition of law valid for all its different forms of realisation (human and divine), was characterised by the pendular movement between rationalism and volontarism, between *ratio* and *voluntas*, both of divine origin and as such open to the idea of mystery. In modern culture, on the other hand, this movement is interrupted firstly by the elimination of every connection between reason and mystery and then by the resultant opposition between *ratio* and *fides*. The former wishing to free itself completely from the latter gets the upper hand as the unique unity of measure of all that is real, as a *norma universi*[82] henceforth placed against the latter. In this context it is evident that the idea of reason, applied to canonical law as a necessary human derivation of the divine law, can no longer have the significance it had in the definition of Saint Thomas.

In fact, still in this modern cultural context, if the eternal law, considered in its philosophical aspect, finds in positive law as an *ordinatio rationis* its human correlative, in as far as it is revealed divine law and – therefore under its theological aspect – this can no longer find its human correlative in reason, but must necessarily find it in another way of knowing: faith, as an *analogatum minus* of the way with which God himself knows[83]. "In fact faith does not know according to the discursive manner of man, whose motivation is the intrinsic demonstrative force of reason, whether specu-

---

[78] *S. Th.*, I-II, q. 90, art. 4.

[79] Cf. for example G. Michiels, *Normae generales iuris canonici, Lublino* 1929, Vol. I, pp. 123-124.

[80] In the protestant camp it is necessary to refer to the work of: U. Kühn, *Via Caritatis. Theologie des Gesetzes bei Thomas von Aquin,* Göttingen 1965.

[81] Sharing this opinion, W. Aymans, *Lex canonica. Considerazioni sulla nozione canonica di legge,* in: *Diritto canonico e comunione ecclesiale. Saggi di diritto canonico in prospettiva teologica,* Torino 1993, pp. 91-112, here p. 110.

[82] On the enormous influence of this concept of Spinoza on western culture up until our day, cf. L. Giussani, *Perché la Chiesa. Vol. 1: La pretesa permane,* Milano 1990, pp. 61-66.

[83] This fundamental affirmation of E. Corecco is to be found in: *Theologie des Kirchenrechts,* op. cit. p. 104 and *"Ordinatio Rationis" o "Ordinatio Fidei"? Appunti sulla definizione di legge canonica,* in: Communio 36 (1977) pp. 48-69, here p. 65.

lative or practical, but by accepting the authority of the *word-witness* of God (=*locutio Dei attestans*), that is of grace. The cause, that is to say the proper motivation of knowledge through faith is not human logic, but divine reason itself inasmuch as it is reason or the ultimate cause of all things, which expresses itself in the world as *ordinatio,* that is as the authority of God, and in which man participates through grace or a supernatural force infused by faith. This means that man knows divine law (expressed historically and embodied in time) not by dint of the stringent logic of the syllogism developed in detail by his own proper reason, but by force of divine motivation, that is by the formal authority of the Word of God, which the impulse of grace makes him accept in the act of faith" [84].

Thus summarised and explained, the proposal of Eugenio Corecco of substituting *ratio* with *fides* in the classical definition of canonical law seems to be a possible ultimate development of the definition of Saint Thomas, a development in which notice is finally taken in a realistic way that the distinction between reason and faith, between philosophy and theology has by now become a clear separation in modern culture. It cannot be deduced however from the invitation to choose to consider canonical law as a disposition of faith and not as an order of reason that the *lex canonica* has nothing to do with seeing with reason and much less that it could be unreasonable. With a similar proposal one does not wish to eliminate the concept of *analogia entis,* as an epistemoligical criterion of Canon Law, but simply to relativise the role of human reason, and with this of natural law, as an obligatory moment of the process of knowledge and a production of positive canonical norm [85]. On the contrary, whoever has opened this way towards a new defintion of the *lex canonica* is immediately preoccupied with developing a critique so radical of the theology of law of Karl Barth [86], in whom the clear refutal of the *analogia entis* ends up by actualising the protestant dualism between *natural* and *supernatural,* as to seem to some excessive and perhaps unjust. In fact, as Hans Urs von Balthasar has acutely observed, however strange and paradoxical it may seem, it is necessary to recognise the existence of an impressive affinity between Saint Thomas and Karl Barth, because, if it is true that the latter defines the *analogia entis* many times as the greatest doctrinal deception of Catholic theology, it is however equally undeniable that the whole of Patristics up until the High Middle Ages – and in part Saint Thomas himself – thought within an *ordo realis supernaturalis* and thus within the *analogia fidei,* which also hides within itself as its integrative moment the *analogia entis* [87]. On the other hand, the *modalità conoscitiva* or *analogia fidei* with which Karl Barth – starting from Christ – understands the revelation of God in creation contains the *analogia entis.* [88]

All this clearly shows that the application of the *analogia fidei* in Canon Law does not eliminate the *analogia entis,* by which proposing the *ordinatio fidei* as a principal element of the definition of *lex canonica* does not at all mean the elimination of the *ratio* of the process of knowledge and production of the law of the Church.

---

[84] E. Corecco, *"Ordinatio Rationis" o "Ordinatio Fidei"?,* op. cit., p. 65.

[85] Cf. E. Corecco, *Theologie des Kirchenrechts,* op. cit., p. 105.

[86] The principal elements of this critique are found in ibid, p. 73 and p. 76.

[87] On this affinity (*anmutende Verwandschaft*) between K. Barth, Saint Thomas and Patristics, cf. H.U. von Balthasar, *Karl Barth,* Einsiedeln 1976, pp. 272-273.

[88] Ibid., p. 390.

Revelation transmitted by the Magisterium being the principal source of knowledge of the latter, canonical law is not therefore either the product of reason, or a product of the so-called "reason illuminated by faith"[89], rather a fruit of faith.[90] The latter never operates however against a correctly understood reason, but on the contrary uses it to advantage in a specific role in the process of historical formation of the concrete positive norm. The faith, in fact, does not threaten either reason or philosophy, but on the contrary defends both from the absolutist claims of gnosis. In other words, faith and theology safeguard philosophy, because not only believing but also thinking belong to the discussion of theology, and the lack of one or the other ends up by dissolving theology itself as a science, which "always looks for a new beginning in thinking, which is not the product of our own proper reflection, but of an encounter with the Word which precedes us"[91]. In as far as it is a theological reality Canon Law carries this truth within itself, because as a structural dimension of the ecclesial communion it is a fruit of the normative proper to Word and Sacrament. Nevertheless, to show that in the so-called *ordinatio fidei* or disposition of faith the principal element of the definition of *lex canonica* simply means leading the rightful consequences from this conception of the law of the Church which, far from being a vague and polyvalent *theologicisation of Canon Law*, represents one of the more authentic attempts to re-establish in a concrete and precise way the connections between canonical norm and Catholic truth[92]. Naturally to develop in detail a true and proper unitary definition of canonical law such connections should be ulteriorly specified, as Winfried Aymans, another disciple of Klaus Mörsdorf, tries to do with courage and lucidity[93].

c) The Essential Internal and External Elements of the *lex canonica*

Beside the central element of the *ordinatio fidei*, two other essential internal characteristics of canonical law can be singled out: its being orientated towards the furtherance of the ecclesial communion and its being configured by reason as a general prescription. Together with the three essential external elements, always traceable in every definition of law (that is to say the competent legislator, the community capable of receiving and promulgating the law), the three internal elements concur in defining canonical law in the following way: "Canonical law is an *ordinatio fidei* orientated towards the futherance of the life of the *communio* and configured by reason as a general prescription, juridically binding, which is issued by the competent authority for a community capable of receiving it and promulgated it in an adequate way"[94].

---

[89] This is the clarification of W. Aymans, *Lex canonica. Considerazioni sulla nozione canonica di legge,* op. cit., pp. 102-104.

[90] Both Augustin and Thomas Aquinas have distinctly demonstrated that *credere* does not mean anything other than *cum assensione cogitare,* cf. J. Pieper, *Lieben, hoffen, glauben,* Munich 1986, pp. 298-304.

[91] J. Ratzinger, *Wesen und Auftrag der Theologie. Versuche zu ihrer Ortsbestimung im Disput der Gegenwart,* Einsiedeln-Freiburg 1993, p. 49; cf. also p. 25 and p. 14.

[92] Cf. G. May, *Enttheologisierung des Kirchenrechts ? ,* in: AfkKR 134 (1965), pp. 370-376, here p. 376; on the necessity of refuting the term theologicisation (=*Theologisierung*), cf. L. Müller, *"Theologisierung" des Kirchenrechts ?,* AfkKR 160 (1991), pp. 441-463, here p. 453 ff.

[93] Cf. above, n. 81 and Aymans-Mörsdorf, KanR I, pp. 142-159.

[94] W. Aymans, *Lex canonica. Considerazioni sulla nozione canonica di legge,* op. cit., p. 112.

Regrettably, although the new process of canonical codification was not guided by the search for a penetration and rational systemisation of the various canonical institutions, but rather by the desire to develop institutionally and juridically the contents of the faith and ecclesial experience[95], so much so that neither the CIC nor the CCEO offer any codal definition of canonical law. Both can. 7 of the CIC and can. 1488 of the CCEO limit themselves to laconically confirming that the laws of the Church are instituted by promulgation. Only in can. 29 of the CIC, on general decrees, which are laws properly called, are the three essential external elements of a canonical law to be found, however even here the ecclesiastical legislator renounces any hint of the internal, certainly primary ordering, of the understanding of the specificity of the laws of the Church compared with all other forms of human laws. In order to grasp this specificity it is necessary therefore to refer either to the ecclesial context of the individual positive norm, or to the doctrine of the study of Canon Law. The latter knows a series of general and particular principles, which direct all the typical institutions of Canon Law, in part maintained also by the normative of the code in force.

3. TYPICAL PARTICULARITIES AND INSTRUMENTS IN THE LAW OF THE CHURCH

The study of the method of the study of Canon Law and the essential contents of canonical law has witnessed sufficiently to how the canonist in order to interpret the positive norm must always refer to the ecclesial context in which this is placed and thus to seek to join together law with life[96]. In fact, in the law of the Church the principle of Roman jurisprudence, according to which "the law is equitable in as much as it is not reduced to abstractions, more or less responding to universal principles, but expresses itself in formulas such as to reveal themselves, in the reality of life, as the actuation of practical principles suitable for satisfying the many exact requirements of intersubjective relationships"[97], finds a very rich field of application, because in the community the *rigor iuris* is constantly called upon to let itself be corrected by the idea of *charitas*. That is amply demonstrated by the important role performed in Canon Law by typical institutions such as the *sensus fidei*, *consuetudo* and *aequitas canonica*.

3.1 PLURALITY IN UNITY AND CANON LAW

Before studying at closer range some of the more typical institutions of Canon Law, capable of documenting in an articulate way the particularity of the *lex canonica*, it is useful to remember how such particularities took root also in other principles which guide the whole juridical system of the Church in its entirety. Among these are pointed out in a particular way: that of an ecclesiological nature, according to which one must always keep in mind the mystery of the Church in the exposition of Canon Law (OT

---

[95]   For a detailed documentation of this general opinion, cf. E. Corecco, *I presupposti culturali ed ecclesiologici del nuovo "Codex"*, in: *Il nuovo Codice di Diritto Canonico*, edited by S. Ferrari, Bologna 1983, pp. 37-68.

[96]   Cf. G. May-A. Egler, *Einführung in die kirchenrechtliche Methode*, op. cit., p. 185.

[97]   P. Fedele, *Equità canonica*, in: EDD, Vol. XV, (Milano 1966), pp. 147-159, here p. 148.

16,4), and that of a liturgical nature, according to which every renewal of Canon Law always arises out of a unique and same intention, that is to say that of wanting to restore Christian life [98].

The former finds its most completed expression in the rule of reciprocal immanence between the Universal Church and the Particular Church (LG 23,1), which impedes the separation of the *ius universale* from the *ius particulare* and vice versa. The central nuclei of both fields of Canon Law form a *corpus legum commune*, in which the fundamental principle *lex universalis minime derogat iuri particulari* is valid [99]. In this common body of ecclesial laws the CIC and the CCEO have the function of a law framework [100], which necessitates, in the respective ecclesial contexts, complementary particular normatives.

The latter, on the other hand, shows all of its importance in the reservation in favour of liturgical law, codified in can. 2 of the CIC and in can. 3 of the CCEO. In the chapters on the normatives of the code relating to the Word of God and the Sacraments the importance of the liturgy for Canon Law will be seen in detail; here it is enough to remember that: "liturgical actions are not private, but are celebrations of the Church" (can. 837 §1) and therefore not only "belong to the whole body of the Church, making it known and influencing it", but in some way guide from within all of Canon Law and not just the *ius liturgicum* [101].

Both principles document then the complexity and multiplicity of the interactions between positive canonical norms and the theological principle of plurality in unity. The nature and function of so many typical institutions of Canon Law confirm it, for which it is worth pausing a little on the better known.

A) *Sensus fidei, consuetudo* AND *aequitas canonica* IN ECCLESIAL LAW

In the ecclesial juridical system the legislative process, as the means for the production of canonical norms, is not a unilateral movement, but rather dialogical and communitarian, because it involves the People of God in its entirety [102]. And this is valid also in the technical sense. Indeed, on the one hand with the promulgation of a canonical law the legislative process in the Church is not yet finished, because to this must be added – albeit not in a constitutive sense, but nevertheless in some way juridically rel-

---

[98]   Cf. the sixth paragraph of : John Paul II, CA *Sacra disciplinae leges*, in AAS 75 (1983), pars II, VII-XIV.

[99]   Cf. can. 20 and the comment of E. Corecco, *Ius universale-Ius particulare,* in: *Ius in vita et in missione Ecclesiae.* Acta Symposii internationalis Iuris Canonici (19-24 aprilis 1993), Città del Vaticano 1994, pp. 551-574, here pp. 561-568.

[100]   Cf. can. 1 of the CIC and the CCEO. The expression *law frame* (=*Rahmengesetz*) is dealt with by: H. Schmitz, *Gesetzgebungsbefugnis und Gesetzgebungskompetenzen des Diözesanbischofs nach dem CIC von 1983,* in : AfkKR 152 (1983) pp. 62-75, here p. 63.

[101]   Cf. P. Stevens, *Die rechtkonstituierende Bedeutung der gottesdienstlichen Versammlung,* in: Liturgisches Jahrbuch 33 (1983), pp. 5-29; G. Lajolo, *Indole liturgica del diritto canonico,* in: La Scuola Cattolica 99 (1971), pp. 251-268.

[102]   Cf. H. Schmitz, *Gesetzgebungsbefugnis und Gesetzgebungskompetenzen,* op. cit., p. 62.

evant – the positive response of the interested ecclesial community or *receptio legis*[103]. On the other hand, this very legislative process, which flows into promulgation, has had its beginning in the fixing of the contents of canonical law, which even when realised outside of the synodal structures can never completely prescind from the *sensus fidei* of the entire People of God. This *sensus fidei*, as will be seen in the sixth chapter dedicated to the institutional organs, expresses itself also on the institutional level through the joint responsibility of all the faithful in the realisation of the mission of the Church. This is however the ultimate root of this communitarian charism, which canonical tradition knows under the name of *consuetudo canonica*[104].

The latter, as an *ordinatio practica* of the *regula fidei* believed by the People of God in its entirety and not only by whoever is invested with imperial power[105], has a very important role in Canon Law. Not only does the *Decretum Gratiani* speak of *consuetudo* as a *lex non scripta*[106], but the codifications of Canon Law known by the Church in the Twentieth Century, in contrast to such as came from the protestant juridical traditions and in the codifications of secular law, recognise in *consuetudo canonica* the *vis legis* and give ample space to customary law[107]. This is documented by different facts.

First of all the Code of Canon Law on the one hand often defers to customary norms, in various of its sectors[108]: on the other hand it only rarely expressly censures as particular custom[109]. In the second place not only a *praeter legem* custom, but most assuredly one *contra legem* can obtain – under determined conditions – the force of law (can. 26). Finally, if canonical law can revoke a custom (cans. 5 and 28), the latter is nonetheless normally considered by the ecclesiastical legislator as "a best interpreter of laws" (can. 27). In the juridical system of the Church, to the correlation *lex-receptio* it then makes in conterpoint another correlation *consuetudo-approbatio*. Both highlight the particularity of Canon Law, whose ultimate aim is the realisation

---

[103] Cf. ibid., p. 62. In this regard cf. also: H. Müller, *Rezeption und Konsens in der Kirche. Eine Anfrage an die Kanonistik,* in: ÖAKR 27 (1976), pp. 3-21. The classical example of a non-received law is the CA *Veterum Sapientia* of John XXIII, cf. AAS 54 (1962), pp. 129-135.

[104] It is the definition of custom given by : R Bertolino, *Il nuovo diritto ecclesiale tra coscienza dell'uomo e istituzione. Saggi di diritto costituzionale canonico,* Torino 1989, p. 56. (Almost as a confirmation of this thesis can. 1506 of the CCEO affirms that only "in the measure in which it responds to the activity of the Holy Spirit in the ecclesial body" a custom "can attain a form of law"!).

[105] Cf. ibid., p. 63.

[106] In this regard cf. R. Weigand, *Das Gewohnheitsrecht in den frühen Glossen zum Dekret Gratians,* in: *Ius Populi Dei. Miscellanea in honorem Raymundi Bigador,* hrsg. von U. Navarrete, Vol. 1, Roma 1972, pp. 91-101.

[107] Cf. cans. 25-30 of the CIC/1917; cans. 23-28 of the CIC/1983 and cans. 1506-1509 of the CCEO.

[108] For example in the codal normative of clerics (cans. 284 and 289 §2), on matrimonial law (cans. 1062 §1 and 1119) and on patrimonial law (cans. 1263, 1276 §2, 1279 §1).

[109] While in the CIC/1917 the ecclesiastical legislator makes recourse to the clause on censure a good 21 times, in the CIC/1983 it happens only 6 times and in the CCEO only 10 times; on the significance of these clauses cf. P. Krämer, *Kirchenrecht II. Ortskirche-Gesamtkirche,* Stuttgart-Berlin-Köln 1993, pp. 62-64.

of the *communio Ecclesiae et Ecclesiarum*. In this "unique and complex reality" (LG 8,1), if to the *lex canonica* belongs on the other hand the function of protecting from the danger of particularism, to *consuetudo canonica* belongs also the function of protecting against the opposite dangers of absolutism or centralism [110]. And thus it is possible only within a juridical system in which the criterion that renders a norm binding that it is not so much the will of the legislator or an exclusively formal value, so much as that of the certainty of law in the state juridical systems, but rather it is the unity or communion which is the essential content of the ecclesial experience itself [111].

Another typical institution of Canon Law, which binds the norm to experience and ecclesial life, is that of *aequitas canonica*. Even if this concept explicitly recurs only twice in the CIC (cans. 19 and 1752), this represents one of the most significant categories in all of the law of the Church and is part of those principles "which are at the base of the canonical system and constitute its specific structure" [112]. In as much as it is corrective and complements the law, *aequitas canonica* allows the ecclesiastical authority to overcome the divarication between the abstractness of the norm and the concrete case, realising a superior form of justice (entered into relationship with the *charitas* and the *misericordia* of God) and developing an analogous function – on the objective level – to that developed by *epikeia* on the subjective level of the conscience decisions of the individual faithful. It was not by chance that Paul VI defined *aequitas canonica* as "one of the most delicate expressions of pastoral charity", which must guide the legislator in the promulgation of laws, the interpreter in explaining them, the judges and the individual faithful in their application [113]. With canonical equity, much more than with canonical custom, the problem of the application and the interpretation of canonical law is then met with, never separable from that of its particularity.

B) CONSEQUENCES FOR THE APPLICATION AND INTERPRETATION OF CANONI-
    CAL LAWS

The particularity of canonical laws is underlined by John Paul II when, promulgating the new Code, he explicitly affirms that this represents "the great effort to transfer into canonical language .... . the ecclesiology of the Council" [114]. Consequently where this translation has not fully succeeded it is evident that whoever is called upon to interpret and apply canonical law must refer to conciliar doctrine. In other words, the particularity of the law of the Church enjoins that the Code of Canon Law is always interpreted and applied in the light of the Vatican Council II. It is in syntony with this fundamental hermeneutical principle that the rules dictated by the ecclesiastical legislator for the interpretation of canonical laws should be read (cans. 16-19).

---

[110] On the structural correlation between law and custom in the Church as a communion, cf. Aymans-Mörsdorf, KanR I, pp. 205-212.

[111] Cf. E. Corecco, *Valore dell'atto "contra legem"*, op. cit., p. 850.

[112] V. del Giudice, *Istituzioni di diritto canonico*, Milano 1936, p. 79. On the canonical significance of equity, cf. H. Müller, *Barmherzigkeit in der Rechtsordnung der Kirche?*, in: AfkKR 159 (1990), pp. 353-367; for a full bibliography, cf. J. Urrutia, *Aequitas canonica*, in: Periodica 73 (1984), pp. 33-88.

[113] Cf. Paul VI, *Discorso ai giudici della Romana Rota dell' 8 febbraio 1973,* in: AAS 65 (1973) pp. 95-103.

[114] *Sacrae disciplinae leges,* op. cit., p. XIII.

Can. 17 chooses five of them, of which the first could be considered as the principal (given its nature of an immediate concretisation of the hermeneutical principle just outlined) and the other four as subsidiary rules[115]. The first, known as a logical-grammatical interpretation, returns to the intrinsic elements of the verbal formula of the law, which can. 17 defines with the two terms text and context, and to the proper sense of the words. The latter is deduced from the etymology of the words, from their usual meaning in the spoken language, from juridical practice. If however this proper sense of the words used in the formulation or text of the canonical law comes out uncertain, it is necessary then to refer to the context, that is to say to the canons that precede or follow the norm in question, as well as to the conciliar principle that inspired it. It is at this level that both the objective-theological interpretation (that is to say the question of the aim and circumstances of the law), or the subjective-theological interpretation (that is to say the question of the intention of the legislator) enter into the game. In order to search out the answer to these three questions it could be useful to compare the norm in question with other canons or canonical laws (the so-called parallel places). Together, these four questions form the group of subsidiary rules for the interpretation of a canonical law, but the aim is to simply indicate that whoever interprets and applies the law must ask himself first of all the question surrounding the text and context and that to respond to them can, and in some cases must, have recourse to them.

This is valid both for the authentic interpretation (can. 16) and for private interpretation, as much doctrinal as usual. The importance of the latter is witnessed to both by the already quoted can. 27 on custom as the best interpreter of canonical law, and by can. 6 §2 on the role of canonical tradition in the interpretation of an *ius vetus*, reprised in the new norms of the code.

3.2 ADMINISTRATIVE ACTS OF CANON LAW

In the Church, in contrast to what happens in the modern State, there is no separation of powers, because – as will be seen in more detail later[116] – the *sacra potestas* is one and unique. Nevertheless, both canonical tradition and the new Code of Canon Law[117] distinguish three functions in the power of government: legislative, administrative and

---

[115] On the point the opinions of the commentators are very discordant; cf. for example Aymans-Mörsdorf, KanR I, pp. 182-185; R. Puza, *Katholisches Kirchenrecht,* Heidelberg 1986, pp. 110-111; G. May-A. Egler, *Einführung in die kirchenrechtliche Methode,* op. cit., pp. 195-200.

[116] cf. below, above all 4. chapter 7.3; on the whole question, cf. K. Mörsdorf, *Heilige Gewalt,* in: *Sacramentum mundi,* Bd. II, Frieburg-Basel-Wien 1968, pp. 582-597; P. Krämer, *Dienst und Vollmacht in der Kirche. Eine rechtstheologische Untersuchung zur Sacra potestas-Lehre des II. Vatikanischen Konzils,* Trier 1973; E. Corecco, *Natura e struttura della "sacra potestas" nella dottrina e nel nuovo Codice di diritto canonico,* in: Communio 75 (1984), pp. 24-52.

[117] Cf. can 135 §1 of the CIC and can. 985 of the CCEO. Although the ecclesiastical administration does not have a simply executive function, enjoying a lot of freedom and full decision making powers, the CIC often uses the term *potestas executiva* (cf. cans 30, 31 §1, 35, 135 §4) and not so often *potestas administrativa* (cf. cans. 1400 §2, 1445 §2). For a full study of all the problems relative to administrative acts in Canon Law, cf. Aymans-Mörsdorf, KanR I, pp. 221-282; for a brief description of the principal forms of a canonical administrative

judiciary. Administrative power has as its immediate aim the realisation and practical promotion of the good of the Church as a *communio*. Its activity is consequently both applicative and creative: the former type of activity marries it with the judiciary power, the latter with the legislative. This is therefore polyvalent to the point that the CIC distinguishes in a clear way the individual administrative acts (decrees, precepts, rescripts, privileges and dispensations) from the general, classified in a separate title (cans. 29-34). In fact, among the latter there are general decrees of a legislative character, which are true legislative decrees and thus are subordinate to the normative of the code on laws (can. 29); the general executory decrees, which determine precisely the manner to be observed in the application of laws (can. 31) and obliging all those who are bound to observance of the laws in question (can. 32); and finally instructions, which oblige the organs proposed for the execution of laws, clarifying their dispositions and ways of realisation (can. 34).

Individual administrative acts, emanating from the competent authority for an individual believer or a group of the faithful and always anyway for a concrete case, must be in conformity with the law and thus are subordinate to a series of common norms (cans. 35-47). Starting from the free or dependent nature of the authoritative intervention, which issued them, these individual administrative acts are distinguished into two categories: decrees and precepts on the one hand (cans. 48-58), and rescripts on the other (cans. 59-93).

A) DECREE AND INDIVIDUAL PRECEPT

The individual decree is the classical instrument of the ecclesiastical administration to regulate a concrete case. In fact, even when the law prescribes the issueing of a decree (can. 57), this always proceeds from the free initiative of the competent authority, albeit with respect to the principle of legality. By its nature, in contrast with a rescript, this does not presuppose any petition, it is given to a physical or juridical person and consists in a decision or provision of the competent authority (can. 48). As such the individual decree prescinds completely from the desire of the interested parties.

A particular type of decree is the individual precept, which is a decisory decree of imperative character with which the competent authority directly and legitimately commands one or more determined persons to do or omit something (can. 49). This specific purpose clearly shows how the individual precept not only does not require any petition or question, but also by its nature is directed to passive non-willing subjects (*in invitos*).

B) RESCRIPT, PRIVILEGE AND DISPENSATION

From Imperial Roman Law the ecclesiastical authority has inherited the custom of giving rescripts, that is to say written replies to questions or requests in which one of the faithful, but also an unbaptised person to whom it has not been expressly forbidden (can. 60), asks for a favour, a privilege or a dispensation. By its nature the rescript is therefore an administrative act dependent upon someone's petition (*in volentes et petentes*) and as such having the character of a written response. This can be conceded directly to the petitioner (forma graziosa) or transmitted by an executor (forma com-

---

act, cf. R.A. Strigl, *Verwaltungsakt und Verwaltungsverfahren*, in: HdbkathKR, pp. 99-113 or the respective voices in the NDDC.

missoria). It is through a rescript that a privilege or dispensation is normally conceded (can. 59 §1). In the former case the competent authority must adhere to the norms contained in cans. 76-84, in the latter case cans. 85-93 are valid.

The privilege, which can be granted in favour of certain physical or juridical persons only by the ecclesiastical legislator or by whoever the legislator has conceded such power (can. 76), is by its nature a typical exception to the general norm. In contrast to the dispensation, which simply frees from the obligation contained in the canonical law, the privilege positively constitutes a special right granted by the legislator to persons, things or places and as such is a norm that modifies the general law (*contra legem*) or goes beyond what the canonical law normally anticipates (*praeter legem*). By its nature it is perpetual (can. 78 §1) and thus normally does not cease by renunciation (can. 80 §1), it is not extinguished if the right of the granter lessens (can. 81) or by disuse (can. 82).

The dispensation is an administrative act with which the competent authority, in particular cases, frees from the obligatory nature of a merely ecclesiastical law (can. 85). In contrast with a privilege, the dispensation has therefore a negative function, because in the concrete case it exonerates from the law without however substituting it with another norm. By its nature it is not permanent and is distinguished into express, tacit, partial (it only frees in part from the obligation of the law), necessary (if it is required by a moral necessity or by canonical equity), free (if it is granted as a favour by a superior). Neither divine laws nor those of natural law can be the object of a dispensation and in order to dispense from merely ecclesiastical laws a just cause proportionate to the importance of the law or the gravity of the concrete case in question is necessary (can. 90). Consequently this ceases with the certain and total cessation of the cause (can. 93).

In respect to the Pio-Benedictine Code the most important innovation in this material is represented by can. 87, which in its first paragraph affirms: "Whenever he judges that it contributes to their spiritual welfare, the diocesan Bishop can dispense the faithful from disciplinary laws, both universal laws and those particular laws ... . not however from those whose dispensation is specially reserved to the Apostolic See or some other authority". This is a direct consequence of the fact that the teaching of the Council on the role of the diocesan Bishop, and of his pastoral ministry [118], obliges the ecclesiastical legislator on the level of the exercise of *sacra potestas* to pass from a sytem of concession to that of reservation, in which "the diocesan bishop in the diocese entrusted to his care has all the ordinary, proper and immediate power required for the exercise of his pastoral office, except in those matters which the law or a decree of the Supreme Pontiff reserves to the supreme or to some other ecclesiastical authority"(can. 381 §1)

3.3 OTHER TECHNICAL-JURIDICAL INSTRUMENTS

If in the normative of the code on the canonical institution of the dispensation it was possible to register an important extremely positive change under the ecclesiological profile, in the remaining titles of the first book of the CIC the cultural and juridical conception of the preceding codification regrettably still prevails. In the name of this

---

[118] Cf. CD 8 and 11 and below in chapter 6 (2.2)

tradition, bound more to the culture of Christianity than to the conciliar vision of the Church, the ecclesiastical legislator reproposes as general norms a whole series of definitions and dispositions regarding the following technical-juridical instruments: statutes and ordinances (cans. 94-95), physical and juridical persons (cans. 96-123), juridical acts (cans. 124-128), the power of governance (cans. 129-144), ecclesiastical offices (cans. 145-196), prescription (cans. 197-199), the computation of time (cans. 200-203). A little analogously to what happens in the CCEO, lacking a section entitled *General Norms*, the most important of these canonical institutions or technical-juridical instruments are here dealt with in those chapters where greater reference is made to them or where it is easier to grasp their particularity and eventually their theological significance. In particular the norms regarding collegial juridical persons, the exercise of the power of governance and ecclesiastical offices are illustrated and explained in the chapters on the institutional organs of the Church[119]. On the other hand, insofar as it concerns the other two most important juridical notions in this section, that is to say that of *person* or *juridical subject* and that of *juridical act*[120], the following observation in this place should suffice.

If it is true that "by baptism one is incorporated into the Church of Christ and constituted a person in it, with the duties and rights which are proper to christians" (can 96), and if it is equally true that in every juridical system in order that a juridical act be valid it is necessary "that it be performed by a person who is legally capable, and it must contain those elements which constitute the essence of the act, as well as the formalities and requirements which the law prescribes for the validity of the act" (can 124 §1), nevertheless both definitions can show the specificity of the ecclesial law only in the measure in which they are interpreted, and eventually reformulated, starting from the principal juridical subject of the whole canonical system: the *Christifidelis*[121]. In fact, only the latter category is in a position to both theologically specify the classical one of *person,* inherited from Roman law, and of liberating that of *juridical act* from emphases that are positivistic or too bound up to the natural law, and as such inadequate to define those which in the Church are juridical acts par excellence, that is to say the Sacraments.

FUNDAMENTAL BIBLIOGRAPHY

Aymans W.-Mörsdorf K., *Kanonisches Recht. Lehrbuch aufgrund des Codex Iuris Canonici,* Bd. I: Einleitende Grundfagen. Allgemeine Normen, Paderborn-München-Wein-Zürich 1991(=KanR I), pp.57-81, pp.141-159 and pp. 205-212.

Corecco E., *"Ordinatio Rationis" o "Ordinatio Fidei"? Appunti sulla definizione di legge canonica,* in: StLT-Communio 36 (1977), pp. 1-22.

Gerosa L., *Grundlagen und Paradigmen der Gesetzesauslegung in der Kirche,* Münster 1999.

---

[119] For a rapid examination of all of these ideas in the Code, cf. F.J. Urrutia, *Il libro 1: norme generali,* in: *Il nuovo codice di diritto canonico. Studi,* Torino 1985, pp. 32-59.

[120] For a full analysis of these ideas in the Code, cf. Aymans-Mörsdorf, KanR I, pp. 283-352.

[121] In the general norms of the CIC this term unfortunately recurs rarely; cf. for example cans. 23, 87 §1, 129 §2, 199 n. 7.

Kasper W., *Per un rinnovamento del metodo teologico*, Brescia 1969.

Kuhn U., *Via Caritatis. Theologie des Gesetzes bei Thomas von Aquin*, Göttingen 1965.

Larenz K., *Methodenlehre der Rechtswissenschraft*, Berlin-Heidelberg-New York 1991 (6. Aufl.).

May G.-Egler A., *Einführung in die kirchenrechtliche Methode*, Regensburg 1986

Muselli L., *Storia del diritto canonico. Introduzione alla storia del diritto e delle istituzioni ecclesiali*, Torino 1992.

Nedungatt G., *Presentazione del CCEO*, in: EV Vol. XII (Bologna 1992) pp. 889-903.

Schmitz H., *Der Codex Iuris Canonici von 1983*, in: HdbkathKR, pp. 33-57.

Urrutia J.F., *Il libro 1: norme generali*, in: *Il nuovo codice di diritto canonico. Studi*, Torino 1985, pp. 32-59.

THIRD CHAPTER: THE JURIDICAL ELEMENTS OF THE PROCLAMATION OF THE WORD

The third book of the CIC, *De Ecclesiae munere docendi,* begins with the affirmation that "Christ the Lord entrusted the deposit of the faith, so that by the assistance of the Holy Spirit, it might conscientiously guard revealed truth, more intimately penetrate it, and faithfully proclaim and expound it"(can. 747 §1). With four words (proclaim, penetrate, expound and guard) the ecclesiastical legislator more or less directly signals as many fundamental forms in which service to the Word of God is realised: proclamation in the liturgy and catechesis (cans. 756-780), the ecclesiastical Magisterium (cans. 748-754), the missionary and educational activity of the Church (cans. 781-822) and finally the juridical protection of the integrity of the faith and the ecclesial communion (cans. 822-833 and 1400-1752). In all these sections it is to be kept in mind that this service to the Word of God in as much as it is a *munus* concerns the whole Church, because this is constantly structured as a reciprocal interaction between the apostolic Magisterium and the *sensus fidei* of all the faithful [1].

1. PROCLAMATION AND MAGISTERIUM

In response to a specific dictate of the Council, contained in no. 44 of the Decree *Christus Dominus* on the pastoral office of bishops, the Congregation for the Clergy published on the 11 April 1971 the *Directorium catecheticum generale* [2]. The latter part of this directory has as its purpose the presentation of the theological-pastoral principles offered by the Vatican Council II to arrange and co-ordinate the different aspects of the evangelizing action of the Church. This is accordingly entirely dedicated to the ministry of the Word: in the first chapter it deals with preaching and in the second with catechesis, that is to say the two instruments of proclamation "which always hold pride of place" (CD 13). The new Code of Canon Law has fully accepted this conciliar vision especially in the way of systemising the material of the first five titles into which *De Ecclesiae munere docendi* is divided. In fact, after some introductory canons on the different levels of responsibility in the exercise of the ministry of the Word, as well as on the sources and on the means of communicating the Christian message, *De divini ministerio* (cans. 756-780) is divided into two chapters: the first dedicated to preaching (cans.762-772), the second to catechetical instruction (cans. 773-780).

---

[1] In this regard cf. W. Aymans, *Begriff, Aufgabe und Träger des Lehramts,* in: HdbkathKR, pp. 533-540 and especially pp. 539-540.

[2] Cf. AAS 64 (1972), pp. 96-176.

In order to be able to analyse the normative of the code as regards these two fundamental forms of the evangelising action of the Church, seeking to understand its profound innovation in comparison with that of 1917, it is timely to make some considerations of a general order on the subject of the Christian proclamation. And that is starting from the principal normative contents both of the quoted canons of the first title, and of the general norms proposed in all of the third book on the teaching function of the Church.

1.1 PROCLAMATION AND ITS UNITARIAN SUBJECT

Both preaching and catechesis, as the "primordial tasks" of the mission of the Church or "essential and different moments ... of one unique movement", are operations "of which the whole Church must feel itself and wish to be responsible"[3]. It is up to the Church as an organic unity or *communio,* that is to say to the Church as a unitary subject animated by the Holy Spirit, to deepen, proclaim and faithfully explain to all the so-called *depositum fidei* (can. 747). To proclaim the Gospel and to teach to all peoples the revealed truth that is Christ Jesus, the Redeemer of mankind, is the task and responsibility of all of the members of the People of God by dint of baptism and confirmation and not only of a "body of pastors who call themselves the teaching Church or simply Church"[4], as taught for example the Catechism of Nancy (1824), but as if it were still in some way traceable to the Pio-Benedictine Code, where such a normative was recorded under the title *De magistero ecclesiastico* and was organised in a casuistic way around the juridical figure of the *missio canonica* of can. 1328.

This common responsibility in comparison with the *ministerium verbi,* exercised according to different levels of representativity or authoritativeness and in conformity with the variety of specific functions, underlies therefore the logic of the ecclesial communion at every level of its different expressions, from the Pope, to whom the *munus Evangelii nuntiandi* is entrusted in a *praecipue* way in relation to the universal Church (can. 756 §1), to the lay faithful, called to be – by dint of baptism and confirmation – witnesses to the Gospel and thus collaborators with the bishop and his priests *in exercitio ministerii verbi* (can. 759). That means that before every subsequent theological legitimisation of speaking in *nomine Ecclesiae,* every believer is bound by dint of the sacrament of baptism – which integrates him into a communion of witnesses[5] – to "proclaim not himself but Jesus Christ" (2Cor 4,5), and that is possible only if he always keeps, also in his own way of acting, communion with the whole Church (can. 209 §1).

It should likewise be observed how the *munus Evangelii nuntiandi,* which the introductory canons 756-761 deal with especially, showing the subjects in a hierarchical perspective, albeit as a general theological notion, that takes in all the aspects of the

---

[3]   The quotes are taken from: Paul VI, Evangelii nuntiandi (8 December 1975), nos. 17-24, in AAS 68 (1976), pp. 17-22; and from John Paul II, *Catechesi tradendae* (16 October 1979), nn. 15-16, 18 and 24, in AAS 71 (1979), pp. 1277-1340.

[4]   E. Germain, *Langage de la foi à travers l'histoire,* Tours 1972, p. 167.

[5]   On how the act of baptismal faith introduces the isolated 'I' to the collective 'I' of the Church, cf. J Ratzinger, *Glaubensvermittlung und Glaubensquellen,* in J. Ratzinger, *Die Krise der Katechese und ihre Überwindung, Rede in Frankreich,* Einsiedeln 1983, pp. 13-39, above all pp. 23-28.

evangelising function of the Church. This is thus less technical than that of the *ministerium verbi*, taking in preaching and catechesis, of which the moderator is the bishop in his own particular Church, as recalled by the §2 of can. 756. Its most authoritative expression, and therefore formally more binding, is the so-called ecclesiastical Magisterium, which is not simply the ministry of the Word, as will be better seen later on. If both are founded on the Sacred Scriptures and Tradition (can. 760), that does not take away from the fact that there is a difference between them. In other words, even if every Magisterium is a ministry of the Word, not every ministry of the Word is a Magisterium. While the Magisterium proclaims, expounds and inteprets the Word of God in an infallible or authentic way – albeit only according to different degrees of intensity and authoritativeness –, the ministry of the Word simply proclaims or transmits. In contrast to the Magisterium, which implies a particular assistance from the Holy Spirit (LG 19 and 24) and therefore a different formal character, the ministry of the Word is thus a particular expression of the proclamation of the Gospel, but in its essential nucleus it is already implicated in the sacraments of baptism and confirmation. As such, this requires particular faculties or a special mandate only when it acquires a greater authority or importance on the liturgical or doctrinal level of the Church (as for example in cans. 767 §1 and 812).

These considerations of a general order being set before us it is possible to illustrate in a more analytical way the principal contents of the new normative of the code regarding the Ministry of the Divine Word as a particular expression of the teaching function of the Church.

1.2 THE FORMS OF PROCLAMATION

Among the different means of proclaiming that the Church can use in order to exercise the ministry of the Word, liturgical preaching and catechetical instruction rightly enjoy primacy[6].

A) LITURGICAL PREACHING

The preaching of the Word of God, as the conciliar decree *Presbyterium Ordinis* teaches in no. 4, has a particular constitutive force in order to build up the *communio fidelium* and therefore is one of the principal duties of ordained ministers (can. 762).

This *praecipium officium* (LG 25,1 and CD 13,3) belongs first of all to the bishops, who have the right (*ius*) to preach the Word of God everywhere (can. 763). Such a right is a direct consequence of the common mandate that Christ gave to the "body of pastors" (LG 23,3) to "proclaim the Gospel in every part of the earth" and is at the same time a duty directly implied by the "solicitude for the whole Church" (LG 23,2) to which every single bishop is bound. The reductive ecclesiological vision of the episcopal office, all concentrated again on the juridical figure of the concession of powers[7], impeded the ecclesiastical legislator of 1917 from highlighting this right-duty of every bishop, reserved as a privilege for cardinals only by can. 239 §1 n. 3.

---

[6]   Cf. can. 761.

[7]   Cf. L. Gerosa, *L'évêque dans les documents de Vatican II et le nouveau code de droit canonique,* in: *Visages de l'Église. Cours d'ecclésiologie* publié par P. De Laubier, Fribourg 1989, pp. 73-89.

Also everywhere, but with the at least presumed consent of the rector of the Church where the ministry is exercised, priests and deacons can exercise the faculty (*facultas*) of preaching, if the competent Ordinary has not taken it from them or restricted the use of such a faculty (can. 764). This means that, despite the concept of *missio canonica* (required by can. 1328 of the CIC of 1917 so that the priest or deacon could preach) being here substituted by that of *facultas*, nevertheless according to the ecclesiastical legislator preaching remains a particular form of evangelisation, which implies the exercise of an originary right, which belongs primarily to the bishop. The change of discipline in comparison with the first canonical codification is not however simply reducible to a radical simplification of the norms relating to preaching but consists above all in the recognition that Holy Orders establish a presumption in favour of the possibility for priests and deacons to preach the Gospel everywhere[8].

Analogously also the normative regarding the preaching of religious in their oratories or churches appears somewhat simplified, given that from now on it only requires the licence of the competent Superior (can. 765). New on the contrary are can. 766 on the preaching of lay people, of which more will be spoken of in detail later, and can 772 §2, which refers back to the dispositions given by the individual Conferences of Bishops concerning preaching by means of radio and television.

B) CATECHESIS

The entire second chapter of the normative of the code on the ministry of the Word is dedicated to catechetical instruction, which is a form of evangelisation more organic and sytematic of preaching. The key to the reading of the new theological-pastoral posting of this normative is given by can. 774 where the ecclesiastical legislator recalls how all the members of the Church are active subjects of its catechetical action (§1) and parents before all others (§2). Moreover this action is efficacious in arranging the growth of faith of the whole people of God only if its two dimensions, the teaching of doctrine and the experience of Christian life (can. 773), are conceived and practiced in a unitarian and integrating way, because orthodoxy and orthopraxis constitute an inseparable unity of every authenic Catholic effort[9].

On the contrary the posting of the Pio-Benedictine normative was very different (cans. 1329-1336), where catechetical action was wholly concentrated on the figure of the parish priest (can. 1330) and the parents were considered only as objects and not subjects of catechesis, among other things reduced it almost exclusively to the catechism of children in function of their participation in the sacraments (cann. 1330-1331). The actual can. 776 on the contrary obliges the parish priest, by virtue of his office, to take care of the catechetical formation of all the members of the People of God, from adults to young people to children, availing himself of the collaboration of all and in particular of catechists, whether they be clerics, religious or lay. It is up to the bishop moreover to provide so that adequate assistance is made available to guarantee an efficacious catechetical work at all levels (can. 775).

---

[8]   The Council teaching of LG 28 is this received by the second Code according to A. Montan, *Il libro III: La funzione di insegnare della Chiesa*, in: *Il nuovo Codice di diritto canonico. Studi*, Torino 1985, pp. 138-163, here p. 147.

[9]   Cf. H. Mussingdorf, in: MK, can 773.

C) THE PROBLEM OF LAY PREACHING

According to the teaching of the Vatican Council II[10], the whole People of God is called to participate in the prophetic office of Christ and therefore in preaching and catechesis. Consequently even the lay faithful can be called to collaborate with the bishop and priests in the exercise of the ministry of the Word[11], whether in catechesis or in teaching, or in liturgical celebrations "even though they are not lectors or acolytes" (can. 230 §3). The acceptance of these conciliar principles in the new Code of Canon Law permits the ecclesiastical legislator not only to abolish the prohibition on preaching imposed on all the laity *etsi religiosi* by the old can. 1342 §2, but also to offer a clear theological foundation to the already quoted can. 766 which states: "The laity may be allowed to preach in a church or oratory if in certain circumstances it is necessary, or in particular cases it would be advantageous, according to the provisions of the Bishops' Conference and without prejudice to can. 767 §1".

According to this norm the preaching of the lay faithful during autonomous celebrations of the Liturgy of the Word, or during other forms of non eucharistic liturgical prayer, does not pose particular problems. Except for priests reduced to the lay state[12], all of the lay faithful can be permitted to do so with respect to the dispositions laid down by the proper Bishops' Conference and whenever they fulfil the conditions of necessity and utility pointed out in line with the principles of the Magisterium. According to no. 17 of the conciliar decree *Apostolicam Actuositatem* a condition of great necessity occurs for example where "the liberty of the Church is greatly impeded", while according to no. 17 of the conciliar decree *Ad Gentes* a condition of true utility occurs where the communitarian prayer is normally presided over by catechists because of the scarcity of priests. The *Directorium de Missis cum pueris* published by the Congregation for Divine Worship on 1 November 1973 indicates in no.24 another condition of utility: liturgical celebrations for children with the participation of their catechists[13]. On the other hand some problems of interpretation of the norm are posed by the expression *admitti possunt laici* and the reservation *et salvo can 767 §1.*

The expression *admitti possunt laici* seems to leave it to be understood that for the ecclesiastical legislator the preaching of one of the lay faithful even in liturgical celebrations only has the value of a personal witness. If for this perhaps the formula *facultas praedicandi laici concedi potest*[14] had been subsituted, it would have been made more evident how also the preaching by one of the lay faithful is never made in his own right but under the commission of the bishop in the name of the Church, without nevertheless impairing with that either the authoritative character of preaching by an ordained minister or the substitutionary character of the preaching of lay people[15].

---

[10]   Cf. LG 33 and 35; AA 3; and can. 204 §1.

[11]   Cf. can. 759; on the whole question of lay preaching cf. L Gerosa, *Diritto ecclesiale e pastorale*. Torino 1991, pp. 58-64.

[12]   Cf. the *Norme della Congregazione per la Dottrina della Fede* of 1971, n. 46, in AAS 63 (1971), p. 308.

[13]   Cf. AAS 67 (1974), p. 37.

[14]   This is the proposal of H. Schmitz, *Die Beauftragung zum Predigtdienst. Anmerkungen zum "Schema canonum libri III de Ecclesiae munere docendi"*, in: AfkKR 149 (1980), pp. 45-63, and in particular p. 60.

[15]   cf. above all Art. 2 §3 of the Instruction: Congregatio pro clericis et aliae, *Instructio De*

The reservation of 767 §1 poses even greater problems of interpretation. In fact, in order to understand the exact normative import of the provision according to which "the homily which constitutes a part of the liturgy itself ... is reserved to the priest or deacon", we need first to determine the significance that the legislator attributes to the expressions *homily, liturgy* and *to reserve*. The *homily*, as emerges both from can. 767 §1 itself (which reprises art. 52 of the Constitution on the Liturgy *Sacrosanctum Concilium*) and from cans. 386 §1 and 528 §1, is an explanation of the truth of the faith, to be believed and applied in customs, derived from Holy Scripture (cf. SC 24). Being one of the more eminent forms of preaching this must be christologically orientated, that is to say presenting "fully and faithfully the mystery of Christ" (can. 760). *Liturgy* is here understood as a eucharistic celebration, either because it is explicitly affirmed in the sections following the canon in question, or because it can be deduced from the explanations proposed by the Pontifical Commission for the Reform of the Code [16]. How on the other hand the verb *to reserve* and thus the idea of *reservation*, introduced by no. 48 of the EA *Catechesi tradendae* of 16 October 1979 and then here reprised by the ecclesiastical legislator, is to be understood is not all that clear and every commentator appears free to be able to intepret, starting from his own theological convictions, as much the text of the code as the history of its composition.

Not even the response of the *Pontificia Commissio Codici Iuris Canonici Authentice Interpretando,* published on 3 September 1987 in the official organ of the Holy See for the promulgation of laws [17], seems to have resolved the question definitively. In fact, to the dubium submitted to it – *Utrum Episcopus diocesanus dispensare valeat a prescripto can.767 §1, quo sacerdoti aut diacono homilia riservatur* –, the quoted Commission replied with a laconic *Negative.* If the absence of motivations is not surprising, this being the normal way in which the decisions of the Commissions were published, nevertheless the missed quotation of the general norm of can. 87 §1, which exactly defines the limit within which the diocesan bishop can validly dispense from canonical laws whether universal or particular, seems to leave the question knowingly open [18]. In fact, it is beyond doubt that the disposition of can. 767 §1 is a *lex mere ecclesiastica* and thus a dispensation from this cannot on principle, be absolutely excluded according to can. 85. In other words, the doubt is at least legitimate of those who considers the reservation in favour of priests and deacons of the so-called homily as not identifiable with an absolute prohibition on the lay faithful from preaching during a eucharistic celebration [19].

---

quibusdam quaestionibus circa fidelium laicorum cooperationem sacerdotum ministerium spectantem, in: AAS 89 (1997), pp. 852-877.

[16]   Cf. Communcationes 7 (1975), p. 152; 9 (1977), p. 161.

[17]   AAS 79 (1987), p. 1249.

[18]   This is the authoritative opinion of H. Schmitz, *Erwägungen zur authentischen Interpretation von c. 767 §1 CIC,* in: *Recht als Heilsdienst; Matthäus Kaiser zum 65. Geburtstag gewidmet,* hrsg. von W. Schulz, Paderborn 1989, pp. 127-143, here p. 143.

[19]   Agreeing with this interpretation: P. Krämer, *Liturgie und Recht. Zuordnung und Abrenzung nach dem Codex Iuris Canonici vom 1983,* in Liturgisches Jahrbuch 34 (1984), pp. 66-83, here p. 77 and O. Stoffel, *Die Verkündigung in Predigt und Katechese,* in: HdbkathKR, pp. 541-547, here p. 543.

The legitimacy of such a doubt, if on the one hand it is consoled by the authoritativeness of a proposal, regrettably not accepted by the ecclesiastical legislator, made in February 1980 by the Congregation for the Doctrine of the Faith to introduce into the text of the Code the addition *ordinarie reservatur*[20], on the other it can rely upon the three following considerations.

Firstly, if it is true that the Council does not speak explicitly of preaching by the laity in eucharistic celebrations, all the same the response to a question on this problem given on 11 January 1971 by the Pontifical Commission for the authentic interpretation of conciliar texts permits that, in special cases, even the lay faithful can preach in eucharistic celebrations[21]. Then a similar interpretation finds its normative confirmation in the quoted no.24 of the *Directorium de Missis cum pueris* which explicitly affirms: "it is by no means forbidden that one of these adults who participates in the Mass, with the assent of the parish priest or rector of the church, can address a word to the children after the Gospel, especially if the priest finds it difficult to adapt to the mentality of the little listeners"[22]. In the third place the concession made by the Holy See to the German Bishops permitting that the laity particularly suited to the ministry of the Word can be called upon, in a subordinate or a subsidiary way, to preach in particular circumstances even in the eucharistic celebration itself has been confirmed many times[23]. After the promulgation of the new Code the normative content of such a concession was only partly modified by the dispositions contained in the *Ordnung für den Predigtdienst von Laien,* prepared by the German Bishops' Conference after long negotiations with the Holy See[24], and came into force on 1 May 1988 in the individual dioceses of West Germany[25]. In fact, in the second paragraph of the first section of these dispositions the German Bishops make clear that, even in eucharistic celebrations, the lay faithful (men or women) can be charged with preaching, in the sense of a *statio* at the beginning of Holy Mass, if at the celebration it is physically or morally impossible to give a homily and there is no priest or deacon available. These dispositions of particular law correspond to article 3 §2 of the Instruction, not like, on the

---

[20]   Cf. H. Schmitz, *Die Beauftragung zum Predigtdienst,* op. cit., p.62.

[21]   Cf. AAS 63 (1971), pp. 329 ff.

[22]   A subsequent and analogous confirmation can be found in the so-called shared-homilies of eucharistic celebrations for small groups (cf. *Richtlinien* published on 24.9.1970 by the Conference of German Bishops, in: *Nachkonziliare Dokumentation,* XXXI, Trier 1972, pp. 54-64).

[23]   The Rescript of the Congregation for the Clergy of 20.11.1973 (cf. X. Ochoa, *Leges Ecclesiae,* V, Roma 1980, n. 4240) was firstly prolonged until 1981 then on the 23.1.1982 it was once again prolonged until the publication of the new Code.

[24]   The last stage in these negotiations is the letter from the Congregation for the Clergy to the President of the German Bishops' Conference, dated 16 February 1988 and containing the communication that the foreseen dispositions did not need any *recognitio* on the part of the Holy See to come into force (cf. P. Krämer *Die Ordnung des Predigtdienstes,* in: *Rechts als Heilsdienst,* op. cit., pp. 115-126, here p. 121). Similar communications leave things perplexed, because according to can. 455 §2 the decrees of a Bishops' Conference obtain their obliging force only after the *recognitio* of the Holy See.

[25]   Cf. for example ABl Eichstätt 135 (1988), pp. 96 ff.

contrary, the practice – abusively spread in some local German language churches –, according to which some of the lay faithful regularly give the homily during the Mass.

All three of the cases indicated underline the character of exceptionality of preaching by lay people in eucharistic celebrations. In particular the latter case underlines also, at least in an indirect way, the general rule according to which the homily should normally be given by whoever presides at the Eucharist because Word and Sacrament are reciprocally ordered one to the other[26]. This character of exceptionality – well highlighted by the Instruction – is enough however to be able to conclude the following: a) The question of the participation of the lay faithful in the ministry of the Word cannot be reduced to the theological-juridical possibility of their preaching within eucharistic celebrations; b) The reservation in favour of priests and deacons, contained in can. 767 §1 must be considered in the measure of a general norm, juridically binding, but which – precisely because it is so – admits exceptions, established by the Bishops' Conference in agreement with the Holy See[27].

D) THE AGGREGATIVE FORCE OF THE AUTHORITATIVE WORD

The lacunae and uncertainties present in the juridical regulation of the preaching by lay people during eucharistic celebrations cannot place in doubt the numerous positive and innovative aspects of the new normative of the Code on the ministry of the Word, whose aggregative force, with a juridical-constitutional value in the arrangement of a formation of *una realitas complexa* (LG 28,1), which is the Church is highlighted in a particular way by can. 762. The latter – which repeats almost letter for letter PO 4,1 – affirms in fact "since the People of God is primarily brought together by the living Word of God, it is wholly legitimate to demand that the sacred ministers have a great regard for the function of preaching, proclaiming the Gospel to all being among their principal duties". The underlining of the aggregative force of the ministry of the Word on the one hand documents its strict link with the Sacrament of Orders, which enables presiding at the Eucharist, and on the other witnesses to the dogmatic root of the authoritative difference between the preaching of priests and that of the laity, ultimately to be found in the difference "of essence and not only of degree" (LG 10,2) between the ministerial and the common priesthood. The latter fact however also constitutes an implicit but specific duty for priests: their preaching represents an explanation of the Holy Scriptures capable of gathering the faithful together re-animating their hearts just like the Words of the Lord to the disciples at Emmaus only if it is deeply directed by the life of that *communio* of witnesses that is the Church. To achieve this result juridical dispositions are not enough, but it is necessary that linked together very much with these are the pastoral action of the whole Christian community and in particular of the pastors in order that the ministry of the Word is

---

[26]   Cf. n.42 of the General Introduction to the Roman Missal of 6.6.1966, in *Nachkonziliare Dokumentation, IX,* Trier 1974, p. 79.

[27]   In this respect it is, of course, legitimate to ask if an "Instructio", which according to the CIC is not a law and, therefore, the dispositions contained in it "legibus non derogant" (can. 34 §2), can any longer abrogate particular laws and customs, as the last phrase of the Instruction of the 13 August 1997 happily seems to demand. Would it not have been enough to recommend to the Bishops that they take care of eliminating all abusive practice?

ever more exercised "in a manner that is suited to the condition of the hearers and adapted to the circumstances of the times" (can. 769).

1.3 THE ECCLESIASTICAL MAGISTERIUM AND GRADUALNESS IN THE ASSENT OF FAITH

In introducing the commentary on the norms of the Code on the Ministry of the Word, there has already been a way of indicating how the most authoritative, and therefore formally most binding, expression of this service or ecclesial ministry is the so-called ecclesiastical Magisterium. Within the communal structure of the faith this has its own proper nature and finality which are expressed in different degrees both in the responsibility of its title-holders and in the assent of faith of all the baptised.

A) NATURE AND FINALITY OF THE ECCLESIASTICAL MAGISTERIUM

What distinguishes the ecclesiastical Magisterium within the general function of teaching of the Church, attributing to it a formal specific character within the "mission to teach all peoples and to preach the Gospel to every creature" (LG 24,1) is its being based on the apostolic mandate and as such in its being assured of a particular help of the Holy Spirit[28]. The specific function of the ecclesiastical Magisterium consists therefore in a particular way of exercising the function entrusted to the Church of protecting the unique *depositum fidei,* that is to say Sacred Scripture and Sacred Tradition, and above all in the exclusive task "of interpreting authentically the written or handed down Word of God" (DV 10,2). This double specific function is strictly bound both to the conferring of the "fullness of the Sacrament of Orders" (LG 21,2) and to the role of whoever is entrusted with being a "visible principle and basis for unity" (LG 23, 1) of the whole Church as a communion. When the Pope and the College of Bishops together with the successor of Peter exercise this function of proclaiming "with a definitive act a doctrine concerning faith or morals" (can 749) they are helped by a singular gift or the "charism of infallibility" (LG 25, 3).

These definitions of the ecclesiastical Magisterium are not new revelations, but have as their aim that of making all the faithful progress in their knowledge of the faith and its contents. At present, just as there "exists an order or rather a *hierarchy* of truths of Catholic doctrine, their connection with the foundation of the Christian faith being different" (UR 11,3) – an order from which a gradualness in the obligation of believing in them derives – so in the development of the ecclesiastical Magisterium by the Bishops and the Pope all the faithful, baptised and confirmed, participate according to their different degrees of responsibility, thanks to the gift of the *sensus fidei* (LG 12,1) and priests and deacons especially by dint of the Sacrament of Orders.

B) THE DIFFERENT DEGREES OF RESPONSIBILITY AND THE ASSENT OF FAITH

Without worrying about defining the nature and finality of the ecclesiastical Magisterium, on the basis of the conciliar lesson just summarised, the ecclesiastical legislator of 1983 in cans. 748-754, placed at the start of the third book on the teaching office of the Church, immediately makes clear the different degrees of responsibility in its exercise, not to mention the different degrees of assent of faith or ecclesial obedience

---

[28]   Cf. LG 19; 21,2; 22,2; 24,1; 25,3; and DV 10, 2 which speaks fully of a *divine mandate* and *help of the Holy Spirit.*

due from all the faithful as taught by the ecclesiastical Magisterium. This strange systematic positioning in a series of introductory canons and not having known how to record all of the normative of the Code on the ecclesiastical Magisterium in its own title, risks perpetrating an ecclesiological equivocation that the ecclesiastical Magisterium is still – contrary to what is taught by Vatican Council II [29] – conceived as an authority exercised over the Church and not within the Church as the ultimate guarantee of its unity. This impression is also confirmed by the fact of having in these canons renounced any reference to the conciliar terms of *sensus fidei* and *infallibilitas in credendo,* in order to theologically establish the communal structure of the community of faith that is the Church, also when exercising its *munus docendi.*

As regards the gradualness of responsibility for the exercise of the ecclesiastical Magisterium the CIC records that both the Pope and the College of Bishops are considered title-holders of the authentic Magisterium (can. 752) on the doctrine on faith and morals. Both the supreme subjects of this responsibility when they make a pronouncement in a definitive manner enjoy infallibility, both gathered together in an ecumenical council, and scattered throughout the world in their sees, but in communion with each other and with the successor of Peter (can. 749). The habitual exercise of the authentic ecclesiastical Magisterium is not however infallible and in fact the third section of this same can. 749§3 makes clear "No doctrine is understood to be infallibly defined unless this is manifestly demonstrated". From this can be deduced the existence of a certain gradualness also in the adhesion on the part of all the faithful to the doctrine of the ecclesiastical Magisterium.

For this reason the legislator prescribes: obedience or the assent of faith, for the truth to be believed in or proposed as divine-catholic faith (can. 751) and for those defined in an infallible way (can. 749 §2); a religious submission of intellect and will faced with the doctrines of the faith proposed by the ordinary ecclesiastical Magisterium, universal and authentic, without being proclaimed with a definitive act (can. 750); a simple submission of intellect and will, faced with the ordinary ecclesiastical Magisterium, universal and authentic, regarding doctrine and morals (can 752); and finally a simple adhesion with an interior religious sense faced with the ordinary authentic Magisterium of the bishop himself (can.753). All of the faithful have, moreover, the obligation to observe the constitutions and decrees with which the competent authority proposes a doctrine or rejects erroneous opinions (can. 754).

Whoever, after having received baptism, totally repudiates the Christian faith, denying in an obstinate way any truth of divine and catholic faith, deliberately removing himself from the communion of faith with the bishops and the Pope is an apostate, heretic and schismatic (can. 751), and incurs the canonical sanction of excommunication according to the norm of can. 1364. Upon whoever, after having received baptism, refutes instead the teaching of the authentic Magisterium of the Pope and the College of Bishops, even if it is not infallible, or obstinately rejects one of the doctrines of which the legislator speaks in can. 752, in accordance with the norm of can. 1371, after admonition, a canonical sanction can be inflicted or applied. Not

---

[29]   Cf. DV 10,2 and the comments of: W. Aymans, *Begriff, Aufgabe und Träger des Lehramts,* op. cit., p. 540; P. Krämer, *Kirchenrecht I,* op. cit., pp. 39-41; A. Montan, *Il libro III, la funzione di insegnare della Chiesa,* op. cit., p. 142.

any denial of a truth of faith, and not even any doubt about any of these truths constitutes an offence of heresy or schism, because even within the *plena communio* of the Catholic Church there exists a legitimate difference between the knowledge of the faith of the individual believer and the faith believed by the Church as a whole [30]. Certainly, if it is true that the general principle according to which every man is bound to embrace and observe by divine law the known truth (can. 748 §1) has a specific juridically binding force for the Catholic faithful, nevertheless the latter must realise that the difference between a serious sin against the faith (or the unity of the Church) and the offence of heresy (or of schism) does not depend on a given dogmatic objective, but on a positive intervention by the ecclesiastical authority [31]. In the normative dimension this positive intervention by the ecclesiastical authority can be expressed on two levels: that of a dogmatic nature of the definition, with a definitive act of the authentic ecclesiastical Magisterium, of the formal limits within which the *communio plena* in the faith is still guaranteed; and that of a legislative nature of providing such formal limits for canonical sanctions. The latter will be studied fully in section 5.3 of chapter 4, in strict connection with the sacrament of penance. Here it is enough to remember that the entire normative of the Code relating to the assent of faith and the total or partial denial of this is seen in the light of the fundamental conciliar principle on the freedom of the act of faith (DH 10), repeated by the ecclesiastical legilator in can. 748 §2, which states: "It is never lawful for anyone to force others to embrace the catholic faith against their conscience". Indeed, the act of faith is always a free and responsible response to the Word of God, which is an event of grace, and therefore has a significance not only for the outside world, but also within the juridical system of the Church, as has already been underlined in a way in the section on the principles for the legitimisation of an ecclesial law.

2. MISSION, EDUCATION AND ECUMENISM

2.1 NORMS OF THE CODE ON MISSIONARY ACTIVITY

The canonical norms on the missionary activity of the Church are grouped together by the ecclesiastical legislator of 1983 in the second title of Book III, according to the following systematic arrangement: after recalling the missionary character of the whole Church (can. 781), the criteria for the different responsibilities in the realisation of the missionary mandate are formulated (cans. 782-785 and can. 792) and finally the different norms that regulate missionary action properly called and its more specific activities (cans.786-791).

Right from the first section of this can. 781 it becomes clear how the ecclesiastical legislator has fully accepted the lesson of the council both on the pilgrim Church, that is "by its very nature missionary since, according to the plan of the Father, it has its

---

[30]   In this regard, cf. K. Rahner, *Häresie in der Kirche heute?* in: *Schriften zur Theologie*, Vol. IX, Einsiedeln 1972 (2. ed.), pp. 453-478, p. 460.

[31]   For a detailed analysis of the whole of this question, cf. L. Gerosa, *La scommunica è una pena? Saggio per la fondazione teologica del diritto penale canonico*, Friburgo 1984, pp. 296-326; Idem, *Schisma und Häresie. Kirchenrechtliche Aspekte einer neuen ekklesiologischen Begriffsbestimmung*, in: ThGl 83 (1993), pp. 195-212.

origin in the mission of the Son and the Holy Spirit" (AG 2,1), and on the work of evangelisation as a fundamental duty of the whole People of God and of each of individual member [32]. From the systematic organisation of the material, and not just from can. 787 §1, the knowledge also emerges that the source of both missionary action in general, and of missionary action properly called, is the witness of life and word of men and women reborn in their humanity through their baptism, by which they are incorporated into the Church as *communio* [33]. The insistence of the ecclesiastical legislator on "a sincere dialogue with those who do not believe in Christ" (can. 787 §1) and on the admission for baptism only of those who have "freely" requested it (can 787 §2), after having received the Gospel proclamation, also fully documents how all of these norms of the Code on the missionary activity of the Church are directed by the conciliar principle of religious freedom.

At the centre of these norms there is rightly found the dispositions concerning the most important and delicate aspect of missionary activity properly called, that is to say the incorporation into the Church of those who have freely welcomed the Christian message. According to the norm of cans. 787-789 after the pre-catechumenate, consisting in the first message or *kerygma*, those who have manifested the will to embrace the faith in Christ are admitted to the catechumenate with a liturgical ceremony. This period of binding instruction in Christian doctrine, of preparation to receive the sacraments and of true and proper apprenticeship of the Christian life is ordered according to statutes and rules emanating from the Episcopal Conferences [34].

Around this central nucleus the ecclesiastical legislator also formulates some norms concerning missionaries (can. 784) and lay catechists (can. 785), as the principal agents of missionary activity properly called (can. 786). The latter has a specific aim: "to implant the Church among peoples or groups who do not yet believe in Christ" (AG 6,3). The formula *plantatio Ecclesiae* of can. 786, from Saint Thomas Aquinas and reprised in many pontifical documents on the missionary activity of the Church, on the one hand describes the responsibility from which such a duty "falls once more upon the universal Church and the particular Churches" [35], and on the other defers to that long and complicated process of inserting the Church into the cultures of different peoples, called inculturation. This process is not a "pure external adaptation", but implies an "intimate transformation of authentic cultural values mediating the integration of Christianity and the rooting of Christianity in the various cultures" [36]. In getting to the end of this long and slow road with the peoples the Church must sustain her missionary action with a specific educational activity also.

2.2 NORMS OF THE CODE ON EDUCATIONAL ACTIVITY

After having fixed in the mind in the three introductory canons (cans. 793-795) of the conciliar principles on catholic education, the 1983 Code gathers together the princi-

---

[32]   Cf. above all AG 11; 35 and 36.

[33]   Cf. LG 14 and AG 11,1.

[34]   On this central nucleus of the norms of the Code on the missionary activity of the Church cf. O. Stoffel, *Der missionarische Auftrag,* in: HdbkathKR, pp. 547-553, above all, pp. 551-553.

[35]   John Paul II, *Redemptoris missio,* in: AAS 83 (1991), pp. 249-340, n. 49.

[36]   Ibid, n. 52; cf. also Paul VI, *Evagelii nuntiandi,* op. cit., n. 20.

pal canonical norms on the educative activity of the Church in three chapters: schools (cans. 796-806), Catholic universities (cans. 807-814), ecclesiastical universities and faculties (cans. 815-821). Given the strict connection of all of this material with the different normatives of the state the ecclesiastical legislator limits himself to offering framed norms and often defers to the particular dispositions of Episcopal Conferences [37]. Of particular importance however is the fact that the ecclesiastical legislator has made proper the conciliar perspective of the right and duty of parents to educate their own children according to their own convictions, from which directly derives the right to freely choose the school best suited to their own children and to receive, on the part of civil society, the assistance necessary to worthily fulfil this difficult task [38]. On the part of the State it would be a grave reduction both of the principle of subsidiarity, and of distributive justice to deny this assistance, invoking the right to a monopoly that does not belong to it or the principle of separation between Church and State, entirely out of place given that it deals not with a prerogative of faith communities, but rather of a fundamental right of parents based on their personal dignity and that of their own children [39].

2.3 CANON LAW AND ECUMENISM

"The restoration of unity among all Christians is one of the principal concerns of the Second Vatican Council" (UR 1,1) The ecclesiastical legislator, bound to look upon the Second Vatican Council as his *alter ego*, can certainly not prescind from this ecumenical inspiration of the entire conciliar teaching. And in fact already in the chapter on the formation of the clergy the necessity is remembered in can. 256 §2 that students are made aware of "missionary and ecumenical questions". Nevertheless, the general norm on the promotion of ecumenical activity has been formulated in a truly unfortunate manner for at least three reasons. First of all can. 755 is placed at the end of the norms of the Code on the ecclesiastical Magisterium, almost as if ecumenical activity has to do exclusively with the *munus docendi*. In second place the same canon being addressed to the Apostolic See, the College of Bishops, Episcopal Conferences and to individual bishops, it seems as if the ecclesiastical legislator forgets the teaching of the council on ecumenical solicitude, "involving the whole Church, faithful and clergy alike" (UR 5). In third place, in contrast to what happens in cans. 902-908 of the CCEO, the quoted canon does not contain any disposition on the instruments and ways of realising ecumenical activity.

Definitively, can. 755 of the CIC, notwithstanding that it certainly represents progress with regard to the prohibition made by the Pio-Benedictine Code on Catholic brethren publicly entering into dialogue with non-catholics without the express per-

---

[37]   The most important example is that of religious instruction given by state school and mentioned by can. 804; on the argument cf. J. Listl, *Der Religionsunterricht*, in: HdbkathKR, pp. 590-605; F. Tagliaferri, *Insegnamento della religione cattolica,* in: Apollinaris 60 (1987), pp 145-150.

[38]   In this regard cf. above all GE 1,1; 2,1; 6,1.

[39]   For a brief illustration of this most important question cf. F.J. Urrutia, *Educazione cattolica,* in: NDDC, pp. 439-440.

mission of the Holy See or the Ordinary[40], in relation to the teaching of the Vatican Council II the general dispositions contained by it are fairly incomplete by way of constituting a solid normative basis for the ecumenical activity of the Catholic Church[41]. This negative opinion is partially mitigated by the presence in the CIC of other norms – fully studied by other authors[42] – decidedly more valid within the ecumenical framework: for example can. 463 §3, where a deep interest and respect for the "other Churches or ecclesial communities which are not in full communion with the Catholic Church" emerges[43]; can 844, which facilitates the relationships between the faithful of the different Christian Churches, above all as regards the reception of some of the sacraments or *communicatio in sacris*[44]; can. 861 §2, which in cases of necessity authorises whoever is moved by the right intention to administer the sacrament of baptism; cans. 1124-1129, which unite in one single chapter all of the canonical normative on mixed marriages, sensibly improved in relation to the preceding norms, as will be seen more fully in 4. chapter (8.3) dedicated to this. If these undoubted improvements within some particular normative sectors had been sustained even by some more specific general norm on the promotion of Christian Unity, it might have been easier for the ecclesiastical legislator to cast a different light, clarifying under the theological profile, also on the full and complex normative of the code on the juridical guardianship of the ecclesial communion.

3. THE JURIDICAL GUARDIANSHIP OF THE ECCLESIAL COMMUNION

In expounding the principles for the legitimisation of the existence of an ecclesial law there is already a way to show how Canon Law thouroughly discharges its function within the community of faith which is the Church, when it simultaneously guarantees the integral handing on of the truth of faith and the free adhesion to this. It is its very purpose to realise this communion of faith and life. To achieve this the ecclesiastical legislator, on the basis of a long canonical tradition, has prepared a series of juridical instruments, which go from the simple *professio fidei* or public profession of faith to the more complex canonical procedures, and in particular that on the *status*

---

[40] Cf. can. 1325 §3 of the CIC/1917 and the comment of P. Krämer, *Kirchenrecht I*, op. cit., pp. 41-42.

[41] This is the opinion of J.L. Santos, *Ecumenismo*, in: NDDC, pp. 437-439.

[42] Besides the indicated literature further on in relation to mixed marriages, among the most important studies which deal with the argument in a general way should be noted: H. Müller, *Der ökumenische Auftrag*, in: HdbkathKR, pp. 553-561; H. Heinemann, *Ökumenische Implikationem des neuen kirchlichen Gesetzbuches*, in: Catholica 39 (1985), pp. 1-26; W. Schulz, *Questioni ecumeniche nel nuovo Codice di diritto canonico*, in: *Vitam impendere vero*. Studies in honour of P. Ciprotti, edited by W. Schulz-G. Feliciani, Roma 1986, pp. 171-184.

[43] Cf. also can. 364 n. 6.

[44] In conformity with the teaching of the council (UR 8,3) there is an exception to this rule in the prohibition made on catholic priests to concelebrate the Eucharist with ministers of Churches or ecclesial communities not in full communion with the catholic Church (can. 908).

personarum, which are more typical because they tend to define or declare the real positioning of one of the faithful within the ecclesial communion.

3.1 SOME JURIDICAL INSTRUMENTS FOR THE DEFENCE OF THE INTEGRITY OF THE FAITH

A) THE PROFESSION OF FAITH AND OATH OF FIDELITY

The bond of the Profession of Faith (can. 205) – together with the sacramental – being at the base of the ecclesial communion, can. 833 imposes on all the faithful who exercise an important ecclesial office in the ecclesial community the obligation to publicly profess the faith of the Catholic Church. Such an obligation juridically binds the individual interested member of the faithful because it cannot be fulfilled by means of a procurator. This implies a public obligation in obedience to Christ and to the Church and is accomplished through a formula approved by the Apostolic See containing the Nicene-Constantinople symbol with a few additions regarding the dispositions contained in cans. 750 and 752.

Notwithstanding that shortly after the closure of Vatican Council II the Congregation for the Doctrine of the Faith supressed the anti-Modernist oath[45], the same Congregation has recently published a document, which came into force on 1 March 1989, with the new formula of the oath of fidelity[46]. The latter is to be considered as the complement of the Profession of Faith imposed by can. 833 on vicars general, episcopal and judicial; on Parish Priests; on the rector and teachers in seminaries; on the rector and teachers in Catholic and ecclesiastical universities; on the superiors of clerical religious institutes and clerical societies of apostolic life; on those promoted to the order of deacon. Beyond the incoherence with which are obliged, without distinction, even the faithful who "do not perform an ecclesiastical office in the name of the Church"[47], it is in any case to be observed how such an oath, of a promissory nature[48], simply reinforces what for the faithful is already an obligation implied by the taking on of that determined ecclesiastical office. For the christian community, on the other hand, it can be a further guarantee of knowing that the bearer of such an ecclesiastical office is pledged also with an oath of fidelity, which while not being a true and proper act of worship to God still assumes the solemnity of a submission to God and to the Church.

B) *Nihil obstat, mandatum* AND *missio canonica*

The technical term *nihil obstat,* the object of not a few discussions and polemics within Catholic post-conciliar theology[49], is used by Canon Law to refer to the commission to

---

[45] Cf. AAS 59 (1967), p. 1058.

[46] Cf. AAS 81 (1989), pp. 104-106. For a critical commentary cf. P. Krämer, *Kirchenrecht I,* op. cit., pp. 61-62; F.J. Urrutia, *Iusiurandum fidelitatis,* in: Periodica 80 (1991), pp. 559-578.

[47] F.J. Urrutia, *Giuramento di fedeltà,* in: NDDC, pp. 546-547, here p. 546.

[48] On the obligations coming from a promissory oath cf. cans. 1199-1204 and above all cans 1200-1202.

[49] Cf. H. Schmitz, *Konfliktfelder und Lösungswege im kirchlichen Hochschulbereich. Bemerkungen zu notorischen aktuellen Problemen,* in: *Eine Kirche – Ein Recht? Kirchenrechtliche Konflikte zwischen Rom und den deutschen Ortskirchen,* hrsg. von R. Puza-A. Kustermann, Stuttgart 1990, pp. 123-128, above all pp. 125-128.

teach theological disciplines either in state universities or faculties or in ecclesiastical superior institutes. Beside the *nihil obstat* conceded by the Apostolic See and known as the *nulla osta romano*, we should not forget the *nihil obstat* of the Ordinary of the place which, according to the concordatory law of many north-European countries, is what has the juridically binding value for the competent state authorities and is practically the equivalent of the *missio canonica*. In both cases however it is a question of a simple negative declaration with which the competent ecclesiastical authority attests that, according to the Canon Law in force, there is no objection as regards an eventual commission to teach for that determined teacher[50].

The *mandatum* is the new technical term that the Commission for the Revision of the Code substituted for the preceding *missio canonica* in can. 812, which states: "Those who teach theological subjects in any institute of higher studies must have a mandate from the competent ecclesiastical authority"[51]. This new canonical institution or juridical instrument for the protection of the ecclesial communion is something more than the simple *nihil obstat,* but at the same time it cannot be considered as a true *missio canonica,* because the latter is prescribed by the CA *Sapientia christiana* only for the teachers of theological disciplines in ecclesiastical universities or faculties[52]. Besides to claim that all teachers of theological disciplines at any type of institute of higher studies must teach in the name of the competent ecclesiastical authority, and not on their own responsibility, would be damaging to the freedom recognised in can. 218 as their right. Beyond the terminological lack of clarity and cohesion of the canonical normative in this sector it can however be affirmed that the mandate is none other than an attestation prior to teaching with which no particular right is conferred on the teacher in question, but it attests positively and publicly to two things: in the first place that the teacher is in communion with the Catholic Church and teaches, therefore, as a Catholic; in the second place that the doctrine proposed by the teacher conforms with the ecclesiastical Magisterium[53].

The technical term *missio canonica* does not have a univocal significance: in the conciliar documents this is used to indicate the manner with which the hierarchy entrusts certain functions to the lay faithful which, by their nature, are more bound to the offices of pastors[54]; in the CIC of 1983 the ecclesiastical legislator makes no reference to this; in canonical tradition with such a term is indicated different forms of participation in the mission of the ecclesiastical hierarchy; finally, in the norms of ecclesiastical law of the state the same expression is used to indicate the ways of collaborating between ecclesiastical and state authorities in the taking on of teachers, lecturers and

---

[50]   Cf. H. Schmitz, *Studien zum kirchlichen Hochschulrecht,* Würzburg 1990, pp. 133-145; I. Riedel-Spangenberger, *Sendung in der Kirche. Die Entwicklung des Begriffes "missio canonica" und seine Bedeutung in der kirchlichen Rechtssprache,* Paderborn-München-Wien-Zürich 1991, pp. 188-191.

[51]   On the sense of the substitution cf. Communicationes 15 (1983), p. 105.

[52]   Cf. AAS 71 (1979), pp. 469-499, here p. 483 (=n. 27,1).

[53]   Agreeing with this definition of the *mandatum*: F.J. Urrutia, *Mandato di insegnare discipline teologiche,* in: NDDC, pp. 661-664, here p. 662; G. Ghirlanda, *Il diritto nella Chiesa mistero di comunione. Compendio di diritto ecclesiale,* Roma 1990, p. 423.

[54]   Cf. AA 24 and the commentary of F.J. Urrutia, *Mandato,* op. cit., p. 662

professors in the various schools and higher institutions[55]. In any case it is a question of different forms, with different juridical consequences, with which the competent ecclesiastical authority commissions one of the faithful to perform a determined function in the name of the hierarchical authority and under the full responsibility of the latter.

Alongside these juridical instruments of a substantially promotional nature, Canon Law recognises other juridical instruments of a more preventative or properly vigilant and defensive nature in order to protect the objective realisation of the ecclesial communion; we are dealing above all with ecclesiastical censure and the procedures for the examination of teaching in theology.

c) ECCLESIASTICAL CENSURE AND THE PROCEDURES FOR THE EXAMINATION OF THE TEACHING OF THEOLOGY

Shortly after the closure of the Vatican Council II, on 14 June 1966, the Congregation for the Doctrine of the Faith abolished the odious index of forbidden books[56] and around ten months later the same Congregation issued the decree *Ecclesiae pastorum*[57], with which it reorganised all the material on the censorship of books. This decree constitutes the principal source for cans. 822-832 on the authorisation for the publication of books and other writings relating to the faith and morals of the Catholic faithful.

The new canonical institutions of *licentia* and *approbatio* are by nature very different from the old *prohibitio*[58] and also have different juridical consequences. For example if a book were published today without the appropriate ecclesiastical approval this would not mean that the book has a prohibited character with all the heavy juridical consequences established by the old can. 1399, that is to say that it cannot be read, printed, conserved, sold or translated by the Catholic faithful[59]. The right and duty of bishops to be vigilant over the writings and the use of the instruments of social communication has an eminently pastoral function, that of preserving "the integrity of faith and morals"(can. 823 §1) soliciting, with the proper interventions, the responsibility of all the faithful. Moreover can. 824 establishes a clear distinction between permission and approval: while with the *licentia* the ecclesiastical authority authorises the publication without making a judgement upon it, the *approbatio* contains such a judgement. The latter is required by the CIC for the publication of the original text of Sacred Scripture, liturgical books, collections of prayers and catechisms. Without approval theology books cannot be used as manuals or teaching textbooks (can. 827

---

[55]   On the whole of this question cf. I. Riedel-Spangenberger, *Sendung in der Kirche*, op. cit., especially pp. 98-144 and pp. 201-281.

[56]   Cf. AAS 58 (1966), p. 445; a little later the same Congregation abrogated can. 1399 of the CIC/1917 on books forbidden by Canon Law and the connected censures (cf. AAS 58 (1966), p. 1186.

[57]   Cf. AAS 67 (1975), pp. 281-284.

[58]   Cf. cans. 1395-1405 of the CIC/1917.

[59]   This does not take away from the fact that even today – according to can. 1369 – a canonical sanction can be applied to the faithful who with their writings gravely wound the catholic faith and morals or rouse up hatred and contempt for the Church.

§2), nor can they be displayed, sold or distributed in Churches or oratories (can 827 §4).

In all other cases permission is sufficient and prior ecclesiastical censorship is only recommended[60].

Alongside these particular juridical institutions, whose application must always come with a full respect for the dignity and the rights of all the faithful – as for example those of immunity from any coercion (can 219), freedom of expression (can. 212 §3) and of research (can. 218) – there also exist in Canon Law determined procedures geared to the protection of the objective realisation and conservation of the ecclesial communion. It is a question of the so-called special administrative procedures – dealt with in the following section together with the other canonical procedures – and of the procedures for the examination of erroneous doctrine.

During the Vatican Council II there was severe criticism of the manner of procedure of the Roman Congregations and in particular the *Sacrum Officium* which, one day before the official closure of the great ecumenical gathering, through the MP *Integrae servandae*[61], received from Pope Paul VI the new name of the Congregation for the Doctrine of the Faith and above all a new organisation. The latter, apart from some light modification, was confirmed by the CA *Regimini Ecclesiae Universae*[62], which obliges the Congregation to give itself a new internal regulation. This happened on 15 January 1971 with the publication of the *Nova agenda ratio in doctrinarum examine*[63], containing the new normative for the procedure of examining doctrines.

If the publication of this *Nova agenda ratio* constitutes without doubt an important step forward towards the full vanquishing of the methods of the Inquisition, characterised by an obscure halo of silence in part inherited by the Holy Office, still some of the norms were strongly criticised, and not always wrongly, as we will see better later on. Among many criticisms, the principal ones relating to a lack of clarity on the role of the diocesan bishop in these procedures and the impression – aroused by the Instruction – that only the Roman Congregation is competent in questions of faith and morals of the Catholic faithful[64]. This role cannot be clarified prescinding from the new theological and juridical statute acquired by the Congregation for Bishops after the Vatican Council II. Neither can it be defined with clarity without a specific positioning within the new and diversified system of canonical procedures. Regrettably, the CIC of 1983 does not offer any help by way of clarifying these problems, being limited to affirming in can. 830 that the right of every Ordinary to entrust to people

---

[60] Cf. can. 827 §3. The importance of these norms of the Code is confirmed by a recent Instruction from the Congregation for the Doctrine of the Faith (30.3.1992), which has clarified the terms of application. For a commentary cf. P. Krämer, *Kirche und Bücherzensur. Zu einer neuen Instruktion der Kongregation für die Glaubenslehre,* in ThGl 83 (1993), pp. 72-80.

[61] The text of this MP of 7.12.65 can be found in: AAS 57 (1965), pp. 952-955.

[62] Cf. AAS 59 (1967), pp. 675-697.

[63] Cf. AAS 63 (1971), pp. 234-236. For a detailed analysis of this text, cf. W. Aymans-E. Corecco, *Kirchliches Lehramt und Theologie. Erwägungen zur Neuordnung des Lehrprüfungsverfahrens bei der Kongregation für die Glaubenslehre,* in: IKZ Communio 2 (1974), pp. 150-170; H. Heinemann, *Lehrbeanstandung in der katholischen Kirche. Analyse und Kritik der Verfahrensordnung (=Canonistica 6),* Trier 1981.

[64] Cf. W. Aymans-E. Corecco, *Kirchliches Lehramt und Theologie,* op. cit., pp. 169-170.

approved by him to judge books remains intact and that the Conference of Bishops can constitute a commission of censors. Consequently, not withstanding its limits, the juridical basis for the procedure for examining doctrines remains – even after the promulgation of the CIC – the *Nova agenda ratio* of 1971.

This regulation for the examination of doctrines envisages two forms of procedure: the extraordinary procedure, to be applied only in cases in which "the opinion gleaned from the examination is clearly and assuredly erroneous and at the same time it is envisaged that from the divulgence of it there could derive or has derived already a real damage to the faithful"(no.1), and the ordinary procedure, to be applied in all other cases. In the first procedure, extremely summary, the Ordinary of the place is immediately notified so that the author can be invited to correct the error. A similar manner of procedure contradicts the fundamental principle, recalled by the same CA *Regimini Ecclesiae Universae* in no. 32, according to which the author, even in the most serious cases, must always be guaranteed the right of defence.

The ordinary procedure, on the other hand, is divided into two phases: an internal (nos. 2-10) and an external (nos. 11-18). The first phase has as its aim that of permitting the Congregation to form for itself – by means of the discussion of the prepared opinions from two experts and from the *pro autore* reporter – a specific opinion on the doctrine under examination and therefore does not envisage an interview with the author and not even necessarily the notification the interested ordinary. The second phase of the procedure, that which addresses the external, comes into play only if after the inquiry carried out in the first phase there are effectively found, in the doctrine under examination, false or dangerous opinions (no.12). The interested Ordinary is then to be notified and "the propositions held to be erroneous or dangerous – in order that he can present in writing, within a working month, his reply" are communicated to the author (no.13). Only if it is deemed to be necessary, the author can be invited to a personal interview with the representatives of the Congregation. After that the Congregation will decide if and how the outcome of the examination should be published (no.17). Finally, once approved by the Pope, these decisions are communicated to the Ordinary of the author (no.15).

As is easily perceivible, even this ordinary procedure has not escaped a lot of criticism, above all because the author's right to defence cannot be reduced to the possibility of a written reply and to that of possibly being invited for an interview[65]. On the other hand there has been a positive acceptance of the fact that this new procedure, of an eminently administrative character, reveals a declarative judgement – juridically binding – which does not directly concern the faith of the author, but the conformity or not of his doctrine to Revelation and to the teaching of the Church.

Of an analogous nature is the judgement, not juridically binding, to which were joined the procedures for the examination of doctrines introduced by some Bishops' Conferences[66]. Here it is simply a question of qualified counsel, given by the Bish-

---

[65] Cf. ibid, p. 166.

[66] Among these procedures, perhaps the most meaningful examples are those formulated by the Conference of the German bishops and the Conference of Swiss bishops. The respective texts were published in: AfkKR 150 (1981) pp. 174-182 and 155 (1986) pp. 165-172.

ops' Conference to the interested Ordinary to offer him some help in his decision[67]. However the applied procedures for accessing this qualified advice are formally more rigorous than those of the Congregation for the Doctrine of the Faith. Indeed, besides having a decidedly synodal character, they guarantee both a greater publicity for the acts and the technical defence of the author. On the contrary, from some standpoints, these particular administrative procedures – but with some elements of an eminently judiciary nature – constitute a clear parallel to the base-structure of canonical procedures, which will be studied in the next section. These seem however to express with greater clarity the procedures for the examination of doctrines, applied by the Congregation for the Doctrine of the Faith, of the particular nature of the law of the Church. For this reason they can provide a valuable point of reference for a future new and more complete normative treatment of all this delicate material on the level of the universal Church as well. And in point of fact on the 29 June 1997, during the work of translating this very manual into Spanish, the Congregation for the Doctrine of the Faith published new procedural norms that – examined at first sight – seem to have welcomed the desired principles manifested in these years, and in particular the right of the author to a technical defence and the direct involvement of his Ordinary[68].

3.2 CANONICAL PROCEDURES

At the heart of the reformation of canonical procedural law it was proposed to entitle this sector of the law of the Church *De modo procedendi pro tutela iurium*[69]. The fact that the last book of the Code instead maintains the title *De processibus* can help the faithful to understand that the aim of the different procedures is not exclusively the protection of legitimate rights and interests, or of the common good, but rather to "promote true reconciliation and to assure full *communio* among all the faithful"[70]. Also on the level of the technical-juridical elements of a process it should nevertheless be possible to perceive the different communitarian and organisational nature characterising the Church before the State. This diversity, founded either on the particular nature of *sacra potestas*, or on the operative unity between Word and Sacrament in the building up of the *communio Ecclesiae*, emerges on three levels: the substantially similar purpose of all the more typical canonical procedures of the juridical system of the Church; the declaritive character of the canonical sentence; the inadequate distinction between the judiciary and administrative nature of the different canonical procedures. The convergence of these three characteristics of canonical procedural law permits the conclusion that there exists a base-structure common to all canonical procedures.

---

[67]   Agreeing with this opinion: H. Heinemann, *Schutz der Glaubens und Sittenlehre,* in: HdbkathKR, pp. 567-578 and P. Krämer, *Kirchenrecht I,* op. cit., p. 60.

[68]   Cf. above all nn. 7 and 17 of the new *Agendi ratio in doctrinarum examine,* the text of which can be found in: AAS 89 (1997) pp. 830-835. For a detailed commentary cf. L. Gerosa, *Grundlagen und Paradigmen der Gesetzesauslegung in der Kirche. Zukunftsperspektiven für die katholische Kanonistik,* Münster 1999, pp. 94-101.

[69]   Cf. Communcationes 1 (1969), p. 83; 10 (1978), pp. 209-216; 15 (1984), p. 52.

[70]   R. Bertolino, *La tutela dei diritti nella Chiesa. Dal vecchio al nuovo codice di diritto canonico,* Torino 1993, p. 16.

A) THE EQUAL AIM OF THE PROCESSES-TYPE OF THE CHURCH

Notwithstanding the pretext, brandished more than once in the preparatory work of the new codification, that Canon Law knows more types of process, the CIC of 1983 presents in fact a unique base-process, the contentious (cans. 1501-1670), to which all the other forms of process – called by the ecclesiastical legislator *special processes* – make constant reference. In the so-called ordinary contentious judgement juridical formalities prevail, and in particular the formality of the written as opposed to oral contentious judgement (cans. 1656-1670). In both forms this has as its object the vindication of the rights of physical or juridical persons, or the declaration of juridical facts[71].

At present, this type of process itself is not only the least frequent but takes up a subsidiary role and as such is also that which the Church can more easily renounce without encountering great difficulties. It is also not by chance that in the *Coetus consultorum* entrusted with the reform of canonical procedural law, there emerged the proposal to substitute it, in its base-process function, with the matrimonial, given that in the Church matrimonial causes are by far the most frequent[72]. The discussion is not however just quantitative. Not just matrimonial causes (cans. 1671-1707), but all the so-called special cases from the under-articulation of matrimonial processes (such as the process for the separation of spouses, that of *ratum et non consummatum* and that of presumption of death of the spouse: cans. 1692-1707) to the process for the declaration of nullity of ordination (cans. 1708-1712) and finally the penal process (cans. 1717-1731), are substantially and in the final analysis causes concerning the *status personarum*. As such these tend to define the real positioning and/or the measure of belonging of one of the faithful to the ecclesial communion and this belongs to the inalienable and typical kernel of the canonical process[73].

The capacity of these causes to distinguish in an irrefutable way the canonical processes regulated by them from the law of the state would have been made more evident if ecclesiastical legislator had not relinquished the codification of canonical processes that not only are conducted by administrative instance but also reflect more clearly the particular nature of the juridical structure of the Church, that is to say the procedure regarding the causes for beatification or canonisation and those – already studied – for the examination of doctrines held to be erroneous. We cannot in fact forget that the canonical procedure for the causes of beatification and canonisation were dealt with in a good 142 canons of the latter part of the fourth book of the CIC/1917 (cans. 1999-2141) and was defined – starting from its formal premises – by an authoritative canonist as "the most rigourous procedural form" known to Canon Law[74]. Placing it at the centre of the new procedural normative of the code would certainly have helped us to understand that the judgement, in which a canonical procedure nor-

---

[71]   Cf. can. 1400 §1.

[72]   Cf. Communicationes 11 (1979), pp. 80-81.

[73]   This is the just consideration of: E. Corecco, *Die richterliche Anwendung der "sacra potestas"*, in: ÖAKR 39 (1990), pp. 277-294, here pp. 284-285.

[74]   Cf. K. Mörsdorf, *Lehrbuch des Kirchenrechts,* Bd. 3, Paderborn-München-Wien 1979 (11. ed.), p. 260 and the comment of W. Schulz, *Das neue Selig- und Heiligsprechungverfahren,* Paderborn 1988, pp. 20-22.

mally unfolds, and in particular those which regard causes on the *status personarum* are the most typical of the procedural system of the Church, is by its nature declarative.

B) THE DECLARITIVE NATURE OF THE CANONICAL SENTENCE

The sentence, in whatever juridical system, represents "the magnetic pole of the entire process" [75] and, as such, reflects the most relevant characteristics of the system in question. This means that the canonical sentence also is the ideal mirror of the juridical structure of the Church, profoundly different – even on the procedural law level – to that of the state.

In fact, in the procedural law of the state the judge, as opposed to the bishop, cannot act if not on condition of placing himself as an organ of formal right which, outside the frame of the law, does not have any power and ceases also to exist [76].

A similar identification between power and developed function, in this case the process, is not possible in the Church because of the particular nature of the *sacra potestas* which, as has already been seen, is one and unique. As such, even when working at the level of the *iuris-dictio*, the *sacra potestas* is never identified either with the organ that exercises it or with its *modus procedendi*. Moreover in the Church – where, as opposed to what happens in the modern State, the division of powers does not exist – the *modus procedendi* of all the organs of government is not determined by the nature of the function developed by it as much as the nature of the object. At present the ecclesiastical judge, whether he proceeds in a judicial manner or in an administrative manner, with his judgement (whether this is under the technical form of a sentence or a decree) is always substantially called to establish the objective facts, such as the validity of the sacraments, the belonging or not to the *communio plena,* the legitimacy of public worship or the orthodoxy of a doctrine. The juridical value of these objective facts transcends the simple private interest of the individual faithful. This touches the reality of the whole of the Church as *communio,* because the juridical structure of the latter has as a *telos* not primarily that of realising the subjective rights of the individual faithful, but rather that of guaranteeing on the constitutional plain or of given objectives the integrity and the truth of the salvific content of Word and Sacrament. This permanence of the *substantia verbi* and of the *substantia sacramenti* is the ultimate aim of the *sacra potestas*, even when this acts as a *potestas iudicaria*. Consequently the canonical sentence, precisely in the most typical processes in the Church, has an eminently declarative character [77]. With a canonical sentence the ecclesiastical authority recognises juridically binding facts and guarantees in this manner the objective realisation of the ecclesial experience, founded on the authenticity of the Word, the validity of the Sacraments, and all those other elements which concern the common vocation of living the faith in the ecclesial communion, which is always a *communio cum Deo* and a *communio fidelium.*

---

[75] R. Bertolino, *Il notorio nell'ordinamento giuridico della Chiesa,* Torino 1965, p. 49.

[76] Cf. for example E. Schumann, *Richter,* in: EvStL³, Bd. 2, Sp. 3010-3016. On the diversity between canonical procedural law and that of the state, cf. also E. Corecco, *L'amministrazione della giustizia nel sistema canonico e in quello statuale,* in: *Amministrazione della giustizia e rapporti umani,* Rimini 1988, pp. 133-140.

[77] Cf. E. Corecco, *Die richterliche Anwendung der "sacra potestas",* op. cit., p. 282; p. 286 and pp.287-289.

These considerations on the declarative nature of the canonical sentence are valid also – as will be seen in the 4. chapter (5.3) – for the sentence (or decree) pronounced at the end of a canonical penal process, and not just when the norms of the code define it as declarative, because it is relative to a *latae sententiae* canonical sanction. Even when the code defines the sentence as to be imposed, because it is a question of a *ferendae sententiae* canonical sanction (for example in can. 1314), this has in fact a declarative character, because the same distinction between *latae sententiae* and *ferendae sententiae* canonical sanctions does not touch their specific nature but their juridical effects exclusively [78].

C) THE INADEQUATE DISTINCTION BETWEEN JUDICIAL AND ADMINISTRATIVE CANONICAL PROCEDURES.

Canon Law, alongside the already studied procedures for the examination of erroneous doctrines and those envisaged by can. 1720 for the application of canonical sanctions, also knows a series of special administrative procedures. There are substantially three of these: the procedure for the removal and transfer of a Parish Priest; the procedure for imposed exclaustration of someone consecrated and finally the procedure for dismissal from the consecrated life.

The normative of the code, which regulates the procedure for the removal or transfer of a Parish Priest, is split into two chapters; removal (cans. 1740-1747) and transfer (cans. 1748-1752). The aim of both procedures is exclusively pastoral: "to assure that is an adequate parrochial ministry for the faithful; so that, not presupposing guilty behaviour of the Parish Priest, one or the other of the procedures cannot be considered as a canonical sanction" [79]. Through a prior and specific investigation the Ordinary must however ascertain the existence of an objective cause which motivates the removal or tranfer. The procedural course prescribes in an obligatory manner both the hearing of two Parish Priest consultors or assessors (can 1742 §1) and the invitation to the Parish Priest to inspect the acts that regard him and to present his written defence (can 1745).

For imposed exclaustration can. 686 §3 demands a grave cause and a procedure that constantly adheres to equity and charity. In accordance with the practise of the Congregation for Religious and Secular Institutes, this procedure poses in the so-called normal cases a double condition prior to the imposed exclaustration, that is to say when illness or abnormality are not relevant components of the case: to have notified the exclaustrant of the reasons and having given them possibility of defending themselves [80]. This tangible safeguard for equity is subsequently reinforced by the fact that the Supreme Moderator cannot ask the Holy See or the diocesan bishop for an imposed exclaustration without the consent of his Council (can. 686 §3).

Finally, the procedure for dismissal from consecrated life – described by can. 697 – permits three distinct stages: that of warnings, that of the decree of dismissal

---

[78] On the whole question, cf. L. Gerosa, *La scommunica è una pena? Saggio per una fondazione teologica del diritto penale canonico*, Friburgo 1984, above all pp. 296-326 and pp. 361-388.

[79] A. Lauro, *I procedimenti per la rimozione e il trasferimento dei parroci*, in: *I procedimenti speciali nel diritto canonico*, Città del Vaticano 1992, pp. 303-313, here p. 304.

[80] For a detailed analysis of this procedure cf. J. Torres, *La procedura di esclaustazione del consacrato*, in: ibid., pp. 315-336, above all pp. 328-329.

and that of its confirmation on the part of the competent authority [81]. Such a procedure guarantees both the right of defence (cans. 695 §2 and 698), and the principle of synodality in the decision (can. 699 §1).

In conclusion, the development in the normative of the code on the three special administrative procedures just examined does not ignore – as a matter of principle – either the synodal dimension of *sacra potestas,* or the right of defence. Especially on the level of the manner of articulating the *ius difensionis,* in these procedures it is not difficult to trace out the analogies with another procedure, of an administrative nature, and totally typical of the canonical procedural system: that prearranged for the ascertainment of the presuppositions necessary for the granting of a dispensation from a ratified and non consummated marriage [82]. In this is excluded the the presence of an advocate, *patronus,* even if in the most difficult cases the technical assistance in the work of a *iusperitus* (can. 1701 §2) is admitted. Still, if it is accepted that the nucleus of the right to defence is extrinsic in the canonical sphere essentially in the principle of the contradictory, then it can be concluded that such a right also finds in this process, so typical of the juridical system of the Church, a concrete and sufficiently guaranteed application. Here, as in the above illustrated administrative procedures, this application would be more complete if beyond the technical defence there was perhaps also a publication envisaged, even were it not *erga omnes,* but still by way of overcoming the strict reserve typical of obsolete curial praxis [83].

The brief analysis of these special administrative procedures has shown that these in substance present all the essential moments of a judicial process. There exists in Canon Law therefore a unique structurisation common to all the different procedures.

D) THE BASE-STRUCTURE OF CANONICAL PROCEDURES

The essential elements of this base-structure of canonical procedures are: the constitutive moment of the process itself (introduction of the cause and delimitation of the terms of the controversy); the instructory phase and the argumentation (presentation of the proofs, defence of the parties, contestations); the valutative and decisory moment (evaluation and weighing up of the proofs on the part of the judges) and finally the issuing of the decree with the part *in iure* and *in facto.* In Canon Law the base-structure of administrative procedures is therefore identical to that of the judicial procedures. The differences are looked for exclusively on the level of the different formalities to be respected. Among these the most important consists in the fact that the norms of the code relating to administrative procedures do not prescribe in an express and binding manner the possibility of recourse to a technical defence. This deficiency is regrettably common both in the normative of the code on administrative procedures for the imposition or declaration of a canonical sanction and the normative of the code relating to the different special administrative procedures described. Nevertheless in

---

[81]   For an analysis of these three stages, cf. J. Beyer, *La dimissione nella vita consacrata,* in: ibid., pp. 337-356, especially pp. 351-353.

[82]   This procedure, which is certainly the most important among the administrative known to Canon Law, the CIC/1983 as opposed to the Code of 1917 has an entire chapter reserved to it (cans. 1697-1706), entirely for the sake of juridical clarity.

[83]   Cf. S. Berlingò, *La diversa natura delle procedure speciali,* in: *I procedimenti speciali nel diritto canonico,* op. cit., pp. 9-23, here p. 22.

the normative of the code relating to all these procedures there exist frequent deferrals to the possibility of preparing written defences or to making recourse to the work of experts. For this reason, to render the canonical administrative and judicial procedures comparable it is enough simply "to take note that when the faculty of a written defence is given it is practically impossible to prevent its composition on the part a technician or patron. It would be enough then to recognise in an obvious manner the legitimacy of this intervention and to concede to it also in other phases of the process" [84].

Once this were done it would no longer be necessary to take the contentious as the abstract basis for canonical procedures. Besides, as has been authoritatively demonstrated and as we shall see better in the section on matrimonial procedures [85], even the process for a declaration of nullity of a marriage, which is by far the most frequent, has little to do with the contentious. Moreover, others already, starting from the oral principle, perhaps a little hastily relegated by the ecclesiastical legislator in the ambit of the contentious process (cans. 1656-1670), have underlined the opportunity for the future of a major diversification of the special procedures in the juridical system of the Church [86]. This cannot come about without a theological-juridical deepening of the base-structure common to all canonical procedures.

Precisely in this sense, given the importance of the material, the auspices formulated at the end of the preceding section which in the future will make up for the serious lacuna of the CIC in order for the possible procedures for examination of doctrines is not to be underestimated. Indeed, if it is true that these days one cannot prescind from respect for the subjective rights of each of the faithful and therefore also of an author, it is equally true that it happens to guarantee to the Ordinary the possibility of free and responsible decisions in order to protect the objective truth of the ecclesial communion. At present, the juridical protection of these two poles, reciprocally immanent, the freedom of the act of faith on the one hand and the objective truth of the ecclesial communion on the other, is precisely the primary purpose of every canonical procedure. The achievement of this purpose can be more easily guaranteed also on the normative level if the study of Canon Law, freed from every inferiority complex as regards the juridical science of the state, were to greatly concentrate its efforts in perfecting, on the juridical-formal level, the base-structure of every canonical procedure, in some way already traceable in the Code of Canon Law actually in force.

FUNDAMENTAL BIBLIOGRAPHY

Aymans W., *Begriff, Aufgabe und Träger des Lehramts,* in: HdbkathKR, pp. 533-540.

Aymans W.-Corecco E., *Kirchliches Lehramt und Theologie. Erwägungen zur Neuordnung des Lehrprüfungsverfahrens bei der Kongregation für die Glaubenslehre,* in: IKZ Communio 2 (1974), pp. 150-170.

---

[84] Ibid, p. 22.

[85] Cf. K. Lüdicke, *Der kirchliche Ehenichtigkeitsprozess – ein processus contentiosus?.* in: ÖAKR 39 (1990), pp. 295-307.

[86] In this regard cf. J. Sanchis, *L'indagine previa al processo penale (cann. 1717-1719),* in: *I procedimenti speciali nel diritto canonico,* op. cit., pp. 233-266, here p. 264.

AA.VV., *I procedimenti speciali nel diritto canonico*, Città del Vaticano 1992.

Bertolino R., *La tutela dei diritti nella Chiesa. Dal vecchio al nuovo codice di diritto canonico*, Torino 1993.

Corecco E., *Die richterliche Anwendung der "sacra potestas"*, in: ÖAKR 39 (1990), pp. 277-294.

Ferme B. E., *"Ad tuendam fidem" – Some Reflections*, Per 88 (1999) pp. 579-606.

Heinemann H., *Lehrbeanstandung in der katholischen Kirche. Analyse und Kritik der Verfahrensordnung (=Canonistica 6)*, Trier 1981.

Krämer P., *Kirche und Bücherzensur. Zu einer neuen Instruktion der Kongregation für die Glaubenslehre*, in ThGl 83 (1993), pp. 72-80.

Stoffel O., *Die Verkündigung in Predigt und Katechese*, HdbkathKR, pp. 541-547.

Urrutia F.J., *Mandato di insegnare discipline teologiche*, in: *Nuovo Dizionario di Diritto Canonico* (= NDDC), edited by C. Curral Salvador-V. De Paolis-G. Ghirlanda, Torino 1993, pp. 661-664.

FOURTH CHAPTER: THE LAW OF THE SACRAMENTS

1. THE CONCEPT OF SACRAMENT IN CANON LAW

After the publication of the *Rituale Romanum* in 1614, with which the Tridentine effort to reform the Roman liturgy ended, it was necessary to await the *Motu Proprio* on liturgical music, published by Pope Pius X on 22 November 1903, in order to record a new and fruitful reawakening of the eminently pastoral character of the so-called liturgical movement[1]. In fact the Latin expression *participatio actuosa* used by Pius X to indicate the active participation of the lay faithful in the liturgy became from that moment a true and proper motto for a vast liturgical-pastoral work which, passing through the influence of great names such as Lambert Beaudivier, Odo Casel and Romano Guardini, resulted first of all in the encyclical *Mediator Dei*, published by Pius XII in 1947, and then in the conciliar constitution *Sacrosanctum Concilium* of 1963. If the earlier writing, in order to avoid the lay faithful considering the liturgy as something accessory and exterior, underlines its Christological dimension, the later, in order to avoid pietistic reductions, greatly underlines the ecclesiological dimension of the Christian liturgy[2].

The understanding of the knowledge of these two constitutive dimensions of the liturgy of the Church permits the Fathers of the Council to theologically define the sacraments simultaneously as signs of the presence of Christ and as fundamental instruments of the self-realisation of the Church[3]. It is necessary above all to refer to this conciliar vision of the liturgy and of the sacramental sign for a first evaluation of the entirety of the normative of the code on the sacraments.

1.1 THE DOCTRINE ON THE SACRAMENTS OF THE VATICAN COUNCIL II AND ITS ACCEPTANCE IN THE CIC

The fact that right from the first section of the dogmatic constitution *Lumen Gentium* the Fathers of the Council speak of the Church as the sacrament, that is to say the

---

[1] For a brief history of the liturgical movement in the XX century up until Vatican II, cf. A. Adam, *Corso di liturgia,* Brescia 1988, pp. 49-59.

[2] Cf. A.G. Martimort, *L'Église en prière. Introduction à la Liturgie,* Paris 1984, pp. 21-28.

[3] Cf. Th. Schneider, *Zeichen der Nähe Gottes. Grundriss der Sakramententheologie,* Mainz 1980 (tr. it. *Segni della vicinanza di Dio,* Brescia 1983, p. 5). On the idea of the sacraments as gifts of the Spirit, not alien to Vatican Council II, cf. on the other hand J.M.R. Tillard, *Les sacrements de L'Église,* in: *Initiation à la pratique de la théologie, Dogmatique II,* published under the direction of B. Lauret-F. Refoule, III (2e édit. corrigée), Paris 1986, pp. 385-466, here p. 402.

sign-instrument through which it manifests itself and realises both its intimate union with God and the unity of the whole human race[4], testifies from the outset to the fundamental characteristic of the conciliar theology of the sacraments: the latter, as with all liturgical actions, "are not private functions but are celebrations of the Church which is the sacrament of unity, namely, the holy people united and ordered under their bishops. Therefore liturgical services pertain to the whole Body of the Church, they manifest it and have an effect on it" (SC 26). In this sense, by means of the sacraments "the sacred and organic character of the priestly community" (LG 11) which is the Church is assisted.

This strong underlining of the ecclesiological dimension of the sacramental sign is a logical consequence of the faith of the Fathers of the Council in the dogmatic given that in every liturgical action, and above all in the sacraments, Christ himself is present and acts who "always associates himself with the Church, his beloved bride who calls to her Lord, and through him offers worship to the eternal Father" (SC 7).

With the conciliar teaching on the *Christus totus* (that is the person of Jesus and the Church united to him) as the principal subject of the sacramental sign the intervention of the Holy Spirit is also highlighted as who, through all of the sacraments and in particular the Eucharist, "gives life to the flesh" (PO 5,2) or the mystical body of Christ which is the Church, right from the beginning of that *communio* that Saint Augustine had already defined as the *opus proprium* of the Holy Spirit.

In its substance this conciliar theology of the sacraments was accepted by the ecclesiastical legislator. In fact, the new Code of Canon Law not only dedicates ample space to the normative of the sacraments (cans. 840-1165), but abandons the traditional civilistic division – which placed the sacraments in *De rebus* – and opts for a more theological systematic organisation of their normative, gathered now in the fourth book dedicated to the *munus sanctificandi*. Moreover, the code's definition of the sacraments gathers in a systematic way all the principal elements of the theology of the sacraments taught by Vatican Council II. In fact, according to can. 840 the sacraments are simultaneously "actions of Christ and the Church", "signs and means with which the faith is expressed and reinforced", gestures which actuate "the sanctification of men" through the consolidation and manifestation of the "ecclesiastical communion".

The particular underlining of the link between sacraments and *communio* is fixed in the mind by can. 843, where with the prescription that "the sacred ministers may not deny the sacraments to those who opportunely ask for them, are properly disposed and are not prohibited by law from receiving them" the legislator echoes the conciliar affirmation of the right of all the faithful to "receive in abundance from the sacred Pastors the spiritual goods of the Church, especially the help of the Word and the Sacraments" (LG 37,1). In this way the CIC impedes the reduction of the sacraments to "private actions" (can. 837 §1) or to a simple *pia exercitia*. These express and actualise the plan of salvation gathering together or reuniting the People of God from the whole of humanity and in this sense are wholly "strictly united and ordered" to the Eucharist, which "presents itself as the source and summit of the whole of evangelisation" (PO 5,2).

---

[4]   Cf. also LG 48, where the Church is defined as the universal sacrament of salvation.

The just underlining of the intrinsic ordination of all of the sacraments to the Eucharist, and with it the structural connection between every sacramental sign and the ecclesial communion, would have better testified to the role of primary importance played by the sacraments in the juridical-constitutional structure of the Church if the idea of a common priesthood (conferred on all the faithful and mentioned only indirectly in can. 836), had been used by the ecclesiastical legislator with all of its ecclesiological value.

The obscuring of such ideas, of primary importance in the *Magna Carta* of Vatican Council II, is aggravated by other incongruences stamped on all of the normative of the sacraments by the debatable systematic choice of placing it exclusively in the viewpoint of the *munus sanctificandi*. In fact this choice, even prescinding from the fact that in the whole Church – including the relationship of possession of material goods – it is functional to the universal vocation to sanctity (LG 40), gives rise to at least two great concerns.

First of all, if it is true that the initial affirmation of the fourth book *De Ecclesiae munere sanctificandi* – according to which "the Church carries out its office of sanctifying in a special way in the sacred liturgy" (can. 834 §1) – reprises almost to the letter no. 7 of the conciliar Constitution *Sacrosanctum Concilium*, nevertheless the ecclesiastical legislator leaves the impression that the ordinary ecclesial actuation of the priestly office to sanctify of Jesus Christ spends its strength exclusively in the sacraments (cans. 840-1165) and in the other acts of divine worship (cans. 1166-1204) or in the times and places ordered by them (cans. 1205-1253). This places in contradiction whether with the fundamental principle of the work of evangelisation – and therefore of sanctification – of the Church, according to which the faith is born and nurtured *praesertim ministerio verbi* (can 836), or with the ecclesiological principle according to which – precisely because every state of ecclesial life "reprises and specifies the sanctifying grace of baptism"[5] -- any of the faithful (lay person, religious, cleric) actualises the *munus sanctificandi* according to the particular means of their own specific vocation. In particular, spouses exercise their priestly office of sanctification primarily not in the active participation in the liturgy but in building up the mystical body of Christ through the daily offering of their being spouses and parents (as is recorded even if in a more bland manner in can. 835 §4), through the full and responsible development of the secular character of their specific ecclesial vocation. Analogously the consecrated faithful exercise their *munus sanctificandi* primarily in following the prophetic charism of the evangelical counsels and clerics in the service of the unity of the entire people of God.

In the second place, the particular viewpoint under which the ecclesiastical legislator deals with the normative of the code on the sacraments, if on the one hand avoids the risk of making them such, as on the contrary the CIC/1917 seems to have done by applying the Justinian tripartition *personae, res, actiones,* on the other hand it does not bring to completion the process extended to render the canonical norm the most possible capable of conveying the theological content that guides its formalisation. In point of fact, between the theological definition of the sacraments given by the eccle-

---

[5]   John Paul II, *Familiaris Consortio,* no. 56; (the complete text can be found in: AAS 74 (1982), pp. 81-191; cf. also LG 11.

siastical legislator in can. 840 (completed as far as regards their validity and liceity by cans. 841 and 838) and the technical-positive of the juridical acts, formulated in cans. 124-126, there is a clear divergence which risks aggravating, rather than resolving, the antinomy denounced even before the Vatican Council II between sacrament and law.

As has been rightly observed, this divergence consists in the fact that, on principle, the quoted general rules on the validity or invalidity of juridical acts are applicable with difficulty to the sacraments, which in the Church are the most frequent juridical acts and with the most constitutive character of the others, given that their juridically binding efficacy does not have a solely social value, but first and foremost soteriological[6]. For the rest the general norms of the code in force on juridical acts, substantially identical to those of the CIC/1917 (as can be noted comparing cans. 124, 125, 126 with cans. 1680, 103 and 104 of the Pio-Benedictine Code), were conceived according to a positivistic mentality which considers juridical affairs especially those of a public character (administrative acts) or those of a private character (contracts) and the sacraments only as particular or secondary juridical acts, with the exception of marriage[7].

Nevertheless the sacraments, together with the Word of God and with charisms, are at the base of the whole juridical structure of the Church, as can be deduced too from Saint Thomas himself, who certainly was not a canonist: *Per sacramenta quae latere Christi pendentis in cruce fluxerunt, dicitur esse fabricata Ecclesia*[8]. In fact, to this affirmation of the sacramental building up of the Church a long canonical tradition has always connected another: "the foundation of any law consists in the sacraments"[9].

1.2 THE INTRINSIC JURIDICAL QUALITY OF THE SACRAMENTS AND THE INTRODUCTORY CANONS ON THE NORMS OF THE CODE ON THE SACRAMENTS

If the sacraments build the Church, and the Code of Canon Law itself leaves it clearly to be understood when it affirms that these "contribute in the most effective manner to the establishing, strengthening and manifesting the ecclesiastical communion" (can. 840), it is because they are its essential constitutive elements even from the point of view of the law[10]. And they are so not just because they produce effects of a juridical character or because, being actions realised by some men – like the ministers of Christ and the Church – in favour of others, they confirm the principle of otherness which is

---

[6]   Cf. E. Corecco, *Aspetti della ricezione del Vaticano II nel Codice di diritto canonico,* in: *Il Vaticano II e la Chiesa,* edited by G. Alberigo-J.P. Jossua, Brescia 1985, pp. 333-397, here p. 342.

[7]   Cf. the commentary on title VII of the first book of the CIC – Arrieta-Lombardia, pp. 122-125.

[8]   Thomas Aquinas, *S. Th.,* III, q. 64, art. 2, ad 3.

[9]   Cf. *In IV Sententiarum,* dist. 7, q. 1, art.1, sol.1, ad 1, and the commentary of C.J. Errazuriz M., *Sacramenti,* in EDD, Vol. XLI (Milano 1989), pp. 197-208, here p. 204.

[10] Cf. above 1. chapter, 3.2; on the whole question, cf. also E. Molano, *Dimensiones juridicas de los sacramentos,* in: *Sacramentalidad de la Iglesia y sacramentos.* IV Simposio Internacional de teologia de la Universidad de Navarra, edited by P. Rodriguez, Pamplona 1983, pp. 312-322.

the presupposition for the existence of an intersubjective relationship of justice [11]. As we have already had a way of underlining in the first chapter, the sacraments are the principal juridical-constitutive acts in the Church because insofar as they are signs of communication they possess a primary and intrinsic emergent juridicality, even if in a diversified manner, on all the levels of the ecclesial communion.

In order to be valid and fruitful the celebration of the sacraments presupposes faith both on the objective level, because the sacraments are always celebrated in the communion of the faith of the Church to which it belongs, and on the subjective level, because in whoever receives them there is the requirement of the *sensus fidei*, that is the free adherence to the *communio Ecclesiae* which is nothing if not "the will at least implicit of accepting God's initiative which leads mankind along the paschal journey of liberation and sanctification" [12].

On the subjective level of faith-sacrament, which substantially coincides with the problem of the necessary requisites for approaching a sacrament, the canonical discourse intersects with the pastoral. In fact, the ecclesiastical legislator after having underlined – in syntony with the Vatican Council II (SC 9) – the importance of the faith in the celebration of the sacraments (cans. 836 and 840), he insists on the duty of evangelisation and catechesis, which all the faithful – and in particular the sacred ministers – must develop in the face of whoever approaches the sacraments (cans. 836 and 843 §2), and finally on the importance of active participation (cans. 837 §1 and §2; 835 §4) in the celebration of the said sacraments.

Among the nine introductory canons in the normative of the code on the sacraments can 842 establishes in having received baptism the general principle for valid admission to all of the other sacraments and can. 844 regulates the sacramental material in relation to ecumenism and to the *communicatio in sacris*, that is to say the admission to the sacraments of the Catholic Church on the part of Christians belonging to other non-Catholic Christian confessions not in full communion with it. Both canons are studied in other sections in this chapter. Here, at the heart of the introduction to the normative of the code on the sacraments, it is more important to briefly analyse can. 843, for its great pastoral importance too.

1.3 THE RIGHT TO THE SACRAMENTS AND ECCLESIAL COMMUNION

The first section of can. 843 states: "Sacred ministers may not deny the sacraments to those who opportunely ask for them, are properly disposed and are not prohibited by law from receiving them". With this norm, inspired by the conciliar teaching concerning the right of all the faithful "to receive in abundance the help of the spiritual goods of the Church, especially that of the Word of God and the Sacraments from the pastors" (LG 37,1), the ecclesiastical legislator intends to remove the admittance to the

---

[11]   It is the pre-eminent tendency of the School of Navarra, which loves to speak of the sacrament as a *res iusta*. In this regard cf. C.J. Errazuriz M., *Sacramenti*, op. cit., p. 204; J Hervada, *Las racies sacramentales del Derecho Canónico, in: Estudios de Derecho canonico y Derecho eclesiástico en homaje al profesor Maldonado*, Madrid 1983, pp. 245-269.

[12]   G. Biffi, *Io credo. Breve esposizione della dottrina cattolica*, Milano 1980, p. 90, annotation 2106.

sacraments from every whimsy. The efficacy of this norm in relation to the possibility of refusing the sacraments (*sacramenta denegare*), strictly subject to the norms in force of the Code (as recalled by the expression *attentis normis* of the second section of the same canon), would have been more incisive if the legislator on the one hand had used the active form, and on the other had explicitly deferred to can. 213, in which the right to the sacraments or the *ius recipiendi spiritualia bona,* envisaged by can. 682 of the CIC/1917 for the lay faithful only is extended to all the faithful. Indeed, this right, being unmistakably bound to the baptismal participation of the faithful in the three offices of Jesus Christ, is to be considered as an declaration deriving from divine law [13], and as such of primary importance for the realisation of the ecclesial communion. The norms of the Code, which limit the exercise of such a right, must therefore be intepreted in the strict sense (can. 18).

The exercise of this right, still according to can. 843, can in any case only be vindicated starting from the fulfilment of three fundamental conditions: the request or *petitio*, the disposition or *dispositio* and the absence of any juridical prohibition and impediment. With the first condition the ecclesiastical legislator intends to underline that the sacraments can be administered only to those who request them freely and in an opportune way (relatively to time, to place and to the manner); the second disposition refers to moral dignity and spiritual preparation of the faithful person who requests to be admitted to the sacrament, both however difficult to determine on the juridical level; the third condition, if we prescind from the faithful hit with excommunication or an interdict and thus excluded from the sacraments [14], is formalised and regulated by the ecclesiastical legislator from time to time for each individual sacrament [15].

All three of the conditions placed by can. 843 §1 for the exercise of the right to the sacraments are different concretisations of two general principles: that according to which all "of the faithful are bound to preserve their communion with the Church at all times, even in their external actions" (can. 209) and that according to which in the exercise of their proper rights the faithful must also take into account "the rights of others and their own duties to others" (can. 223 §1). Moreover, in this case it is more evident than ever that it is a question of a right which is nothing if not the speculative dimension of a duty, that of taking care of one's own sanctification and that of the Church (can. 210), which in the Catholic vision also implies "the greatest reverence and due care" (can. 840) in preparations for the celebration of the sacraments. This due care is not only an obligation for the faithful who ask to be admitted to a sacrament, but also a specific duty for pastors, as §2 of can. 843 specifies, almost wanting to underline that the responsibility for evangelisation, precisely because it is communal,

---

[13] This is the opinion of E. Corecco, *Il catalogo dei doveri-diritti del fedele nel CIC, in: I diritti fondamentali della persona umana e la libertà religiosa.* Atti del V Colloquio giuridico (8-10 marzo 1984), Città del Vaticano 1985, pp. 101-125, here p. 111.

[14] Cf. can. 1331 §1 no.2 and can. 1332.

[15] In relation to the Eucharist (cf. can. 912) and marriage (can. 1058) the general norm is repeated earlier in the introductory canons and then latterly specified; in this regard cf. H. Reinhardt, *Recht auf Wortverkündigung und Sakramentenempfang,* in: MK, can. 213/2 and 4; P. Krämer, *Kirchenrecht I. Wort-Sakrament-Charisma,* Stuttgart-Berlin-Köln 1992, pp. 65-66.

demands both on the subjective and objective level the exclusion of every whimsy in the important field of admission to the sacraments.

2. THE EUCHARIST

In the Dogmatic Constitution on the Church the Vatican Council II defines the Eucharist as the "source and summit of the whole of Christian life", that is to say as the sacrament which "admirably expresses and realises" the unity of the People of God [16]. The Eucharist is therefore at the centre of all of conciliar ecclesiology and as such also globally directs the juridical structure of the Church [17]. It is worth the effort however to consider more closely the fundamental directives of this conciliar teaching and its importance for Canon Law before analysing the norms of the Code on the Eucharist.

2.1 THE EUCHARIST IN THE VATICAN COUNCIL II

A) *Communio Eucharistica* AND *communio Ecclesiae*.

Many and varied are the contexts in which the Fathers of the Council speak of the Eucharist with the double intention of unitarily summing up the essential elements of Catholic Eucharistic theology and to offer starting points for new and deepened developments of the same. In particular the sacrificial aspect (SC 7) and that of memorial (SC 47) many times come to be reproposed in synthetic and unitary formulas proper to the Dogmatic Constitution on the Church. For example in LG 28 it is affirmed that priests "exercise their sacred function above all in the Eucharistic cult or *synaxis*, where, acting in the person of Christ and proclaiming his mystery, uniting the votive offerings of the faithful to the sacrifice of their head" (LG 28,1); on the other hand the participation in the Eucharist of the latter is not passive, but rather a *participatio actuosa*, because they "by virtue of their royal priesthood, participate in the offering of the Eucharist" (LG 10,2). The latter "admirably expresses and realises" (LG 11,1) the unity of the People of God. The Eucharistic celebration is thus no longer presented as a liturgical action of the priests, but as the principal liturgical action of the whole Church, in which every one of the faithful is invited to actively take part "not in an indiscriminate way, but each according to his proper role" [18].

---

[16] Cf. LG 11,1 and SC 10,1.

[17] In this regard cf. K. Mörsdorf, *Kirchenverfassung. I Katholische Kirche* in: LThK, Bd. VI. (Freiburg im. Br. 1961) pp. 274-277 and in particular p. 275; H. Müller, *Zugehörigkeit zur Kirche als Problem der Neukodifikation des kanonischen Rechts*, in: ÖAKR 28 (1977), pp. 81-98; P. Krämer, *Theologische Grundlegung des kirchlichen Rechts. Die rechtstheologische Auseinandersetzung zwischen H. Barion und J. Klein in Licht des II. Vatikanischen Konzils*, Trier 1977, p. 141; R. Ahlers, *Eucharistie*, in: *Ecclesia a sacramentis. Theologische Erwägungen zum Sakramentenrecht*, hrsg. von R. Ahlers-L. Gerosa-L. Müller, Paderborn 1992, pp. 13-25, above all p. 15.

[18] LG 11,1. On the link between the ecclesial dimension of the action of the priest and the communitarian structure of the Eucharistic celebration, cf. W. Haunerland, *Die Messe aller Zeiten. Liturgiewissenschaftliche Anmerkungen zum Fall Lefèbvre*, in: *Das Bleibende im Wandel. Theologische Beiträge zum Schisma von Marcel Lefèbvre*, hrsg. von R. Ahlers-P. Krämer, Paderborn 1990, pp. 51-85, here p. 71.

In the ecclesiology and theology of the sacraments developed by the Vatican Council II the Eucharist is therefore "the centre of the community of the faithful presided over by the priest" (PO 5,3). As such this directs the whole sacramental structure of the Church and consequently "all of the sacraments, as indeed all ecclesiastical ministries and works of the apostolate are bound up with the Eucharist and are directed towards it" (PO 5,2).

It is not therefore arbitrary to give a systematic priority – whether on the dogmatic or juridical level – to this sacrament [19]. On the contrary, this is fully justified by the fact that the two constitutive and in part reciprocally immanent aspects (*communio cum Deo* and *communio fidelium*) of the *communio Ecclesiae,* as the central idea of the whole of conciliar ecclesiology, find their fullest synthesis in the *communio Eucharistica.* In fact, as the Fathers of the Council still teach, "in the breaking of the Eucharistic bread we are taken up into communion with him (the Lord Jesus Christ) and with one another" (LG 7,2). In other words: "There is an indissoluble bond between the mystery of the Church and the mystery of the Eucharist, or between the ecclesial communion and the Eucharistic communion; by itself the Eucharistic celebration signifies the fullness of the profession of faith and the ecclesial communion" [20].

This does not mean that all that the term *communio* indicates must necessarily be formalisable also in the juridical level, but simply that in the "community of the altar" (LG 26,1) or the *communio Eucharistica,* the constitutive and juridically binding force of the sacrament of the Eucharist, is manifested in an eminent way. Moreover, it is not either exaggerated or mistaken to affirm that, according to the conciliar teaching, where the Eucharist is no longer celebrated in any way the Church itself ceases to exist as a communion [21].

B) CHRISTIAN PRIESTHOOD AND EUCHARISTIC COMMUNITIES

The new People of God, which is the Church, according to the Vatican Council II is by its nature a "priestly people" (LG 10,2), because "remaining one and unique, is to be spread throughout the whole world and to all ages in order that the design of God's will may be fulfilled: he made human nature one in the beginning and has decreed that all his children who were scattered should be finally gathered together as one" (LG 13,1). Within this one and unique priestly people the differentiations are always secondary, structurally ordered one to the other, functional and relative to the priestly and

---

[19]   This systematic order is for example proposed by: K. Rahner, *Kirche und Sakramente,* Freiburg-Basel-Wien 1968 (3. Aufl.), p. 73; it is however repeated in the documents of the Holy See, cf. for example nos.. 5-15 of the Instruction *Eucharisticum mysterium* (AAS 59 [1967], pp. 539-573) and no. 58 of the *Directorium catechisticum generale* (AAS 64 [1972], pp. 97-176).

[20]   Secretariat for Christian Unity, *Nota su alcune interpretazioni della "Istruzione sui casi particolari di ammissione di altri cristiani alla communione eucaristica nella chiesa cattolica",* in AAS 65 (1973), pp. 616-619, here p. 616 (n. 3a).

[21]   In this regard cf. R. Ahlers, *Communio Eucharistica. Eine kirchenrechtliche Untersuchung zur Eucharistielehre in Codex Iuris Canonici,* Regensburg 1990, above all pp. 81 and 185.

universal mission of the whole of the new People of God [22]. Thus is also explained the difference "of essence and not only of degree" (LG 10,2) between the common priesthood of all the faithful and the ministerial priesthood of the faithful invested with Sacred Orders. In the common priesthood of all the baptised in "their own way and on their own behalf" (LG 31,1) the participation of all the faithful in the subjective dimension of the priesthood of Christ is realised; in the ministerial priesthood, on the other hand, the participation of clerics in the priesthood of Christ is realised in its objective dimension. These two forms of priesthood consist in a diverse participation in the unique priesthood of Christ and as such cannot be either disjoined or opposed. The correct interpretation of the texts of Vatican Council II imposes the consideration of their distinction "as the fruit of a particular richness of the very priesthood of Christ" [23]. This does not mean however to theologically establish this *distinctio* on the somewhat pragmatic affirmation "according to which the ministerial priesthood has as a specific function the representation of Christ as the head of the Mystical Body, which is the Church, while the common priesthood has as its aim the representation of Christ according to a more generic reason" [24]. In the Church there is no principle of ecclesiological representation which is not contemporaneously christological also, because the principle *in persona Ecclesiae* is not possible as such in the sacramental reality prescinding from the principle *in persona Christi* and vice versa. Thus indeed the simple statement that the ministerial priesthood is conferred with the sacrament of Orders, while the common priesthood is conferred by the sacrament of baptism, while being exact does not explain in an exhaustive way under the theological outline the difference of the sacramental effects of Orders and baptism. The theological reason discriminating the difference of essence between the two concrete forms of Christian priesthood is to be sought therefore in the very nature of the unique priesthood of Christ, which participate in a direct manner, in their respective specificity, both the priesthood founded on baptism and that founded on Holy Orders: "both in fact, each in its own proper way, shares in the one priesthood of Christ" (LG 10,2).

As it is possible that the unique priesthood of Christ communicates itself directly in two different ways, reciprocal and complementary, this can be deduced from the texts of the third and fourth chapter of *Lumen Gentium*, where the conciliar fathers speak of the different modalities of participation of the laity and ordained ministers in

---

[22] For a deeper commentary on the whole of the second chapter of the dogmatic constitution *Lumen Gentium*, cf. G. Philips, *La Chiesa e il suo mistero nel Concilio Vaticano II. Storia, teso e commento della Costituzione Lumen Gentium*, 2 Voll., Milano 1969, here Vol.I, pp. 119-196.

[23] John Paul II, *Novo incipiente. Ad universos Ecclesiae sacerdotes adveniente feris V in coena Domini* (8 April 1979), in AAS 71 (1979), pp. 392-417, here quoted by EV, Vol. VI, no. 1296. Previously also the *Commissione Theologica Internationalis* in its document *Themata selecta de ecclesiologia*, published on 7 October 1985 on the occasion of the XX anniversary of the Conclusion of the Vatican Council II, had explicitly affirmed: "Evidens est utrumque habere suum fundamentum et fontem in unico sacerdotio Christi" (EV, Vol. IX, no. 1688).

[24] E. Corecco, *Riflessione giuridico-istituzionale su sacerdozio comune e sacerdozio ministeriale*, in: *Popolo di Dio e sacerdozio*, edited by ATI, Padova 1983, pp. 80-129, here p. 80.

the *tria munera Christi* according to a terminological perspective characterised as subjective and objective[25]. Summarising: Jesus Christ is a priest because in the essence of his personal structure He is the one who gives himself totally to the Father. It is in this love of Christ for the Father, fully realised in the total obedience of the Cross, that the two fundamental aspects of his priesthood are both expressed: the subjective of the one who offers himself, and the objective of the one who lets himself be sacrificed; the subjective of the dedication and love towards the Father, proper of the sacrificing, and the objective of the obedience or oblation to the Father, proper to the sacrificed or the victim on the cross for the expiation of the sins of all. In the priesthood of Christ, this second objective aspect of expiatory obedience is not added in an extrinsic and accidental way as in the Old Testament, but constitutes together with the first aspect, the subjective aspect of love, the very essence of the unity of the person of Christ, which is one sole existence with the Father.

In Christ, and only in Christ, is realised the perfect unity between the sacrificing and the sacrificed. In the passage from the priesthood of Christ to that of the Church the two elements are distinguished once again, but differently from what occurs in the Old Testament, these remain strictly complementary and not extrinsic to each other. By dint of the principle of reciprocal immanence, implicit in the structure of *communio* characterising the ecclesial reality on all levels, the Church as a People of priests cannot renounce one of the two concrete forms of Christian priesthood without contemporaneously also eliminating the other.

In fact, as the baptised believer, in order to realise his own common priesthood according to all the subjective radicality postulated by love, has need of an objective authority which is legitimised to concretely challenge him, just as the Father challenged the Son to his death on the cross, so the ordained minister has need of the baptised, or at least catechumens, in order to concretely develop the function of service proper to the ministerial priesthood within the ecclesial *communio*.

In this sense, the perfect unity in Christ of the subjective element with the objective of the priesthood of the New Covenant, on the ecclesial level finds its analogical comparison in the following double fact. On the one hand the common priesthood of the faithful, in as much as it is a participation in the formal subjective aspect of the priesthood of Christ, continues to subsist in whoever also receives the ministerial priesthood, which is in its turn the participation in the formal objective aspect of the priesthood of Christ. On the other, the ministerial priesthood while not subsisting in the common priesthood of all the faithful cannot, in its turn, prescind from this because in the Church the ministerial priesthood *non existit nisi in ordine ad exercitium sacerdotii communis*[26]. Indeed, in the plan of the New Covenant, the ministerial priesthood is not necessary for offering sacrifice through an intermediary, as in the pre-Christian religions, nor in the name of the People, as in the Old Testament, but so that all the faithful, together with Christ, can offer themselves in the full objectivity of obedience to the Father.

---

[25]   On the dogmatic level the most convincing attempt at explaining this fundamental aspect of conciliar teaching on the priesthood of Jesus Christ is certainly that developed in detail by: H.U. von Balthasar, *Christlicher Stand,* Einsieldeln 1977, pp. 145-202.

[26]   Commissio Theologica Internationalis, *Themata selecta de ecclesiologia,* in: EV, Vol. IX, no. 1734.

The underlining of this substantial complementarity and this reciproal correlation explains how the difference *essentia et non gradum tantum* between the two concrete forms of Christian priesthood does not imply either a clear separation or much less an opposition between them.

The separation between common priesthood and ministerial priesthood is only partial. To understand in the subjective and objective element of the priesthood of Christ the ultimate theological reason for this partial separation does not in any way mean that the Christian priesthood " ... in the ministry would have the aim of commanding, while in the priesthood of the faithful it would have the aim of obeying"[27]. A similar opinion, more than critical, appears as a coarse reduction of the theory just expounded, in which the contents of the *missio* of the whole people of God are not absolutely neglected, but simple seen as fundamental components of the *communio*. In the Church there is no mission or *plantatio Ecclesiae* which is not a realisation of the universal ecclesial communion, in a concrete and particular place, just as there is no authentic experience of communion in the particular without openness to the universal mission. This realisation of the ecclesial communion finds, as seen in the preceding section, its maximum expression in the *communio Eucharistica*. This truth would have been placed more greatly highlighted if the Fathers of the Council had also deepened more greatly the study of the pneumatological dimension of the Christian priesthood, because the *communio* being the so-called *opus proprium* of the Holy Spirit[28], such a dimension cannot not defer constantly to the structural functionality of both the forms of Christian priesthood in respect to the building up of the Christian community, which finds in the Eucharist its source and summit.

This pneumatological dimension is however underlined by the conciliar Fathers in the texts where they speak of the Eucharist as the primordial and indispensible gathering factor[29]. Among these the most significant is the Decree on the ministry and life of priests: "No Christian community is built up which does not grow from and hinge on the celebration of the Most Holy Eucharist. From this all education for community spirit must begin" (CD 6,5). In fact, in the Eucharist is manifested the "genuinam verae Ecclesiae naturam" (SC 2) in its human and divine elements. It is above all from this that the canonist must therefore draw the criteria to distinguish the properly constitutional elements from the merely associative of the different forms of communities of the faithful.

The importance of the Eucharist at the level of the constitutional structure of the Church is highlighted with extreme clarity also in CD 11,1 where the Diocese as the principal juridical form of a particular Church finds in the Gospel and the Eucharist its

---

[27] S. Dianich, *Teologia del ministero ordinato. Una interpretazione ecclesiologica,* Roma 1984, p. 87.

[28] Cf. J. Ratzinger, *Der Heilige Geist als "communio". Zum Verhältnis von Pneumatologie und Spiritualität bei Augustinus,* in: *Erfahrung und Theologie des Heiligen Geistes,* hrsg. von C. Heitmann-H. Mühlen, München 1974, pp. 223-238, here p. 226.

[29] Cf. above all LG 11,1, but also CD 30,6 and SC 10,1. For an analysis of these texts and a deepened study of the pneumatological dimension of the Christian priesthood, cf. L. Gerosa, *Carismi e diritto nella Chiesa. Riflessioni canonistiche sul "carisma originario" dei nuovi movimenti ecclesiali,* Milano 1989, pp. 135-156.

principal gathering factors [30]. For the same reason the parish has a pre-eminent place in the different Eucharistic communities into which a *portio Populo Dei* divides itself [31]. As the conciliar Fathers explicitly affirm, the parochial sense of community flourishes above all "in communi celebratione Missae dominicalis" (CD 42,2).

In conclusion: the correct interpretation of the conciliar texts on the connections between the two forms of Christian priesthood and the building up of the ecclesial community confirms the lesson of the Vatican Council II on the centrality of the Eucharist directed to the *communio Ecclesiae*. The principles, which govern the communio Eucharistica, must therefore direct the whole juridical structure of the Church and not just the norms of the Code regarding the sacrament of the Eucharist. The verification of this necessarily implies however an analysis of the way with which the ecclesiastical legislator has accepted in these norms the conciliar lesson on the *augustissimum sacramentum* (LG 11,1).

2.2 NORMS OF THE CODE ON THE EUCHARIST

A rapid glance at the systematic order of the normative of the Code on the Eucharist (cans. 897-958) is more than enough to grasp the unitareity with which the ecclesiastical legislator of 1983 deals with the material. In particular it appears at last as definitively overcome the dualism, present in the old Code, between the sacrifice of the Mass and the sacrament of the Eucharist [32]. The unitary vision of this sacrament – at the same time sacrifice, memorial, summit and source of the ecclesial communion – developed in detail and proposed by the Vatican Council II appears therefore to have been accepted. The introductory canon confirms this, offering a clear and complete synthesis of the conciliar doctrine: "The most august sacrament is the blessed Eucharist, in which Christ the Lord himself is contained, offered and received, and by which the Church continually lives and grows. The Eucharistic Sacrifice, the memorial of the death and resurrection of the Lord, in which the Sacrifice of the cross is forever perpetuated, is the summit and the source of all worship and Christian life. By means of it the unity of God's people is signified and brought about, and the building up of the body of Christ is perfected. The other sacraments and all the ecclesiastical works of the apostolate are bound up with, and directed to, the blessed Eucharist" (can. 897). As can be seen the centrality of the Eucharist (founded upon its being at one and the same time *sacrificium, memoriale, culmen et fons* of worship and Christian life) is underlined by a repetition almost to the letter of the conciliar teaching on the fact all the other sacraments are directed to this: so too the tridentine triad *continere, offrire, sumere* has lost its individualistic and clerical emphases in order to be developed and integrated into the ecclesial and constitutive dimension of the Eucharist, through which *continuo vivit et crescit Ecclesia*.

---

[30] Cf. infra 6.chapter 2.2

[31] Cf. SC 42.

[32] In the CIC/1917 the norms on the Eucharist are collected in two chapters: the first, entitled *De sacrosancto Missae sacrificio* (cans. 802-844), and the second entitled *De sanctissimo Eucharistiae sacramento* (cans. 845-869). The questions relative to the reservation and veneration of the *Sanctissimum Sacramentum* (cans. 1265-1275) are dealt with completely detached from these.

Consequently the dualism is also overcome between the *celebratio* of the Mass, the exclusive competence of the priests[33], and the *auditio* of the same, to which the faithful are individually bound[34]. In fact, right from the start of the new normative of the Code on the Eucharist the legislator affirms in clear terms that this "is the action of Christ himself and of the Church" (can. 899 §1) and at its celebration "all the faithful present, whether clerics or lay people, unite to participate in their own way, according to their various orders and liturgical roles" (can. 899 §2).

The people of God, called into unity under the presidency of the bishop or the priest, is the unitary subject of the Eucharist and is therefore from this perspective, of the contitutional type, that happens to start by gathering all of the juridical and pastoral significance of the canonical norms on the "most august sacrament" (can. 897), collected by the new Code of Canon Law according to the following system-atic arrangement: after two introductory canons – the first (can. 897) on the intimate connection between Eucharist and ecclesial mystery, the second (can. 898) on the fundamental importance of this sacrament for the life of all the faithful, called to par-ticipate actively in its celebration –, the first chapter (cans. 899-933) is dedicated to the celebration of the Eucharist (with norms on the minister of the Eucharist; on the active participation of all of the faithful; on rites, time and place of the celebration), the second chapter (cans. 934-944) deals with the reservation and veneration of the Eucharist (cans. 945-958), and finally the third chapter gathers together the juridical rules on the offerings for the celebration of Holy Masses.

A) THE JURIDICAL-CONSTITUTIONAL ROLE OF THE EUCHARIST

Although in the introductory canons on the Eucharist, while rich in ecclesiological relevance, the ecclesiastical legislator does not explicitly repeat the conciliar affir-mation according to which in all the "communities of the altar ... though they may often be small and poor, or existing in the diaspora, Christ is present through whose power and influence the One, Holy, Catholic and Apostolic Church is constituted" (LG 26,1), still the constitutional role of this sacrament within the *communio Ecclesiae et Ecclesiarum* is certainly highlighted by many other norms of the Code, even if – as will be better seen later on – the balance between the universal Church and particu-lar Churches is not always guaranteed. For example the legal definition of Diocese, which is the most important institutional form of a particular Church, indicates in the binominal *Evangelium et Eucharistia* (can. 369) the magnetic pole around which is gathered the *portio Populo Dei* in question. Analogously can. 528 §2 affirms, even if only indirectly, that the Eucharist is the centre "of the parish community of the faith-ful" and cans. 327 and 298 §1 invite the faithful to hold in high esteem especially the associations with spiritual purposes or tied up with the promotion of public worship, and therefore in some way bound to the experience of a community of the altar.

The juridical-constitutional role of the Eucharist is underlined by the CIC also on the subjective level that is to say of the ecclesial life of the faithful which, according to the norm of can. 209 §1, is always bound to preserve in their way of acting the communion with the Church. Indeed, the Eucharist is at one and the same time the

---

[33] The introductory canons of the two chapters of the CIC/1917 leave this proposition in no doubts, cf. cans. 802 and 845.

[34] Cf. can 1248 CIC/1917.

sacrament in which develops Christian initiation, the food that sustains the faithful through the whole of life and the viaticum, which comforts at the moment of death [35] . While baptism and confirmation constitute the irrepetible sacramental element of the process of Christian initiation, the Eucharist represents the dynamic moment. These "so complement one another that all three are required for full Christian initiation" (can. 842 §2) and consequently can. 866 prescribes that the baptised and confirmed adult, immediately afterwards "participates in the celebration of the Eucharist and receives Holy Communion". This participation, if it is active through the whole of life, leads then all the faithful to receive "this sacrament frequently" (can. 898) and priests to celebrate it frequently and, as far as is possible daily [36]. Finally, the importance of the Eucharist in the life of the Christian faithful is underlined by the right of the sick and dying to receive *viaticum* [37] and of the respective duty to bring it to them imposed by the legislator on pastors, vicars, chaplains and – in cases of necessity – "any other priest or other minister of holy communion" (can. 911).

With this brief reference to the Eucharist as *viaticum* another problem of constitutional relevance is touched upon, that relating to the right to receive holy communion and the duty of participating in the Sunday Eucharist.

The right of every baptised person to receive the sacraments from their own proper pastors, established by can. 213, is specified in relation to the Eucharist by can. 912, which states: "Any person who is not forbidden by law may and must be admitted to Holy Communion". The fact that in this the legislator does not mention the proper disposition as can. 843 §1 on the other hand does, reinforces such a right taking away the decision on the subjective disposition of the faithful from the minister of Holy Communion. This decision, according to the norm of can. 916, belongs to the believer himself who wants to receive communion and an eventual limitation of this right on the part of the minister is subject to objective criteria, fixed by can. 915, which states: "Those upon whom the penalty of excommunication or interdict has been imposed or declared, and others who obstinately persist in manifest grave sin, are not to be admitted to Holy Communion". The making clear of the legislator concerning the necessity that the canonical sanction be imposed or declared, not to mention the insistence on the fact that the serious sin be objectively such and known to the whole community, clearly highlights how the possibility on the part of the minister to refuse communion to the faithful has been submitted to juridical criteria more formally rigorous than in the normative of the old Code [38].

---

[35] In this regard cf. R. Ahlers, *Communio Eucharistica,* op. cit., pp. 111-125; P. Krämer, *Kirchenrecht I,* op. cit., pp. 71-72.

[36] Cf. cans. 904 and 276 §2 n.2. Unfortunately this orientation of the ecclesiastical legislator of 1983 confirmed both by can. 917 (on the possibility of receiving communion twice on the same day) and by can. 905 (on the possibility of celebrating twice a day), is interrupted by the little obscure norm of can. 920 on the obligation on all the faithful to receive communion at least once a year during Eastertide.

[37] Cf. cans. 213 and 912.

[38] Cf. can. 855 CIC/1917.

In conformity with the apostolic tradition represented by the Vatican Council II [39], cans. 1246-1248 reaffirm the obligation on all of the Christian faithful to observe Sunday as the "primordial feast day", in which the "paschal mystery" is celebrated in the Holy Eucharist, in which all of the faithful must "participate". In comparison with the 1917 Code the new normative of the Code regarding the obligation of the festive precept – regrettably not recalled in can. 920 – is much simplified: first of all the ecclesiastical legislator no longer speaks of *omnes et singuli dies dominici* [40], rather simply of Sundays; in the second place this obligation does not concern the mere *auditio* of Holy Mass, but the *participatio* (can. 1248) at the same, in the conciliar (and therefore active) sense of the word [41]. It is a question of an obligation which has very little in common with a casuistic morality of other times and which manifests, on the contrary, a clear significance of the juridical-constitutional type, because it recalls every one of the faithful to his proper responsibility in order to build up the ecclesial communion as the place for his own sanctification, responsibility which finds precisely in the Eucharistic celebration its particularly important and efficacious moment.

B) THE EUCHARISTIC CELEBRATION

After having put into relief in the first two sections of can. 899 the juridical-constitutional character and the public nature of the Eucharist, the sacrament of the unity of the People of God, in the third section of the same canon the ecclesiastical legislator affirms: "the Eucharistic celebration is to be so ordered that all the participants derive from it the many fruits for which Christ the Lord instituted the Eucharistic sacrifice". The Eucharistic assembly in order to express and effectuate the unity of the Church, with all the graces connected to this, must therefore be ordered. In its communional structure is reflected that of the Church, at the same time universal and particular, and vice versa, in accordance with the constitutional principle of reciprocal immanence, suggestively translatable in the Eucharistic formula: "The whole in the fragment" [42]. Of the elements of this structure the normative of the Code on the Eucharistic celebration mentions and regulates only the principals, deferring for the juridical regulation of all the other elements to the liturgical laws in force [43].

---

[39] Cf. SC 106. Outside of the feast days chosen in the first section of can. 1246, the diocesan Bishop can announce particular feast days for his own diocese (cf. can. 1244 §2) and Episcopal Conferences have the faculty to suppress or transfer to the following Sunday some days of precept (cf. can 1246 §2); on the whole of this argument cf. P. Krämer, *Kirchenrecht I*, op. cit., pp. 75-79.

[40] Can. 1247 CIC / 1917.

[41] The *participatio* is called *plena* if it involves holy communion, cf. Communicationes 15 (1983), p. 195.

[42] It is also the title of a book: H.U. von Balthasar, *Das Ganze im Fragment. Aspekte der Geschichtstheologie*, Einsiedeln 1963 (tr. it. *Il tutto nel frammento*, Milano 1970).

[43] Cf. can. 2. These liturgical laws are collected in: R. Kaczynski, *Enchiridion documentorum instaurationis liturgicae, I* (1963-1973), Torino 1975, *I praenotanda dei nuovi testi liturgici*, edited by A. Donghi, Milano 1989. Of particular importance, and with a juridically binding character (cf. Notitiae 5 (1969), p. 417) is the general introduction to the: *Missale Romanum ex decreto Sacrosancti Oecumenici Concilii Vaticani II instauratum auctoritate Pauli PP. VI promulgatum, Ordo Missae*, Città del Vaticano 1069 (editio iuxta typicam alteram 1977).

The first element mentioned by the ecclesiastical legislator is the role of the faithful who have received Holy Orders. By dint of this sacrament these are called to preside over the Eucharistic assembly and as such to be the first servants of the unity of the Church, because they live out this function "in the person of Christ" and therefore "not looking to things that are their own but the things that are Jesus Christ's" (PO 9,2). The power to preside and to *make* the Eucharist is therefore " necessarily associated with priestly ordination"[44] and consequently the first section of can. 900 establishes: "The only minister who, in the person of Christ, can bring into being the sacrament of the Eucharist, is a validly ordained priest". If this is the indispensible condition for the validity of the Eucharistic celebration, the second section of the same canon specifies the two indications for liceity: the absence of any impediment for the priesthood and the observance of the prescriptions of the Code. The first condition is complied with when the priest is not impeded in the exercise of his function by any irregularity (can. 1044 §1) or by a canonical sanction (can. 1333 §1). The second condition, on the contrary, concerns multiple prescriptions different among themselves: the principals are established by can. 903 (which prescribes the rector of a Church to admit to the Eucharistic celebration only known priests or those able to show commendatory letters) and by can. 906 (which recommends to priests to celebrate only with the participation of at least one of the faithful). Both prescriptions underline the public character of the Eucharist and therefore its being a liturgical action of the entire People of God. That is reinforced by the fact that the measure of obligation of the recommendation, contained in can. 904, concerning the daily celebration of priests, increases if the latter have assumed an ecclesiastical office, as for example that of Parish Priest[45].

A second important element of the communal structure of the Eucharistic celebration is that regarding the distribution of holy communion. In this regard can. 910 distinguishes between ordinary ministers (bishop, priests and deacons) and extraordinary ministers (acolytes or other members of the faithful upon whom a ministry has been conferred in accordance with can. 230 §3). The reference to this last canon is important because, despite the ecclesiastical legislator in can. 899 §2 speaking of "various orders and liturgical roles", these different offices are not then either mentioned or listed in the normative of the Code on the Eucharistic celebration. In can. 230 on the other hand, in syntony with the MP *Ministeria quaedam* published on 15 August 1972 by Pope Paul VI[46], three types of ministry conferred on the laity are distinguished: the stable ministries of acolyte and lector, conferrable only on the lay faithful of the male sex; temporary ministries, conferrable also on women; extraordinary or supplementary ministries, conferrable on all the lay faithful, even without being lectors or acolytes. Alongside these *ministeria* are added the *munera* or functions (can. 230 §2), such as for example commentator or cantor. Among the latter, of lesser importance and conferrable on *omnes laici* (therefore as much on men as on women), can be added also altarboys and altargirls[47]. The importance of the first, and

---

[44] Cf. the letter *Sacerdotium ministeriale,* published by the Congregation for the Doctrine of the Faith on 6 August 1983, in :AAS 75 (1983), p. 1000.

[45] Cf. cans 528, 530 no.7, 534 §1.

[46] Cf. AAS 64 (1972), pp. 529-534.

[47] This is the just observation with which H. Reinhardt (cf. MK, can. 230/7) seeks to put an end to a sad and far from understandable diatribe.

in particular the stable ministry of acolyte, is on the other hand highlighted by the norms that regulate the admission to holy communion, studied in the next section and in some way also bound to the modalities of the distribution of the same.

A third and last important element of the order of Eucharistic assemblies is constituted by the rites and ceremonies with which the same are celebrated. Having established the obligation to keep to the liturgical books "lawfully approved" (can. 928), the ecclesiastical legislator limits himself to recalling some of the principal liturgical norms, as for example that the "Eucharistic sacrifice must be celebrated with bread and wine" (can. 924 §1), following the example of Jesus Christ himself[48]. These norms are then completed by a series of prescriptions regarding the time and place of the Eucharistic celebration (cans. 931-933), as well as the custody and adoration of the most holy Eucharist (cans. 934-944). Among the latter, can. 935 on the non-liceity for anyone to "keep the blessed Eucharist in personal custody" clearly underlines how the worship of the Eucharist *extra Missam*, that is outside the sacrifice of the Holy Mass, is also strictly bound to the celebration or eucharistic assembly itself.

2.3 PARTICULAR QUESTIONS

In every Church or ecclesial communion the celebration of a sacrament has always been a sign of unity in faith, in worship and in community life: "Insofar as they are signs, the sacraments, and in particular the Eucharist, are sources of unity of the Christian community and of spiritual life and means of increasing them. Consequently, the eucharistic communion is inseparably bound to full ecclesial communion and its visible expression."[49]. Does this mean that all which is opposed to the *plenitudo* of the *communio* limits the exercise of the right of every baptised person to receive from their proper pastors such spiritual food? In this regard, as has already been seen, can. 912 affirms that only the impediments fixed by law prohibit the baptised from being admitted to holy communion; can. 18 specifies moreover that all of the norms limiting the exercise of a right are to be interpreted in the strict sense. Contemporaneously applying these two criteria it follows that the following three categories of the baptised are impeded in their exercise of the right to be admitted to the Eucharistic table: first of all non-Catholic Christians (can. 844 §1); in second place Catholic Christians who have not yet acquired "sufficient knowledge and careful preparation" (can. 913 §1); and finally the Catholic faithful who by dint of a canonical sanction or in manifest grave sin, in which they obstinately persist, cannot be admitted to holy communion (can. 915).

Being impeded in the exercise of this right does not however necessarily mean not being admitted to holy communion. In fact, as is easily deducible from can. 916, the circle of the non-authorised faithful is always greater than that of the faithful who cannot be admitted to the eucharistic communion[50], because the minister of holy com-

---

[48] Cf. Mt 26,26-29; Mk 14,22-25; Lk 22,18-20; 1Cor 11,23-24. In this regard cf. A. Mayer, *Die Eucharistie*, in: HdbkathKR, pp. 676-691, especially pp. 683-687.

[49] Pontifical Council for the Promotion of Christian Unity, *Direttorio per l'applicazione dei principi e delle norme sull'ecumenismo*, Città del Vaticano 1993, no. 129.

[50] Concurring with this opinion: H. Schmitz, *Taufe, Firmung, Eucharistie. Die Sakramente der Initiation und ihre Rechtsfolgen in der Sicht des CIC von 1983*, in: AfkKR 152 (1983), pp. 369-408, here pp. 398-404; P. Krämer, *Kirchenrecht I*, op. cit., pp. 73-74.

munion in distributing it must hold rigorously to the objective criteria of can. 915. Now, precisely at the level of interpretation of the objective criteria on the basis of which it is possible to limit the exercise of the right to be admitted to the eucharistic communion two particular questions are posed, particularly delicate under the pastoral outline: that of the eucharistic hospitality of non-Catholic Christians and that of the faithful who are divorced and remarried.

A) THE EUCHARISTIC HOSPITALITY OF NON-CATHOLIC CHRISTIANS

As a matter of principle the Catholic Church admits to the eucharistic communion and to the sacraments of penance and annointing of the sick the Catholic faithful exclusively, that is to say those who are in its unity of faith, worship and ecclesial life [51]. By way of exception, and under determined conditions, she can authorise and even recommend [52] the admission to these sacraments even non-Catholic Christians. Evidently as much the authorisation as the recommendation are applicable only whenever the double demand is protected at the same time: that of the integrity of the ecclesial communion and that of the good of souls [53].

In syntony with the special considerations shown by the Vatican Council II towards the non-Catholic Eastern churches, which "although separated from us, yet possess true sacraments, above all – by apostolic succession – the priesthood and the Eucharist" (UR 15,3), in can. 844 the ecclesiastical legislator distinguishes in this respect two types of juridical norm which regulate the extraordinary admission to the Eucharistic communion of the faithful members of the Eastern churches (can. 844 §3) and those which govern the extraordinary admission of other Christians (can. 844 §4).

In the first case there are two conditions fixed by the ecclesiastical legislator for licit admission: first of all the faithful members of the non-Catholic Eastern churches must spontaneously ask to be admitted to the Eucharist, and in second place must be properly disposed. In the second case, on the other hand, there are four conditions for licit admission, which are valid only in determined circumstances. In fact, only in danger of death or when prompted by some other grave necessity can Christians not belonging to the Eastern Churches and not being in full communion with the Catholic Church be admitted to holy communion if the following conditions are observed in their totality and contemporaneously: 1. the impossibility of approaching a minister of their own Church or ecclesial communion; 2. the spontaneous request for admission; 3. the demonstration of a personal faith conforming to that of the Catholic Church concerning the sacrament of the Eucharist; 4. the proper disposition. The issuing of general norms which permit discernment, in cases of grave necessity, and the verification of the listed conditions, repeated exactly in no. 131 of the new Directory on Ecumenism, is the competence of the diocesan Bishop, keeping in mind the norms that can be established in this matter by the Conference of Bishops. This specification

---

[51] Cf. UR 8; can. 844 §1/CIC and can. 671§1/CCEO.

[52] *Direttorio per l'applicazione dei principi e delle norme sull'ecumenismo*, op. cit., no. 129. The celebration of the Eucharist with ministers of Churches or ecclesial communions not in full communion with the Catholic Church remains however forbidden for Catholic priests (cf. can. 908).

[53] Cf. *Instructio "De peculiaribus casibus admittendi alios Christianos ad communionem Eucharisticum"* in: AAS 64 (1972), pp. 518-525, here no. 4.

concerning the competence of the diocesan Bishop is very important especially for the particular churches which find themselves in countries where the contact between Christians of different confessions are so frequent as to render less easily comprehensible what is meant by grave necessity, as well as for the impossibility of approaching a minister of their own Church.

B) DIVORCED AND REMARRIED AND THE EUCHARIST

In the Apostolic Letter *Familiaris Consortio* of 22 November 1981 Pope John Paul II explicitly stated that the entire community of the faithful must help the divorced, and in particular the divorced and remarried, to not consider themselves as "separated from the Church, for as baptised persons they can, and indeed must, share in her life"[54]. The faithful and pastors must therefore do their utmost, untiringly, to welcome them and place at their disposal the means of salvation of the Church, keeping in mind the reasons which have brought about the ruin of the first marriage and the contracting of a second union may be very different among themselves. On the contrary, some of these faithful "are sometimes subjectively certain in conscience that their previous and irreparably destroyed marriage had never been valid"[55]. Nevertheless the Pope reaffirms the practice of the Church, "based on Sacred Scripture, of not admitting to the Eucharistic communion divorced persons who have remarried. They are unable to be admitted thereto from the fact that their state and condition of life objectively contradict that union of love between Christ and the Church, which is signified and effected by the Eucharist. Besides this, there is another pastoral reason: if these people were admitted to the Eucharist, the faithful would be led into error and confusion regarding the Church's teaching about the indissolubility of marriage"[56].

Notwithstanding the clarity of this document, whose principal contents have been reaffirmed by the Pope on other occasions too[57], both on the scientific-theological level and on the level of concrete application of the canonical norms in force, the debate has not diminished. Within it can be distinguished at least three great orientations[58]; before summarising them briefly it is perhaps opportune to recall the principal norms of the Code actually in force on this matter.

First of all it is underlined that, in contrast to the Pio-Benedictine Code, the CIC of 1983 and the CCEO of 1990 do not envisage any canonical sanction for the divorced and remarried[59]. Another important difference in comparison with the normative of the old Code consists in the fact that, as has already been seen, the conditions for the non-admission to holy communion have become formally more rigorous, in order to avoid any abuse on the part of the minister of communion and to guarantee a fair protection of the right of the baptised to receive the sacraments. On the contrary,

---

[54] John Paul II, *Familiaris Consortio*, in: AAS 74 (1982), pp. 81-191, here no. 84,3.

[55] Ibid., no. 84,3.

[56] Ibid., no.84,3.

[57] Cf. for example John Paul II, *Ansprache von 19.06.1987 an die österreichischen Bischöfe anlässlich ihres ad limina Besuches,* in : AAS 80 (1988), pp. 17-25, no. 36.

[58] Even if with different emphases, the summarising scheme of these orientations can be found in: R. Ahlers, *Communio Eucharistica*, op. cit., pp. 168-189; P. Krämer, *Kirchenrecht I,* op. cit. pp. 135-139; R. Puza. *Katholisches Kirchenrecht,* Heidelberg 1986, pp. 356-364.

[59] This was on the contrary envisaged by can. 2356 of the CIC/1917.

notwithstanding the Commission for Reform having explicitly affirmed that among the faithful who persist "obstinately in grave sin" are certainly to be numbered also the divorced and remarried [60], there is no lack of those who affirm that the subjective elements contained in can. 915 are such as to legitimise a differentiated valuation in individual cases [61]. According to these, on the one hand holy communion can be refused exclusively to the faithful who are responsible – in a manifest way – for a grave offence in which they persist without any sign of repentence; and on the other precisely this cannot be stated with certainty under the subjective outline for all the divorced and remarried. Consequently the ultimate disposition of can. 915 is to be interpreted more as an appeal to the minister of communion, wishing to clarify in a pastoral dialogue the conditions for admission in the light of can. 916 too, than not an immediately applicable juridical normative. Now, it is precisely on the level of the applicability of this norm of the Code that there constantly re-emerge the three orientations indicated above and hereafter briefly summarised.

The first of these orientations, in syntony with the traditional Catholic doctrine [62], in every way considers the second marriage after civil divorce as adultery, that does not cease to be so – and thus is in contradiction with the objective moral order established by God – even if it lasts through time and is lived with responsibility, assuming all the obligations deriving from its own complex situation. Any prescription of adultery and invalid marriage does not exist. Nevertheless as long as this state of life persists the premises for admission to the sacraments and in particular the Eucharist are lacking. The only possible solution is to search in the internal forum starting from the so-called *probata Ecclesiae praxis*, according to which once the existence of determined conditions has been verified, and in particular the serious amenability to the *cohabitatio fraterna*, in the sacrament of confession together with the sacramental absolution the permission is also given to approach holy communion. According to the best known representative of this orientation [63], the conditions for admittance to the Eucharist for the divorced and remarried must be fulfilled contemporaneously and are the following three: 1. their total separation is impeded by grave reasons, as for example the education of the children and their reciprocal assistance; 2. the renunciation of conjugal relations is reciprocal and seriously demonstrated; 3. the possibility of giving rise to scandal in the community is opportunely avoided.

Decidedly different is the orientation of those canonists who, starting from the contestation according to which the second marriage of whoever is bound by a previous matrimonial bond, while being juridically illegitimate and invalid is no longer subject to canonical sanctions, believe in being able to leave exclusively to moral theology the judgement on its legitimacy or not [64]. Although on the external forum having

---

[60]   Cf. Communicationes 15 (1983), p. 194; the interpretation of the Commission not only is in syntony with no. 84 of *Familiaris Consortio* but is also repeated in no. 17 of the apostolic exhortation *Reconciliatio et Paenitentia,* cf. AAS 77 (1985), p. 223.

[61]   Cf. P. Krämer, *Kirchenrecht I,* op. cit. pp., 137.

[62]   Cf. for example Paul VI, *Litterae circulares,* in: AfkKR 142 (1973), pp. 84 ff.

[63]   Cf. H. Flatten, *Nichtigerklärung, Auflösung und Trennung der Ehe,* in: HdbkathKR, pp. 815-826, here p. 818.

[64]   Among these is to be pointed out A. Zirkel, *Schließt das Kirchenrecht alle wiederverheirateten Geschiedenen von den Sakramenten aus?,* Mainz 1977.

contracted this second marriage makes the presumption of an offence, however in per-during and the consolidation of this state of life new elements can enter in which permit it to be judged in a different manner. In particular if the ruination of the first marriage is absolutely irremediable and the second marriage is lived in the faith as a responsible reality, the latter should be legitimised by the Church as a new sacramental reality from which there arise new moral obligations. This legitimisation based on the infinite mercy of God, imposes however the obligation both to heal the consequences of the wound connected to the ruin of the first marriage, and to exercise pardon and reconciliation.

Between these two extreme positions is located a crowded group of theologians and bishops who, without placing directly under discussion the official teaching of the Church on the sacramentality and indissolubility of marriage, retain that the full applicability to individual concrete cases of the canonical norms actually in force in this matter is a strictly pastoral problem[65]. The pastoral solutions developed in detail by them start from the conviction that from the teaching of the apostolic exhortation *Familiaris Consortio* (especially regarding the fact that the divorced and remarried are not excommunicated and therefore excluded in principle from all of the sacra-ments) the following conclusions can be drawn: respect for the conditions placed by the *probata praxis Ecclesiae* cannot be indiscriminately asked of all the divorced and remarried, but it is necessary to work with the differentiations. It is Pope John Paul II himself who explicitly reminds pastors that, for love of the truth, they are obliged to discern the situations well. There is in fact a difference between those who sincerely made the effort to save the first marriage and were wholly unjustly abandoned, and those who by their own serious fault have destroyed a canonically valid marriage[66]. Consequently to fix the criteria so that a careful evaluation of individual cases is possi-ble does not mean introducing arbitrariness into such a delicate and important matter, rather it indirectly affirms that either a formal general authorisation or a formal and unilateral authorisation on the part of the Church in the individual concrete case is not possible. Indeed, even in the case in which there is a deep subjective conviction concerning the nullity of the first narriage as well as the concrete demonstration that the second union is lived out in the faith as a moral reality, the ultimate decision on the possibility of participating at the Eucharistic table, even if all of the conditions of the *probata praxis Ecclesiae* are complied with, must be left to the "personal conscience of the individual believer" who in any case can take such a decision only after a deep-ened "pastoral dialogue" with a priest[67]. The latter, after the pastoral dialogue, not only cannot grant a formal permission, but in the more complex cases is called upon no matter what to respect the decision of the faithful.

---

[65] For a list of the principal theologians who sustain this pastoral orientation, cf. R. Puza, *Katholisches Kirchenrecht*, op. cit., pp. 358-359; among the pastoral documents of bish-ops are to be pointed out: H. Krätz, *Seelsorge an wiederverheirateten Geschiedenen*, Wien 1979 and W. Kasper-K. Lehmann-O. Saier, *Grundsätze für eine seelsorgliche Begleitung von Menschen aus zerbrochenen Ehen und Wiederverheirateten Geschiedenen in der Ober-rheinischen Kirchenprovinz*, in: HK 9 (1993), pp. 460-467.

[66] John Paul II, *Familiaris Consortio*, op. cit., no. 84,2.

[67] W. Kasper-K. Lehmann-O. Saier, *Grundsätze für eine seelsorgliche Begleitung*, op. cit., p. 465 (n. IV,4).

Notwithstanding the laubable effort to render the most operative possible the accompaniment and the care of the Church towards these faithful in irregular matrimonial situations, the pastoral solutions developed in detail by the third group of theologians and bishops are not all that convincing neither on the moral level, nor on the juridical nor finally on the sacramental.

On the moral level the deferment to the "personal conscience of the individual believer" of a similar decision can not only lead the latter to practically fulfil, with a good conscience, what is contrary to the teaching of the Church, but can also develop into other "pastoral solutions" contrary to the teaching of the magisterium and to thus justify "a creative hermeneutic, according to which the moral conscience would not be entirely obligated, in all cases, by a particular negative precept"[68]. On the juridical level, even if it cannot be denied that the widening of the rules for the dissolution of a valid matrimonial bond, in the cases in which the *privilegium petrinum* is applicable, should make for a reconsideration of the whole question relative to the divorced and remarried[69], still canonical tradition has always held valid both the principal that marriage enjoys the *favor iuris* (can. 1060), for which in cases of doubt and until it cannot be proved to the contrary, the validity of the contract bond has to be recognised, and the principle according to which the subjective conviction concerning the nullity of the marriage does not necessarily exclude the matrimonial consent[70]. Consequently, rather than insisting on this premise pastoral charity, precisely by dint of the alarming statistics, should suggest counselling these faithful with greater frequency and an insistence on the introduction of cases of matrimonial nullity, also because, in syntony with the conciliar teaching, the new canonical matrimonial law envisages a greater number of nullity cases than in the normative of the old Code. Finally, on the sacramental level the pastoral solutions proposed present not a few defects.

First of all, these pastoral solutions are too unilaterally concentrated on the admittance to the Eucharistic communion, forgetting that the ordinary way of reconciliation is represented by the sacrament of penance, resulting in sacramental absolution, which "can only be granted to those who, repenting for having broken the sign of the Covenant and of fidelity to Christ, are sincerely ready to undertake a way of life that is no longer in contradiction to the indissolubility of marriage"[71]. In the second place, all of the sacraments being directed to the Eucharist, admission to the Eucharistic communion cannot be spoken of avoiding comparing the problem of the sacramentality of the second union of the divorced and remarried faithful, sacramentality which is certainly found in only one flesh being its one concrete, fundamental and constitutive expression. Finally, the Eucharistic communion is the centre and not the whole of Christian life, by which the underlining that the divorced and remarried are not separated from the Church and therefore can and must participate in its life, means for example that they are "encouraged to listen to the Word of God, to attend to the Sacrifice of the Mass, to persevere in prayer, to contribute to the works of charity and to community efforts in favour of justice, to bring up their children in the Christian faith,

---

[68]   John Paul II, *Veritatis splendor*, Roma 1993, no. 56.

[69]   This is the opinion of K. Walf, *Kirchenrecht*, Düsseldorf 1984, p. 142.

[70]   Cf. can. 1100.

[71]   John Paul II, *Familiaris Consortio,* op. cit., no. 84,5.

to cultivate the spirit and practice of penance and thus implore, day by day, God's grace"[72]. The divorced and remarried faithful are neither explicitly excused from the possibility of exercising ecclesial functions or of participating in parochial or diocesan councils. Even when the ecclesiastical legislator requires for the exercise of such functions "a life in keeping with the faith"[73], it is the competent ecclesiastical authority which must decide if a divorced and remarried believer is to be excluded or not.

In conclusion, the pastoral solutions to the sad and complex problem of the divorced and remarried, precisely because dictated by pastoral charity must take into consideration all the moral, juridical and sacramental aspects of the situations for these faithful, in order to avoid at the same time both every violation of their rights and every confusion in the ecclesial communion. In their formulation neither the unilateral accentuation of one aspect of the problem, nor the yielding to the analogous and opposed temptations of laxism and rigorism are of any help. Fundamental remains the preoccupation of avoiding that any solution of this problem can falsify on the objective level, but on the measure of the possible also on the subjective, the significance of the sacramental structure of the Church and in particular the Eucharist, its source and summit because it is the sign par excellence of the *communio Ecclesiae*, that is to say the unity of the entire People of God.

2.4 EUCHARIST, COMMUNION OF GOODS AND CANONICAL PATRIMONIAL LAW

The sacrament of the Eucharist, as the "source and summit of the whole of Christian life" (LG 11,1), has to do with all of the concrete aspects of life of the men and women that God, through baptism, calls to form "a unity which is no longer according to the flesh but in the Spirit, that is the new People of God" (LG 9,1). The experience of the ecclesial communion and above all of the Eucharistic communion, directs in a new way – *Gratia perficit, non destruit naturam* – all the relationships of the *Christifideles*, even that of their material goods. Not by chance, precisely in connection with the Eucharistic celebration a tradition was born of offerings and collections, from which in the course of the centuries the Church has gradually drawn the criteria and principles which still today form the basis of its patrimonial law.

Certainly, the use of goods, and in particular the use of money, being subject to the temptations of greed and cupidity, it is not difficult to trace in the Gospels an attitude of scepticism on the part of Jesus Christ in relation to money and riches[74]. Nevertheless he did not exclude the rich from the community of his disciples[75], and he introduces into the same the practice of a common fund[76]. Moreover, while on the one hand he addresses to the Apostles the warning "Freely you have received, freely give" (Mt 10,8), on the other he recognises their right to receive from the other disciples their proper sustenance, "because the worker deserves his wages" (Mt 10,10; Lk 10,7)

---

[72] Ibid., no. 84,3.
[73] Cf. for example cans. 874 §1 n. 3 and 893 §1.
[74] Cf. for example Mt 6,24; Mk 8,36; Lk 6,20 and 12,13-21.
[75] Cf. for example Lk 8,3; 19,1-9; Mt 27,57 and Jn 19,38-42.
[76] Cf. Jn 12,6 and 13,29.

These principles are not juridical norms, but are accepted by the first Christian community as an invitation to wish to express in concrete gestures the meaning of the common listening to the Word of God and the common Eucharistic celebration or "breaking of the bread" (Acts 2,42). It is in the Eucharist that the principle of the communion of goods is based, to have "everything in common" (Acts 2,44); it is from the experience of fraternal union generated by this that collections and offerings started as an expression of *Koinonia* (Rom 15,26) and *Diakonia* (Rom 15,31 and 1Cor 8,4). It is worth the effort therefore to reflect briefly on the more important juridical aspects of this long tradition to be able to grasp in this the inspiratory principles of all of the canonical normative relative to patrimonial goods.

A) MASS OFFERINGS

With his customary geniality St Thomas Aquinas summarises in one phrase the significance of the custom of the faithful of giving an offering for the celebration of Holy Mass: *Sacerdos non accipit pecuniam quasi pretium Eucharistiae ... , sed quasi stipendium suae sustentationis*[77]. If then such an offering is not needed for the sustenance of the priest, the latter is bound to transfer the same, or part of it, in favour of the poor[78]. These principles, reconfirmed and reread by Pope Paul VI in the light of conciliar Eucharistic theology[79], constitute the basis of the new normative of the code on offerings for the celebration of Mass (cans. 945-958) as explicitly recalled by can. 946 which states "Christ's faithful who make an offering so that Mass can be celebrated for their intention, contribute to the good of the Church, and by that offering they share in the Church's concern for the support of its ministers and its activities". This norm has a double constitutional type foundation: on the one hand it obliges each of the faithful to "provide for the needs of the Church, so that the Church has available to it those things that are necessary for divine worship, for works of the apostolate and of charity and for the worthy support of its ministers" (can. 222 §1); and on the other the right of clerics, who exercise a ministerial service, to "a remuneration that befits their condition, taking into account both the nature of their office and the conditions of time and place, because it is to be such that it provides for the necessities of their life and for the just remuneration of those whose services they need" (can. 281 §1). The sobriety with which the legislator describes this right of clerics who exercise an ecclesiastical office – underlined by the corresponding obligation to pledge any eventual surplus "for the good of the Church and for charitable works" (can. 282 §2) – is certainly inspired by the teaching of the council on the "standard of living" of priests, characterised by "voluntary poverty" and by a "use of property in common" (PO 17,5), as well as by the principle of the communion of goods, as can easily be deduced from the recommendation, formulated in the same context, "of practicing some manner of common life" (can. 280).

---

[77] *S. Th.* II-II, q. 100, art. 2 ad 2.

[78] Cf. Thomas Aquinas, *S. Th.* II-II, q. 86, a. 2 and the commentary of K. Mörsdorf, *Erwägungen zum Begriff und zur Rechtfertigung des Meßstipendiums,* in: K. Mörsdorf, *Schriften zum kanonischen Recht,* hrsg von W. Aymans-K. Th. Geringer-H. Schmitz, Paderborn-München-Wien-Zürich 1989, pp. 499-581.

[79] Cf. Paul VI, MP *Firma in Traditione,* in: AAS 66 (1974), pp. 308-311.

All of the other norms relating to offerings for Holy Masses are directed towards guaranteeing the correct following of the fixed purposes of the quoted can. 946. This is not given without the contemporaneous respect of the evangelical principle *Gratis accepistis, gratis date* (Mt. 10,8) and of the canonical tradition that considers the goods of the Church as a *patrimonium pauperum* [80]. For these reasons the ecclesiastical legislator demands without half measures that "any semblance of trafficking or trading" (can. 947) be carefully avoided.

B) GENERAL PRINCIPLES OF CANONICAL PATRIMONIAL LAW

What has been said on the significance of offerings for the celebration of Holy Masses finds a substantial confirmation in the inspiratory principles suggested by Vatican Council II for the reform of canonical patrimonial law. In the knowledge that "private property or some sort of ownership of external goods assures a person a highly necessary sphere of autonomy" (GS 71,2), the Fathers of the Council affirm in clear terms that the Church also "uses temporal realities as often as its mission requires it" and that it must do so "using all and only those means which are in accord with the Gospel and for the welfare of all according to the diversity of times and cirumstances" (GS 76,5). From these affirmations at least three fundamental or inspiratory principles of canonical patrimonial law can be deduced: 1. all ecclesiastical goods have an instrumental destination and thus are to be used always keeping in mind the mission of the Church [81]; 2. their conferral and use are directed towards the witness and realisation of the ecclesial communion [82]; 3. their administration must keep in mind the customs of the place and particular canon law [83], even if it must progressively overcome the system of benefices [84].

In their substance these principles were accepted by the ecclesiastical legislator in the fifth book *De bonis ecclesiae temporalibus* (cans. 1254-1310), which is therefore to be considered as a blueprint law for the particular normatives of individual Dioceses or particular Churches [85]. The importance of the first principle is underlined right from the introductory canons, and especially where the ecclesiastical legislator defines the proper ends of the patrimonial goods of the Church (can. 1254 §2). The connection of the use of patrimonial goods with the realisation of the *communio Ecclesiae* is witnessed to above all by the constitution in every single Diocese of an institution for the sustenance of the clergy (can. 1274) and by the more general correlation between

---

[80] Cf. GS 88; the principles are confirmed by the ecclesiastical legislator both in can. 945 §2 and can. 282 §2.

[81] Cf. PO 17, 3-4 and 20,1; CD 6,3.

[82] Cf. above all PO 8,3; but also PO 21 and LG 13,2.

[83] Cf. for example PO 21,2; CD 12,2. In this regard the Synod of Bishops of 1967 states: "cum regimen bonorum temporalium iuxta leges propriae nationis magna ex parte ordinari debeat" (= no.5, of the *Principia quae Codicis Iuris Canonici recognitionem dirigant,* in: Communicationes 1 (1969), p. 81).

[84] Cf. PO 20,2.

[85] This is the opinion of W. Schulz, *Grundfragen kirchlichen Vermögensrechts,* in: HdbkathKR, pp. 859-880, here p. 864. For a rapid examination of the novelties introduced by the CIC in this material, cf. V. De Paolis, *De bonis Ecclesiae temporalibus in novo Codice iuris canonici,* in: Periodica 73 (1984), pp. 113-151; for a deeper study, cf. *Handbuch des Vermögensrechtes der katholischen Kirche,* hrsg. von H. Heimerl-H. Pree, Regensburg 1993.

the administration of the goods of the Church and the vigilance of the "supreme authority of the Roman Pontiff" (can. 1256). The role of particular law in patrimonial matters is then highlighted by continual deferments to the norms emanating from the Conferences of Bishops or from individual diocesan bishops [86]. Finally, the conciliar direction to progressively abandon the system of benefices is entrusted in can. 1272 to the Confernces of Bishops. Even if in this last canon *suppressionem* is not spoken of explicitly, because in many cases it would come into collision with concordatory norms and acquired rights [87], still this reveals in a clear way the intention of the legislator to overcome with the new norms all the limits connected with the benefice system, sometimes still predominating, that is to say: its being a cause of unequal distribution among the clergy and thus an obstacle to common life; its incapacity to guarantee sufficient sustenance for all of the priests; the not few difficulties implicated on the level of administration and thus greater possibilities of disputes between priests and parishioners; its insufficient transparency, often the cause of suspicions about the real poverty of the Church [88].

The intention to overcome this obsolete system is confirmed by the care with which the ecclesiastical legislator diversifies and defines the many "lawful ways by either natural or positive law" (can. 1259) at the Church's disposition to acquire temporal goods. These legitimate ways can be gathered together into two major categories. Belonging to the first category, which has precedence because it conforms more to the principle of the prevalence in the Church of the oblative criterion over the contributive, are both "the offerings given by the faithful for a specified purpose" (can. 1267 §3) and the offerings made in favour of a "special collection" (can. 1266). These two types of offering are both founded on the obligation by which every one of the faithful is bound "to provide for the needs of the Church" (can. 222 §2 of even c. 1262). Belonging to the second category are the following four types of offering: the so-called special appeals or *subventiones rogatae* (can. 1262); offerings on the occasion of the adminstration of the sacraments (stole fees) or *oblationes* (can. 1264 n. 2); the taxes for acts of executive power and for the execution of rescripts or *taxae* (can. 1264 n. 1); the ordinary levies imposed on physical persons, called simply *tributum* (can. 1263). All four types of offering are founded not so much on the principle that all of the faithful must contribute to the realisation of the ecclesial communion as much as on the inherent right of the Church "to require from the faithful whatever is necessary for its proper objectives" (can. 1260).

Are ecclesiastical taxes, very diffuse in European state ecclesiastical law, therefore to be considered simply as an extraordinary means for acquiring temporal goods on the part of the Church? The clause *salvis legibus et consuetudinibus particularibus quae eidem potiora iura tribuant"* [89], introduced at the suggestion of the German bishops into can. 1263 permits considering them, at least on the level of particular canon law,

---

[86]   Cf. for example cans. 1262 and 1263.

[87]   In this regard cf. V. De Paolis, *Beneficio,* in: NDDC, pp. 91-95.

[88]   Cf. V. De Paolis, *Sostentamento del clero,* in: NDDC, pp. 1014-1017, here p. 1015.

[89]   For the editing history of this clause, which provides a foundation in the Code for the particular custom of worship tax, cf. Communicationes 12 (1980), pp. 401-403.

as an ordinary means of providing for the needs of the Church in determined cultural contexts [90].

Finally it is to be demonstrated how the CIC of 1983 not only made its own the inspiratory principles fixed by the Vatican Council II for the reform of canonical patrimonial law, but has also accepted the more general principles of synodality and joint responsibility above all on the administrative level of the temporal goods of the Church. In fact, can. 1280 prescribes that every juridical person must have a proper "finance committee" or at least "two counsellors", and nothing prevents the latter being lay faithful, expert in financial matters. Moreover, the dispositions of the code concerning the constitution and composition of the diocesan finance committee (can. 492) and the parish finance committee (can. 537), in which the principles mentioned find a clear and efficient application, correspond to this general norm, documenting once more the importance of the *communio* as the formal principle of the whole of Canon Law.

3. BAPTISM

If the Eucharist is at the same time the source and summit of the whole of Christian life, as has been fully seen in the preceding section, the sacrament of baptism is always to be considered as the foundation of this life, that is to say "the gateway to life in the Spirit" and "the door that opens up access to the other sacraments" [91]. The Vatican Council II and the Code of Canon Law theologically and juridically specify the meaning of these suggestive traditional images.

3.1 BAPTISM IN VATICAN COUNCIL II AND IN THE CIC

A) THE COUNCIL TEACHING

Among the most authoritative commentators on conciliar baptismal theology there is no lack of those who have acutely observed how the necessity for the sacrament of baptism in the order of salvation has been illustrated by the Fathers of the Council in a not too happy manner [92]. And in fact this was made clearer by the Catechism of the Catholic Church in the sense that "Baptism is necessary for salvation for those to whom the Gospel has been proclaimed and who have had the possibilty of asking for this sacrament" [93]. Prescinding from this, all the other fundamental elements of the rich Catholic baptismal theology have been represented and reexplained in a wonderful way in the various documents of the Vatican Council II. The elements, which have a more direct relationship with the canonical normative, can be summarised thus: 1. Mankind, "reborn through the Word of God" (AG 6,3) and "regenerated by means of

---

[90] This is the opinion of W. Aymans repeated by: H. Hollerbach, *Kirchensteuer und Kirchenbeitrag,* in: HdbkathKR, pp. 889-900, here p. 891.

[91] The expression *vitae spiritualis ianua* is found in the first article (=n. 1213) on baptism of the *Catechism of the Catholic Church,* Città del Vaticano 1992; the expression *ianua sacramentorum* is found on the other hand in can. 737 §1 of the CIC/1917.

[92] Cf. LG 16 and the commentary of J. Ratzinger, *Der Kirchenbegriff und die Frage nach der Gliedschaft der Kirche,* in: Idem, *Das neue Volk Gottes. Entwürfe zur Ekklesiologie,* Düsseldorf 1970 (2. Aufl.), pp. 90-104 and especially p. 101.

[93] *Catechism of the Catholic Church,* op. cit., no. 1257.

baptism in Christ" (AG 14,2), are introduced "into the People of God" (PO 5,1), and "incorporated into the Church" (LG 11,1); 2. Once " become a member of the Church, the person baptised belongs no longer to himself"[94], but to Jesus Christ, because with the sacrament of baptism "man is truly incorporated into the crucified and glorified Christ" (UR 22,1); 3. This being "conformed to Christ" (LG 7,2), through baptism, not only purifies from all sins, but also makes of the neophyte a "new creature" (2Cor 5,17), with his own dignity and personality, "common to all the faithful" (LG 32,3) and articulated in a series of rights and duties, according to the fundamental principle that "in the Church there is a diversity of ministry, but united in one mission" (AA 2,2); 4. Of "the bond of sacramental unity" the sacrament of baptism is simultaneously the indispensible constitutive element and also only "a beginning and a point of departure for it is wholly directed towards the acquiring of fullness of life in Christ" and is therefore "ordained towards a complete profession of faith" and "a complete integration into the Eucharistic communion" (UR 22,2); 5. Finally, the sacrament of baptism impresses on the believer an "indelible sacramental character which appoints him to celebrate Christian worship" (LG 11,1) and to exercise the common priesthood, that is that "holy priesthood" which permits the "offering in spiritual sacrifice all the works of Christian men, and proclaims the wonders of him who has called them out of darkness into his own marvellous light (cf. 1 Pet 2,4-10)" (LG 10,1).

This new synthesis of the Catholic doctrine on the sacrament of baptism has directed both the editing of the new *Ordo baptismi parvulorum,* published on the 15 May 1969 and the normative of the code entitled *De baptismo* (cans. 849-878).

B) THE FUNDAMENTAL CANONICAL NORMS

Claiming to wish to sythesise in only one introductory canon all these elements of the conciliar doctrine on baptism and to attempt at the same time to join them with the conditions for the valid administration of the sacrament, the sole preoccupation of can. 737 of the old Code of 1917, cannot but lead to a hybrid and incomplete result. In fact, can. 849 states: "Baptism, the gateway to the sacraments, is necessary for salvation, either by actual reception or at least by desire. By it people are freed from sins, are born again as children of God and, made like to Christ by an indelible character, are incorporated into the Church. It is validly conferred only by a washing in real water with the proper form of words." As can be seen, of the five elements of the conciliar theology on baptism the fourth is wholly missing, that is to say the reference to the fact that this sacrament is the foundation of the ecclesial communion, because it constitutes the first sacramental bond of unity. Moreover, the first element – that of incorporation into the Church – is robbed of its intrinsic connection with being reborn in listening to the Word of God and the fifth element is deprived of its most significant aspect for Canon Law, that of the common priesthood. Even the third element of the baptismal theology of the Council, being conformed to Christ, is presented in this canon completely separated from the rights and duties of the Christifidelis. In order to recapture this ecclesial and juridical-constitutional dimension of the sacrament of baptism reference has to be made to two other canons, placed by the ecclesiastical legislator in other sections of the normative of the code: can. 204 and can. 96.

---

[94]   Ibid., no. 1269.

The first section of can. 204 states: "Christ's faithful are those who, since they are incorporated into Christ through baptism, are constituted the people of God. For this reason they participate in their own way in the priestly, prophetic and kingly office of Christ. They are called, each according to his or her particular condition, to exercise the mission God entruted to the Church to fulfil in the world". The imnportance of this norm for all of constitutional canonical law would have been more greatly evident if the ecclesiastical legisaltor had made it follow immediately that of can. 96, inexplicably placed in the title dedicated to physical and juridical persons[95], and which states: "By baptism one is incorporated into the Church of Christ and constituted a person in it, with the duties and rights which, in accordance with each one's status, are proper to Christians, in so far as they are in ecclesiastical communion and unless a lawfully issued sanction intervenes". Both the norms of the code would moreover have been more efficacious in order to determine the rights bound to belonging to the Church if it were not undervalued that such a belonging finds its full expression in the other two sacraments of Christian initiation: confirmation and the Eucharist, as is indirectly recorded in both can. 866 and the disposition about entrusting to the diocesan bishop of the "baptism of adults, at least of those who have completed their fourteenth year" (can. 863).

c) THE OTHER NORMS OF THE CODE

Notwithstanding the inadequacy of the introductory canon, the other norms of the Code on baptism seem to have accepted the substance of the conciliar doctrine on this sacrament[96]. This shows first of all the fact that the point of departure for their organic self-articulation is now the baptism of adults[97]. This does not detract anything from the legitimacy of baptism of children, as can be immediately deduced from the disposition of can. 867 §1 which obliges parents to "see that their infants are baptised within the first few weeks". However, this perspective accentuates the importance of the "catechumenate" (can. 851 n. 1) and of all the dispositions relative to adequate preparation and to instruction, which must precede the celebration of baptism[98]. This responsibility is not only that of the parents, but also of the godparents (can. 872) and of the minister of baptism[99], as well as the whole ecclesial community in which the baptism will be celebrated, because these "are there also as representatives of a community of faith, guarantors of the faith and the desire for ecclesial communion of the candidate"[100].

---

[95] Cf. H. Schmitz, *De ordinatione systematica novi CIC recogniti*, in: Periodica 68 (1979), pp. 171-200, here p. 175; Idem, *Taufe, Firmung, Eucharistie*, op. cit., p. 380.

[96] For a detailed analysis of these norms on baptism, cf. A. Mostaza, *Battesimo*, in: NDDC. pp. 80-91; P. Krämer, *Kirchenrecht I*, op. cit., pp. 71-85; A.E. Hierold, *Taufe und Firmung*, in: HdbkathKR, pp. 659-675, especially pp. 660-667.

[97] Cf. cans. 851-852 and can. 865.

[98] Cf. can. 851 n.2 but also cans. 865, 867 and 868.

[99] For the new Code the ordinary minister of baptism is no longer only the bishop and priests, but also deacons (can. 861 §1). Can. 861 §2 makes clear however that the responsibility for baptismal instruction is above all up to the parish priests.

[100] *Directory for the application of the principles and norms of ecumenism*, op. cit., no.98.

Within this perspective, which witnesses to the character of the *sacramentum fidei* of baptism, the conditions for the licit and valid administration of this sacrament are rendered more rigorous. For the adult can. 865 prescribes the following four conditions: 1. The free manifestation of the wish to receive baptism; 2. Adequate instruction in the fundamental truths of the faith and the duties connected with it. 3. The passing through a period of testing or catechumenate; 4. Being cautioned as to the necessity for repentence for their personal sins. For the baptism of children the ecclesiastical legislator prescribes on the other hand the following three conditions: 1. The consent or the request from at least one of the two parents for the baptism of their own child; 2. Adequate preparation for the celebration of the sacrament; 3. The existence of a realistic hope that the child will receive instruction and a Catholic education[101]. Except for the conditions concerning the freedom of the request by an adult to be baptised, as well as the presupposition that the candidate, whether an adult or a child, has not already received baptism (can. 864), all the other conditions regard only the liceity of the sacrament. Nevertheless these positively underline the necessity of avoiding a sacramentalisation at any cost, because as has been rightly observed "a sacramentalisation without prior evangelisation makes a contribution towards de-Christianisation"[102].

To be positively hailed also are the dispositions of can. 877, which exclusively oblige the parish priest of the place where the celebration took place to register the baptism avoiding the inconveniences of a double registration, and of can. 871 which overcomes at a stroke the painful and obsolete casuistry of aborted foetuses. To be criticised on the other hand are the following three deficiencies or downright contradictions into which the legislator has fallen.

The first regards the non-acceptance of the liturgical norm contained in no. 27 of the general introduction to the *Rite of Christian Initiation of Adults*, published by the Sacred Congregation for the Sacraments and Divine Worship on 6 January 1972 and which states: "As far as is possible, all the children born within a given period of time are to be baptised on the same day with a common celebration. The sacrament is not to be celebrated twice in the same church on the same day, unless for a just cause".

The second norm of the code that gives rise to justified worries is that of can. 868 §2 which admits the liceity of the baptism of a child, even against the wishes of the parents, whether they are Catholics or not. Indeed, a similar attitude would seem to be in open contradiction with can. 748 §2 where the ecclesiastical legislator proclaims that it is never lawful for anyone "to force others to embrace the Catholic faith against their conscience", without the clarification that the legitimacy of such a sacramental gesture is placed under the reservation that the extraordinary minister does not have any intention of proselytising or of *Zwangskatholisierung*[103].

Finally, also the norm of can. 1366 – which provides for a canonical sanction for the parents who consign their children to be baptised into a non-Catholic community – without the double clarification that this refers only to Catholic parents who commit

---

[101] Cf. cans. 851 no.2, 867 and 868 §1.

[102] A. Mostaza, *Battesimo,* op. cit., p. 84.

[103] In the schema of preparation of the new Code, sent out for consultation in 1975, the canon in question was formulated in a different way, cf. Communicationes 13 (1981) p. 223. Agreeing in this criticism: P. Krämer, *Kirchenrecht I,* op. cit., p. 82 and H. Schmitz, *Taufe, Firmung, Eucharistie,* op. cit., pp. 383-384.

this gesture with a clear anti-Catholic intentionality, demonstrates scant ecumenical sensibility and gives rise to some concerns in the realm of the full acceptance of the conciliar lesson on the sacrament of baptism.

Of an entirely different content, on the other hand, is the first section of the already quoted can. 868, which in no.2 provides the possibility of a deferral of the baptism of a child, as well as can. 869 on the validity of baptism celebrated in a non-Catholic ecclesial community.

D) THE POSSIBILITY OF A DEFERRAL OF THE BAPTISM OF CHILDREN.

This is a question of an absolutely new norm, introduced for the first time in the new *Ordo baptismi parvulorum* of 1969. In order to interpret it correctly we need to compare it with another norm of the code, new and of fundamental importance, that of can. 843 §1 on the impossibility of refusing the sacraments to the faithful who ask for them opportunely, with the proper disposition and who are not impeded by law from receiving them. It seems then immediately in an unequivocal way that the ecclesiastical legislator in can. 868 §1 no.2 is not speaking of a "refusal", rather of a "deferral" of baptism. In order that such a serious decision not be subject to whim in the same canon the three conditions which render such a deferral possible and legitimate are specified: 1. It must be established that the hope of the child being educated in the Catholic faith is totally lacking (*prorsus deficiat*); 2. That the parents be advised of the reasons for the deferral; 3. That the latter be done "in accordance with the provisions of particular law".

The first condition testifies to the special nature of this deferral, which is nothing if not a proposal, prolonged over time, to live baptism as a sacrament of the faith, proposed so that it solicits the educative responsibility not only of the parents but of all of the people in the environment of the life of the child [104]. The dialogue with the parents prior to the celebration of the baptism can be interpreted as a second indispensable condition, only if there exists some doubt based on the possibility that the child will be educated in the Catholic faith. Finally, the third condition is a direct consequence of the fact that baptismal incorporation into the Church always comes about through the gathering together of a determined ecclesial community. According to the rules fixed by the Conference of German bishops [105], the deferral of the baptism of a child is possible only under these conditions: 1. The dialogue with the parents must always have the character of a proposal of baptism and not of a placing under tutelage; 2. The aim of such a dialogue is that of deepening the reasons for asking for baptism; 3. The deferral of baptism can only be decided after the refusal of this dialogue on the part of the parents and having established that none of the godparents is disposed to assume the responsibility of educating the child in the Catholic faith; 4. The parish priest or minister of baptism cannot take this decision on his own but must consult the dean; 5. The parents must be advised of the reasons for the deferral; 6. An annual report of

---

[104] In this regard, cf. *Pastorale Anweisung der Deutschen Bischofskonferenz an die Priester und Mitarbeiter im pastoralen Dienst vom 12. Juli 1979 über die rechtzeitige Taufe der Kinder,* in: AfkKR 148 (1979), pp. 466-475, no. 3.7, p. 474.

[105] For a commentary on these norms, cf. P. Krämer, *Kirchenrecht I,* op. cit., pp. 83-85; H. Schmitz, *Taufe, Firmung, Eucharistie,* op. cit., pp. 384-386.

the eventual deferrals of baptism of children must be presented to the Ordinary of the place.

E) THE VALIDITY OF BAPTISM IN OTHER CHRISTIAN CHURCHES AND ECCLESIAL
   COMMUNITIES

In the knowledge that the "one Church of Christ ... subsists in the Catholic Church, governed by the successor of Peter and the Bishops that are in communion with him" (LG 8,2), the Fathers of the Council recognise that even in the other Churches or ecclesial communities not in full communion with the Church of Rome there exist "numerous elements of sanctification and truth" (LG 8,2) among which the sacrament of baptism certainly excels. Given that because the different divisions known throughout the centuries by the Church " differ greatly from one another not only by reason of their origin, place and time, but still more by reason of the nature and seriousness of questions concerning faith and the ecclesiastical structure" (UR 13,4), the Council Fathers adopted a distinction between the Eastern Churches not in full communion with the Church of Rome and the other Churches or ecclesial communities [106]. This distinction also has consequences on the level of the evaluation of the validity or not of baptism. According to no. 99 of the *Directory for the application of the principles and norms on ecumenism* for the first group there is no problem because the validity of the baptism conferred by them is absolutely not an object of doubt and it is enough to establish that this has been effectively administered. For the second, on the other hand, a distinction has to be made between those Churches or ecclesial communities with which the Catholic Church has reached an agreement on baptism and the others.

For the validity of baptism conferred by Churches or ecclesial communities with which such an agreement is in force the principle holds according to which "when an official ecclesiastical certificate has been released, there is no reason to doubt ... as long as, for a particular case, an examination does not reveal that there is a serious reason to doubt the matter, the formula used for the baptism, the intention of the adult being baptised or of that of the baptising minister" [107] In this particular case, and only in this, can. 869 §1 is to be applied, which provides for the conferral of conditional baptism. For all the other Churches or ecclesial communities the "serious enquiry" envisioned by this canon, concerning the effective conferral of the sacrament of baptism and the validity of the same it is always necessary first to proceed to a possible conditional baptism. For the enquiry concerning the validity the second section of the same canon demands that there be "an examination of the matter and the form of words used" as well as "the intention of the adult being baptised and of that of the baptising minister".

The ecumenical importance of can. 869 would have been placed in a greater light if the ecclesiastical legislator had emphasised these fundamental ecclesiological distinctions and had explicitly deferred these agreements to the Conferences of Bishops. The latter in proceeding to such forms of agreement on the validity of baptism must keep in mind the following: " a) Baptism by immersion or by infusion, with the trinitarian formula is, in itself, valid. Consequently, if the rituals, the liturgical books or

---

[106] Cf. UR 14-18 for the Eastern Churches and UR 21-23 for the others.

[107] *Directory for the application of the principles and norms on ecumenism*, no. 99 c); cf. also can. 869 §2.

the customs established by a Church or ecclesial community prescribe one of these modes of baptising, the sacrament must be held to be valid, except when there are sound reasons to place in doubt that the minister has observed the norms of his own community or Church. b) The insufficient faith of a minister in what concerns baptism, of itself has never rendered a baptism invalid. The sufficient intention of the baptising minister must be presumed, as long as there is not a serious reason for doubting that he wanted to do what the Church does. c) If doubts arise on the use of water and the manner of making use of it, respect for the sacrament and deference towards the ecclesial communities implicated requires that a serious enquiry be conducted concerning the practice of the community in question prior to any judgment on the validity of the baptism administered by it" [108].

3.2 CONSTITUTIONAL TYPE QUESTIONS

A) RELIGIOUS SECTS AND ECCLESIAL COMMUNITIES

Much more radical and deeper than the distinction between Churches and ecclesial communities, just examined in relation to the problem of the validity of baptism, is the distinction that this sacrament introduces between religious and ecclesial realities or complex social structures. The first, known also as Christian sects, are constituted by dint of their faith in Jesus Christ based exclusively on the Word of God and sometimes are reduced to vague forms of 'Jesusism'; the second, on the other hand, are true and proper ecclesial communities because besides the Word of God they also celebrate baptism and possibly other sacraments. Baptism, incorporating the human person in Jesus Christ and in His one Church, introduces the baptised into the institutional structure of the *Ecclesia Christi*, which is historically realised in different forms and in different degrees of ecclesiality or of ecclesial communion [109]. The latter reaches a degree of an objective and structural *plena communio* only in the Catholic Church, which – at the constitutional level – is at the same time universal and particular, as can easily be deduced from the conciliar formula according to which in the particular Churches and from the particular Churches the "one and unique Catholic Church" is realised (LG 23,1).

It is in this perspective that the rights and duties based on the sacrament of baptism are to be studied, a perspective with an important ecumenical significance [110] and certainly not without juridical relevance even for non-Catholic Christians who, precisely by dint of their baptism, are not excluded on principle from the exercise of some of such rights.

B) RIGHTS AND DUTIES OF THE *Christifidelis*

By divine institution the People of God is unique: "One Lord, one faith, one baptism" (Eph. 4,5). Consequently, according to the Vatican Council II, in the Church on the one hand "there is a common dignity of members deriving from their regeneration in Christ" (LG 32,2), adopted by the sacrament of baptism, and on the other there is no

---

[108] Ibid., no. 95.

[109] Cf. E. Corecco, *Taufe*, in: *Ecclesia a Sacramentis*, op. cit., pp. 27-36, especially pp. 28-29.

[110] In this regard, cf. H.J.F. Reinhardt, *Reflexionen zur ekklesiologischen Stellung der nichtkatholischen Christen im CIC/1983*, in: *Ministerium Iustitiae*. Festschrift für H. Heinemann, hrsg. von A. Gabriels-H.J.F. Reinhardt, 1985, pp. 105-115.

room for any "inequality arising from race or nationality, social condition or sex" (LG 32,2). The affirmation of this principle of true equality and common dignity among all the members of the Church is repeated almost to the letter by the ecclesiastical legislator in can. 208, the first of the titles of the Code of Canon Law containing the rights and duties of all the faithful (cans. 208-233). And with reason, because if the faithful do not enjoy this equality, founded in the sacrament of baptism, every discourse on the rights and duties of all of them would be in vain. This fundamental equality is not unlimited but extends to all that is common to the state of the *Christifidelis*, immanent and distinct from all the other vocational states, each having its own list of specific rights and duties: that of the laity (cans. 224-231), the clerical (cans. 273-289) and the religious (cans. 662-672).

The fact that the list of the rights and duties of all of the faithful is found in the CIC / 1983 at the beginning of the chapter *De Populo Dei* undoubtedly constitutes a progress with respect to the systematic of the Dogmatic Constitution *Lumen gentium*. More than that, to tell the truth, the conciliar Fathers being rightly occupied with promoting above all the laity, did not always succeed "in doctrinally isolating the figure of the faithful from the three states of life" [111] and they sometimes fell into overlapping. Nevertheless all the cases in point formulated by the ecclesiastical legislator of 1983 in this first list have an explicit foundation, sometimes even literal, in the various conciliar documents: the right-duty to express one's own opinion on what relates to the good of the Church, formulated in can. 212 §3, is stated in LG 37,1; in the same conciliar text is also found the right to receive the sacraments from the pastors of the Word of God, codified in can. 213; the right-duty to give worship to God according to the proper right and a proper spirituality, formulated in can. 214, is founded both in UR 4,5 and LG 41; the freedom of assembly and the right to associate freely, guaranteed by can. 215, are stated in AA 19,4; the right-duty to promote and sustain apostolate initiatives is affirmed for the laity in AA 3,2 and extended by can. 216 to all the faithful; the right to a Christian education of can. 217 is evidently presupposed by the duty, repeated by the Council, to "judge and interpret everything with an integrally Christian sense" (GS 62,7); the freedom of research in the theological field, guaranteed by can. 218, is recognised as a "lawful freedom" in GS 62,8; the right to free choice of one's own state of life (can. 219) is confirmed by the Council in relation to all three vocational states; matrimonial (GS 49,1), clerical (OT 6) and religious (PC 24). Finally, the right to the protection of one's good name and one's own privacy (can. 220), as well as the right to legitimately defend all these rights before the competent ecclesiastical forum (can. 221) are direct implications of the principle of religious freedom strongly stated by the Vatican Council II in no. 10 of the declaration *Dignitatis humanae*. Missing, from the list of the CIC of 1983, at least on the explicit level, is the right-duty to follow one's proper charism, affirmed on the other hand by the conciliar Fathers many times and in particular in LG 12,2 and AA 3,4. This lack and the missing explicit reference to the theological categories of the *sensus fidei* and the *sacerdotium commune*, with which the Vatican Council II starting from baptism

---

[111] E. Corecco, *Il catalogo dei doveri-diritti del fedele nel CIC*, in: *I diritti fondamentali della persona umana e la libertà religiosa*. Atti del V Colloquio giuridico (8-10 March 1984), Città del Vaticano 1985, pp. 101-125, here p. 104.

has defined the ecclesiological positioning of the *Christifidelis* [112], risk impoverishing the constitutional value of this listing in a catalogue of the rights and duties of all the faithful, as well as of exposing the same catalogue to readings extraneous to the communional nature of the Church. To avoid this it is indispensable to keep in mind the following three observations concerning the special nature of these rights and duties of the faithful.

First of all, from cans. 209 and 223 it can clearly be deduced that all of these rights of the *Christifidelis* are directed by the constitutional principle of *communio*. In fact, if "the faithful are bound to preserve their union with the Church at all times, even in their external actions" (can. 209 §1), this means that their rights, in as much as they are based more or less on the sacrament of baptism, have not been formalised by the ecclesiastical legislator in a list in order to create spheres of autonomy of the individual in relation to the ecclesial community, but to guarantee at one and the same time his active participation "as one of the faithful in the building up of the mystical body of Christ" (CD 16,5), and the exclusion of any whim on the part of the ecclesiastical authority in relation to the correct exercise of these rights. Such an exercise is in fact juridically regulated by two fundamental principles or reservation clauses; that of self-limitation and that of authoritative moderation. The former is formulated by the ecclesiastical legislator in can. 223 §1, which reserves by law in favour of three protected juridical spheres: the common good of the Church, the rights acquired by others and the duties towards others; the latter, on the other hand, is fixed by can. 223 §2 as follows: "Ecclesiastical authority is entitled to regulate, in view of the common good, the exercise of rights which are proper to Christ's faithful". The complete lack of specifications concerning the legislative or administrative instruments with which the ecclesiastical authority is authorised to intervene is surprising. In fact, such a lack risks compromising the credibility of the list and to make the clause itself seem like a blank cheque in the hands of a superior. However, in evaluating the effective import of this clause the following data must be kept in mind: 1. In Canon Law divine law, whether positive or natural, enjoys a clear priority not only in relation to purely ecclesiastical norms but also in relation to their possible formal juridical listing as constitutional norms; 2. The ontological structure of every single right-duty of the *Christifidelis* is determined with precision starting from the conciliar texts by which the ecclesiastical legislator was inspired for his listing in the code [113]; 3. Natural rights, and in particular those commonly known as human rights, have in the law of the Church a more inter-

---

[112] Cf. E. Corecco, *Taufe*, op. cit., pp. 29-30.

[113] In this regard three categories of rights of the faithful can be distinguished: the first comprises the expressions deriving exclusively from positive divine law (as for example the duty to live in communion or the right to the sacraments); the second comprises the duties-rights whose structure exists of per se also in the framework of natural law (as for example the right of association and the duty-right to express your own opinion); the third category comprises finally the matter in hand of true and proper natural law (as for example the right to the freedom of research and the right to a free choice of the state of life). Apropos of this, cf. E. Corecco, *Il catalogo dei doveri-diritti del fedele nel CIC*, op. cit., pp. 111-112.

locutory than subsidiary significance, that is of juridical relevance only in the measure in which they help to clarify and realise the specific mission of the Church [114].

In the second place the rights of the faithful are ontologically based in the Church as communion, whose beginning and preamble is baptism, also because they are often nothing other if not the mirror image of a duty. For example the right to the sacraments (can. 213), which we have seen the importance of, is so founded in baptism but is also necessarily implicated in the duty of all the faithful to tend towards sanctity (can. 210). The priority of duties over rights in the constitutional structure of the Church is not however based upon the positivist interpretation of the axiom: *si nulla esset obligatio, nec ius allum foret* [115]. In fact in the Church "the priority of duty over right arises from the same reference of all the faithful, and thus also of Pastors, to Christ who redeems and calls to live in communion with the Father. The *communio cum Deo* determines the existence and the nature of the *communio cum hominibus*. The faithful must live the communion among themselves because with baptism, which renders them participants in the unique priesthood of Christ, even if with modalities different in essence, they are ontologically inserted into the communional trinitarian structure" [116].

In the third place it can be observed that, even if there is no unanimity on the application or not of the qualification of fundamentals to the rights of the faithful [117], the post-conciliar canonist certainly recognises in the latter in their totality a special nature in relation to the fundamental rights of the citizen within the juridical system of the state. In fact, in relation to the Church the *Christifidelis* as a juridical subject does not enjoy an analogous pre-existence to that which on the other hand the human person possesses in respect to the State. Their rights do not constitute spaces of autonomy because the *Christifidelis* is not a simple individual, but a new subject, by its nature communional, by dint of the sacrament of baptism, which establishes a reciprocal immanence of the faithful in the Church and the latter in the faithful.

In order that the special nature of the rights of the faithful are not however erroneously interpreted as a trivialisation of their constitutional significance, can. 221 provides for the possibility of their legitimate juridical defence. While the legislator of 1983 has not provided a true and proper administrative procedure for the protection of the rights of the faithful, still the normative of the Code on hierarchical recourse against administrative decrees (cans. 1732-1739) certainly demonstrates a certain sensibility towards the urgency of making ready ever more efficient juridical instruments in order to overcome the dialectic between person and collectivity and therefore ever more suitable for efficaciously realising the *bonum communionis* of the Church.

---

[114] Cf. P. Krämer, *Kirchenrecht II. Ortskirche-Gesamtkirche,* Stuttgart-Berlin-Köln 1993, pp. 28-32, above all p. 30.

[115] On how it was Hegel who considered, positivistically, how the highest duty of the individual, that of being a member of the State, bearer of the supreme right against the single, cf. A. Verdross, *Abendländische Rechtsphilosophie,* Wien 1963, pp. 128-163.

[116] E. Corecco, *Il catalogo dei doveri-diritti del fedele nel CIC,* op. cit., p. 116.

[117] A summarising schema of the different positions is proposed by: H.J.F. Reinhardt, in: *MK, Einführung vor 208/7.*

4. CONFIRMATION

Confirmation is not a useless ceremony or a simple catechesis, but a *verum et proprium sacramentum*[118]. This tridentine definition is the fruit of a long and complex history, which begins, in the early centuries of the Christian era when in the liturgical rite of this sacrament it was still difficult to establish with exactitude where baptism ended and confirmation began. In fact, the first conciliar text that distinguishes with clarity the rite of baptism from the "laying on of hands or benediction" proper to confirmation is due to the Council of Elvira, celebrated in the IV Century, which was also followed a little later by the progressive prevalence of the use (except in Italian) of the term confirmation over that of *chrism*[119]. The Vatican Council II repeated in a few lines the essential doctrinal contents of this long becoming aware of the fact that confirmation is a true and proper sacrament and not simply a development of baptism, and in doing so opened up the way towards a more precise determination of its juridical effects.

4.1 CONFIRMATION IN THE VATICAN COUNCIL II AND THE CIC

A) CONCILIAR TEACHING

The Fathers of the Vatican Council II after having stated that with baptism the faithful are "incorporated into the Church" (LG 11,1) immediately specify that "with the sacrament of confirmation they are more perfectly bound to the Church and are endowed with the special strength of the Holy Spirit. Hence they are, as true witnesses of Christ, more strictly obliged to spread the faith by word and deed" (LG 11,1). This specification contains the three fundamental elements of Catholic doctrine on the sacrament of confirmation: 1. This sacrament strengthens the bond with the Church; 2. It communicates a gift or special strength of the Holy Spirit; 3. It enables the spreading and defence of the faith as true witnesses of Jesus Christ.

The first element, that fixed by the expression *perfectius Ecclesiae vinculantur*, on the one hand defines confirmation as the crowning and perfection of baptism, and on the other shows how the conciliar ecclesiological teaching on the gradualness of communion also has a meaning too within the *communio plena* of the Catholic Church. Belonging to this is not something exact and static, but a dynamic progress within which each of the three sacraments of Christian initiation has a specific role. That of confirmation is specified by the second and third element of the conciliar definition. The gift of a special strength of the Holy Spirit through this sacrament, comparable with the experience of Pentecost[120], is something different from the gift of the same Holy Spirit in the washing and regeneration of baptism because "whoever is born by baptism into the Christian life (1Cor 12,13) must grow and mature in his life until he becomes a perfect Christian in the likeness of Christ and reaches the age of adulthood through the fullness of the Holy Spirit (Eph 4, 13-14)"[121]. The specificity of this gift

---

[118] Cf. *Tridendinum*, Sess. 7, *De sacr.*, can. 1 (=DS, no. 1628).

[119] On the historical evolution of the sacrament, cf. A. Montaza, *Confermazione*, in: NDDC, op. cit., pp.262-276, above all pp. 263-264.

[120] Cf. P. Fransen, *Firmung*, in: LThK, Vol. IV (Freiburg im Br. 1960), pp. 145-152, here p. 150.

[121] A. Mostaza, *Confermazione*, op. cit., p. 265. For an analysis of LG 11,1 cf. G. Philips, *La Chiesa e il suo mistero nel Concilio Vaticano II*, op. cit., pp. 142-143.

of the Holy Spirit is seen above all in the fact that the believer is enabled to spread and defend the faith as a qualified witness, because if in baptism he is reborn *ad vitam* in the sacrament of confirmation he is strengthened *ad pugnam*, as the Fathers of the Church stated. Through "the anointing with chrism on the forehead, which is done with the laying on of the hand and through the words: *Receive the seal of the gift of Holy Spirit*" [122], the believer becomes a *miles Christi* and as such deputed "to the apostolate by the Lord himself" (AA 3,1)

This right-duty to the apostolate, in which is expressed the "participation in the saving mission of the Church" (LG 33,2) of all the faithful, if on the one hand is based on the sacrament of baptism, on the other receives its full legitimisation in confirmation because strengthening the bond of belonging to the Church it realises in a wholly special way the conciliar principle according to which the sacraments "communicate and nourish the love of God and of man which is the soul of the whole apostolate" (LG 33,2).

Alongside this synthesis of Catholic doctrine on confirmation, in the conciliar texts are also found some suggestions concerning one of the thorny theological questions relative to the administration of this sacrament: that of the minister. In LG 26,3 it is stated that bishops are "the original ministers of confirmation"; in no. 13 of the *Decree on Eastern Catholic Churches* it is specified however that: "The discipline concerning the minister of holy chrism, in force from ancient times among the Eastern Churches, is to be fully restored. Therefore the priests have the power to confer this sacrament using the chrism blessed by their patriarch or the bishop" (OE 13). On the problem, never definitively resolved, of the age of those to be confirmed, the conciliar Fathers make no explicit reference. This indirect relativisation of the problem then develops into the attempt, made by Pope Paul VI in the new *Ordo confirmationis* [123], to reconcile the two predominant ways of posing the question; that of those who hold that confirmation should be administered at the age of discretion and that of those who instead prefer to defer the celebration of this sacrament to the age of adolescence.

B) THE PRINCIPLE NORMS OF THE CODE

The three fundamental elements (the more perfect bond with the Church, the special gift of the Holy Spirit and being deputed to witness) of the conciliar definition of the sacrament of confirmation are, at least on the general level, accepted by the ecclesiastical legislator of 1983 in can. 879, which states: "The sacrament of confirmation confers a character. By it the baptised continue their path of Christian initiation. They are enriched with the gift of the Holy Spirit, and are more closely linked with the Church. They are made strong and more firmly obliged by word and deed to witness to Christ and to spread and defend the faith". In the remaining norms of the Code on confirmation (cans. 880-896) the ecclesial dimension of this sacrament and its link with the rights and duties of the faithful lay person [124] is neither mentioned not testified to in a sufficient way.

---

[122] Paul VI, CA *Divinae consortium naturae*, in: AAS 63 (1971), pp. 657-664, here p. 663.

[123] The *editio typica* was published in the Vatican City in 1971 and entered into force on 22 August 1971 (cf. AAS 64, 1972, p. 77).

[124] Cf. can. 225 §1.

If the strict rapport of confirmation with baptism is underlined by can. 893 §2, in which the ecclesiastical legislator rightly advises that those who assumed the same obligation in baptism should be chosen as the godfather or godmother, the conciliar suggestions concerning the solution of the problem of the minister of this sacrament and the age of those to be confirmed are accepted only in part [125].

In can. 882 once again the tridentine term of *minister ordinarius* is preferred to the conciliar term *minister originarius*, undervaluing the fact that with the latter not only did they wish to simply respect the discipline of the Eastern Catholic Churches, but also to say something both about the power of priests in the ordering of the administration of confirmation and on the ecclesial dimension of this sacrament. In fact, on the one hand, all Eastern priests can validly confer this sacrament, whether together with baptism or separately, to all of the faithful of whatever rite, the Latin not excluded, observing for liceity the prescriptions of both common and particular law [126], and on the other in order to testify to the link of the significance of confirmation with a more complete insertion into the ecclesial communion provoked by this could suffice for a more marked underlining of the following criteria. First of all, only the diocesan bishop always administers confirmation validly in every circumstance and in every place (can. 886), while priests can do it only by dint of a special relationship (based on a *mandate* or by virtue of an *office*) with the diocesan authority and exclusively within the limits of the territory designated by them (can. 887). In the second place, this link with the particular Church [127] is already highlighted by the disposition according to which "The chrism to be used in the sacrament of confirmation must have been consecrated by a Bishop, even when the sacrament is administered by a priest" (can. 880 §2). Still, even if the ecclesiastical legislator has not formally accepted the term of original minister, he ended up by making the principal consequences of this conciliar teaching his own, as demonstrated in can. 882, which surprisingly does not apply to the priest armed with the faculty to administer this sacrament the opposite term of extraordinary, and cans. 883 and 884, in which is enormously widened the circle of priests who, either *ipso iure* or by *particular concession* or finally because associated for a serious reason, can validly administer confirmation. Besides, except there be the extension of a mandate or a concession coming substantially into play here, in case of error or doubt there is nothing against the application of the principle *supplet Ecclesia*, as can. 144 §2, among others, explicitly states.

Also in reference to the age of those to be confirmed, by nature substantially pastoral, the CIC does not prescribe anything taxative. While can. 842 §2 affirms that baptism, confirmation and Eucharist are "required together for full Christian initiation", from this disposition the ecclesiastical legislator does not draw the consequence that the order of the triad be taxative [128]. More so, after having stated that the sacra-

---

[125] For a detailed analysis in this regard, cf. R. Ahlers, *Firmung*, in: *Ecclesia a Sacramentis*, op. cit., pp. 37-52, especially pp. 43-50.

[126] OE 14; cf. also can. 694/CCEO.

[127] Agreeing on the necessity of emphasising this link and the particular responsibility of the diocesan bishop: H. Schmitz, *Taufe, Firmung, Eucharistie*, op. cit., p. 390; Y. Congar, *Der Heilige Geist*, Freiburg 1982, p. 458.

[128] Of another opinion seems to be: F. Hölzl, *Die Sakramente der Eingliederung in ihrer rechtlichen Gestalt und ihren rechtlichen Wirkungen vom zweiten Vatikanischen Konzil bis*

ment of confirmation is to be administered to the faithful at the age of discretion and therefore only after the completion of the seventh year [129], he leaves, however, to the Conferences of bishops the faculty to determine another age and this certainly does not exclude a priori that the liturgical order of the sacraments of Christian initiation can be inverted, in the sense that confirmation can be administered even after first communion, a usage that was widespread for the first time in France only towards the middle of the XIX Century [130].

The uncertainty over the question of the age at which this sacrament must be administered and especially concerning its link with the Eucharist does not impede the legislator however from seeing in confirmation the premise for the liceity of determined acts of the faithful.

C) CONFIRMATION AS THE PREMISE FOR DETERMINED JURIDICAL ACTS

If without baptism it is not possible to be admitted validly to the other sacraments, confirmation included [131], this latter is in its turn required for the liceity of determined juridical acts. And more precisely for the following: Admission to a major seminary (can. 241 §2); 2. Admission to the novitiate (can. 645 §1); 3. Assumption of the obligation of godfather or godmother to a candidate for baptism (can. 874 §1,3) and a candidate for confirmation (can. 893 §1); 4. Promotion to Holy Orders (can. 1033); 5. Admission to the sacrament of marriage (can. 1065 §1). The insistence of the Vatican Council II on the fact that confirmation realises a more perfect belonging to the Church should have suggested to the ecclesiastical legislator the reservation of the fulfilment of some services or the assumption of some offices, as for example the participation in various synodal councils or consultative organs [132], exclusively to the baptised who have also received the sacrament of confirmation. Besides the Eucharistic communion being the fullest form of the ecclesial communion, the fact that can. 912 on the admission to holy communion and can. 914 on admission to first communion do not make any reference to confirmation certainly does not facilitate the understanding of what the conciliar principle according to which all of the sacraments "are bound up with and directed to the blessed Eucharist" (can. 897) means on the structural and juridical level.

The insufficient clarity on the links between confirmation and the Eucharist, as well as between this sacrament of Christian initiation and the communitarian and missionary life of the Church has prevented the ecclesiastical legislator from specifying deep down the juridical consequences of this sacrament and in particular its role in the constitution of the Church.

4.2 CONSTITUTIONAL TYPE QUESTIONS

On the constitutional level there are two fundamental questions connected with the administration of the sacrament of confirmation: that of the reception of a baptised

---

zum Codex Iuris Canonici von 1983, Regensburg 1988, p. 187.

[129] Cf. cans. 891 and 97 §2.

[130] In this regard, cf. A. Mostaza, *Confermazione*, op. cit., pp. 272-274.

[131] Cf. cans. 889 §1 and 842 §1.

[132] In this regard, cf. H. Schmitz, *Taufe, Firmung, Eucharistie*, op. cit., p.391.

non-Catholic into full communion with the Church and that relating to the full exercise of the rights and duties of the lay faithful.

A) THE RECEPTION OF BAPTISED NON-CATHOLICS INTO FULL COMMUNION WITH THE CHURCH

Every baptised person outside of the Catholic Church "has the right, for reasons of conscience, to freely decide to enter into the full Catholic communion"[133]. In the knowledge that it was dealing with a very important and delicate question, the Vatican Council II has fixed three fundamental criteria to conveniently regulate this reception of the non-Catholic baptised into full communion with the Church. First of all it has to be kept in mind that "the work of preparing and reconciling those individuals who wish for full Catholic communion is of its nature distinct from ecumenical action" (UR 4,4); in the second place, precisely because it is such and of great constitutional relevance, this work must be developed with absolute respect for the principle according to which no-one "can be forced to embrace the faith against his will" (DH 10); in the third and last place " in order to restore communion and unity or preserve them, *one must impose no burden beyond what is indispensable* (Acts 15,28)" (UR 18). Specifying these criteria, in the *Rite for the Christian Initiation of Adults* the Sacred Congregation for Divine Worship has provided a special *Rite for the Reception into Full Communion with the Catholic Church of those who have already been Validly Baptised.*

In the Code of Canon Law, in contrast to the CCEO, which dedicates the whole of Title XVII to this theme (cans. 896-901), no emphasis is made of this. It is necessary therefore to make reference to the liturgical and ecumenical norms, without forgetting how much is laid down in can. 869 concerning the validity of baptism, to resolve this question. In particular with reference to the recognition of the validity of confirmation, an indispensable premise for admission into full communion with the Catholic Church, it is once again necessary to distinguish between the Eastern Churches and the other Churches or non-Catholic ecclesial communities. For the former it needs to be kept in mind that in these "the sacrament of confirmation (chrismation) is lawfully administered by a priest contemporaneously with baptism; it can however happen with a certain frequency that the canonical certification of the baptism does not make any mention of confirmation. This does not in fact authorise the putting in doubt that the confirmation has also been conferred"[134]. For the latter, on the other hand, the following has to be kept in mind: "To the actual state of our relations with the ecclesial communities coming from the Reformation of the XVI Century, we have not yet arrived at an agreement either on the meaning, or on the sacramental nature or on the administration of the sacrament of confirmation. Consequently, in the actual circumstances, the persons who would enter into the full communion of the Church and who should come from these communities, must receive the sacrament of confirmation according to the rite and teaching of the Catholic Church before being admitted to the Eucharistic Communion"[135].

---

[133] *Directory for the application of the principles and norms on ecumenism*, op. cit., no. 99.

[134] Ibid., no. 99 a).

[135] Ibid., no. 101.

B) THE RIGHTS AND DUTIES OF THE LAY FAITHFUL

The suggestion of LG 33,2 concerning the possibility of seeing in the sacrament of confirmation the legitimisation of the full exercise of the rights and duties, founded in baptism, on the part of all the faithful, and in particular on the part of the lay faithful, finds a partial confirmation in the beginning of can. 225 §1, which states: "Since lay people, like all Christ's faithful, are deputed to the apostolate by baptism and confirmation, they are bound by the general obligation and they have the right, whether as individuals or in associations, to strive so that the divine message of salvation may be known and accepted by all people throughout the world. This obligation is all the more insistent in circumstances in which only through them are people able to hear the Gospel and to know Christ". To place the study of the rights and duties of the *Christifidelis laicus* in this chapter is not only legitimate but could help to overcome the dialectic between those who want them to be exclusively linked to baptism and those who on the other hand want to relegate them exclusively to the sphere of the married lay faithful.

In fact in the conciliar vision of the People of God, as can easily be deduced from LG 31, the states of life with their rights and duties are not watertight compartments opposed to one another. All three states of life have a constitutional character and are connected to each other in a circular relationship of reciprocal integration, because "in the church-communion the states of life are so bound up together among themselves as to be directed one to the other. Certainly common, even more so unique is their deep meaning: that of being the manner according to which the equal Christian dignity and the universal vocation to sanctity in the perfection of love are to be lived. They are modalities at the one time diverse and complementary, so that each one of these has its own original and unmistakable physiognomy and at the same time each of these can place itself in relation to the others and at their service" [136]. In this way, the clerical state of life by dint of the exercise of the ministerial priesthood is primarily bound to guarantee the permanent sacramental presence of Jesus Christ and the unity of the whole ecclesial community; the religious state through the charism of the evangelical counsels is primarily called to testify to the eschatological character of the Church; the lay state on the other hand finds "its specificity in its secular character and performs a ecclesial service in witnessing to and recalling for, in its own way, priests, male and female religious the meaning that earthly and temporal realities have in God's salvific plan" [137].

The Vatican Council II had already underlined that "their secular character is proper and peculiar to the laity" that is to say that "they are to seek the Kingdom of God by engaging in temporal affairs and directing them according to God's will" (LG 31,2). The quoted EA *Christifidelis laici* deepens however the reflection on the indoles saecularis of the state of life of the lay faithful by employing two important specifications: 1. Secularity as a specific and proper form of the lay state of life can be lived as a value in the wide sense in the other ecclesial states of life also and knows therefore a certain gradualness in its realisation; 2. This is not simply a sociological note but a theological category, which as such characterises not only the mission of the

---

[136] John Paul II, *Christifideles laici, no. 55.*, in: AAS 81 (1989) 393-421.
[137] Ibid., no. 55.

Church in the world but also its self-structuring as a unitarian missionary subject. The first specification – based on LG 35,2 – means that the secularity of the lay person is the missionary element that guarantees to the Church, and therefore to the whole plan of redemption, a structural and permanent link with the plan of creation, that is to say with natural and historical reality [138]. The secularity of the laity, thus conceived, finds therefore in the sacrament of marriage its ecclesiologically most relevant expression, because through this the essential constitutive elements of secularity (liberty, fruitfulness, propriety) are thoroughly realised. The second specification means that, even on the juridical level, the secular character is the specific and prevalent manner in which the lay faithful are called to participate – by dint of baptism and above all confirmation – in the exercise of the *tria munera*, and therefore also in the exercise of the *munera regendi*. In fact, pastors "helped by the experience of the laity, are in a position to judge more clearly and appropriately in spiritual as well as in temporal matters" (LG 37,4)

Unfortunately these two fundamental clarifications on the specific constitutional significance of the very secularity of the lay faithful, already substantially traceable in the conciliar texts, are evidently ignored by the ecclesiastical legislator who, in compiling the list of the rights and duties of the lay faithful (cans. 224-231), allows himself to be guided more by the contingent intention of promoting their active participation than by the desire to define with precision their juridical statute [139]. As a result of this of all of the cases in point of the rights and duties listed in this catalogue at least six are attributable indiscriminately to all of the faithful: the right-duty to "strive, whether as individuals or in associations, so that the divine message of salvation may be known and accepted by all people throughout the world" (can. 225 §1); the right to be admitted, if suitable, to ecclesiastical offices and functions (can. 228 §1); the faculty of being actively consulted as experts (can. 228 §2); the right to the study and teaching of theology (can. 229 §2 and §3); the right to exercise liturgical ministries (can. 230); and finally the right to a worthy remuneration for those who perform particular services (can. 231 §2). Moreover among the cases in point attributable to the lay faithful, some – as for example those provided for in cans. 228 and 230 – are attributable both to the laity living in the world and members of Institutes of consecrated life and others – as for example those provided for in can. 226 – are attributable both to lay people married and living in the world and married clerics [140]. In conclusion, only two rights and duties are attributable in an exclusive way to the laity faithful by dint of their secular character: the duty to "permeate and perfect the temporal order of things with the spirit of the Gospel" (can. 225 §2) and the right to enjoy the freedom necessary to fulfil this mission in an adequate manner (can. 227). Making up part of this freedom is also the right to gather together for this purpose, as an important lay specification of the freedom of association recognised for all the faithful by can. 215.

---

[138] For a full development of this conception of lay secularity, cf. H.U. von Balthasar, *Christlicher Stand,* Einsiedeln 1977, pp. 51-314 and E. Corecco, *I laici nel nuovo Codice di diritto canonico,* in: La Scuola Cattolica 112 (1984), pp. 194-218.

[139] For a detailed analysis of this catalogue in the light of conciliar teaching, cf. E. Braunbeck, *Der Weltcharakter der Laien. Eine theologisch-rechtliche Untersuchung im Licht des II. Vatikanischen Konzils,* Regensburg 1993, pp. 133-136 and pp. 262-270.

[140] These matters in hand are then developed in cans. 793-806.

All the other rights and duties of the lay faithful contained in the Code's list are not based on the secular character of their ecclesial state of life, but more or less directly on their sacramental participation (that is to say by dint of their baptism and confirmation) in the exercise of the three offices of Jesus Christ. As such they are not specific to the laity but common to all the faithful not invested with the sacrament of orders, and for that reason the argument will also necessarily be repeated in the chapter dedicated to *sacra potestas*. Here it is sufficient to point out how the specific participation of the laity in the exercise of these offices, and above all in the office of governance, is not juridically regulated in an organic way in the CIC[141]. On the contrary, precisely on this level, the ecclesiastical legislator sometimes falls into contradiction with the conciliar principles, accepted in the same Code of Canon Law. For example to limit to the laity of the male sex the possibility of stably assuming the ministries of lector and acolyte (can. 230 §1) is in clear contradiction not only with the principle of equality among all the faithful (can. 208), but above all with the principle of distinction between these ministries, conceived as autonomous liturgical services, and the same ministries conceived as important stages or moments in the formation for the diaconate and priesthood[142], a distinction adequately guaranteed by can. 1035.

5. PENANCE

Both the new *Ordo Paenitentiae* (1973), and the Code of Canon Law of 1983 reaffirm on the one hand that "individual and integral confession, with its relative absolution, remain the ordinary means, thanks to which the faithful are reconciled with God and with the Church", and on the other that this free personal choice has a specific ecclesial dimension, rooted in baptism and flourishing in the Eucharist[143]. Indeed, the Church has always been conscious of the analogy existing between the sacrament of baptism and that of penance, so much so that the latter represents a *renovata gratia* of the former, in relation to which it has also been defined as *paenitentia secunda*[144]. This means that the sacrament of penance, to the same degree as baptism, is an act at the same time personal and communitarian, as for every other authentically ecclesial action and especially the sacramental. It is therefore under this double perspective that its theological contents and juridical outlines are briefly to be illustrated.

---

[141] For an articulated documentation of this opinion, cf. E. Corecco, *I laici nel nuovo Codice.* op. cit., pp. 213-218.

[142] Cf. Paul VI, MP *Ministeria quaedam*, in: AAS 64 (1973), p. 533 and the commentary of: H.J.F. Reinhardt, in: *MK, can. 230/3*; P. Krämer, *Kirchenrecht II*, op. cit., pp. 33-34.

[143] Cf. *Ordo Paenitentiae* no. 31 and nos. 1-2; cans. 959 and 960.

[144] Cf. Tertullian, *De Paenitentiae, 7, 10.* Particularly suggestive is the way with which Saint Ambrose explains the link between baptism and penance: "Water and tears are not lacking in the Church: the water of baptism, the tears of penance" (*Epist.* 41, 12: PL 16, 1116). On the baptism-penance-Eucharist link, cf. F. Sottocornola, *Penitenza (Sacramento della)* in: *Dizionario Teologico Interdisciplinare*, Torino 1977, Vol. II, pp. 690-706, here p. 691. For the doctrinal history of the sacrament, the work of B. Poschmann, *Paenitentia secunda,* Bonn 1940 remains fundamental.

5.1 THE THEOLOGICAL-JURIDICAL STRUCTURE OF THE SACRAMENT

A) THE TEACHING OF THE VATICAN COUNCIL II

The inseparability of the personal element from the ecclesial in the sacrament of penance was highlighted in its canonical significance by Klaus Mörsdorf before the Vatican Council II when he explicitly states that "the *pax cum Ecclesia* is the sacramental cause of the *pax cum Deo*"[145]. The Fathers of the Council speak of this link, without exactly determining its nature: "Those who approach the sacrament of penance obtain pardon from God's mercy for the offence committed against him, and are, at the same time, reconciled with the Church which they have wounded by their sins and which by charity, by example and by prayer labours for their conversion" (LG 11,2). The expression *simul reconciliatur* cum Ecclesia (substantially identical to that of PO 5,1) contains a fundamental theological truth: in the Church sin, insofar as it is a personal fault, is never a private matter. This, when it is serious, cuts deeply into the communion not only between the faithful and Christ, but also between the individual baptised and the Church, because full incorporation into this – as LG 14,2 teaches – presupposes the possession of grace, highlighted by the conciliar expression *qui Spiritum Christi habentes*[146]. Consequently "anyone who is conscious of grave sin, without having been to sacramental confession" (or made an act of perfect contrition which includes the resolve to go to confession as soon as possible) cannot approach – as established by can. 916 – Eucharistic communion. This reciprocal connection between the personal and communal aspect of the sacrament of penance is also reflected in the rest of the normative of the code relative to this.

B) THE PRINCIPAL NORMS OF THE CODE

Right from the systematic imposition of the matter (cans. 959-997) we can sense that the ecclesiastical legislator has substantially accepted the conciliar teaching on the sacrament of penance: after an introductory canon and a first chapter on the different liturgical forms of the sacrament of penance, an entire chapter (the second) is dedicated to its ecclesial value, emerging above all in sacramental absolution bestowed by the ordained minister, and another (the third) to the personal dispositions the faithful must assume as a penitent to effectively receive the sacrament of penance. The addition of a fourth chapter on indulgences does not change the substance of the discussion.

Can 959, which introduces the normative of the Code on penance, states: "In the sacrament of penance the faithful who confess their sins to a lawful minister, are sorry for their sins and have a proper purpose of amendment, receive from God, through the absolution given by that minister, forgiveness of sins they have committed after baptism, and at the same time they are reconciled with the Church, which by sinning they wounded". Notwithstanding a little complex stylistic form, this canon enumerates all the essential elements of theological teaching on the sacrament of penance:

---

[145] K. Mörsdorf. Lb. Vol. II, p. 63.

[146] For an analysis of LG 14,2 cf. F. Coccopalmerio, *Sacramento della penitenza e communione della Chiesa*, in: Strumento internazionale per un lavoro teologico: Communio 40 (1978), pp. 54-64.

the element formed by the actuation of the common priesthood, which expresses the necessary personal and active collaboration of the penitent in the sacramental act, and the element constituted by the sacramental absolution in which is expressed the ministerial priesthood, and which represents the very form of the sacrament.

The parts forming the first element are: the accusation or *confessio* of sins before a lawful minister, that is authorised by the Church according to the specific norms established by the ecclesiastical legislator in cans. 965-986; contrition or *contritio*, which constitutes the very principle of conversion or evangelical *metanoia*, only if it is at one and the same time "a clear and decisive repudiation of the sin committed"[147]; the satisfaction or *satisfactio* which concretises the "purpose of amendment" by dint of justifying grace, with which the sacrament transforms simple penance into a gesture of love for Christ, according to the Thomist adage: *ex atritio fit contritus*[148].

The second element, that is sacramental absolution or *absolutio*, which can only be validly bestowed by a priest invested with the necessary faculties (can. 966), is "a sort of judiciary action" which not only possess "a therapeutic or medicinal character"[149], but brings about a full reincorporation into the ecclesial communio according to all its dimensions, as the same introductory canon testifies to with the emphases on the forgiveness of God and reconciliation with the Church after baptism.

5.2 PARTICULAR QUESTIONS

A) GENERAL ABSOLUTION

Already the first of the *Normae Pastorales Sacramentum Paenitentiae*, issued on the 16 June 1972 by the *Sacra Congregatio Pro Doctrina Fidei*[150], affirms in a lapidary manner that in the celebration of the sacrament "the teaching of the Council of Trent must be firmly retained and faithfully applied in practice", according to which by "divine precept" and for the "greatest good of souls" it is necessary that "individual and integral confession with absolution" remains "the only ordinary means, thanks to which the faithful are reconciled with God and with the Church, unless a physical or moral impossibility excuses them from such a confession". This norm is repeated almost to the letter both in no. 31 of the *Ordo Paenitentiae* and in can. 960. This means that in the celebration of the sacrament of penance the first liturgical form – that is the reconciliation of the individual penitent – "constitutes the only normal and ordinary manner of the sacramental celebration, and it can be neither allowed to fall into disuse or be neglected", while the third liturgical form – that is to say the reconciliation of more than one penitent with general confession and absolution – "takes on a character of exceptionality, and is not, therefore, left to free choice but is regulated by an appropriate discipline"[151].

---

[147] Cf. John Paul II, *Reconciliatio et paenitentia*, in: AAS 77 (1985), pp. 185-275, no. 31.

[148] Cf. for example IV Sent. d. 22 q. 2a. 1 sol. 3, quoted by K. Rahner, *Penitenza (Sacramento della)*, in: *SacrM*, Vol. VI (1976), coll. 305-332, here coll. 326; cf. also cans. 959 and 987.

[149] Cf. John Paul II, *Reconciliatio et paenitentia*, op. cit., no.31.

[150] Cf. AAS 64 (1972), pp. 510-514 and EV Vol. IV, pp. 1042-1053, here p. 1045.

[151] John Paul II, *Reconciliatio et paenitentia*, op. cit., no. 32. The second liturgical form: the reconciliation of more than one penitent with individual confession and absolution, even if it underlines greatly the communitarian aspect of the sacrament of penance, is not even mentioned by can. 960, because it is *equiparata alla prima forma per quanto riguarda la*

This latter form requires from the penitent believer – so that he does not fall under the prohibition of can. 915 – not only the normal personal dispositions for validly making use of sacramental absolution, but also the obligation to go to individual confession as soon as possible (can. 962 §1), at least before receiving another general absolution according to the norms of cans. 963 and 989. To the minister of the sacrament, on the other hand, the same discipline records in can. 961 §1 that general absolution can be granted in only two cases: firstly, when there is imminent danger of death; secondly, when there is a serious need, that is when the two different circumstances are simultaneously verified such as the absence of a sufficient number of confessors and the deprivation for a long time of sacramental grace and Eucharistic communion, through no fault of the penitents. This state of necessity, still according to the canonical legislator, is not however normally verified on the occasion of solemnities or pilgrimages with a great gathering together of people. It is up to the diocesan bishop nevertheless (can. 961 §2) to issue a judgment concerning the concrete verification or not of the conditions established by the law for collective absolution in cases of necessity. The responsibility for this judgment is exercised not only keeping in mind the criteria agreed upon with the other members of the conference of bishops, but also with respect to the specific warning of the Bishop of Rome: "The exceptional use of the third form of celebration must not lead to a lesser respect, far less an abandonment of the ordinary forms, nor to a retention of such a form as an alternative to the other two; it is not, in fact, left to the freedom of pastors and the faithful to choose between the mentioned forms of celebration which is held to be the most opportune" [152]. The choice revolves exclusively upon the verification or not in a given particular Church of the so-called cases of necessity.

In this regard the European Conferences of Bishops are divided and have created a situation that is unclear both on the normative level and much less so on the pastoral level [153]. We can therefore ask ourselves if faced with the rapid decrease in individual confessions the Swiss and Austrian Conferences of Bishops, recognising in their territory the possibility that the state of necessity provided for in can. 961 can be verified on the vigil of great feasts, have not deep down yielded to the temptation of going out to meet this serious situation seeking to assure for the most possible sacramental value in every form of penitential celebration and therefore have not fallen back into the old pastoral model of sacramentalisation, nowadays more and more held to be inadequate for an authentic work of evangelisation [154].

B) THE FACULTY TO HEAR THE CONFESSIONS OF THE FAITHFUL

In comparison with the 1917 Code the new normative of the code on the valid administration of the sacrament of penance (cans. 965-986) is notably changed and simplified. This rests everything on two pillars: can. 966 on the necessity *ad validitatem* of the

---

normalità del rito. (*Reconciliatio et paenitentiia,* op. cit., no. 32). Consequently, by dint of can. 2, it is necessary to return again to the *Ordo paenitentiae,* op. cit., nos. 22-30.

[152] John Paul II, *Reconciliatio et paenitentia,* op. cit., no. 33.

[153] For a detailed analysis of this complex juridical-pastoral situation, cf. L. Gerosa, *Diritto ecclesiale e pastorale,* Torino 1991, pp. 176-180.

[154] Cf. Ch. von Schönborn, *Sacramento della penitenza, celebrazioni penitenziali ed evangelizzazione,* in: Communio 40 (1978) pp. 65-77, here p. 71.

so-called faculty to habitually hear the confession of the faithful, and can. 967 §2 on the possibility of exercising it *ubique terrarum* [155]. With these two norms the valid administration of the sacrament of penance is more clearly anchored in the sacrament of orders, even if the faculty to hear confessions is not conferred with priestly ordination. In fact, in accordance with can. 966 §2, this is conferred *ipso iure* or by concession of the competent authority. In conformity with the Council's teaching on the unity of *sacra potestas*, can. 966 §1 presupposes that the priest has received with priestly ordination all of the *munera* – and thus also the *munus* to remit sins – of which the *sacra potestas* is made, but specifies at the same time that in order to validly exercise this *munus* [156] he needs to receive the *facultas* to exercise it. In other words, this faculty is not something that is added to the outside of the sacred power given by the sacrament of orders, but simply the capacity to validly exercise this sacred power in the service of building up the ecclesial communion [157].

This interpretation of can. 966 based on the fact that the Vatican Council II never made reference to the traditional distinction between *potestas ordinis* and *potestas iurisdictionis,* is confirmed by the absolutely new disposition of can. 967 §2, according to which priests enjoy the "faculty habitually to hear confessions, whether by virtue of their office or by virtue of a concession of the Ordinary of either the place of incardination or that in which they have a domicile, can exercise that faculty everywhere". Finally, both can. 976 (according to which every priest, even if he is deprived of the faculty to hear confessions, validly and licitly absolves all penitents who find themselves in danger of death), and can. 144 §2 (which explicitly applies to this matter the principle of *supplet Ecclesia*), permit the conclusion that nothing is opposed under the theological outline to the ever more explicit underlining in the Code of the strict connection between priestly ordination and the administration of the sacrament of penance [158].

C) THE SACRAMENTAL SEAL AND THE OTHER DUTIES OF THE CONFESSOR

Can. 983 distinguishes the sacramental seal from the obligation of the secret of confession. The former is inviolable and prohibits the confessor from betraying the penitent, even partially, by words or in any other way and for any other reason; the second is the obligation to which a possible interpreter is bound as well as everyone else who through a confession in any way comes to the knowledge of sins. For the direct violation of the sacramental seal can. 1388 §1 provides for excommunication *latae sententiae* reserved to the Apostolic See; for the indirect violation of the sacramental seal as well as for any violation of the secret of confession the same canon provides for the possibility of applying a canonical sanction *ferendae sententiae,* not excluding excommunication.

---

[155] For a clear and concise presentation of this normative of the code, cf. L. Mistò, *Il libro IV: La funzione di sanctificare nella Chiesa,* in: *Il nuovo Codice di diritto canonico. Studi,* Torino 1985, pp. 165-193, here pp. 185-188.

[156] The legitimacy of this specification is based on can. 841.

[157] Cf. H. Müller, *Die Ausübung der geistlichen Vollmacht im Sakrament der Versöhnung,* in: *Erfahrungen mit dem Bußsakrament,* hrsg. von K. Baumgartner, Bd. II, München 1979, pp. 432-445, here p. 440.

[158] This is the conclusive opinion of P. Krämer, *Kirchenrecht I,* op. cit., p. 92.

Besides this fundamental obligation, the confessor is also bound to a series of other juridical-pastoral obligations listed in cans. 978-982 and 984-986. Among these acquire a particular importance, in the light of what has been said of the right to the sacraments and on the protection of the rights of the *Christifidelis*, both can. 980 and can. 984. The former affirms that if the confessor does not have any doubts about the disposition of the penitents and these ask for absolution, the latter cannot either be deferred or much less denied. The latter, on the other hand, affirms that the confessor, and in particular one who is constituted in authority, is absolutely forbidden to use the knowledge gained from a confession to the detriment of the penitent, even if any danger of violation of the confessional secret is excluded.

5.3 PENANCE AND CANONICAL SANCTIONS

In the law of the Church from the Council of Trent on the distinction between the *forum externum* and the *forum internum*, unknown as much to Roman jurisconsultants as the modern civilists, has been ever more affirmed. This is the daughter of the distinction between the *forum paenitentiale* and the *forum iudiciale*, with which the classical study of Canon Law determined the distinction between canonical penitential discipline and procedural law. Unfortunately in the modern era the internal forum has been erroneously reduced to the *forum conscientiae* and consequently the binominal external forum and internal forum has been identified with that of law and morality. Conscience, on the other hand, as the place for the direct relationship of the individual with God can never be mistaken for the internal forum which simply represents a manner, different from the external forum, with which the ecclesiastical authority acts out its *sacra potestas*. The latter always binds the conscience of whoever acts in the external or internal forum and therefore the two fora cannot be separated one from the other, more so that both, and not just the external forum, are of a juridical nature [159].

Analogously, as can easily be deduced from the ancient discipline of public penance, the sacrament of penance and the system of canonical sanctions while being two distinct realities are not separate, but have different points of contact and therefore common: on the one hand in the Church every crime presupposes a serious fault, which as such defers always to the sacrament of penance; on the other the canonical sanction which the delinquent incurs can – under determined conditions – also be remitted to the internal sacramental forum and therefore during the act of confession. This possibility is nothing less than an anomalous fact within the Church and in some way reveals the strange nature of canonical sanctions. It is however legitimate to take the starting point of this in order to understand the ecclesial significance of the whole system of canonical sanctions.

A) THE SACRAMENT OF PENANCE AND THE REMISSION OF A CANONICAL SANCTION

A canonical sanction can cease through the death of the culprit or simply by the fact that the determined time has expired for which it was imposed. More often it ceases

---

[159] In this regard cf. K. Mörsdorf, *Der Kirchenbann im Lichte der Unterscheidung zwischen äußerem und innerem Bereich,* in: Idem, *Schriften zum kanonischen Recht,* hrsg. von W. Aymans-K.Th. Geringer-H. Schmitz, Paderborn-München-Wien-Zürich 1989, pp. 864-876, especially p. 875.

through the remission in the external forum on the part of the competent authority, either through dispensation, if it is a question of a disciplinary type of sanction (can. 1336), or through absolution if it is a question of medicinal sanctions. For the latter absolution often comes in the internal forum and then this is not an act of grace but a juridical act by law up to the culprit who withdraws from the contempt and thus is truly penitent (can. 1358 §1). In any case, can. 1354 states three general principles for the remission of a canonical sanction: 1) all those who can dispense from a law or liberate from a precept can also remit a canonical sanction; 2) the law or precept which constitutes a canonical sanction can moreover also give to others the power to remit it; 3) if the Apostolic See has reserved to itself or others the remission of a canonical sanction, the reservation must be interpreted in the strict sense [160]. On the basis of these principles the Code of Canon Law not only gives full faculty to remit a canonical sanction in the external forum even to whoever is not the author of the law or precept [161], but extends this possibility also to whoever, while not having particular faculties, can still under determined conditions remit a canonical sanction on the internal forum.

In fact there are not a few cases in which a canonical sanction, and especially an excommunication or an interdict, can be remitted in the internal forum for pastoral reasons. These can be summarised thus: 1) A canonical sanction *latae sententiae*, not declared and not reserved to the Apostolic See can be remitted by any bishop or canonical penitentiary in the act of sacramental confession (cans. 1355 and 508); 2) in hospitals, prisons and sea voyages the chaplain has analogous faculties (can. 566 §2); 3) in a *casus urgentior*, that is when it is hard for the penitent to remain in a state of grave sin for the time necessary until the competent superior can provide, any confessor can absolve on the internal forum a *latae sententiae* canonical sanction (excluding suspension), if the same is neither declared nor reserved (can. 1357 §1), and the obligation stands firm to have recourse within a month, under the pain of the reimposition of the sanction; 4) in danger of death every priest, even if deprived of the faculty of hearing confessions, validly and licitly absolves from any canonical sanction (can. 976). These being the essential elements of the normative of the Code relative to the remission of a canonical sanction it is not difficult to intuit the wholly particular nature of the same and above all of excommunication, for ever the sanction-type of the Church.

B) NATURE AND APPLICABILITY OF CANONICAL SANCTIONS

The sixth book of the CIC is entitled *De sanctionibus in Ecclesia* (cans. 1311-1399), almost as if to indicate that there are no true and proper penalties in the Church, but only sanctions. We will see later on the difference between the two ideas, but here it is necessary to remember right from the start that the Code of Canon Law still

---

[160] By law five excommunications are reserved to the Holy See: that relating to the profanation of the Eucharistic species (can. 1367); that for whoever uses physical violence against the Roman Pontiff (can. 1370); that for an episcopal consecration without a mandate (can. 1382); that for violation of the sacramental seal (can. 1388) and finally that envisaged for the absolution of an accomplice (can. 1378 §2). On the whole argument cf. V. De Paolis, *Cessazione della pena*, in: NDDC, pp. 147-152.

[161] Cf. cans. 1355-1356.

speaks of penalties. Can. 1312 distinguishes them into three fundamental categories: censures (cans. 1331-1335), expiatory penalties (cans. 1336-1338) and penal remedies or penances (cans. 1339-1340). The former, known also as medicinal penalties, have as a direct aim the correction or emendation of the offender; the second, previously named *vendicative*, tend directly on the other hand to the reparation of the damage brought upon the community and only indirectly to the conversion of the offender; the third constitute an instrument both to prevent possible crimes and to apply in a manner pastorally consonant with the first two categories of canonical sanctions. Precisely on the level of the applicability of these sanctions what follows has to be kept in mind.

In Canon Law the ultimate criterion for establishing the applicability of a norm is given by the capacity of the latter to express, transparently, the particularity of the ecclesial juridical direction which, as we saw in the first chapter, is not generated by the natural dynamism of human society, but by that specific to grace, knowable only through faith. The question on the applicability of the penal sanctions decreed by the new Code defers therefore to the more general one, issued in all of its radicality within the conflicts and tensions of the process of ecclesiastical renewal initiated by Vatican Council II, concerning belonging to the Church with its own sacramental structure, and its own mission of salvation, when she inflicts penalties upon whoever disobeys canonical laws.

In other words, *De sanctionibus in Ecclesia* would be much more applicable in the actual ecclesial reality the more the ecclesiastical legislator would keep in mind, in the development in detail of this new normative of the code, that the force imprinted by the Council in the axiom *credere non potest homo, nisi volens* (DH 10) was such that many theologians and bishops felt duty bound to ask not only for a revision, but a drastic reduction, if not a downright abrogation, of canonical penal law [162].

If we compare the normative on excommunication of the CIC with the Code's notion of penalty, expressed in *De sanctionibus in Ecclesia*, it appears however difficult to hide their deep divergence and, consequently, the ambiguity of the reply of the ecclesiastical legislator to the insistent request to make clear the ecclesiological significance of the presence of sanctions in the juridical ordering of the Church, in order to avoid rendering insurmountable the ever latent divergence between law and sacrament [163].

From one standpoint, the new CIC threatens excommunication always as a *latae sententiae* sanction, except in two cases: where this is envisaged as possibly making the situation worse, after the interdict and the suspension also inflicted *latae sententiae* (can. 1378 §3), and when the real offence is more serious than the case in hand provided for (can. 1388 §2). In point of fact, even in these cases excommunication

---

[162] There were many interventions on this argument by the bishops of the Synod 1967: cf. G. Caprile. *Il Sinodo dei Vescovi. I. Assemblea generale* (29.9-19.10.1967), Roma 1968, pp. 87-139.

[163] This is the principal content of the vote expressed by the special Committee of the Canon Law Society of America, forwarded to the Holy See together with the official replies of the Committee of American Bishops for Canonical Affairs; cf. J. Provost, *Reaktionen auf den Entwurf zu einem neuen Strafrecht*, in: Concilium 11 (1975), pp. 508-512. On the whole question cf. also: L. Gerosa, *Strafrecht und kirchliche Wirklichkeit. Die Anwendbarkeit der vom neuen Kodex vorgesehenen Strafen*, in: Concilium 22 (1986), pp. 198-204.

can be sanctioned latae sententiae and then, given the seriousness of both offences, the competent authority must declare the same with a decree or sentence. In this way the ecclesiastical legislator, conforming to the principle according to which in Canon Law juridical certainty can never prevail over objective and theological truth, indicates, even if only indirectly, that the canonical institution of the *excommunicatio* is, by its nature, a mere *declaratio*. Further proof of this is the fact that *latae sententiae* excommunication is upheld also in the cases of the so-called crimes of apostasy, heresy and schism, highlighting the theological foundations of the declarative nature of excommunication. This is not an evil inflicted by the will of the ecclesiastical authority, but rather the establishment of a fact: that of non communion, in which the believer places himself by his anti-ecclesial attitude. Even John Paul II has expressed himself in this sense in his first discourse to the Rota: " ... the penalty threatened by the ecclesiastical authority (but which is in reality a recognition of a situation in which the subject himself has placed himself) is to be seen ... as an instrument of communion"[164]. The ecclesiastical authority does not on the whole constitute the situation of a break of the communio, but establishes it and eventually declares it, so that this emerges in the consciousness of the faithful and in that of the whole Church.

On the other hand, the notion of canonical penalty underlying the new CIC is substantially identical to that of the *De delictis et poenis* of the 1917 Code, as can easily be deduced from cans. 1311, 1312, 1341 and 1399. In particular, can. 1341, where the spirit which directs the whole discipline of the Code on canonical sanctions is *maxime perfusus, in recto* invites the Ordinary to inflict or declare a canonical penalty only after having established the failure of all the other ways dictated by pastoral care, while *oblique* affirming that the *reparatio scandalum*, the *restitutio iustitiae* and the *emendatio rei* are the ends of every ecclesiastical penalty; exactly as in the CIC of 1917, in which the legislator made his own the mixed penal theories (and in particular that of the juridical tutelage) developed above all by Catholic penal studies at the end of the 19th century and then systematically integrated into canonical legislation by the educated men of the IPE[165]. But is such a conception of penalty truly applicable to *excommunicatio*, considered by the new Code as a mere *declaratio*?

The response can be nothing other than negative, if we consider the principle effect of excommunication, which consists in the prohibition placed on the excommunicated person of freely approaching the sacrament of penance. In fact, the necessity of obtaining first of all, and in the external forum, the legitimate absolution from the excommunication is not a true and proper *retributio*. Its finality is also not either the *reparatio scandali* or the *restitutio iustitiae*, but rather the protection of the *communio* by means of the full amendment of the faithful, for whom such a prohibition constitutes a motive of greater difficulty, which renders more credible his desire for reconciliation with the Church. On the contrary, precisely this medicinal character does not qualify the prohibition as an *effectum poenale* of excommunication, but rather as an *aggravatio paenitentiae*, that is to say an anticipated penance, analogous with what

---

[164] AAS 71 (1979), p. 415.

[165] For a full analysis of the role of these penal theories in the CIC/1917, cf. L. Gerosa, *La scommunica è una pena? Saggio per una fondazione teologica del diritto penale canonico*, Fribourg 1984, pp. 192-213.

takes place prior to the separation between the sacrament of confession and canonical penal law.

A hypothesis of this nature is not ventured, if we consider it taking can. 1344 as the reading key for *De sanctionibus in Ecclesia*, according to which the ecclesiastical judge, even when the law uses preceptive terms, can substitute a canonical sanction with a *paenitentia*, which formally is not part of the *poenae strictae dictae*. Moreover, this is legitimate both under the historical outline and the systematic, being evident the basic parallelism between the ecclesiastical juridical obligation to request the legitimate absolution from excommunication and the necessity, of a dogmatic order, of approaching the sacrament of penance, when the believer, conscious of having committed a serious sin, wishes to return to full communion with God and the Church. Finally, such a hypothesis is confirmed by the fact that, as we have seen in the previous section, the CIC has increased the *extraordinarias circumstantias* in which the penitent accused can avoid, even if not finding himself in danger of death, recourse to the competent Superior and receive in the internal sacramental forum absolution from a latae sententiae canonical sanction.

This last observation focuses on the fact that, the judgment in which excommunication consists being of a declarative nature, the establishment of full communion depends primarily on the free will of the excommunicate. In fact, in the very moment that the excommunicate withdraws from the contempt he enjoys the so-called *ius absolutionis* and the *remissio poenae* (consisting in another judgment of the declarative type that opens the way to full reconciliation with God and the Church, put into effect by sacramental absolution) cannot be refused him by the legitimate ecclesiastical authority (can. 1358 §1).

Excommunication, sanction-type of the juridical ordering of the Church, is therefore a good way from realising the conception in the Code of penalty, expressed in particular in can. 1341. Far less, being based on a declarative judgment, can this be considered as a must be, as a juridical-moral necessity analogous with a state penalty. On the contrary, keeping in force *latae sententiae* excommunication, of particularly ecclesial origin, the CIC testifies to the substantially declarative nature, as well as the medicinal character of its principal juridical effect, and therefore highlights how this type of canonical sanction does not correspond to the juridical notion of penalty. By the same standard even the other ecclesiastical censures, interdict and suspension, having to be remitted as soon as the offender withdraws from the contempt (can. 1358 §1), are not penalties. A little different is the discourse on the so-called *poenae expiatorie*, which nevertheless – differently from *excommunicatio* – could also not exist. These on the one hand can be applied by the administrative method and on the other can be remitted by means of a *dispensatio*[166]. Moreover for at least two reasons they can be considered as disciplinary measures *sui generis*. In fact, in the first place these do not have any direct influence on the reception of the sacraments, but only on their administration and are therefore normally only applied to clerics, religious and lay people exercising a particular ecclesiastical ministry. In the second place these prohibitions or deprivations, listed in can. 1336 §1, can be applied by the ecclesiastical

---

[166] Cf. A. Arza, *De poenis infligendis via administrativa*, in: *Questioni attuali di diritto canonico*, Roma 1955, pp. 457-476; cf. also can. 1342.

authority only on the basis of the establishment – of certain pastoral relevance – of the non-suitability of the subject of assuming or continuing to fulfil the obligations bound to a determined ecclesiastical ministry [167].

In conclusion, the three censures (excommunication, interdict, suspension) and the disciplinary type sanctions of can. 1336 together form a system of canonical sanctions, which cannot be defined either as true and proper penal law, or as an exclusively disciplinary arrangement.

The equidistance from the two extreme poles, penal and disciplinary, imposed by the particular theological nature of excommunication, guarantees a specific originality to the entire system of sanctions in the Church. This system must be considered for what in fact it is, in the light of its own indispensable relationship with the sacrament of penance: a system of canonical or penitential sanctions of a pastoral-disciplinary character.

5.4 THE PROCEDURES FOR THE DECLARATION OR IMPOSITION OF A CANONICAL SANCTION

In the CIC the fourth part of the seventh book *De processibus* is entitled *De processu poenali* (cans. 1717-1731). In the CCEO the corresponding normative of the Code is entitled *De procedura in poenis irrogandis* (cans. 1468-1487), almost as if wishing to underline a clearer separation from the contentious process which, as has been seen in §9.2, is to be applied as seldom as possible in the Church, it being difficult to reconcile the *strepitus iuris* with pastoral demands. The particular nature of canonical sanctions and a greater attention to the punitive character quoad modum of a true and proper penal process should impose the use of more adequate terms, as for example those proposed in the title of this section. With the common term of canonical procedures there would be thus designated as much the administrative procedure as the judicial process for the declaration or the imposition of a canonical sanction. Regrettably all this is not made clear not even in the systematic order adopted by the ecclesiastical legislator of 1983. In fact the 15 canons dedicated to the material are gathered together in the following three chapters: the first on *The Preliminary Investigation* (cans. 1717-1719), the second on *The Course of the Process* (cans. 1720-1728) and the third *The Action for Damages* (cans. 1729-1731).

The canonical institution dealt with in the last chapter is a contentious action and as such not only is it not an integral part of the penal process, but the judgment on this does not refer to the eventual declaration or imposition of the canonical sanction. This can therefore be resolved outwith the procedural method *ex bono et aequo* (can. 1718 §4), or postponed by the judge even until after the issuing of the definitive sentence (can. 1730 §1), with the aim of avoiding excessive delays. The preliminary investigation, on the other hand, plays a decisive role in directing the possible declaration or imposition of a canonical sanction, because it must furnish the judge above all with the necessary indications concerning the procedure to follow: judicial or administrative. The latter are both then regulated, even if regrettably not in a sufficiently precise systematic order, by the second chapter (cans. 1720-1728).

---

[167] In this regard cf. L. Gerosa, *Diritto ecclesiale e pastorale,* op. cit., pp. 191-192.

A) THE PRELIMINARY INVESTIGATION AND THE CHOICE OF THE ADMINISTRATIVE OR JUDICIAL METHOD

This choice must be made by the Ordinary at the end of the preliminary investigation, common to both the procedures for the declaration or imposition of a canonical sanction, and which can therefore be considered an autonomous juridical institution, with its own nature and finality. Its conclusion represents the true critical point of the canonical penal process and puts into play also the pastoral credibility of the whole procedural law of the Church. It is worth the effort therefore to study separately the norms of the Code which regulate it.

It is a question of cans. 1717-1719, which constitute the normative reply to the pastoral demands placed by can. 1341, which invites the Ordinary to promote one of the two procedures established for the declaration or imposition of a canonical sanction only after having established the failure of fraternal correction and the other methods of pastoral care. The norms contained by these three canons substantially deal with three themes: 1. the acts (notice of the offence and denouncement) which precede the investigation; 2. the object and subjects of the investigation; 3. the different phases of the preliminary investigation. Their normative treatment is directed by the two following fundamental principles: the discretion of whoever conducts the investigation and the protection of the rights of the suspect. Both direct the purposes of the preliminary investigation, as is underlined by the expression *caute inquirat* of can. 1717 §1. These purposes can be thus summarised: "The investigation is directed to furnishing the Ordinary with the information necessary for the assessment of the truth about the committed facts and their author, that is, if the notification of the committing of a crime is or is not with foundation, and to be able in such a way to decide upon the measures to take" [168]. In other words if the object of the investigation is threefold (facts, circumstances, imputability), its ultimate aim is unique: to inform the Ordinary of the certain existence of an offence. In fact, the latter has been committed for certain only if all three of the constitutive elements are simultaneously documented, that is to say: 1) the certain establishment of facts that constitute an external violation of norms protected by a canonical sanction (can. 1321); 2) the absence of circumstances which eliminate the imputability or punishabilty of such violations (cans. 1322-1327); 3) the existence of a serious imputability (can. 1321 §1). At the end of the preliminary investigation, in accordance with can. 1718, the Ordinary must decide on a threefold object: if the elements exist for a process directed to the declaration or imposition of a canonical sanction; if there is the opportunity to do so on the basis of can. 1341 and finally if the judicial or administrative method should be activated. In both of its forms, this process has as its proximate and immediate aim the declaration or the imposition of the canonical sanction, therefore it cannot prescind from the examination also of the culpability of the suspected believer.

In the choice of the judicial or administrative method, being in conformity with the already quoted can. 1718 §1 no.3 it would seem that the Ordinary is completely free and that his choice is subject only to a few restrictions. However, such a canon – as

---

[168] J. Sanchis, *L'indagine previa al processo penale (cans. 1717-1719)*, in: *I procedimenti speciali nel diritto canonico*, Città del Vaticano 1992, pp. 233-266, here p. 241.

has been rightly underlined by various authors [169] – is to be interpreted in the light of the dispositions of can. 1342. At present §2 of this last canon states: "Perpetual penalties cannot be imposed or declared by means of a decree; nor can penalties which the law or precept establishing them forbids to be applied by decree" [170]. The §1 of the same canon moreover specifies the criteria for the choice of one or other procedure in the remaining cases: "Whenever there are just reasons against the use of a judicial procedure, a penalty can be imposed or declared by means of an extra-judicial decree". Within these fundamental co-ordinates, fixed by the ecclesiastical legislator, the freedom of choice or the discretion of the Ordinary remains truly great. More so, from a close analysis of the tenor of can. 1342 and the history of its editing it can be deduced that the radius of action of this discretion is even greater, because the much declaimed preferential choice of the ecclesiastical legislator for the judicial procedure in the application of any type of canonical sanction seems to be more theoretical than practical [171]. In fact, even if the proposal to standardise the two methods was not formally accepted by the *Coetus studiorum* [172], with regard to the history of the editing of this canon De Paolis himself states: "The general principle of can. 1342 §1 is the fruit of a long and wearisome elaboration. The initial intention was very clear: to favour the judicial process in comparison with the administrative. However in the successive elaborations such an intention became ever more weakened, until it remained less and less perceivable from the formulation itself. The first editing spoke of *causae graves* that must exist for the abandonment of the judicial process in favour of the administrative, and more so required *probationes de delicto evidentes*" [173]. The long discussion emerging from the *Coetus* did however bring about a very different final editing, because " ... the final text in place of *graves causae* has only *iustae causae* and the phrase *et probationes de delicto evidentes sint* has totally disappeared" [174]. Rather, for remedial penalties and penances just causes are not even needed, and consequently the preference for the judicial method for the application of a canonical sanction can be held to be truly only theoretical or in any case reduced to minimal terms.

This conclusion has a double confirmation. First of all it conforms to the desire of the ecclesiastical legislator to operate in a way that the new system of canonical sanctions " ... be truly applicable, through an efficacious process, and constitute con-

---

[169] Cf. for example J. Sanchis, *L'indagine previa*, op. cit., p. 260; V. De Paolis, *Processo penale*, in: NDDC, pp. 850-864, here pp. 856-857; K. Lüdicke, *Strafverfahren*, in: MK, 1718/3 and 4.

[170] This holds for example for the declaration or imposition of an excommunication because the application of this canonical sanction is reserved to a collegiate tribunal of three judges (can. 1425 §1 no. 2).

[171] That the ecclesiastical legislator prefers the judicial procedure to the administrative is the common opinion of the doctrine according to J. Sanchis, who in note 65 (cf. *L'indagine previa*, op. cit., p. 261) quotes the following authors: F. Coccopalmerio, F. Nigro, J. Arias, V. De Paolis, A Marzoa, G. Di Mattia. This preference is however not explicitly confirmed either in the Code or much less in practice.

[172] Cf. Communcationes 9 (1977), pp. 161-162.

[173] V. De Paolis, *Processo penale,* op. cit., p. 856.

[174] Ibid., p. 857.

sequently a useful pastoral tool for the good of the People of God" [175]. In the second place this is confirmed by the, fairly surprising, result emerging from the comparison of the normative of the code regarding the two procedural methods, the judicial and the administrative [176].

B) THE COMMON BASIS OF THE TWO PROCEDURES

The judicial penal process, in accordance with the norms of can. 1728, develops according to the norms of the *Trials in general* (cans 1400-1500) and *The Ordinary Contentious Trial* (cans. 1501-1655), as long as they do not oppose the nature of the thing itself or any law relating to the public good of the Church. We must turn to these norms for everything regarding the libellus, the citation, the contestatio litis, the instruction of the case, the conclusion, the argument and the sentence. Among these those which regulate *ex professo* the function of the promoter of justice (cans. 1430-1437) assume a particular importance, in so far as penal causes relate to the public good. And in fact can. 1721 provides for the Ordinary transmitting the acts to the promoter of justice, who has the obligation of encouraging the penal action, presenting the petition of accusation to the judge.

Another specific norm of the judicial penal process is represented by can. 1723, which not only assures the accused of a legitimate defence but provides a technical defence for him, that is to say an advocate. Moreover the accused, who is not bound to confess his own offence (can. 1728), always has the right – either by himself or through his own advocate or procurator – to speak and to write last (can. 1725), and this is contrary to the provision of can. 1603 §3, the promoter of justice being in penal cases a party in the case, insofar as he is the titleholder of the public accusation.

Finally, the punishment of the accused not being the principal aim of the penal judicial process, rather it is that of protecting the ecclesial communion by means of the possible declaration or imposition of the canonical sanction, the norms of the Code relative to the declaration of innocence (can. 1726) acquire a particular importance, in whatever stage of the process, and for the possibility of renunciation of the same (can. 1724 §2). Both norms, as underlined by the word *debet* used by the ecclesiastical legislator, have as their aim the protection of the reputation and good name of the accused. Are the rights of the latter protected just as much by the norms, which regulate the administrative procedure for the declaration or imposition of a canonical sanction?

Once the choice has been made – in accordance with the norms of can. 1718 §1 n. 3 – to follow the administrative method, the Ordinary cannot proceed arbitrarily, because also in this case it is a question of a canonical process, that is a series of formal and necessary acts prior to the pronouncement of a judgment, by means of a decree or sentence. In other words, the administrative procedure also has specific juridical-formal outlines, which render it very different from the abolished procedure *ex informata conscientia*, through which according to the CIC/1917 "neque formae iudiciales neque canonicae monitiones requiruntur" (can. 2187). In fact, the new can. 1720 fixes the following steps, which the Ordinary must necessarily fulfil before issuing the final

---

[175] J. Sanchis, *L'indagine previa*, op. cit., p. 263, note 73.

[176] For a deepened study of this argument, only summarised here, cf. L. Gerosa, *Exkommunikation und freier Glaubensgehorsam. Theologische Erwägungen zur Grundlegung und Anwendbarkeit der kanonischen Sanktionen*, Paderborn 1995, pp. 367-379.

decree: 1) notification of the accusation to the accused believer; 2) offering the same the possibility of defending himself; 3) evaluation with two assessors of all the proofs and arguments; 4) certain establishment of the offence and the non-cessation of the criminal action; 5) written exposition of the reasons in law and in fact; 6) issuing of the decree in accordance with the norms of cans. 1342-1350.

Although the debatable choice of gathering all these passages in only one canon has impeded the ecclesiastical legislator from specifying with due care the normative content of each one of these, still the complex nature of the extra judicial decree is evident enough with which a canonical sanction is declared or imposed. This presupposes all one procedure, "which includes many passages and perhaps many other decrees, instrumental to the last and definitive" [177]. In particular can. 1342 §3 establishes that the Ordinary who proceeds by the administrative method "is equivalent to the judge who proceeds by the judicial method and must offer all the guarantees that the judge in a judicial process offers" [178]. Moreover the same Ordinary in the issuing of the decree in the external forum and in its written formulation must pay rigorous attention to all the norms which regulate singular administrative acts (cans. 35-93) and above all singular administrative decrees (cans. 48-58). Among these can. 50 states: " Before issuing a singular decree, the person in authority is to seek the necessary information and proof and, as far as possible, is to consult those whose rights could be harmed". Given that no. 1 of can. 1720 speaks of *vocare* and *comparare* it is to be supposed that this right to be heard should be interpreted as a fundamental element of the right of defence, affirmed in a general way by can. 1481 §2 in the penal field and provided for by the same can. 1720, even if only with the bland expression *facultate sese defendendi*. However, in the case in which the canonical sanction provided should be a censure, this finds its possible confirmation also in can. 1347 §1, which expressly establishes the necessity of a prior warning, to be carried out before the start of the process. Finally, it must not be forgotten that the rights of the accused, in as far as they are the carrying out of the natural right of defence, find their subsequent reinforcement in the importance given to the administrative procedure for the evaluation of the proofs. In accordance with the norm of no. 2 of can. 1720 the Ordinary must in fact accurately consider all of the arguments with two assessors and, in accordance with the norm of can. 127 §2 no.2 the omission of such an obligation would render the decree null. Certainly, can. 1720 does not contain *expressis verbis* a norm on the right to a technical defence, however neither does it exclude that the accused can be assisted by an *advocatus* [179].

Therefore the fear is only partially justified of those who believe that an administrative procedure cannot just as well protect the rights of the faithful and in particular the accused as a judicial procedure. This possibility of the technical defence of the accused should be guaranteed in the future also on the normative level, so that the difference between the two procedures for the declaration or imposition of a canonical sanction should be reduced only to the extent of their field of application, given

---

[177] V. De Paolis, *Processo penale,* op. cit., p. 858.

[178] A. Calabrese, *La procedura stragiudiziale penale,* in: *I procedimenti speciali nel diritto canonico,* op. cit., pp. 267-281, here p. 278.

[179] For this interpretation of the text of the code, cf. K. Lüdicke, *Strafverfahren,* op. cit., 1720/3 Nr. 5.

that – as has already been seen – can. 1425 §1 reserves to a tribunal of three judges the cases which provide for the possibility of dismissal from the clerical state and the imposition or declaration of excommunication. Even here however, at least under the theoretical outline, it cannot be seen why the said judging college must necessarily issue a sentence – even if only of a declarative nature – and not a decree. Synodality, as will be seen later in 6. chapter 1, is an ontological constitutive dimension of the *sacra potestas*, and as such expresses itself also on the level of its administrative function and not only on the judicial level. The choice of one of the two possible procedural methods should then be on the one hand undramatised by dint of the basic structure common to all canonical procedures, and on the other should be dictated solely by pastoral reasons, entirely for the advantage of the efficacy and ecclesial transparency of canonical sanctions.

6. THE ANOINTING OF THE SICK

6.1 THE THEOLOGICAL-JURIDICAL STRUCTURE OF THE SACRAMENT

In the numerous post-conciliar publications on the theology of the fifth sacrament, and above all in those that have appeared after the promulgation of the new *Ordo unctionis infirmorum* [180] , the denomination *Anointing of the Sick* has by now definitively substituted the ancient expression *Extreme unction*. This authentification would seem on its own to confirm the judgment of those who state that the council Fathers had made their own the new conception developed in detail by the liturgical movement and pastoral theology in the Fifties, according to which the danger of death is no longer – in conformity with the praxis of the primitive Church witnessed to by the letter of James (5, 14-15) – a necessary condition for reception of the sacrament of the anointing of the sick [181]. On the contrary, the new pastoral orientation has made itself so predominant that the position of those who on the other hand see in the sacrament of the anointing of the sick a crowning or completion of baptism for the faithful at the point of death appears almost to be considered as not conforming to the teaching of the Vatican Council II [182]. Such a conclusion is however hasty, and partly erroneous,

---

[180] The full title is: *Ordo unctionis infirmorum eorumque pastoralis curae*, Città del Vaticano 1972; the promulgation of this new *ordo* or *Rituale* (7 December 1972) corresponds to the principles of the CA *Sacram Unctionem infirmorum*, published by Paul VI on the 30 November 1972, cf. AAS 65 (1973), pp. 5-9. For a review of the principal literature cf : O. Stoffel, *Die Krankensalbung*, in: HdbkathKR, pp. 712-714; V. Ramallo, *Unzione degli infermi*, in: NDDC, pp. 1085-1091.

[181] Already perceptible in the Directory on the pastoral use of the sacraments published by the French episcopate in 1951 are the influences of these forces, cf. J. Feiner, *La malattia e il sacramento della preghiera dell'unzione*, in: MySal, hrsg von J. Feiner-M. Löhrer, Zürich-Einsiedeln-Köln 1976. Ed. it. a cura di D. Pezzetta, Vol. X (Brescia 1978), pp. 595-662, here p. 628.

[182] Among the most prominent theologians who before the Vatican Council II maintained this thesis are to be recorded Karl Rahner, Alois Grillmeier and Michael Schmaus. Their opinions were reviewed by B. Studer, *Letzte Ölung oder Krankensalbung?*, in: Freiburger Zeitschrift für Philosophie und Theologie 10 (1963), pp. 33-60. Among the upholders of

as is fully demonstrated in a careful reading of the conciliar texts on the sacrament of
the anointing of the sick.

A) THE TEACHING OF THE VATICAN COUNCIL II

There are three conciliar texts on the sacrament of the anointing of the sick: articles
73, 74 and 75 of the Constitution *Sacrosanctum Concilium* on the Sacred Liturgy, art.
11 of the Dogmatic Constitution *Lumen Gentium* on the Church and art. 27 of the
Decree *Orientalium Ecclesiarum* on the Eastern Catholic Churches.

The last text states that, whenever access to a priest of the proper Church is physically or morally impossible, then the faithful of a non Catholic Eastern Church can
request the anointing of the sick from a Catholic priest just as the Catholic faithful can
ask for it from a non-Catholic minister. In this way the Fathers of the Council therefore
implicitly recognise the liturgical practice of the Eastern Churches. The latter normally
requires that the anointing of the sick takes place in church and consequently underlines the ecclesial dimension of this sacrament, as well as its not being conditioned by
the presence of the danger of death.

The condition of the danger of death, even if very minimised in its rigour, is on the
other hand recorded already in the first article in which the Constitution *Sacrosanctum
Concilium* mentions the sacrament of the Anointing of the Sick, which in fact repeats:
"*Extreme Unction*, which may also and more fittingly be called *Anointing of the Sick*,
is not a sacrament for those only who are at the point of death. Hence if any one of
the faithful begins to be in danger of death from sickness or old age, the fitting time
for him to receive this sacrament has certainly already arrived"(SC 73). With this text
the Vatican Council II affirms two things: 1) on the terminological level the preference
is to give it the name *Anointing of the Sick*; 2) on the pastoral level such an anointing is to be administered not only to the dying, but to all the faithful who, because
either of a dangerous illness or very advanced age, are physically or spiritually faced
with the reality of death [183]. Precisely because such a sacrament is not to be offered
indifferently to any sick person or to any old person, the successive article of the same
Constitution on the liturgy distinguishes first of all the rite of Anointing from Viaticum
and then reintroduces the ancient *Continuous Rite*, in which the Anointing of the Sick
"is conferred on the sick man after Communion and before receiving Viaticum" (SC
74). The opportune adaptations of the rite of the anointing of the sick "correspond to
the varying conditions of the sick who receive the Sacrament" (SC 75) are provided
for in the new Ritual of Pope Paul VI, which decreed the new sacramental formula
and absolutely provides for the possibility of a communitarian celebration in a great
assembly of the faithful.

It is however art. 11 of the Dogmatic Constitution *Lumen Gentium*, which offers a
clear synthesis of the Catholic doctrine on this sacrament, formulated by the Council
of Florence (1439) and by the Council of Trent (1551). This states in fact: "By the
sacred anointing of the sick and the prayer of the priests the whole Church commends

---

this thesis after the Council, cf. for all D.N. Power, *Das Sakrament der Krankensalbung.
Offene Fragen*, in: Concilium (1991), pp. 154-163, here p. 154.

[183] Cf. G. Greshake, *Estrema unzione o unzione degli infermi? A difesa di una teoria e una
practica sacramentale differenziata*, in Communio 70 (1983), pp. 25-44, above all pp. 43-
44.

those who are ill to the suffering and glorified Lord that he may raise them up and save them (Jas. 5,14-16); and indeed she exhorts them to contribute to the good of the People of God by freely uniting themselves to the passion and death of Christ (Rom 8,17; Col. 1,24; 2 Tim, 2,11-12; 1Pet. 4,13)" (LG 11,2). There are two principal contents of this conciliar synthesis. First of all the ecclesial and communitarian dimension of the anointing of the sick is based in its theological dimension, that is to say in the sacramental conformity of the sick member of the faithful, after the anointing, to the passion and death of Jesus Christ. In second place, precisely because the spiritual good of the individual sick member of the faithful is strictly connected to the good of the People of God, the latter by means of the minister who anoints "with the oil of the sick" can bring to him "relief and salvation"[184]. Both dogmatic meanings are subsequently specified by the new Ritual, which on the one hand underlines the communitarian character of this sacrament, and on the other witnesses how the grace conferred by this has strong analogies with that conferred by baptism and the sacrament of penance, because from the anointing of the sick the believer "obtains new strength against the temptations of the Evil One and against anxiety over death; thus the sick person is able not only to bear suffering bravely but also to fight against it. A return to physical health may follow the reception of the sacrament if it will be beneficial to the sick person's salvation. If necessary the sacrament also provides the sick person with the forgiveness of sins and the completion of Christian penance"[185].

B) THE NORMS OF THE CODE

The principal liturgical indication of the Vatican Council II, and that is that holy anointing of the sick is not a sacrament only (*tantum*) for the faithful at the point of death, was fully accepted by the ecclesiastical legislator in 1983. In fact can. 1004 §1 explicitly states: "The anointing of the sick can be administered to any member of the faithful who, having reached the use of reason, begins to be in danger by reason of illness or old age". Therefore the expression *nisi qui*, with which the ecclesiastical legislator of 1917 in can. 940 §1 restrictively interpreted the more generic *praesertim* used by the Council of Trent falls by the wayside[186].

Consequently not only can the sacrament be repeated (can. 1004 §2), but it can be administered in a common celebration to different sick people together, "well prepared and duly disposed" as well as "in accordance with the regulations of the diocesan bishop" (can. 1002). Preparation and disposition prevent the reduction of the communitarian celebration of the sacrament for more of the faithful into a mass administering. If all of the faithful, and in particular pastors (can. 843 §2) and the relatives of the sick person (can. 1001) are responsible for the remote and proximate preparation, the due disposition to receive the oil of the sick normally presupposes sacramental con-

---

[184] cf. PO 5,4.

[185] Paul VI, *Ordo unctionis infirmorum*, op. cit., no.6; cf. also no. 33.

[186] While the Council of Florence admitted the administration of *Extrema unctio* only to the sick whose death is to be feared (*nisi infirmo, de cuius morte timatur*, DS 1324), the Council of Trent shows a greater opening and declared that this anointing must be administered to the sick, above all to those (*illis vero praesertim*, DS 1698) whose status is perilous and appear to have reached the end of their lives.

fession [187]. Naturally this is also valid for the sacramental anointing of an individual member of the faithful.

Like all the other sacraments the anointing of the sick also always possesses a communitarian dimension which must emerge, as far as is possible, in its liturgical celebration. In fact, for the latter, notably simplified in words and gestures, the CIC on the one hand prescribes oil blessed by the bishop (can. 999) and on the other states that every priest, and only the priest [188], "validly administers the anointing of the sick" (can. 1003 §1). Both dispositions of the code indicate a relationship with the community of the faithful.

Even the norms of the code (cans. 1004-1007) relative to the conditions for admission to the sacrament of the anointing of the sick have been notably simplified. The sick person must be evidently baptised (can. 842 §1) and have reached the use of reason (can. 1004 §1). If the ill believer, because of the illness, has lost the use of his faculties, the sacrament can and must be administered when the intention can be presumed, at least implicitly, of receiving it (can. 1006). Presupposing this intention the sacrament can be administered even in cases of doubt concerning the use of reason, the seriousness of the illness or the effective death of the faithful (can. 1005). This sacrament cannot on the other hand be administered when it is certain that the faithful sick person is already dead and to those who "obstinately persist in a manifestly grave sin" (can. 1007). This does not mean depriving them of any religious assistance, but simply that in administering to them the anointing of the sick the rules for the administration of the sacrament of the Eucharist are to be applied, studied in the commentary on can. 915. A particular point in the normative of the Code on the anointing of the sick refers to can. 998 which, with words taken from LG 11, establishes the matter (the holy oil) and the form (the words prescribed in the liturgical books) of this sacrament. Regrettably however not only does it not define but also it exhortatively reduces the finality of the sacrament itself, dropping both its christological foundation and its ecclesiological dimension, clearly highlighted by the conciliar Fathers. In this way the aim of the sacrament *ut eos allevet et salvet* – that is to relieve and save the seriously ill faithful – loses much of its specific significance and its efficacy, both for the individual member of the faithful and for the whole Christian community. Firstly to receive the holy anointing of the sick is not simply a relief comparable with the visit of a friend and secondly the celebration of this sacrament is not simply the fulfilment of a good action or moral duty. Both are called upon to participate, even if in different ways, in a specific and sacramental confirmation of that ecclesial community which all of the faithful are bound to preserve (can. 209), in order to enjoy the salvation effected by the death and resurrection of Christ.

6.2 PARTICULAR QUESTIONS

The true theological questions, left open by the Vatican Council II and totally ignored by the ecclesiastical legislator, are not those relating to knowing whether the blessing

---

[187] Cf. *Erklärung der Deutschen Bischofskonferenz zur Krankenpastoral* (20.11.1978), in: ABl Eichstätt 9 (1979), pp. 170-174.

[188] That such a positive norm does not prejudice for the future the possibility that even a deacon could validly administer the anointing of the sick is confirmed by the same Commission for the reform of the CIC, cf. Communicationes 9 (1977), p. 342.

of the oil must necessarily be done by the bishop or not and if the *minister proprius* (DS 1719) of the sacrament must necessarily be a priest or not. They are rather those, which arise from the rediscovered christological foundation and the rediscovered ecclesiological dimension of the anointing of the sick and are thus in some way bound to the specific nature of the grace conferred by means of this sacrament. What are the pastoral and ecclesial consequences of the presentation and of the acceptance of the illness as a concrete possibility of participating in a specific way and in the faith in the passion and death of Christ? What does it mean that the celebration of this sacrament relates to the whole Church and as such has its natural place in the liturgical assembly of the faithful? It is not up to the canonist to give an exhaustive response to these questions. However, even in this domain it is possible to offer some starting points for reflection on the constitutional role of the fifth sacrament, as well as on the meaning of this role for the juridical regulation of the sacramentals and in particular of ecclesiastical funerals.

A) THE CONSTITUTIONAL SIGNIFICANCE OF THE ANOINTING OF THE SICK

Without having to refer back to the categories of moral theology, which distinguished between *sacramenta maiora* and *sacramenta minora* [189], it is evident that the seven sacraments do not all have, on the ecclesiological level, the same constitutive importance. However none of them is deprived of a certain value of a constitutional order, as underlined by the principle *Ecclesia a sacramentis*, fully revaluated by the Vatican Council II both by means of the rediscovery of the fundamental sacramentality of the Church "sign and instrument of the intimate union with God" (LG 1) and by means of the synthetic description which LG 11 offers for every single sacrament a further and specific deepening of belonging to Christ and the Church, inaugurated by baptism. Not even the holy anointing of the sick is deprived of this ecclesial and constitutive worth, as result already partially in its constant systematic positioning in fifth place, after the sacrament of penance and therefore half way between the so-called sacraments of initiation (baptism, confirmation, Eucharist) and those of status (orders and marriage). In fact, analogously to the sacrament of penance, the holy anointing of the sick introduces the faithful who receive it into a particular form of belonging to the Church, which on the one hand is not simple reducible to the primary one of baptism and on the other nor is it entirely assimilable to a state of ecclesial life based on a sacrament (orders and marriage) or on a charism (evangelical counsels). The theological reasons for this double diversity are multiple.

First of all, serious illness (with its reminder of death) by means of the sacrament of the anointing of the sick is sort of consecrated, that is assumed and presented to God by the Church, and becomes thus a "salutary reality" [190]. For the believer anointed with the oil of the sick this salutary reality consists in a sort of "renewal of baptism

---

[189] In this regard, cf. Y. Congar, *Die Idee der "sacramenta maiora"*, in: Concilium 4 (1968), pp. 9-15.

[190] The expression is presented almost as a dogmatic definition by: J. Nicolas, *Synthèse dogmatique*, Paris 1985, p. 1072.

in the face of death" [191] , for the other faithful, on the other hand, this same salutary reality consists in indicating to them how the anointed or consecrated sick person has become "in a special manner the way of the Church" [192], which leads to a definitive and eschatological encounter with Christ.

In second place the anointing of the sick, while being a specific and particular restitution of the first participation in the death of Christ given at baptism, evidently does not confer a character and is thus a repeatable sacrament. Consequently the state of sacramental consecration, and thus ecclesial, of the believer who has received the anointing of the sick ceases with his healing. The particular modality of being a member of the Church on the part of the faithful sick person consecrated with the anointing of the sick is not moreover entirely immune from every constriction, at least in its natural order premise, as is on the other hand necessarily required by all of the states of ecclesial life (can. 219).

The ecclesial positioning of the believer consecrated by the anointing of the sick is therefore entirely special. This presents not a few analogies with the repentant believer, as follows from the dogmatic-canonical tradition arising from the Council of Trent [193]. The latter, by reason of the evident expiatory and purificatory meanings of suffering consecrated and offered up, not only has always considered the fifth sacrament as a complement to the sacrament of penance, but also holds – especially in antiquity – that the believer anointed with the oil of the sick, even after healing, has been bound (in the same measure as the public penitent) to the obligations of the *conversio*, because of which the administration of the anointing of the sick was ever more postponed until it became the so-called *extreme unction* offered to the faithful at the point of death.

Just as the believer who approaches confession sacramentally, and thus ecclesially, verifies the necessity that the whole of Christian life be a constant conversion or *perpetua penitentia*, so the believer who receives the anointing of the sick sacramentally, and thus ecclesially, verifies the necessity that the whole of life, from baptism to death, be a progressive conforming to the death of Christ, so that the Christian can "live a new life" (Rom 6,4). Both roads lead to the Eucharist, which is the sacrament of integration of all the other sacraments. Both roads have their archetype in the *homo viator*, interpreted and symbolised ecclesially in the itinerant condition of the *peregrinus*. In the Middle Ages the latter assumed a special *status* in ecclesial life, analogous to that of religious, with their proper rights and duties [194]. The strong analo-

---

[191] This is the conclusive definition of the anointing of the sick proposed by G. Greshake, *Estrema unzione o unzione degli infermi?*, op. cit., p. 44; in this regard cf. also G. Lohfink, *Der Ursprung der christlichen Taufe*, in: ThQ 156 (1976), pp. 35-54.

[192] John Paul II, *Salvifici doloris*, no. 3; the text of the apostolic letter can be found in: AAS 76 (1984) pp. 201-250.

[193] Cf. DS 1694 and among the copious deserving literature: B. Poschmann, *Buße und Letzte Ölung*, in: *Handbuch der Dogmengeschichte*, Bd. IV/3, hrsg. von M. Schmaus-J.R. Geiselmann-H. Rahner, Freiburg 1950, pp. 125-138; J. Auer-J. Ratzinger, *Kleine Katholische Dogmatik*, Bd. VII: *Die Sakramente der Kirche*, Regensburg 1979/2, pp. 197-202.

[194] For a more detailed description of the state of life of the pilgrim, cf. *Guida del pellegrino di Santiago. Libro quinto del Codex Calitinus* (XII Century), edited by P. Caucci von Saucken, Milano 1989, pp. 31-46; for an argument between the juridical status of the pilgrim and the faithful anointed with the oil of the sick, cf. L. Gerosa, *Krankensalbung*, in: *Ecclesia a*

gies between the situation of the faithful anointed with the oil of the sick and that of the pilgrim permit the witnessing to how the sacrament of the anointing of the sick confers on the condition of this believer the characteristics of a particular and specific state of ecclesial life, also signalled by the spirituality of detachment and of parting. The specific consists in the verification in a dramatic, but salutary, way of the christo-logical form common to the three fundamental vocations known by the Church (lay, priestly and religious), retrievable in substance in the total and absolute adhesion to the "Follow me" (Mk 2,14) which Christ addresses to every one of his disciples. Thus understood, the constitutional role of the sacrament of the sick represents a concrete realisation of the *gradualitas in communione* with which the Vatican Council II has introduced a dynamic and progressive concept of belonging to the Church, not lack-ing in juridical consequences also for the Catholic faithful. By means of the canonical description of this role a more exact evaluation both of the ecclesial and constitutive worth of every single sacrament and of the so-called sacramentals is possible.

B) SACRAMENTALS

Precisely because the ecclesial communion is not a static but rather a dynamic reality, which realises itself in stages and directs the whole life of the faithful, the Vatican Council II not only bears witness to the ecclesial dimension of every sacrament, but also re-evaluates the role of the sacramentals as signs and instruments with which the faithful "are disposed to receive the chief effect of the sacraments, and various occa-sions in life are rendered holy" (SC 60). For this reason at the end of the normative of the Code on the sacraments as much in the CIC (cans. 1166-1172) as in the CCEO (cans. 867 §§1 and 2) some general dispositions regarding the sacramentals are gath-ered together[195]. Among these can. 1166 states: "Sacramentals are sacred signs by which, somewhat after the fashion of the sacraments, effects, especially spiritual ones are signified and are obtained through the intercession of the Church". In contrast to the CIC/1917 the ecclesiastical legislator of 1983 uses here for the first time the con-ciliar term *signa sacra* concerning sacramentals. The latter are therefore signs of the faith, which verify in an entirely special way the sacramental and salvific structure of the Church. In other words it is a question of the means for obtaining a specific grace through the entreaty of the Church (*ex Ecclesiae impetratione*). And precisely on the level of their modality of intervention and their efficacy the sacramentals differ sub-stantially from the sacraments[196]. While the latter have an irreversible eschatological validity, because they act *ex opere operato*, the sacramentals have a limited efficacy,

---

Sacramentis, op. cit., pp. 71-82, above all pp. 76-80.

[195] Even if in this regard only the CCEO defers explicitly to the norms of particular law (can. 867 §2), in principal this deferral holds also for the CIC, which in can. 1167 §2 prescribes the accurate observance of the rites and formulas *approved by the authority of the Church* in the administration of the sacraments. This authority can of course be the Conference of Bishops or the diocesan bishop.

[196] These differ also in number (there are seven sacraments, while the number of sacramen-tals is indefinite) and in origin (the sacraments were instituted by Jesus Christ, while the sacramentals – as explicitly stated in can. 1167 §1 – are instituted, interpreted, changed and abolished by the Church). The last question is however controversial, cf. M. Löhrer, *Sakramentalien*, in: LKD, pp. 449-451.

because they act *ex opere operantis Ecclesiae* [197]. The efficacy of the spiritual effects can. 1166 speaks of is in fact obtained only by dint of the moral dignity of the minister who conducts the rite and the believer who receives it.

Also the normative of the code in force is subject to the distinction between the two fundamental types of sacramentals: *consecrationes* and *benedictiones*. Through consecration (*consecratio* or *benedictio constitutiva*) a person (by free choice) or a thing (by legitimate choice) is destined in a lasting way to worship or to the world of the sacred of the praying Church: for example the consecration of virgins or of an altar; religious profession or the blessing of an Abbot. Through simple blessing or *benedictio invocativa*, like a special prayer of a minister of the Church, can be obtained a particular divine protection and particular divine benefit on persons or things.

A special form of consecration is dedication, that is to say the solemn and sacred rite with which the Church removes from profane use a place or a thing in order to set it apart it in a permanent way to divine worship. A particular form of invocatory blessing is on the other hand the rite of ecclesiastical funerals.

C) ECCLESIASTICAL FUNERALS

With the celebration of ecclesiastical funerals "the Church prays for the spiritual support of the dead, it honours their bodies, and at the same time it brings to the living the comfort of hope" (can. 1176 §2).

Precisely because with this rite honour is also rendered to the bodies of the faithful departed, the Church still recommends interment, that is to say the custom of burying the bodies of the faithful departed, however "it does not forbid cremation, unless this is chosen for reasons that are contrary to Christian teaching" (can. 1176 §3). On the other hand, precisely because in this rite the Church intends first of all to pray for spiritual help for the faithful departed, the ecclesiastical legislator in cans. 1183-1185 in accordance with the principle of gradualness in the communion dictates the norms, which need to be held to in the granting or refusal of ecclesiastical funerals. Not only catechumens, who "are to be reckoned among Christ's faithful" (can. 1183 §1) but also "children whose parents had intended to have them baptised but who die before baptism" (can. 1183 §2) and baptised non-Catholics can be granted ecclesiastical funerals. On the other hand these are to be denied, but only "if they did not give some sign of repentance before death" (can. 1184 §1 n. 1) to the faithful notoriously apostate, heretic or schismatic (can. 1184 §1); the faithful who have chosen cremation of their own bodies for reasons contrary to the Christian faith and finally the so-called *pecatores manifesti*, whenever the celebration of their ecclesiastical funeral could not take place "without public scandal to the faithful" [198]. Pastoral charity demands that in cases of doubt the presumption should be in favour of the granting of an ecclesiastical funeral; can. 1184 §2 invites however consultation with the Ordinary of the place, almost as if to underline how even in these pastorally delicate situations we need to let ourselves be guided in the formulation of our judgments by the principles of the ecclesial communion.

---

[197] Cf. H.J.F. Reinhardt, *Die Sakramentalien*, in: HdbkathKR, pp. 836-839, here p. 836.

[198] On how this specification by the ecclesiastical legislator can lead to different solutions in the various local communities, cf. H.J.F. Reinhardt, *Das kirchliche Begräbnis*, in: HdbkathKR, pp. 840-844, here p. 842.

7. HOLY ORDERS

"Through regeneration and the anointing of the Holy Spirit" all the baptised acquire a holy priesthood in order to "be able to offer in spiritual sacrifice all the human activities of the Christian" (LG 10,1) and together form the People of God, organically structured as a "priestly community" (LG 11,1). With these statements, based in the teachings of the Apostle Peter [199], the Fathers of the council did not want to make their own the identity established by Luther between being a Christian and being a priest [200], but rather to free the Catholic theology on the ministerial or hierarchical priesthood from the too apologetic emphases which have regrettably characterised it from Trent up until the Pio-Benedictine Code. This new ecclesial positioning of the ministerial priesthood presents a notable relevance on the juridical level, too: this allows finally abandoning the ancient canonical tradition of the *duo genera Christianorum* [201] and so the move forward towards a different understanding both of the status of clerical life and of the links between holy orders and *sacra potestas*. In order to define the juridical outlines of all these realities it is therefore indispensable to fix first of all the fundamental tracts of the conciliar teaching on holy orders and on *sacrum ministerium*.

7.1 THE THEOLOGICAL-JURIDICAL STRUCTURE OF THE SACRAMENT

A) THE TEACHING OF THE VATICAN COUNCIL II

Once it proclaimed the sacerdotal character of the whole People of God and with this the constitutional priority of the common priesthood of all the baptised over the ministerial, totally at the service of the former [202], the Vatican Council II states in clear terms that both are ordered each to the other and differ *per essentia et non gradu tantum* (LG 10,2). This formula means that the sacred ministry is not derived from the community, nor does it represent a simple increment in the common priesthood of all the faithful, but rather constitutes a different participation in the unique priesthood of Christ. As such the ministerial priesthood *pertinet ad structuram essentialem Ecclesiae* [203] and possesses its own specificity. This fulfils a particular function within

---

[199] Cf. 1 Pet 2,4-10.

[200] It is above all in the writing *De captivitate babylonica ecclesiae*, published in 1520, that Martin Luther established this equation, cf. L. Müller, *Weihe*, in: *Ecclesia a Sacramentis*, op. cit., pp. 103-123, above all pp. 107-108. On how Catholic theology on the ministerial priesthood has been too long conditioned by the anti-reformation preoccupation, cf. J. Ratzinger, *Il sacramento dell' ordine*, in: Communio 59 (1981), pp. 40-52, here p. 51; K. Lehmann, *Das dogmatische Problem des theologischen Ansatzes zum Verständnis des Amtspriestertums*, in: *Existenzprobleme des Priesters*, hrsg. von F. Henrich, München 1969, pp. 121-175, here p. 150.

[201] Cf. *Decretum Gratiani* C. 12 q.1 c.7; can. 948 of the CIC/1917.

[202] In this regard cf. above §11.1b): on how the priestly ministry is instrumental in the service of that common to all the faithful, cf. also: Gemeinsame Römisch-Katholische/Evangelisch-Lutherische Kommission, *Das geistliche Amt in der Kirche*, Paderborn-Frankfurt a. M. 1981, p. 21, note 23.

[203] Commissio Theologica Internationalis, *Thema selecta de ecclesiologia*, in: EV, Vol. IX, no. 1735.

the ecclesial communion radically different from that of the common priesthood and realised according to a growing intensity in its three degrees: diaconate, presbyterate and episcopate [204].

In the light of the ecclesiology of communion taught by the Vatican Council II, even if the decrees *Optatam totius* and *Presbyterorum ordinis* – the first on priestly formation and the second on the ministry and life of priests – do not succeed in overcoming entirely the worship-priestly vision of the *Tridentinum*, it is possible to retrace in the totality of the conciliar texts the essential elements of the specific ecclesial function of the sacred ministry. Already in LG 10,2 it is stated that the sacred minister fulfilling the Eucharistic sacrifice in the person of Christ "offers it to God in the name of all the people" and then in LG 28,1 it is made clear that the priests "acting in the person of Christ and proclaiming his mystery, unite the votive offerings of the faithful to the sacrifice of Christ their head". In the two quoted decrees, finally, the conciliar fathers make clear simultaneously both the theological foundation of this specificity and in what this concretely consists. Above all, by means of the laying on of hands on the part of the bishop, priests are "made participants in a special way in the priesthood of Christ" and thus "in the Eucharistic celebrations they act as ministers of him who in the liturgy uninterruptedly exercises his priestly office in our favour by means of his Spirit" (PO 5,1). The specificity of the function of priests in the realisation of the ecclesial communion consists therefore in their participation, conferred by the sacrament of orders, in the "authority with which Christ himself builds up and sanctifies and rules his Body" (PO 2,3). Precisely because all sacred ministers, and in particular bishops having received the fullness of sacred orders (LG 21,1), with the *sacra potestas* in which they are vested form and direct the priestly people (LG 10,2), it is necessary in their education and formation to make of them "true pastors of souls" (OT 4,1), so that they can achieve " sanctity in their own way" (PO 13,1).

This new definition of the specific ecclesial function of the sacred minister is a consequence of the dynamic and communitarian conception that the conciliar Fathers had of holy orders [205]. In fact such a sacrament not only adopts a particular configuration to Jesus Christ, but also enriches "by a special outpouring of the Holy Spirit" (LG 21,2), which imprints the *sacrum characterem* and renders participant in the *tria munera* of Christ the priest, master and shepherd, that is to say in the functions of sanctifying, teaching and ruling. This threefold mission of the sacred minister "divinely instituted" (LG 28,1) is exercised above all by bishops, upon whom is conferred "the fullness of the sacrament of orders" (LG 21,2), and then by priests, who participating "in the same and unique priesthood and ministry of Christ" (PO 7,1) are the *necessarios adiutores* (PO 7,1) of their own bishop. Finally, but in a different way and in an inferior measure, deacons also participate, upon whom hands are laid "not for priesthood, but for service" (LG 29,1). In order to carry out this threefold mission, conferred upon them by the sacrament of orders, the sacred minister by means of his

---

[204] This distinction in degrees is not to be confused therefore with the difference in essence between the two forms of Christian priesthood: cf. E.J. De Smedt, *Das Priestertum der Gläubigen*, in: *De Ecclesia. Beiträge zur Konstitution "Über die Kirche" des II Vatikanischen Konzils*, hrsg. von G. Baraúna, Bd. I, Freiburg-Basel-Wien 1966, pp. 380-392, here p. 382.

[205] This is the opinion of: H. Müller, *Die Ordination*, in: HdbkathKR, pp. 715-727, here p. 715.

cooptatio in an *ordo,* is inserted into a reality of hierarchical communion of a sacramental nature. In particular the priests "constitute together with their bishop a unique presbyterate" (LG 28,2) and thus form a "sacramental fraternity" (PO 8,1).

As much the dynamic element of the gradualness of the participation in the exercise of the ecclesial function of the sacred minister as the communitarian element of the method of realising such a mission directs the conciliar conception of the status of clerical life and of the specific road to holiness of priests. If in PO 13,1 it is stated unequivocally that the exercise of the *tria munera,* carried out with a constant and untiring commitment, is the primary and specific source for the sanctification of sacred ministers [206], the Synod of Bishops of 1990 points out: "In the unity of the diocesan presbyterate around their bishop" [207], is the privileged place for acquiring all the instruments and assistance necessary for the realisation of their own mission and for the personal sanctification of their own particular state of life.

As far as regards the criteria for admission to sacred orders the conciliar Fathers underline above all how this always presupposes a *vocation* [208], which is "recognised and examined by means of those signs which the Lord makes use of every day to let his will be known to prudent Christians" (PO 11,2). Among the so-called *criteria manifestative* with which to judge the authenticity of a priestly vocation the Vatican Council II points explicitly to full "freedom, both external and internal" (PO 11,1) of the call [209].

Among the special demands in the life of the priest the Vatican Council II, while stating that the permanent diaconate can also be conferred on married men [210] and also respecting the traditions of the Eastern Catholic Churches among whose sacred ministers "there are also some very good married priests" (PO16,1), recommends ecclesiastical celibacy in a special way. It is silent however on the question of the admission of women to holy orders, emerging later in relation to the Anglican Communion and the Declaration *Inter insigniores* of the Congregation for the Doctrine of the Faith [211]. The latter, reprising the fundamental reasons – taken from Sacred Scripture and Tradition – with which Paul VI explains the Catholic doctrine on the ministerial priesthood reserved to the male faithful, arrives at the conclusion that the Church "does not acknowledge within herself the authority to admit women to priestly ordination" [212]. The ultimate reason for this conclusion, confirmed on more than one occasion by Pope

---

[206] Regrettably neither the Council nor the CIC knew how to bring all of the consequences of this principle to the level of the norms which regulate the education of the clergy, cf. E. Corecco, *Sacerdozio e presbiterio nel CIC,* in: Servizio Migranti 11 (1983), pp. 354-372, above all pp. 355-356.

[207] Synod of Bishops 1990, *La formazione dei sacerdoti nelle circostanze attuali.* Lineamenta, no. 7; cf. also the Congregation for the Clergy, *Directory for the ministry and life of priests,* Città del Vaticano 1993, no. 19 and no. 27.

[208] Cf. OT 2.

[209] Cf. also SCInstCath, *Ratio fundamentalis institutionis sacerdotalis,* no.39, in: AAS 62 (1970), p. 349.

[210] Cf. LG 29,2 and Paul VI, *Sacrum diaconatus ordinem,* in: AAS 59 (1967), pp. 597-698.

[211] The former text is found in: AAS 68 (1976), pp. 599-600; the latter in: AAS 69 (1977), pp. 98-116.

[212] Ibid., p. 100

John Paul II[213], lies in the fact that Jesus Christ himself, "giving to the Church her fundamental constitution, her theological anthropology, followed always by the Tradition of Church, has established it thus"[214]. Being a question of a sort of voluntaristic *ratio theologica,* among other things not yet sufficiently studied in all its aspects, the ecclesiastical Magisterium has up until now tended to define this truth as dogma. This does not prevent on the one hand various theologians seeing in the same a strict connection with the mystery of the Word of God Incarnate, that is with the mystery of the Man-God Jesus Christ, and therefore with what most greatly distinguishes Christianity from all other religions[215], and on the other John Paul II declaring it a definitive decision: "Consequently, with the aim of removing every doubt on a question of great importance, which belongs to the divine constitution of the Church itself, by virtue of my ministry of reaffirming the brethren (cf. Lk 22,32), I declare that the Church does not in any way have the faculty to confer sacred ordination on women and that this decision must be adhered to in a definitive way by all the faithful of the Church"[216].

B) THE NORMS OF THE CODE

In the new Code the norms on the sacrament of orders are gathered together in three chapters: the celebration of ordination and the minister (cans. 1010-1023); those to be ordained (cans. 1024-1052); the registration and evidence of ordination (cans.1053-1054). To these the ecclesiastical legislator has put forward two canons of notable importance in order to understand in what measure the conciliar lesson, just summarised, has been accepted in the norms of the Code on holy orders.

The first of these norms, can. 1008 states: "By divine institution some among Christ's faithful are, through the sacrament of orders, marked with an indelible character and are thus constituted sacred ministers; thereby they are consecrated and deputed so that, each according to his own grade, they fulfil, in the person of Christ the Head, the offices of teaching, sanctifying and ruling, and so they nourish the people of God". Under the constitutional outline the first innovation, compared to can. 948 of the CIC/1917, is that contained in the expression *inter Christfideles*[217]. With this the ecclesiastical legislator intends to underline the connecting link existing between the sacred ministers and the other faithful, members of the ecclesial community, within which there is in force a *vera aequalitas* (can. 208). Every believer cooperates in the building up of the Church according to his own place in the *communio* and his proper function, based on the gift of a charism or of a sacrament. In the case of sacred ministers the difference from all the other members of the faithful is determined by the

---

213 Cf. no.16 of the Apostolic Letter *Mulieris dignitatem* of the 15 August 1988; no.51 of the Apostolic Exhortation *Christifideles laici* of the 30 December 1988, no.1577 of the *Catechism of the Catholic Church* of 1992; no.2 of the Apostolic Letter *Ordinatio sacerdotalis,* op. cit., no.2.

214 John Paul II, *Ordinatio sacerdotalis,* op. cit., no.2.

215 Cf. for example: L. Bouyer, *Frau und Kirche.* Übertragen und mit einem Nachwort versehen von H. U. von Balthasar, Einsiedeln 1977, pp. 69-70 and pp. 87-95; P. Grelot, *Y aura-t-il des "femmes prêtres" dans l'Église?,* in: NRT 111 (1989) pp. 842-865, above all p. 863.

216 John Paul II, *Ordinatio sacerdotalis,* op. cit., no.4.

217 This recurs also in can. 207 which, albeit in a more balanced way in comparison with its antecedent can. 107 of the CIC/1917, speaks of the difference between the laity and clerics; cf. L. Müller, *Weihe,* op. cit., p. 105.

sacrament of orders received from the former, which confers on them in an indelible way a function of service, that of spiritual paternity in relation to the whole community. It is a question therefore of a functional difference, that is to say structurally finalised towards the effective realisation of the ecclesial communion[218]. The second innovation, also inspired by conciliar teaching on the sacrament of orders, consists in making prominent the fact that such a sacrament delegated the sacred ministers to be an authority in the ecclesial community, that is to say to the exercise *in persona Christi Capitis* the three functions of teaching, sanctifying and ruling. By means of the application in this canon of the *tria munera Christi* the ecclesiastical legislator succeeds in freeing himself from the start from a worship-priestly conception of the sacred minister and in underlining how the latter by dint of the sacrament of orders is placed at the service of the global growth of the ecclesial communion[219]. This sacrament, then, is only one, even if it is administered in three different degrees: episcopate, priesthood and diaconate (can. 1009 §1).

Concerning this the question arises whether the deacon is called to exercise as an *auctoritas*, even if only to a much lower degree, the three functions of teaching sanctifying and ruling to which *sacra potestas*, conferred by the sacrament of orders, delegates and therefore is constituted guide and shepherd of the community and as such to be part of the apostolic succession. The redeeming clause *pro suo quisque gradu* of can. 1008 and the fact that the first paragraph of can. 1009 does not speak of degrees but rather simple of *ordines* prevents thinking that the legislator wanted to present in these introductory canons a definition of orders indiscriminately valid for the episcopate, the priesthood and the diaconate[220]. For example the formula *in persona Christi Capitis* is not applicable to the deacon, because these cannot preside at the Eucharist, so also it is not certain that diaconal ordination imprints an indelible character. What is certainly indiscriminately valid for all three degrees of sacred orders is how much can. 1009 §2, conforming to the teaching of the ecclesiastical Magisterium[221], establishes concerning the matter (laying on of hands) and the form (prayer of consecration) of this sacrament.

According to can. 1012, then, in each of the three degrees the minister of sacred ordination is the consecrated bishop. The use of the latter term permits the conclusion that even a bishop suspended, excommunicated or not in full communion with the Catholic Church can administer the sacrament of orders in a valid way. For the liceity of ordination, on the contrary, the two following criteria must be observed: 1) without the pontifical mandate no bishop can administer the sacrament of the episcopate (can. 1013) and if he does it anyway he incurs the sanction of excommunication *latae sententiae* (can. 1382); 2) without dimissorial letters and the respect of the norms relating to his own bishop (can. 1015) no bishop can licitly administer the priesthood and the diaconate. Dimissorial letters are the written authorisation from a Bishop or a major Superior to his own subject faithful so that he can receive one of these two orders

---

[218] In this regard cf. G. Ghirlanda, *De Ecclesiae munera sanctificandis. De ordine-Adnotationes in Codicem*, Romae 1983, p. 4; idem., *Ordine sacro*, in: NDDC, pp. 737-746, here p. 739.

[219] Cf. P. Krämer, *Kirchenrecht I*, op. cit., pp.98-99.

[220] This opinion of H. Müller (cf. *Die Ordination*, op. cit., p. 718) corresponds with the intention of the legislator, cf. Communicationes 10 (1978), pp. 179ff.

[221] Cf. Paul VI, CA *Pontificalis Romani*, in: AAS 60 (1968), pp. 369-373.

(cans. 1018-1023). Can. 1016 establishes who is to be considered the proper bishop: in the case of diaconal ordination it is the bishop of the diocese in which the one to be ordained has domicile or the bishop of the diocese in which the one to be ordained wishes to exercise his ministry; in the case of priestly ordination it is the bishop of the diocese in which the one promoted to orders was ordained deacon. Naturally for those ordinands who do not have their own bishop, such as members of religious or secular institutes, the members of societies of apostolic life or personal prelatures, any bishop in full communion with the Catholic Church can administer the diaconate and the priesthood after having verified the authenticity of the dimissorial letters of the competent superior (can. 1022). In cases where these norms are not respected can. 1383 envisages for the bishop a prohibition on conferring orders for a year and for the ordained suspension from the order received.

Among the norms of the Code relating to those to be ordained (cans. 1024-1052) are to be singled out above all can. 1024, according to which only a baptised man validly receives sacred ordination, and can. 1037 which prescribes the public assumption before God and the Church of the obligation of celibacy before diaconal ordination, with the exception evidently of whoever intends to enter the permanent diaconate as a married man. For the latter can. 1031 §2 prescribes on the other hand that he has completed at least his thirty-fifth year and has obtained the consent of his wife. If baptism is the indispensible condition in order to be able to validly receive the sacrament of orders in all its degrees (can. 849), by contrast holy confirmation is required by can. 1033 solely for the liceity of ordination. This is somewhat incomprehensible because, as has been seen, the sacrament of confirmation reinforces the belonging to the Church, obliges to the apostolate and is consequently fundamental for the exercise both of the common priesthood and the ministerial priesthood[222]. Also scarcely understandable is the fact that the ecclesiastical legislator both in the article on the requistes for ordination (cans. 1026-1032) and in can. 1051 on the examination of the qualities required in one who is to be ordained does not make any reference to the conciliar texts on vocation, notwithstanding the copious emphases on piety and good morals. Appearing more positive on the educational level on the other hand is can. 1035 §1, which for promotion to the diaconate demands having previously received and exercised for an adequate time the ministries of lectorate and acolytate[223].

Finally it is to be noted how the norms of the Code relating to the impediments to holy orders have been notably simplified and purified from discriminatory elements such as the candidate being born outside of wedlock or his bodily impairment[224]. Among the impediments provided for the Code distinguishes irregularities, or impediments of a permanent character which render access to holy orders (cans. 1041 and 1043) and their exercise (can. 1044) illicit, and simple impediments, which also render illicit access to holy orders and their exercise, but can however cease without the

---

[222] Cf. L. Müller, *Weihe*, op. cit., p. 122.

[223] The canon makes its own the teaching of Pope Paul VI which clearly distinguishes these *ministeria*, conferred with the *institutio*, of the three *ordines*, conferred by *ordinatio*; cf. Paul VI, MP *Ministeria quaedam*, in: AAS 64 (1972), pp. 529-534. Can. 230 §1 extends to all the laity of the male sex the possibility of assuming these ministries of lector and acolyte.

[224] For an analysis of the list of a good 21 impediments recorded in the CIC/1917 (cans. 984-987), cf. K. Mörsdorf, Lb. Bd. II, pp. 111-118.

need for a dispensation, when the cause which determines them lessens (can. 1042). Both categories of impediments to holy orders are differentiated in their turn from matrimonial impediments because they concern only the liceity and not the validity of ordination. On the part of the one who is to receive ordination the illiceity of the ordination (cf. 1025 §1) is given only when there occurs a lack of freedom of choice, either by the existence of some external constriction (can. 219 and 1036), or by reason of a serious illness or psychological infirmity (can. 1041 n. 1). Once the ordination is complete, the names of the individual ordained and of the ordaining minister, together with the place and the date of the ordination are to be "entered in a special register which is to be carefully kept in the curia of the place of ordination" (can. 1053 §1).

7.2 HOLY ORDERS AND THE *communio fidelium*

In the sixth title *De ordine* of the book on the sanctifying office of the Church the ecclesiastical legislator of 1983 has substantially accepted the conciliar teaching on the sacrament of orders. It remains now to examine in what measure such an acceptance has also directed the norms of the Code on the clerical state of life, which in the CIC are regrettably gathered together in separate sections from those on holy orders.

A) HOLY ORDERS AND THE CLERICAL STATE OF LIFE

Even if the Vatican Council II and the CIC have not directly resolved the question surrounding knowing whether the *status vitae* of the evangelical counsels is of divine right like the lay and clerical [225], nevertheless it is beyond doubt that such a state of life is founded on the example of Jesus Christ and as such represents a *donum divinum* made to the whole Church [226]. As a gift of the Holy Spirit to the Church, the state of life founded on the charism of the evangelical counsels "while not relating to the hierarchical structure of the Church, still belongs indisputably to her life and her holiness" (LG 44,4). This represents therefore a structural reality with a constitutional-juridical character different from the lay and clerical states of life [227]. This ecclesiological and juridical recognition of the "divine foundation for the evangelical counsels has the advantage of removing the constitution of the Church from the bipolar dialectic, by now become fruitless, on clerical-lay relationships. It allows on the other hand the development of a triangular or circular dialectic among the three states of life in the Church, in this way to expropriate the hierarchy from the prerogative of being the only point of reference for measuring the value and specific ecclesiological weight of the other two states" [228].

The three states of ecclesial life are structurally reciprocal and complementary: each of these – as has already been seen when speaking of the rights and duties of the lay faithful – enjoys a given primacy over the other two in the ecclesial communion. If the state of life of the evangelical counsels enjoys the primacy on the level of the

---

[225] Cf. can. 207 §1 according to which these last two states exist in the Church *ex divina institutione.*

[226] The expression of LG 43,1 is reprised in can. 575, at the beginning of the normative of the Code on the institutes of consecrated life.

[227] In this regard cf. H.U. von Balthasar, *Christlicher Stand,* Einsiedeln 1977, pp. 225-279; L. Gerosa, *Carisma e diritto nella Chiesa,* op. cit., pp. 231-236.

[228] E. Corecco, *I laici nel nuovo Codice di diritto canonico,* op. cit., p. 202.

prophetic-eschatalogical dimension of the Church and the lay state on the level of the missionary dimension, the clerical state of life enjoys in its turn the primacy in the ordering of the unity of all the faithful and of the Church. It is not by chance in the light of the conciliar lesson on the theological-juridical structure of the sacrament of orders the sacred ministers appear undoubtedly as the only "true shepherds of souls" (OT 4,1) and, in the measure in which they are invested with the "fullness of the sacrament of orders" (LG 21,2), they constitute the "visible principle and the foundation of unity" (LG 23,1) of the Church.

The corresponding norms of the Code on the formation of clerics (cans. 232-264) and on the clerical state of life (cans. 273-293) appear on the other hand to be inspired by very different principles.

As regards the former, in conformity with the principle established in the conciliar decree on priestly formation according to which not being possible in this field "to sanction laws if not of a general character" it is necessary to develop in every nation or rite a particular *Sacerdotalis Institutionis Ratio* (OT 1), it would have been more than legitimate to wait first and foremost for a normative much more sober and capable of leaving ample space for the *sacerdotalis rationes* of the individual Conferences of Bishops, whose competence is still recognised in can. 242. In the latter, in the light of the conciliar teaching we cannot understand why the legislator wanted to shift the emphasis from the objective formation of developing the function of pastors or sacred ministers to the subjective of the spiritual attitude in order to exercise it in a spiritually fruitful way. From the descriptions of the "spiritual formation" and of the "doctrinal preparation of the students in a seminary " (can. 244) we can glean the clear impression that in general in the CIC, and not just in cans. 245 and 258, "the fruitfulness of the apostolate is seen first of all in function of the subjective sanctification. Evidently the subjective aspect and the objective are independent, but the emphasis placed upon the former rather than the latter is a clear indication of the fact that the CIC faces up to the problem first of all with the concern of forming the students to live out well their own *status vitae*, the clerical, rather than their apostolic function, remaining bound to a perspective nearer to the tridentine than to that of the ecclesiology that arose from Vatican II" [229].

Unequivocal indications of this orientation not in any way conforming to the teaching of the Vatican Council II are easily to be found both in the norms on the formation of the clergy and in those relating to their state of life. Two emblematic examples are offered by cans. 276 §2 and 245 §2.

In the former the ecclesiastical legislator, in the attempt to formalise on the normative level the directions of PO 13,1 concerning the centrality of the pastoral function for the whole life of the cleric and therefore also for his sanctification, in comparison with the conciliar text substituting *fideliter* for the adverb *sincere* and substituting *officia* (in the sense of duties of state) for the substantive *munera*. Analogously in the latter the legislator instead of reporting word for word the expression *necessarios adiutores et consilarios*, used in PO 7,1, in order to define the ecclesial positioning of priests, speaks simply of *fidi cooperatores*. In both cases the constitutional perspective of the conciliar texts, capable of redefining the function of clerics within the *commu-*

---

[229] E. Corecco, *Sacerdozio e presbiterio nel CIC*, op. cit., p. 356.

nio fidelium and therefore of directing the latter as to a place and method for their personal sanctification, is reduced to a moral exhoration, of a subjective type, and as such incapable of constituting a programmatic principle for the life and spirituality of the diocesan clergy. Consequently the catalogue of the rights and obligations of clerics (cans. 273-289) also has more of the appearance of a *vade mecum* of recommendations and advice and not of a true and proper juridical statute for clerics. Certainly more in conformity with conciliar ecclesiology, and in particular the concept of mobility of the clergy introduced by PO 10, are on the other hand the norms of the Code relating to the incardination of clerics (cans. 265-272), more than anything decidedly simplified in comparison with the corresponding norms of the CIC/1917.

B) HOLY ORDERS AND ECCLESIASTICAL OFFICE

Differently from the Code of 1917, according to which any ecclesiastical office carried a certain participation in the power of orders and jurisdiction [230], the CIC of 1983 defines the ecclesiastical office in can. 145 in a more generic way and without making any mention of *sacra potestas*. For this reason the study of ecclesiastical offices, that is to say those charges stably constituted for spiritual ends, is deferred to the chapter on the institutional organs of the Church. However it remains an indisputable given fact that the greater part of ecclesiastical offices bear an intimate connection with the *sacra potestas* of sacramental origin [231]. Not by chance one of the first norms in the catalogue of the rights and duties of clerics expilicitly states: "Only clerics can obtain offices the exercise of which requires the power of orders or the power of ecclesiastical governance." (can. 274 §1). Even if the ecclesiastical legislator again prefers to use a terminology that, as shall be seen in the following section, has been abandoned by the Vatican Council II, here in fact he refers to all those offices which bear the full care of souls and thus presuppose the possession of *sacra potestas*. Consequently only priests can for example be validly nominated as parish priests (can. 521 §1), as vicars forane (can. 554 §1) or as members of a chapter, whether cathedral or collegial (can. 503). Under the theoretical outline the link between these ecclesiastical offices and *sacra potestas* poses not a few problems. For example canonists are somewhat in disagreement over the interpretation of the term *cooperare*, used by can. 129 §2 to open up the way to some form of participation, and not just of joint responsibility, of the lay faithful in the exercise of the power of governance in the Church. A help to the development of correct solutions to all these problems can of course come from the deepened study of conciliar teaching on the nature and form of the exercise of *sacra potestas*, as well from a careful examination of the debate that such teaching has given rise to in the post-conciliar study of Canon Law. In this area some brief emphases can and must suffice.

7.3 *Sacra Potestas*: ITS NATURE AND FORMS OF EXERCISE

A) THE LESSON OF THE VATICAN COUNCIL II ON THE UNITY AND ORIGINALITY
OF *sacra potestas*

The unitarian idea of *sacra potestas* is based by the Vatican Council II on two fundamental principles: the sacramental origin of ecclesial power and the inseparability

---

[230] cf. above all can. 145 of the CIC/1917.

[231] Cf. cans. 129 §1 and 150.

of its personal importance from the synodal. Both principles testify to the originality of this power, different from every other form of power, and determined both in its different functions and in its different forms of exercise. The essentials of these two principles can be thus briefly illustrated.

In the Dogmatic Constitution on the Church the Vatican Council II on the one hand represents the Catholic tradition that considers the bishops as "fathers", "shepherds" and "representatives of the Lord"[232], in the etymological sense of those who "in the midst of believers" render him "present" (LG 21,1), and on the other states that this representation is possible because "in episcopal consecration the fullness of the sacrament of orders is conferred" (LG 21,2). It is therefore the latter that confers upon bishops the total reality of the sacred ministry. This means that episcopal consecration confers upon them the threefold office of Christ, who is at the same time priest, prophet and king. But these *tria munera Christi* are nothing other than three aspects of only one mission, as Pope John Paul II will comment later, or three different expressions of a one and only ecclesial power[233].

The introduction of this unitarian idea of *sacra potestas* has given rise to passionate debates within and outside the conciliar assembly. In fact, in the scholastic doctrine which divides the canonical power of the bishop into *potestas ordinis* (which the bishop receives with consecration) and *potestas iurisdictionis* (which the bishop receives with his *missio* from the Pope), some theologians and bishops refute the doctrine of the *tria munera*, developed above all by Calvin and entered into Catholic theology only in the last century. Since the former distinction appears to be dictated by the different origin of the two powers and the latter seems to insist rather on the difference of function or scope of the various powers, the Fathers of the Council were able to attempt a synthesis of the two doctrines in the direction proposed by some canonists, that on the one hand attaches the *munus sanctificandi* to the *potestas ordinis* again and on the other points out in the *potestas iurisdictionis* the foundation for the *munus regendi* and the *munus docendi*[234]. Despite this possibility the Council has avoided entering into the heart of the discussion and limited itself to speaking either of the *triplex munus Christi* or *sacra potestas* not precisely in an explicit way if it necessitates the substitution of the model of the *tria munera* with the traditional distinction between the power of orders and the power of jurisdiction. It is on the other hand certain that the latter two terms do not ever coincide in the conciliar texts, while that of *sacra potestas* is found in LG 10 and 18. Moreover, as an idea, this underlies LG 21 and appears again wherever the Fathers of the Council explain how the *sacra potestas* is at the service of the building up of the *communio Ecclesiae*: "The bishops, as vicars and legates of Christ, govern the particular Churches assigned to them by their counsels, exhortations and example, but over and above that also by the authority

---

[232] On the meaning of the term *representation* applied to the ecclesiastical function of bishop, cf. G. Philips, *L'Église et son mystère*, I, Paris 1967-1968, pp. 248-251.

[233] In this regard John Paul II affirms: "Analysing the conciliar texts with care, it is clear that we need to speak of a threefold dimension of service and the mission of Christ, rather than of three different functions" (*Letter to all of the priests of the Church*, in: EV, Vol. VI, no.3, pp. 905-906).

[234] In this regard, cf. K. Mörsdorf, *Potestà sacra nella Chiesa*, in SacrM, Vol. VI (1975), coll. 415-432 and in particular coll. 428.

and sacred power which indeed they exercise exclusively for the spiritual development of their flock in truth and holiness" [235].

With the introduction of this unitarian idea of sacred power the Fathers of the Council open up to theologians the possibility of considering the classical distinction between the power of orders and the power of jurisdiction no longer as a material distinction but simply formal: it is not a question of two different powers, but of two formally distinct modalities of exercising a unique power with the same salvific content. The former modality of the *sacra potestas* participates according to the logic of the communication of gesture and sacrament, the latter on the other hand according to the logic of the communication of the word (*iuris dictio*). Both are always sufficiently efficacious in order to generate the Church of Christ if they are exercised in the *communio plena* with the other bishops and with the Pope. This means that the functions of teaching and sanctifying (*munera docendi et sanctificandi*) cannot be exercised in a fully efficacious way outside of the *communio* in the same measure as the *munus regendi*, which in its turn is not a merely organisational task and as such juridical. For example the government of the particular Church entrusted to the bishop is a natural complement of the sacramental reality in which these participate with his insertion in the *ordo episcoporum*, that is in the community of those who have been called to exercise in the Church the *summum sacerdotium* or the fullness of the sacred ministry [236]. Analogously priests, and in particular parish priests, "carry out their ministry of teaching, sanctifying and governing" (CD 30,1) under the authority of their bishop, with whom "they form one priestly body in the diocese" and are united by a "sacramental fraternity" (PO 8,1).

The second principle used by the Vatican Council II in order to explain the unity and originality of the *sacra potestas* is the inseparability between the personal element and the synodal element of the same. It would have been wrong to set one against the other because between the two there always exists a reciprocal immanence, even if at the level of the exercise of power one can prevail over the other [237].

On the universal level if the personal element prevails in the function of the Bishop of Rome, the synodal element prevails on the other hand in the supreme power enjoyed by the episcopal College called to realise in common the missionary precept directed to the Apostles (LG 23). If it is undoubtable that such a power expresses itself in a solemn way in ecumenical Council (LG 22), it is on the other hand still an open theological question knowing in what way such a power expresses itself in the new ecclesial institutions of the Synod of Bishops and Episcopal Conferences.

On the particular level the personal element of episcopal power is highlighted by the Council with the specification that the bishop possesses all the faculties required for the full exercise of the apostolic ministry in his particular Church not by virtue

---

[235] LG 27,1. Among the first canonists to have identified the unitarian notion of ecclesial power developed by the Vatican Council II are to be pointed out: P. Krämer, *Dienst und Vollmacht in der Kirche. Eine rechtstheologische Untersuchung zur "Sacra Potestas" – Lehre des II. Vatikanischen Konzils,* Trier 1973; E. Corecco, *Natura e struttura della "Sacra Potestas" nella dottrina e nel nuovo Codice di diritto canonico,* in: Communio 75 (1984), pp. 24-52.

[236] Cf. LG 21 and CD 2.

[237] For a fuller analysis of the question, cf. L. Gerosa, *Diritto ecclesiale e pastorale,* op. cit., pp. 77-90 and pp. 93-110; cf. also below, section 20.1 a) of the last chapter.

of a delegation by the Pope, but thanks to his sacramental consecration (LG 27). The Vatican Council II here effects a radical change: from a regime of concession of powers on the part of the Pope to bishops it passes to a regime of reservation [238]. Always within the particular Church the synodal element of episcopal power is given value by the theological depiction that the Council gives to the *presbyterium* [239] and to its representative structure, that is the presbyteral Council. In point of fact the principle of the *communio*, that characterises in a constitutive way relationships within the college of bishops, also regulates the relationships between the bishop and his priests, as his *necessarios* collaborators (PO 7,1). The qualification of 'necessary' underlines that the episcopal ministry is not just personal but essentially synodal and thus the bishop needs his priests in order to fulfil his pastoral assignment in the particular church. On the other hand the presyteral ministry without this specific link with the bishop would be incomplete.

B) THE CONTRADICTORY ACCEPTANCE OF THE CONCILIAR IDEA OF *sacra potestas* IN THE NEW CODE OF CANON LAW

Regrettably on the level of the juridical structurisation of the power of the Church the most important innovation of the Vatican Council II on the origin and nature of this *potestas spiritualis* (PO 6,1), that is the unitary idea of *sacra potestas*, was not assumed by the new Code. It is true that can. 375 §2 asserts that "by their episcopal consecration, Bishops receive, together with the office of sanctifying, the offices also of teaching and ruling". It is also true that, in consequence of this, can. 379 prescribes that designated bishops receive episcopal consecration prior to taking possession of their office. It is finally true that can. 381 explicitly dictates that in the particular Church entrusted to him the bishop possesses "all the ordinary, proper and immediate power required for the exercise of his pastoral office". However, the idea of *potestas* the ecclesiastical legislator is working with is not unitarian. On the contrary, surprisingly he never uses the expression *sacra potestas* and reintroduces the traditional distinction, abandoned by the Council, between power of orders and power of jurisdiction, which he calls among other things *potestas regiminis* [240].

This debatable option does not only not completely reflect the teaching of the Council, also summarisable with the suggestive formula *qui reget vel docet, sanctificat* [241], but leads the ecclesiastical legislator into coming more than once into conflict with his own general principles. This could have negative consequences on the pastoral level, above all in the sphere of Canon Law relating to the proclamation of the Word and the celebration of the sacraments, where in no canon is any mention made

---

[238] Cf. H. Schmitz, *Der Diözesanbischof*, in: HdbkathKR, pp. 336-348.

[239] In this regard, cf. O. Saier, *Die hierarchische Struktur des Presbyteriums*, in AfkKR 136 (1967), pp. 341-391.

[240] Cf. can. 129 §1: it should however be noted that following on the ecclesiastical legislator no longer speaks of *potestas iurisdictionis* but only of *potestas regiminis*, in order to avoid confusing it with *potestas iudiciaria*, cf. Communicationes 9 (1977), p. 234 and 14 (1982) p.146. On how all this represents a regression in comparison with conciliar teaching, cf. P. Krämer, *Kirchenrecht II*, op. cit., pp.45-57.

[241] Thus can be reformulated in the light of conciliar teaching the old adage *qui regit docet, qui docet, regit*: cf. J. Beyer, *De natura potestatis regiminis seu iurisdictionis recte in Codice renovato enuntianda*, in: Periodica 71 (1982), pp. 93-145, here pp. 118-119.

of the combined action of the two powers of order and jurisdiction, underlined on the other hand also in the canonical tradition which maintains this distinction. Analogously the normative of the Code relating to the exercise of *sacra potestas* in the non-sacramental sphere is also not without its contradictions.

Within the first framework, that is to say the sacramental, the CIC regularly replaces the term *potestas* with that of *facultas*[242]. With this term, whose meaning is closer to that of authorisation or *licentia* than to that of *potestas*, the ecclesiastical legislator does not necessarily wish to indicate something that is added on from the outside to ecclesial or spiritual power but rather its jurdical concretisation and as such conferred by the sacrament of orders[243]. In fact, for example, the *facultas absolvendi* which a bishop enjoys is valid for the whole Church, even if he should not be the holder of any office (can. 967 §1), and if that of a priest can be withdrawn, that depends solely on the fact that he does not possess the fullness of the sacrament of orders. Moreover in the context of the sacrament of marriage the CIC combines the term *facultas* with that of *delegatio,* traditionally used to designate the transmission of a *potestas* and not of a simple *facultas*[244]. It is therefore legitimate to conclude that in the new Code "the administration of the sacraments is not considered as an act combined with the power of orders and of jurisdiction, but rather as an exclusive effect of the power of orders. Like the systematic recourse to the term *facultas* instead of that of *potestas* (much more frequent on the other hand in the old CIC, even if in an exclusive way), the new CIC leaves it to be understood that the *potestas iurisdictionis* does not operate intrinsically in the realisation of the sacraments but only extrinsically; it is not a power that merges with a material content exactly as an efficent cause of the sacrament, beside that of orders, but only an extrinsic formal power, preferred for the correct administration of the sacraments"[245].

Within the second framework, that is to say the non-sacramental, the ecclesiastical legislator on the other hand uses the term *potestas* in a rigorous manner in relation to all acts of ecclesiastical authority, traditionally held as certain emanations of the power of jurisdiction. For example for the granting of indulgences (can. 995) or for the *potestas dispensandi* from vows (can. 1196), from swearing an oath (can. 1203) and from matrimonial impediments (can. 1079 §2 and §3). Only in the case of the dispensation from the irregularities or from the other impediments to receiving holy orders (can. 1047) is recourse not made to the term *potestas,* not even when it is replaced with that of *facultas,* but it remains however evident that in this case the dispensation, according to the norm of can. 85, is to be considered an act typical of the *potestas regiminis executiva*. There is the clear impression therefore that in the norms of the code relating to the non-sacramental framework the *potestas iurisdictionis* possesses its own material content, distinct from that of the *potestas ordinis.*

---

[242] This systematic substitution is already intuitable starting from the general norm of can. 144 §2 according to which the prescriptions of the law which hold for the power of governance are applicable also to the faculties required for the administration of the sacraments; cf. can. 995 of the CCEO, where in this field the legislator has adopted the same solutions.

[243] Cf. P. Krämer, *Kirchenrecht II,* op. cit., p. 51.

[244] Cf. cans. 1111-1114. This contradiction is even more serious if one thinks that according to the norm of can. 1112 §1 the delegation can also be given to the laity.

[245] E. Corecco, *Natura e struttura della "Sacra potestas",* op. cit., pp. 48-49.

In conclusion we cannot share in the opinion of those who retain that in the new CIC the ecclesiastical legislator does not only distinguish with clear rigidity the power of orders from that of jurisdiction, but also dares to separate them one from the other, almost as if they were two different and autonomous *potestates*, of which the latter (that of jurisdiction) appears downrightly to have two contrasting meanings: a solely extrinsic or formal meaning in the sacramental framework and a contained or material one, on the other hand, in the non-sacramental framework[246].

c) *Communio* AND THE EXERCISE OF THE *potestas regiminis*

The dualism characterising the ideas of the Code of *potestas ordinis* and of the *potestas regiminis* is aggravated by the fact that the ecclesiastical legislator places the Title *De potestate regiminis* (cans. 129-144) in Book II, dedicated to the general norms, as if it were a question of a more technical-juridical than constitutional problem. This does not just reveal a positivist conception of ecclesial power but in fact accentuates rather than resolves the dialectic between clerics and the laity[247], because it impedes understanding that "it is not the communion that is to be determined by the *sacra potestas*, but the latter by the former"[248]. In point of fact, in both these frameworks, the sacramental and the extra-sacramental, if the liceity of the acts of the unique *sacra potestas* can also be determined with criteria of an exclusively disciplinary nature, the validity of the same acts, on the other hand, depends on the presence or not of all the objective elements of the *communio*.

The latter principle directs all the forms of the exercise of the *sacra potestas* and in a particular way those relating to the so-called *potestas regiminis*, which is nothing if not a particular function of the former[249]. As such according to can. 135 §1 of the CIC and can. 985 §1 of the CCEO, this distinguishes itself – albeit in an inadequate and somewhat different way from the power of the State – into legislative, executive and judicial. The last two are normally exercised by different and independent institutionally representative organs; the legislative function, on the other hand, is exercised directly by the subjects of the power of government (Pope, Bishops and Councils). Actually, however, all three functions of the *potestas regiminis* possess a synodal dimension that shows itself in two ways.

On the one hand these three functions, both in the Latin and the Eastern tradition[250], can be exercised by institutional organs of a synodal nature, because if it is true that the plenary and the provincial Council possess above all legislative competence (can. 445/CIC) nothing nevertheless goes against their also exercising the other two functions, and analogously this is also valid for the episcopal Synod of the East-

---

[246] Ibid., pp. 50-51.

[247] Cf. L. Müller, *Weihe*, op. cit., p. 118.

[248] E. Corecco, *Natura e struttura della "Sacra potestas"*, op. cit., p.43.

[249] That in the Church the power of governance is profoundly different from the executive power of a State appears also from the fact that this can have juridical effects not only in the external forum, but also in the internal forum (can. 130).

[250] Cf. in this regard: W. Aymans, *Das synodale Element in der Kirchenverfassung*, München 1970, pp. 159-171; G. Nedungatt, *Synodalität in den katholischen Ostkirchen nach dem neuen Kodex des kanonischen Rechts*, in: Concilium 28 (1992), pp. 396-408, here pp. 398-401.

ern Patriarchal Churches (can. 110/CCEO). On the other, the disposition of the Code according to which the exercise of the *potestas regiminis* concerns only the faithful distinguished by holy orders (can. 129 §1/CIC) does not mean that the *ceteri christifideles* (can. 979 §2/CCEO), and in particular the laity, are excluded from any *cooperatio* in the exercise of this power[251]. Indeed, as will be seen in more detail in the chapter on the institutional organs or government, in the Church the synodal element of the *sacra potestas* always presupposes the joint responsibility, based on baptism and confirmation, of all the faithful.

8. MARRIAGE

8.1 CATHOLIC DOCTRINE ON MARRIAGE IN THE LIGHT OF THE VATICAN COUNCIL II

During the whole of the first millennium the Church always considered marriage as a reality founded in the mystery of creation and therefore, as such, intrinsically holy even before it was elevated by Jesus Christ to the dignity of a sacrament. In particular Patristics not yet clearly distinguishing natural law from positive divine law did not know how to single out a natural-contractual element and a divine-sacramental element in this holy reality of marriage. Only scholastic theology began, on the purely conceptual level, to make use of this distinction, without however impairing the unity of marriage by dint of the principle *Gratia perficit, non destruit naturam*[252]. In the modern epoch, after the Reformation of Martin Luther, for whom marriage was only a mundane reality, but most of all after the secularist evolution of the State in the XVIII and XIX centuries, this distinction was reduced to a radical separation. On the one hand the sacred character of marriage is confined within only the sacramental element, albeit reduced to a simple accidental aspect in comparison with the contract, and on the other ending up by denying to marriage as such every sacred and religious character[253]. From the end of the last century onwards for the pontifical Magisterium it has not therefore been easy to recapture the doctrine of the first millennium on the sacredness of marriage. If a first attempt in this direction was made by Pope Leo XIII in the encyclical *Arcanum divinae* of the 10 February 1880, it was nevertheless only Pius XI who succeeded in specifying the thought, affirming explicitly, in the encyclical *Casti connubii*, that the sacred and religious character of marriage is not derived just from its having been elevated to being a sacrament but to its very nature, which right from the start could be considered a *quaedam incarnationis Verbi Dei obumbratio*[254]. This recapturing of the intrinsic sacredness of marriage and the explicit affirmation of

---

[251] For example the office of judge in a judging tribunal can be assumed even by a lay person. cf. can. 1421 §2/CIC and can. 1087 §2/CCEO.

[252] Cf. E. Corecco, *L'inseparabilità tra contratto matrimoniale e sacramento alla luce del principio scolastico "Gratia perficit, non detruit naturam"*, in: Communio 16 (1974), pp. 1010-1023.

[253] Cf. J. Basdevant, *Des rapports de l'Église e de l'État dans la législation du mariage du Concil de Trente au Code Civil*, Paris 1900; H. Dombois, *Kirche und Eherecht. Studium und Abhandlungen 1953-1972*, Stuttgart 1974.

[254] Pius IX, *Casti connubii*, in AAS 22 (1930), pp. 539-592, here p. 570.

its complement in the elevation to a sacrament allow the Vatican Council II to gather together in the notion of a covenant and in the ecclesial role of this sacrament two fundamental elements of the whole of Catholic theology on marriage [255].

A) MARRIAGE AS A COVENANT AND ITS RELIGIOUS DIMENSION

The Vatican Council II – having taken as read that in contemporary society marriage as an institution is constantly called into question by "polygamy, the plague of divorce, by so-called free love and by other blemishes", as well as ever more often "dishonoured by selfishness, hedonism and unlawful contraceptive practices" (GS 47,2) – reproposes in various texts some fundamental points of the Catholic doctrine on marriage [256]. In particular, in the Pastoral Constitution on the Church in the Modern World the Fathers of the Council offer a definition of marriage of great importance even under the canonical outline: "The intimate community of life and love which constitutes the married state has been established by the Creator and endowed by him with its own proper laws: it is rooted in the covenant of its partners, that is, in their irrevocable personal consent. It is an institution confirmed by the divine law and receiving its stability, even in the eyes of society, from the human act by which the partners mutually surrender themselves to each other; for the good of the partners, of the children, and of society this sacred bond no longer depends on human decision alone" (GS 48,1).

In this conciliar definition alongside elements forever present in the Catholic doctrine on marriage there are others totally new. Among the former are numbered the fact that marriage is seen as a stable or lasting institution, ordered for the good of the partners and the children [257] , with an intrinsically sacred character and thus regulated by its own laws not subject to human decision while being in itself activated by the free consent of the partners. Among the latter emerge the fact that this institution is defined as a community of life and love, for which the object of consent that institutes it is not simply the so-called *ius in corpus* [258], but the reciprocal gift of themselves which, as such, involves the totality of the human person of the spouses. The accent on the personal character of this institution, at the base of every human society, casts a different light also on the traditional elements and is *in nuce* entirely contained in the idea of a matrimonial covenant (*foedus coniugii*), that the Fathers of the Council prefer to the traditional Latin concept of *contractus matrimonialis* [259]. Even if a more detailed analysis of the conciliar text shows that the terminological change does not mean a complete abandonment of the idea of contract, however it cannot be denied that the term 'covenant' is theologically more adequate for expressing the personal

---

[255] For a synthesis of the same, cf. W. Kasper, *Zur Theologie der christlichen Ehe*, Mainz 1981 (2. ed.)

[256] Cf. for example LG 11,2; 35,3 and 41,4: AA 11 and 29; GS 12,4; 61,2; 67,3; 87 and above all 47-52.

[257] In this regard it is to be observed however that the Vatican Council II no longer speaks of the primary end (*procreatio*) and secondary end (*mutuum adiutorium*) as in can. 1013 §1 of the CIC/1917.

[258] Cf. can. 1081 §2 CIC/1917.

[259] Among the different studies published recently on this thematic, cf. J. Eder, *Der Begriff des "foedus matrimoniale" im Eherecht des CIC*, St. Ottilien 1989; N. Lüdecke, *Eheschliessung als Bund. Genese und Exegese der Ehelehre der Konzilskonstitution "Gaudium et spes" in kanonistischer Auswertung*, Würzburg 1989.

and religious reality of marriage. Moreover, this recaptures in itself also the elements that make of the institution of marriage a *sui generis* contract, that is to say a contract whose duration and whose essential juridical effects are removed from the whim of the contractants [260]. In other words, the fact that according to the conciliar text those to be married do not stipulate a contract but a matrimonial covenant means that the peculiarity of the reality called by Latin matrimonial law *contractus sui generis* is better expressed in the fuller concept of covenant, whose biblical origin better underlines that it is God himself who is the creator and founder of the institution of marriage: *Ipse vero Deus est auctor matrimonii, variis bonis ac finibus praediti* [261]. With the introduction of the new expression *foedus matrimoniale* the Vatican Council II not only fully recaptures the sacred character of the institution of marriage but also singles out the *proprium* which distinguishes marriage from any other contract and thus open up the way towards a correct conception of marriage-sacrament. The latter is not an accidental addition but the development of that *proprium* in a radically new and deeper dimension as regards the order of creation [262]. As has been rightly observed: " If marriage had not been elevated as a sacrament the man-woman relationship would have remained removed from the specific restoration of Grace: too corrupt to be still capable of fulfilling the cultural function assigned to them by God for the destiny of humanity. Without the sacrament of marriage the Church too would remain discarnate and in an extrinsic position as regards the historical experience of humanity, within which marriage has preserved, albeit in a non-exclusive way, the centrality of meaning accepted in the plan of creation. The Church would become in this way a simple superstructure as regards the real history of man, because it would not permeate it with the efficacy of its Grace in one of its inseparably constitutive elements" [263].

The *proprium* of the sacrament of marriage, primary object of canonical matrimonial law, is not therefore separable from its constitutional role in the Church, highlighted by the Vatican Council II both in Dogmatic Constitution on the Church and in the Decree on the Apostolate of the Laity.

B) THE SACRAMENT OF MARRIAGE AND ITS ECCLESIAL DIMENSION

If speaking of the apostolate of the laity the Vatican Council II defines the family *tamquam domesticum sanctuarium Ecclesiae* (AA 11,4), in describing the constitutional structure of the People of God the same institution is designated downrightly as *velut Ecclesia domestica* (LG 11,2). Although it is not easy to establish exactly the theological significance of these two conciliar formulas, and above all to measure their consequences for Canon Law, still the intention of the conciliar Fathers seems clear: to underline the ecclesial dimension of conjugal society and through this the

---

[260] In this regard, cf.. P. Krämer, *Kirchenrecht I,* op. cit., p.103; H. Zapp, *Kanonisches Eherecht,* Freiburg 1988 (7. ed.), pp 22ff.

[261] GS 48,1; cf. the commentary of W. Aymans, *Il matrimonio-sacramento: alleanza istituita da Dio e forma di attuazione della vita della Chiesa,* in: Idem, *Diritto canonico e communione ecclesiale. Saggi di diritto canonico in prospettiva teologica,* Torino 1993, pp. 187-221, here pp. 190-192 and p. 220.

[262] Cf. J. Auer-J. Ratzinger, *Kleine Katholische Dogmatik,* Bd. 7, Regensburg 1972, p. 249.

[263] E. Corecco, *Il sacramento del matrimonio: cardine della costitutzione della Chiesa,* in: Communio 51 (1980), pp. 96-122, here p. 108.

constitutional role of the sacrament of marriage. The non-identification of the latter with the Church, albeit only in its domestic realisation, is documented by two facts. First of all in both conciliar texts the term *ecclesia* is applied directly to the family and not to marriage; moreover the use of the words *tamquam* and *velut* testify that it is a question not just of an analogous application, because the family while being founded in the sacrament of marriage, which renders the love of Christ for the Church present in history, is not capable of realising in itself either the structure of the *communio hierarchica*, or the specific eschatological dimension of the evangelical counsels [264].

These dutiful clarifications do not however subtract anything from the importance that the Vatican Council II wanted to give to the ecclesiological role of the family and the sacrament of marriage. For the family such a role is at the base of the publication (22 October 1985), by the Holy See, of the *Charter of the Rights of the Family*. Regrettably however in *De matrimonio* of the CIC the Latin substantive *familia* occurs only twice and without exhibiting any particular ecclesiological significance [265]. For the sacrament of marriage, on the other hand, the rediscovery of its ecclesial dimension impedes on a general level the legitimisation of the different easy intimate distinctions that often nowadays are come across even in the Church. On the more strictly canonical level such an ecclesial dimension allows moreover the understanding that even the evaluation of the sacramentality of marriage can no longer be separated from belonging to the ecclesial communion, regulated by the Vatican Council II with the principle of *gradualitas in communione*.

C) PRINCIPAL CONSEQUENCES FOR CANONICAL MATRIMONIAL LAW

The introduction of the idea of conjugal covenant as well as the recapturing of the ecclesial dimension of the sacrament of marriage are certainly of great importance for an ever more correct theological evaluation of the fundamental principles that govern the whole of canonical matrimonial law. Although a careful analysis of the norms of the Code on the sacrament of marriage (cans. 1055-1165) would regrettably be destined to confirm the opinion of those who hold that canonical matrimonial law, compared to the rest of sacramental law, is a juridical framework that has remained rigidly anchored to the principles of its own tradition, nevertheless the indications of the Vatican Council II have given rise to a scientific debate that sooner or later will bring the study of Canon Law to develop "on the one hand a doctrine of marriage centered more on ecclesiology than on sacramental theology, and on the other a juridical system based more on the idea of sacrament than on that of contract, which runs the risk of contaminating the very idea of covenant. In particular the study of Canon Law must reexamine

---

[264] Agreeing in this analysis of the conciliar texts: E. Corecco, ibid., pp. 114-116 and W. Aymans, *Il matrimonio-sacramento,* op. cit., p. 188.

[265] Cf. cans. 1063 no.4 and 1152 §1: the adjective *familiaris* recurs also in can. 1128 on mixed marriages and in can. 1071 we find the term *filii familias*, evidently even less significant than the others; cf. in this regard U. Navarrete, *Diritto canonico e tutela del matrimonio e della familia,* in: *Ius in vita et in missione Ecclesiae. Acta Symposii Internationalis Iuris canonici* (19-24 aprilis 1993 in Civitate Vaticana celebrata), Città del Vaticano 1994, pp. 987-1062, here pp. 991-992. On the canonical significance of the conciliar doctrine on marriage, cf. also U. Navarrete, *Structura iuridica matrimonii secundum Concilium Vaticanum II,* Romae 1968, above all pp. 108-127.

motivations and criteria in order to be able first and foremost to formulate matrimonial impediments (deduced up until now more from natural law than from the specific nature of the sacrament), secondly canonical form (which instead of being sacramental and liturgical is still juridical and extrinsic to the sacrament) and then to fix the content of the consent, developed more from natural law than from the specific contents of the faith" [266].

Some traces of how this important work of renewal has already also begun to bite, albeit sometimes in a contradictory way, on the normative level, are nevertheless visible in the formulation of some canons of the new canonical matrimonial law, above all in the preliminary canons (cans. 1055-1062).

In relation to the conciliar lesson on marriage as a covenant a first trace can already be found in the first paragraph of can. 1055, which states: "The marriage covenant, by which a man and a woman establish between themselves a partnership (*consortium*) of their whole life, and which of its own very nature is ordered to the well-being of the spouses and to the procreation and upbringing of children, has, between the baptised, been raised by Christ the Lord to the dignity of a sacrament". At first sight the formulation of the first section of this introductory canon appears to reveal a great effort at an adaptation to the conciliar teaching on marriage. In point of fact, the term *contractus*, with which the first canon of the old canonical matrimonial law referred to marriage, has been subsituted with the conciliar term of *foedus* [267]; the hierarchisation of the ends of marriage [268] has also disappeared and certainly diminished is the distance between the constituent act of marriage (or marriage *in fieri*) and marriage *in facto esse* [269]. Nonetheless for the conciliar term of *communitas vitae et amoris* the ecclesiastical legislator has preferred the classical expression of Roman Law of *consortium* [270] , and in the second section of the same canon not only does he use once again the term *contractus* but repeats exactly the text of can. 1012 §2 of the CIC/1917. Moreover the relative proposition *quo vir et mulier ... constituunt* risks leaving it to be understood that it is the parties that conclude the covenant, while in the New Covenant or the plan of Redemption this covenant becomes a sacramental reality and it is thus God himself who, under human signs such as the exchange of consent, is the author of it [271]. If it

---

[266] E. Corecco, *Il sacramento del matrimonio: cardine della costitutzione della Chiesa, op.* cit., p.117.

[267] Cf. can. 1012 §1 of the CIC/1917; that such a solution, taking place after a long debate, was finally accepted only as a more adequate linguistic expression but without particular juridical consequences results clearly from the accounts published by the Commission for reform, cf. Communicationes 9 (1972) pp. 120-122; 10 (1978), pp. 125-127.

[268] Cf. can. 1013 §1 of the CIC/1917.

[269] In fact the canon puts together concepts and realities of the two moments of the conjugal covenant, such as the *costituzione dell'alleanza* and the *consorzio di tutta la vita* between a man and a woman, cf. in this regard M. Serrano Ruiz, *Ispirazione conciliare nei principi generali del matrimonio*, in: *Il Codice del Vaticano II. Matrimonio canonico tra tradizione e rinnovamento*, edited by A. Longhitano, Bologna 1985, pp. 17-78, here p. 36.

[270] In Modestino the expression *consortium omnis vitae* appears to indicate the participation in the *stato civile*, cf. P. Bonfante, *Istituzioni di Diritto Romano, Torino* 1957, pp. 180 ff.

[271] This is the commentary on the canon by W. Aymans, *Il matrimonio-sacramento, op.* cit., p. 195.

is right to underline right from the start that the idea of covenant constitutes the *proprium* of every marriage it is therefore erroneous, or at least insufficient with regard to the sacrament of marriage, to place such a covenant exclusively at the level of human action.

The new canon law of the Eastern Catholic Churches in can. 776, the first in the chapter dedicated to marriage, adopts a clearer distinction between a marriage covenant, as an institution of the plan of creation, and the sacrament of marriage. In fact, on the one side it deals with the two matters in hand in two distinct sections and on the other does not limit itself to affirming that the marriage covenant validly concluded between a man and a woman, both baptised, is a sacrament, but specifies what is concretely put into operation by this sacrament: through the sacramental sign "the spouses are united to God in the image of the indefectible union of Christ with the Church and are almost consecrated and strengthened by sacramental grace" (can. 776 §2 /CCEO). On the basis of this formula, " ... even the doctrine of the contract can be correctly interpreted. The marriage contract, and more precisely the personal consent or matrimonial consent of the parties, appears almost as the substratum for the irrevocable action of God, who founds the matrimonial covenant. The theological value of the consensualist theory can be seen in the fact that it manifests the modality with which God acts in relation to man. God does not violate man but calls him to a collaboration with his plan for salvation. The Christian faithful, united to each other by God in marriage, follow in their own way the permanent call of God"[272]. This reciprocal binding themselves of the spouses and their being united by God is very perceptible in the Roman Ritual which, after the manifestation of the matrimonial will of the partners, for the realisation of the sacrament of marriage envisages the following words of the priest: *Ego coniugo vos in matrimonium. In nomine Patris, et Filii, et Spiritus Sancti. Amen*[273].

Regrettably, unlike what happens in can. 828 of the CCEO and contrary to what is required in the conciliar Constitution on the Sacred Liturgy[274], very little remains of this conception of the sacrament of marriage in the CIC, as will be seen in more detail in the section dedicated to the form of marriage. This is not only certainly not in conformity with the intention with which the Vatican Council II introduced the notion of a marriage covenant, but also could prove to be dangerous for the future of the sacrament of marriage itself. In point of fact, in a cultural period such as that characterising the end of the twentieth century, in which the matrimonial law of the State is ever more dominated by the tendency to permit that the partners be the absolute arbiters not only of the duration but also of the contents of the effects of the marriage contract, the Church cannot any longer permit that her own matrimonial law be substantially inspired by a juridical-contractual conception in which on the one hand the sacred dimension of marriage, recaptured by the Vatican Council II with the notion of

---

[272] W. Aymans, ibid., p. 197.

[273] On the importance of the liturgical rite for the canonical form of the sacrament of marriage still remain a sure point of reference the studies of Klaus Mörsdorf, both republished in: K. Mörsdorf, *Schriften zum kanonischen Recht,* edited by : W. Aymans-K.Th. Geringer-H. Schmitz, Paderborn-München-Wien-Zürich 1989, pp. 575-590 and pp. 591-605.

[274] Cf. SC 77, where it is asked whether the grace of the sacrament is more clearly expressed in the rite of celebration.

covenant, is obscured, and on the other the ordinary canonical form of the sacrament ever still remains separated from the liturgical form of its celebration.

As regards the ecclesial dimension of the sacrament of marriage, highlighted by the Vatican Council II, its evaluation on the normative level appears to present still more problematic aspects. Indeed, starting from the traditional conception of the contract-sacrament relationship, reproposed in can. 1055 §2, it seems we have to conclude that "the sacrament of Christian marriage arises exclusively, almost in a sacramental casuality, from the fact of the baptism of the partners"[275]. On the applicative level this would be confirmed by the fact that an error concerning the "sacramental dignity, provided it does not determine the will, does not vitiate matrimonial consent" (can. 1099). Consequently it would seem necessary to conclude that for canonical matrimonial law the sacramentality of this covenant is totally independent from the faith of those to be married and exclusively bound to the faith of the Catholic Church. To such a conception many parties have objected, not without foundation, to an excessive automatism[276]. This is however in contradiction both with some dispositions of the Code and above all with the ecclesiology of communion and the rediscovered ecclesial dimension of the sacraments, both developed by the Vatican Council II.

For Catholic sacramental theology it is certainly not an innovation that the personal faith of the individual has a relatively subordinate role to that of the believing community in the realisation of a sacrament, as for example in the baptism of children. Nevertheless this does not mean either that the faith of the individual baptised person is generally without relevance for the valid administration of the sacraments, or that such an irrelevance is to be particularly underlined in the canonical norms relating to the sacrament of marriage, which must evidently guarantee in the best of ways juridical security, in order to avoid invalid marriages as much as possible. In point of fact, both the error on the sacramentality which determines the will of one of those to be married (can. 1099), and the positive act of the will with which one of the two excludes sacramentality (can. 1101 §2) strikes matrimonial consent at the root and prevents the valid constitution of a marriage. Therefore, at least on the negative level, the faith of the individual if it determines the matrimonial will makes an impression upon the valid or non-valid realisation of the sacrament[277].

Now, in the light of conciliar ecclesiology deeply directed by the principle of gradualness in the communion, this faith of the individual believer even in relation to the sacramentality of marriage can no longer be completely separated from its concrete ecclesial belonging. In other words, individual non-Catholic Christians can no longer be considered as believers isolated from every ecclesial context, almost as if they were juridically impeded Catholics[278]. The fact that these live separated from the

[275] W. Aymans, *Il matrimonio-sacramento*, op. cit., p. 200.

[276] Cf. for example L.M. Groghan, *Ist die Taufe der entscheidende Faktor?*, in: *Wie unauflöslich ist die Ehe?*, edited by J. David (and others), Aschaffenburg 1969, pp. 238-248; P. Huizing, *Kirchenrecht und zerrüttete Ehe*, in Concilium 9 (1973), p. 458.

[277] Rotal jurisprudence also confirms it; cf. M. Weber, *Die Totalsimulation. Eine Untersuchung der Rechtsprechung der Römischen Rota*, St. Ottilien 1994, pp. 164-179.

[278] This is the conception of belonging to the Church underlying can. 87 of the CIC/1917; cf. K. Mörsdorf, *Persona in Ecclesia Christi*, in: *Schriften zum kanonischen Recht*, op. cit., pp. 99-147.

communio plena of the Catholic Church does not mean that they are excluded from every experience of ecclesial communion, in which the constitutive elements of the Church of Christ are more or less present. For these the fact that the Vatican Council II recognises that they live in separate Churches or ecclesial communions cannot be ignored on the juridical level [279], not even in canonical matrimonial law. Consequently in the evaluation of the sacramentality of a marriage of non-Catholic Christians it is necessary to keep in mind that such a "marriage cannot be judged without reference to the profession of faith, from which it arises and in which it is inserted. In this perspective marriage is comparable to baptism itself. It would not occur to anybody to recognise as a sacrament the baptism of an ecclesial community for whose profession of faith this is explicitly only a human pentitential act, not an action of God under a visible sign. To the capacity to be a sacramental sign even marriage can arrive only as a form of actuation of the ecclesial communion, when this belongs to the creed of that confession, around which the concrete ecclesial life develops" [280]. If then such an evaluation should lead to the conclusion that it is a question of a valid but non-sacramental marriage, this would not be anything truly new, because Canon Law has always known a similar case in point, as marriages concluded with the dispensation from the impediment of *disparitas cultus* show (can. 1086 §2). Acknowledging besides the latter other exceptions to the principle of the inseparability of the contract and the sacrament in Christian marriage (can. 1055 §2), does not mean to deny such a traditional doctrine, never dogmatised, but becomes nonetheless an integrating part of the ecclesiastical magisterium on marriage. The latter assertion is confirmed in its validity by at least three motives.

Firstly, even the International Theological Commission while holding firm the principle of the inseparability between contract and sacrament in Christian marriage in its document of December 1977 does not deny to the baptised, who have completely lost the faith and do not have any intention of celebrating their marriage in Church, the natural right to a marriage [281]. In second place if can. 1059 of the CIC – which in contrast to the old can. 1016 limits itself to regulating the marriage of Catholics and not of all the baptised – shows a great respect for the matrimonial rights of the other Christian confessions, can. 780 of the CCEO states absolutely explicitly in its second section that "the marriage between a Catholic party and a non-Catholic baptised party, except staying the divine law, is regulated also by the proper law of the Church or Ecclesial Community to which the non-Catholic party belongs". Finally, as much as was stated on the necessity of evaluating the sacramentality of marriage starting also from the faith of the Church or Ecclesial Community to which the members belong it is not a denial but rather a further specification, in the light of the Vatican Council II, of the principle of the inseparability between contract and sacrament in the sense that the believer belonging to the *plena communio* cannot choose between

---

[279] In this regard cf. O. Saier, *"Communio" in der Lehre des Zweiten Vatikanischen Konzils. Eine rechtsbegriffliche Untersuchung*, München 1973, pp. 103-132.

[280] W. Aymans, *Il matrimonio-sacramento: alleanza istituita da Dio e forma di attuazione della vita della Chiesa*, op. cit., p. 211.

[281] Cf. Commissio Theologica Internationalis, *Propositiones de quibusdam quaestionibus doctrinalibus ad matrimonium Christianum pertinentibus*, in: Z. Grocholewski, *Documenta recentiora circa rem matrimonialem et processualem*, Vol. II, Roma 1980, pp. 22-32.

a sacramental marriage and a non-sacramental marriage. In the full ecclesial communion marriage is per se and not by the will of the spouses a sacrament, but this per
se is possible without any proper automatism because such a communion is full and
therefore naturally presupposes the minimum intention to do what the Church does [282].
In non-Catholic Christians, who as such are not in full communion with the Catholic
Church, it is not however possible to presume this minimum intention because this is
"(...) in indissoluble dependence on the faith of the Church; this must necessarily
be understood in its ecclesiological context. The tridentine minimum form, according
to which the intention *saltem faciendi quod facit Ecclesia* is required of the minister
of the sacrament, must be understood differently, after the Vatican Council II, in relation to the concept of Church which subtends it all. In this context *Ecclesia* cannot
come to be understood in the meaning of the Church of Jesus Christ, to which all
of the baptised belong, independently of their profession of faith and, absolutely, of
their personal salvific situation; in the opposite case, the action of the Church would
be completely relativised. This however does not mean, on the other hand, that such
an intention exists or can only exist in the *plena communio* of the Catholic Church.
The intention, which relativises the faith of the individual, serves, from a juridical-
constitutional point of view, to assign the individual Christian to his community and
with this to a determined profession of faith" [283].

This rereading of the tridentine doctrine on the minimum intention in the light of
the ecclesial dimension of the sacrament of marriage could be allowed to overcome
every automatism and every subjectivism even in the difficult evaluation of the sacramentality of the marriage of those faithful who have abandoned the Catholic Church
with a formal act and who thus – according to the norms of can. 1117 – are dispensed
from canonical form. Even in these cases it cannot be seen why civil marriage cannot
be recognised as valid without however being sacramental [284]. Naturally, as in the cases
envisaged by can. 1086 §2, to the unity and indissolubility of these marriages that *pe-
culiare fermitatem* is missing which these assume in Christian marriage by reason of
the sacrament (can. 1056).

8.2 THE JURIDICAL CONFIGURATION OF MARRIAGE-SACRAMENT

Right from its origins canonical matrimonial law has been divided into three major
sectors: the norms relating to matrimonial capacity, those on matrimonial consent and
finally, especially from the Council of Trent onwards, the norms which regulate the
form of marriage. Before examining the norms of the Code relating to these three
sectors it is necessary pause briefly on the primary subjective right of every person to
marriage or the *ius nubendi*.

A) THE RIGHT TO MARRIAGE

The natural and inalienable right of every human person to marriage was accepted by
the CIC in can. 1058, which states: "All can contract marriage who are not prohib-

---

[282] The Council of Trent formulated this principle of sacramental theology apropos of the minister of a sacrament in can. 11 of the VII Session *De Sacramentis in genere*; cf. DS 1611.

[283] W. Aymans, *Il matrimonio-sacramento*, op. cit., pp. 218-219.

[284] Many authors agree on this point, cf. for all: P. Krämer, *Kirchenrecht I*, op. cit., p. 108; R.
Puza, *Katholisches Kirchenrecht*, Heidelberg 1986, p. 274.

ited by law". This right had already been affirmed with the same identical formula by the Code of 1917 in can. 1035 at the beginning of the chapter on matrimonial impediments. Having changed its systematic positioning, moving it to the preliminary canons, greatly highlights its constitutional character [285]. The latter is simultaneously reinforced and specified by cans. 219 and 842 §1. The former affirms the right of every believer to the free choice of his or her state of life and therefore also implicitly takes in the fundamental content of can. 1058; the latter, on the other hand, specifies more implicitly that in the order of marriage-sacrament such a right belongs only to the baptised. As much the natural right of every man to marriage as the right of the Christian to the sacrament of marriage can thus be subjected only exceptionally to limitations and the latter, once positively fixed by Canon Law, must be – according to can. 18 – interpreted in the strict sense.

A further reinforcement of the so-called *ius nubendi* can be seen in can. 1060, where it is stated that marriage enjoys the *favor iuris*, whenever it is wished to give this expression a fuller meaning than that which it usually has in the procedural field, and therefore in some way relevant for the whole of Canon Law. In a wholly exceptional way the protection of the right to marry must direct all of the norms of the Code relating to the preparatory pastoral care of marriage (cans. 1063-1072), among which do not take a secondary place can. 1071, which regulates those marriages which can be assisted at licitly only with the permission of the Ordinary of the place, and can. 1066, which states: "Before a marriage takes place, it must be established that nothing stands in the way of its valid and lawful celebration".

B) MATRIMONIAL IMPEDIMENTS

A typical case of a limitation of the right to marriage is constituted by matrimonial impediments. In old Canon Law the concept of *impedimentum* was all encompassing of everything that in some way is opposed to the birth of marriage and also thus took in lack of consent and the defects of canonical form. The Code of 1917 on the other hand introduced a juridical notion of matrimonial impediment in the strict sense, substantially underlying also the new normative of the Code on this theme (cans. 1073-1094). From the examination of these canons can be deduced, in the absence of a legal definition, that by matrimonial impediments the Code means all "those circumstances relating to the person, which by divine or human (ecclesiastical) law stand in the way of the valid celebration of marriage. This is the concept of impediments under the material aspect; under the formal aspect they are, on the other hand, the legal interdicts to validly contracting marriage imposed by divine or human law by reason of the aforesaid circumstances" [286].

Analysing more deeply the nature of these legal interdicts it is possible to conclude that these represent disabling laws, given that can. 1073 too speaking of the diriment impediment states that this "renders a person incapable of validly contracting a marriage". However even the incapacities which constitute a lack of matrimonial consent touch upon the person of those to be married, although for determining primarily the act they are classified as "invalidating laws" (can. 10). Consequently

---

[285] Agreeing with this evaluation: P. Krämer, *Kirchenrecht I*, op. cit., p. 113 and J.M. Serrano Ruiz, *Ispirazione conciliare nei principi generali del matrimonio canonico*, op. cit., p. 59.

[286] L. Vela, *Impedimenti matrimoniali*, in: NDDC, pp. 551-554, here p. 552.

a further effort is necessary in order to make precise the specific juridical nature of matrimonial impediments with respect to lack of consent; while the latter are referred to persons inasfar as they are subjects of marriage, impediments refer to those to be married inasfar as they are objects of marriage itself, in conformity with can. 1057 §2 which states: "Matrimonial consent is an act of the will by which a man and a woman by an irrevocable covenant mutually give and accept one another for the purpose of establishing a marriage".

In all of the *corpus matrimoniale canonicum* matrimonial impediments have the function of "safeguarding the internal good of the community, but also of preventing that it incur personal and direct damage to the other party" [287]. Moreover: for as far as their constitutive source is concerned they can be of divine law (positive or natural) or of human ecclesiastical law; as for personal circumstances these can be absolute (age, bond, vow) or relative (consanguinity, crime); starting from their temporal duration they are divided into perpetual (consanguinity) and temporal (age). Furthermore can. 1074 distinguishes the public impediment, which can be proved in the external forum, from the occult. More important is however the distinction between dispensable impediments and those that are not dispensable, which however does not coincide with the first of the distinctions listed. In point of fact, if all the impediments of divine law cannot never be an object of a dispensation, not all those of ecclesiastical law are dispensable, as is specified for example in can. 1078 §3 in the matter of consanguinity in the second degree of the collateral line, which while being only, probably, an impediment of divine law, is still never subject to a dispensation. Again in the matter of the dispensation from matrimonial impediments it is to be pointed out that the fundamental rule of can. 87, according to which the diocesan bishop can dispense from all impediments, comes across three limitations in matrimonial impediments coming respectively from holy orders, from public perpetual vows and from crime, whose dispensation is reserved to the Apostolic See (can. 1078 §2).

The CIC lists 12 diriment impediments, which render the person incapable of validly contracting marriage: age (can. 1083); impotence (can. 1084); the bond of a previous marriage (can. 1085); *disparitas cultus* (can. 1086); sacred orders (can. 1087); public vow (can. 1088); abduction (can. 1089); crime (can. 1090); consanguinity (can. 1091); affinity (can. 1092); public propriety (can. 1093); legal relationship (can. 1094). In contrast to the Code of 1917 the new matrimonial law no longer speaks of impedient impediments, which render the marriage illicit but not invalid, even if in fact the matrimonial impediment then called of *mixtae religionis* (can. 1060 of the CIC/1917) was transformed into a simple prohibition, as will be seen in the next section dedicated to mixed marriages (cans. 1124-1125).

In contemporary society the diriment impediment of impotence (can. 1084) has acquired a particular importance. In fact, it is not seldom in the matter of the marriage of handicapped people (paraplegics, etc.) that the Church is accused of violating with this canon the fundamental right of every person, and therefore also the handicapped, to marry. In this regard we can briefly record the following: 1. The impediment in question only relates to copulative and not procreative incapacity; 2. This impotence

---

[287] J.M. Castano, *Gli impedimenti matrimoniali*, in: *Il Codice del Vaticano II. Matrimonio canonico*, op. cit., pp. 101-131, here p. 109.

to complete the conjugal act must be not only antecedent but also perpetual; 3. In a case where a doubt exists, whether of right or of fact, according to can. 1084 §2 the marriage cannot be impeded [288].

c) MATRIMONIAL CONSENT

Starting from Saint Thomas Aquinas, who without making his own the principle of Roman Law *solus consensus facit nuptias* had however an intuition that the *causa efficens* of the individual and concrete marriage is the consent of those to be married [289], the latter has become ever more the central nucleus of canonical matrimonial law [290]. Practically from then matrimonial consent has become by a long way the matter upon which both the study of Canon Law and rotal jurisprudence have worked and published most [291]. Moreover, while the Catholic doctrine on consent is not inseparably bound to contractualistic matrimonial theory, and excluding neither on principle that in the constituting itself of the sacrament of marriage an instrumental cause can intervene (such as the blessing of the priest or deacon), it is evident that the conciliar lesson on marriage as a *foedus* has accentuated the personalistic characteristics of matrimonial consent and has thus had in this field a stronger impact than in others [292].

In point of fact, as has already been seen, can. 1057 does not only indicate firstly the efficient cause of marriage in the consent of the parties, but in the second section specifies that it is a question of a qualified consent. As such this must be between two people of different sexes, that is between a man and a woman, who with a free act of the will mutually give and accept one another with an irrevocable covenant. Precisely in as much as it is a giving of themselves, and therefore a choice of life that involves the entirety of their person, marriage "cannot spring up from anything but an act of the will, conscious and intentional, of those to be married themselves" [293]. In order to integrally guarantee this, the ecclesiastical legislator formulates the normative of the Code on matrimonial consent basing himself on three principles: the principle that consent cannot be substituted (can. 1057 §1), the principle of the perfection of consent (cans. 1095-1107) and the principle of the stability of the marriage born from a valid consent (cans. 1056; 1107 and 1134). In any case can. 1057 remains fundamental, placed by the ecclesiastical legislator among the preliminary or introductory canons in order to

---

[288] On all this question, cf. P. Krämer, *Kirchenrecht I*, op. cit., pp. 129-131.

[289] Cf. Thomas Aquinas, *IV Sent.*, D. 28, qu. unic., art.3.

[290] In this regard, cf. G. Dauvillier, *Le marriage dans le droit classique de l'Église depuis le décret de Gratien (1140) jusqu'à la mort de Clément V (1314)*, Paris 1934, above all pp. 76-90.

[291] Useful bibliographical directions are to be found in: P.A. Bonnet, *Introduzione al consenso matrimoniale canonico*, Milano 1985; K. Lüdicke, *Eherecht*, in: *MK, Literaturverzeichnis vor 1055; Incapacidad consensual para las obligaciones matrimoniales*, edited by J.A. Fuentes, Pamplona 1991; M. Wegand, *L'incapacité d'assumer les obligations du marriage dans la jurisprudence récente du tribunal de la Rote*, in: RDC 28 (1978), pp. 134-157. In this area we should limit ourselves however to briefly illustrating only some of the more important aspects of this rich canonical patrimony and refer therefore to the copious literature indicated by these writings for deeper study.

[292] Cf. B. Primetshofer, *Der Ehekonsensus*, in: HdbkathKR, pp. 765-782, here p. 765.

[293] P.A. Bonnet, *Il consenso*, in: *Il Codice del Vaticano II. Matrimonio canonico*, op. cit., pp. 149-216, here p. 153.

increase its importance; logic would therefore have suggested entitling chapter IV *De consensu matrimoniali* in a different way, because these canons contain in fact only the norms of the Code relating to defects and lack of consent. Although one or the other qualifaction is not always attributable in an exclusive way to each of the different cases in point envisaged by the CIC, these canons can be gathered together in the following way: 1. an absence of consent through psychic or psychological incapacity (can. 1095); 2. an absence of consent through defect of knowledge (can. 1096-1100); 3. an absence of consent through a lack of the will (cans. 1101-1103); 4. special modalities of consent (can. 1102 §2 and cans. 1104-1106); 5. permanence of matrimonial consent (can. 1107).

The first of these canons, can. 1095, is assuming an ever more important role in marriage nullity processes; and it could not be otherwise its normative contents being a fruit of many decades of work of the judges of the Roman Rota, developed with the intention of applying ever more correctly the results of the scientific researches in the psychiatric, psychological and psychoanalytical fields to canonical matrimonial law[294]. In fact, in contrast with the Code of 1917 which provided only for cases of *defectus consensus ob amentiam* (can. 1982), in this new canon the legislator of 1983 establishes a triple incapacity to give a valid matrimonial consent: the first (insufficient use of reason) and the second (grave defect in discretion of judgement) directly relating to the subject as the producer of an inadequate psychological act, the third (inability to assume the essential obligations of marriage) on the other hand relates to " once again formally the subject, but placed in relation with the object to which he is unequal"[295]. As can easily be deduced from the latter specification, although the basis of the three types of incapacity is still the classical and rigidly intellectualistic schema, of knowing-wishing-acting, all the same the legislator is deeply conscious that one cannot establish in matrimonial consent either a clear cut between subject and object or a radical break between the critical-evaluative capacity and affectivity[296]. The judge must keep this in mind in his evaluation of possible experts' reports, even if all the psychoses and pathological illnesses (as for example schizophrenia) can normally be covered under the first type of incapacities, under the second type every serious form of neuroses or psychopathy (as for example depressions, insecurities and fanatics), and finally under the third type all the pathological and psychopathological forms of destructurising of the personality or psychosexual anomalies which render

---

[294] On the question cf. A. Dordett, *Eheschließung und Geisteskrankeit Eine Darstellung der Rechtsprechung der Sacra Romana Rota,* Wien 1977, above all pp. 14-19. From the annual reports sent to the Apostolic Signatura there still emerges the dangerous tendency to overvalue the import of can. 1095; for example in the USA the number of declarations of nullity for psychic incapacity is immensely greater than the number of decisions relating to other headings of nullity: cf. Z. Grocholewski, *Processi di nullità matrimoniale nella realtà odierna,* in: *Il processo matrimoniale canonico,* Città del Vaticano 1988, pp. 11-24, here p. 14.

[295] M.F. Pompedda, *Incapacità di natura psichica,* in: *Il Codice del Vaticano II. Matrimonio canonico,* op. cit., pp. 133-147, here p. 134.

[296] Cf. on the point L. Vela, *Incapacità di contrarre matrimonio,* in: NDDC, pp. 561-567, above all pp. 563-564.

the person incapable of interpersonal relationships (as for example homosexuality, nymphomania and masochism).

In the remaining canons, the ecclesiastical legislator alongside the classical forms of lack of consent, as for example the exclusion by a positive act of the will either marriage itself (total simulation) or some essential element of it (partial simulation), also choses new topics such as deceit (can. 1098) and error determining the will (can. 1099). The introduction of deceit as a cause for nullity of marriage represents an absolute innovation, which breaks in some way the contractualistic conception of marriage and constitutes a clear exception to the general norm of can. 125 §2, according to which the juridical act made by grave fear or by deceit remains in any case valid. Nevertheless, not every deceitful error, caused in order to obtain matrimonial consent is juridically relevant, because – according to the norms of can. 1098 – only if this spills onto a quality by its nature such as to be able to gravely disturb the community of conjugal life does it render the marriage null. Among these qualities is to be numbered sterility (can. 1084 §3), religious convictions, the habitual or professional state of delinquency, a physical or psychological illness (as for example alcoholism or drug dependence) and finally the state of a pregnancy hidden or falsely attributed to the deceived one about to be married[297]. Even the clarification made by can. 1099 on the problem of the juridical relevance of error concerning the essential properties (unity and indissolubility) and on the sacramental dignity of marriage when it determines the consensual will is certainly as a result of rotal jurisprudence[298]. And it is an important result, because with its practice the Roman Rota has clearly highlighted that "as much more error over the principles from which the essential properties arise is inveterate and rooted in the person, so it is becoming more difficult to maintain that this remains extraneous to matrimonial will. One must in fact maintain that man acts in a coherent manner, willing in conformity with the intelligence he has of the act. On the other hand when an error over the principles which constitute the necessary presupposition of the essential properties is so deeply seated in the mind, becoming one almost with the person, only with much effort could it be maintained that this erroneous configuration has not become identifying for the will, distorting in an essential way the essence of the marriage and making it become something else compared to that prefigured by God"[299].

D) THE CANONICAL FORM OF MARRIAGE

By dint of the Pauline parallel between the sacrament of marriage and the union of Jesus Christ with the Church (Eph 5,21-32), right from the early days of Christianity in order to conclude the nuptials of two baptised people much importance has been given to the fact that they should be celebrated publicly before the Church. Notwithstanding the numerous testimonies of the Fathers of the Church concerning the importance given by the faithful to the laying on of hands or the priestly blessing when in the

---

[297] For a detailed commentary on can. 1098, cf. P.A. Bonnet, *Il consenso,* op. cit., pp. 185-189; F. Bersini, *Il nuovo diritto canonico matrimoniale. Commento giuridico-teologico-pastorale,* Torino 1985, pp. 104-105.

[298] Cf. Z. Grocholewski, *Relatio inter errorem et positivam indissolubilitatis exclusionem in nuptiis contrahendis,* in: Periodica 69 (1980), pp. 569-601.

[299] P.A. Bonnet, *Il consenso,* op. cit., p. 179.

XVI Century the Church, for reasons of public order, was forced to make canonical form (exchange of matrimonial consent before the parish priest, or his delegate, and two witnesses) obligatory, the Council of Trent did not think of unifying this juridical form with the liturgical-sacramental form [300]. The ambiguities connected to this situation suggested, during the period of the Vatican Council II, to some theologians to request downrightly the abolition of the tridentine form almost as if it were a juridical superstructure not up to the sacramental character of the gesture; others on the other hand were more inclined to ask for the unification of the canonical form with the liturgical, because it is not only up to the Christian community to verify if the dispositions of those to be married really correspond to the baptism they have received, but also in their exchange of consent, which makes the marriage, the Church "also remains the sign and guarantee of the gift of the Holy Spirit which the spouses receive committing themselves to each other in as far as they are Christians" [301]. In the CIC of 1983 the ecclesiastical legislator has decided once again to confirm the compulsory character of canonical form for the validity of the marriage (can. 1108), without however uniting it with the liturgical form, required only for liceity (can. 1119). Rather, in this sector of matrimonial law the contractualistic conception has once again prevailed, because not only does it provide for an extraordinary form (exchange of consent before witnesses only) in cases of "grave difficulty in reaching a competent assistant" (can. 1116), but also the latter can even be a lay person (can. 1112) and those to be married can express their consent through a procurator (cans. 1104-1105). Moreover the cases of dispensation from the canonical form have been increased, because over and above danger of death (can. 1079 §1 and §2) and mixed marriages (can. 1127 §2) must now be added the case of the faithful who by a formal act have abandoned the Catholic Church (can. 1117). Even if in this case we cannot speak of a dispensation in the proper sense, but of a true exception to can. 11, under the sacramental outline the substance of the discourse remains the same. In point of fact, it is legitimate to wonder if canonical form is simply a juridical superstructure, or if you will an "invalidating law, with which one regulates and thus one limits the exercise of a fundamental right" [302], or an intrinsic element of the liturgical form of a sacrament and, as such, a constitutive element of the mediating and instrumental will of the Church, in conformity with the conciliar principle that all of the sacraments are "actions of Christ and of the Church" (can. 840).

E) THE EFFECTS OF MARRIAGE AND METHODS FOR ITS CONVALIDATION

One of the principle consequences of the conciliar lesson on marriage for canonical matrimonial law has been – as has been seen commenting on can. 1055 – the potential overcoming of the distinction between *matrimonio in fieri* and *matrimonio in facto esse*. Nevertheless the norms of the Code (cans. 1134-1140) which regulate the effects of marriage have remained substantially those of the 1917 Code, thus risking once

---

[300] On the whole of this question cf. E. Corecco, L'inseparabilità *tra contratto matrimoniale e sacramento,* op. cit., pp. 360-361; F. Bersini, *Il nuovo diritto canonico matrimoniale,* op. cit., pp. 140-142.

[301] G. Martelet, *16 Tesi cristologiche sul sacramento del matrimonio,* in: Il Regno-Documenti 23 (1978) pp. 391-392, thesis 10.

[302] V. De Paolis, *Forma canonica,* in: NDDC. pp. 516-524, here p. 521.

again separating the effects of marriage from all that relates to the conjugal state of life and the family as a *velut Ecclesia domestica*[303]. Among the principle effects to be pointed out are: the equality of rights and duties of the man and the woman in the community of conjugal love (can. 1135); the joint responsibility of the partners in the exercise of the right-duty of educating the children (can. 1136); the legitimacy of the children conceived or born from a valid or putative marriage (can. 1137).

An invalid marriage is called putative, "if it has been celebrated in good faith by at least one party. It ceases to be such when both parties become certain of its nullity" (can. 1061 §3). Once certain of nullity the marriage ceases to be putative, but remains nevertheless written in the canonical register as valid. In order to put a stop to this appearance of validity the partners have two possibilities: either to separate, and then a legitimate declaration of nullity would be necessary (can. 1085 §2) before being able to enter into a new marriage, or they can convalidate their marriage. According to canonical matrimonial law, besides the cessation of the impediment or the dispensation from the same, in order to convalidate a null marriage it is necessary to resort to one of the two following methods: simple convalidation (cans. 1156-1160) or retroactive validation (sanatio in radice) (cans. 1161-1165). The former method always implies the renewal of consent with a new act of the will (can. 1157), and depending on the reason for which the marriage is invalid (impediment, defect of consent, defect of form) can happen in three different ways, that are spoken of in cans. 1156, 1159 and 1160 respectively. The latter method, on the other hand, is employable only when the natural consent validly expressed perdures (cans. 1162 §1, 1163 §1), and its juridical inefficacy is curable[304]. This special convalidation is called retroactive validation (sanatio in radice) because it removes, through the intervention of the competent ecclesiastical authority, the cause of nullity and has a retroactive effect (can. 1161).

8.3 MIXED MARRIAGES

Even if the conciliar documents *Unitas redintegratio* on Ecumenism and *Dignitatis humanae* on Religious Liberty do not contain explicit norms relating to mixed marriages, in the postconciliar period the latter were the object of a full discussion and of a deepened re-examination[305]. The principal stages of this reform, expounded in the chapter *De matrimoniis mixtis* (cans. 1124-1129) of the CIC, are as follows: 1. the MP *Pastorale munus* of the 30 November 1963, with which the faculty to dispense from the impediments relating to mixed marriages passed to residential bishops[306]; 2. the instruction *Matrimonii sacramentum*, issued by the Congregation for the Doctrine of the Faith on the 18 march 1966, which abolishes excommunication for those Catholics who celebrate their own mixed marriage before a non-Catholic minister and mitigates

---

[303] For a detailed analysis of the effects of marriage, cf. J. Prader, *Das kirchliche Eherecht in der seelsorglichen Praxis*, Bozen 1983, pp. 147-149.

[304] Cf. can. 1163 §2 and the commentary of J. Prader, ibid., pp. 163-164.

[305] On the origin and dynamism of the postconciliar reforms in this regard, cf. Z. Grocholewski, *Matrimoni misti*, in: *Il Codice del Vaticano II. Matrimonio canonico*, op. cit., pp. 237-256, especially pp. 242-245.

[306] Cf. AAS 56 (1964), here p. 8.

the demand for the promises of the non-Catholic party [307] ; 3. the MP *Matrimonia mixta* of the 31 March 1970, whose norms practically constitute the basis of those actually in force, and distinguishes three types of mixed marriage: the marriage between Catholics and non-Catholic Eastern Christians; the marriage between Catholics and Christians not of the Eastern Rite; the marriage between Catholics and the non-baptised [308]. In the first two types it is a question of sacramental marriages and thus they are to be considered together.

A) MARRIAGE BETWEEN CATHOLICS AND THE BAPTISED OF ANOTHER CHRISTIAN CONFESSION

Differently from both, the Code of 1917 and the law depicted by the MP *Matrimonia mixta*, the CIC of 1983 has abolished the impedient impediment that was opposed to the celebration of the marriage between Catholics and the baptised of another Christian confession. In point of fact, can. 1124 uniquely states that such a marriage "is prohibited without the express permission of the competent authority". From the juridical point of view, the fact that the legislator no longer speaks of an impediment but of a simple prohibition has its importance, because while in the former case a dispensation would still be necessary to enter into marriage, now a permission is enough. By its nature the latter can be conceded much more easily and even if there is not a grave cause (can. 1061 of the CIC/1917), being to such an end the existence of a "just and resonable cause" (can. 1125) is sufficient. On the contrary, given that these marriages, notwithstanding their particular difficulties, "present numerous elements which it is good to evaluate and develop, both for their intrinsic value, and for the contribution they can make to the ecumenical movement" [309], the ecclesiastical legislator could undoubtedly have refrained from the mention of a just and reasonable cause and opted for a negative formulation, in the sense that such a permission can be refused only if there are serious reasons against the marriage itself [310]. Certainly positive on the other hand is the fact that in the concession of this licence, otherwise required simply for the liceity of the marriage, the ecclesiastical authority does not impose anything on the non-Catholic party, demanding only that the same be informed of the promises made by the Catholic party (can. 1125 no.2) concerning the preservation of their own Catholic faith and their commitment to do all that is within their own powers " in order that the children be baptised and brought up in the Catholic Church" (can. 1125 no.1). It is up to the Conferences of bishops to fix the modalities with which the Catholic party must make this declaration and these promises (can. 1126). On the other hand the right to possibly dispense from canonical form is up to the Ordinary of the place of the Catholic party, if grave difficulties (can. 1127 §2) should arise for its observance. In these cases for the validity of the marriage some sort of public form of celebration,

---

[307] Cf. AAS 58 (1966), pp. 235-239.

[308] Cf. AAS 62 (1970), pp. 257-263.

[309] John Paul II, *Familiaris consortio*, op. cit., no. 78.

[310] This is the opinion of P. Krämer, *Kirchenrecht I*, op. cit., p. 121; the same author rightly observes that in Germany the faculty to dispense from the impediment now abolished, already after the publication of the MP *Matrimonia mixta* in 1970, was conceded by the Conference of Bishops to all the priests having faculties to bless marriages, cf. AfkKR 139 (1970), pp. 538-548.

and therefore uniquely civil marriage too, is enough. When it is a question however of a not only valid but also sacramental marriage (can. 1055 §2), one cannot make out why the ecclesiastical legislator did not have the courage to demand also for these marriages that which he requires for the validity or sacramentality of the marriages between Catholics and non-Catholic Christians of the Eastern Rite, that is to say the intervention of the *minister sacer* (can. 1127 §1).

The importance and the actuality of mixed marriages should have suggested a more precise formulation of can. 1366. Indeed, the possibility of applying canonical sanctions to parents who present their children to be baptised or educated in a non-Catholic religion relates first of all to those Catholic faithful who actively put into action this choice and only in second place to those Catholic spouses who, living in a mixed marriage, have deliberately not done all within their power to keep faith in their promises [311].

B) MARRIAGE BETWEEN CATHOLICS AND THE NON-BAPTISED

According to cans. 1086 and 1129 the norms relating to mixed marriages between Catholics and the baptised of other Christian confessions apply also to marriages between Catholics and the non-baptised. These marriages, which are only celebrated validly after having obtained the dispensation from disparity of cult, are not sacramental and represent for the Catholic party bigger risks and greater responsibilities. In point of fact, in Europe these marriages are more and more often celebrated between Catholics and muslims, who have a very different conception both of marriage and the family [312]. According to the muslim conception of marriage, not only does the woman not have equal rights with the man "to whatever pertains to the partnership of conjugal life" (can. 1135), but the clan the muslim man belongs to has rights over his children, for which reason it seems almost unthinkable that these could be educated in a religion different from that of their father. On the other hand the latter, according to the Koran, can have up to four wives. For all these reasons before granting the dispensation the competent ecclesiastical authority must: 1. examine the effective will of the non-Catholic party to recognise unity and indissolubility as essential qualities of their own marriage; 2. require from the non-Catholic party the promise to respect such commitments even in the case of a return to their own country of origin [313]. On the Catholic party are imposed the same commitments envisaged by can. 1125 in mixed marriages between Catholics and the baptised of other Christian confessions.

8.4 MATRIMONIAL PROCEDURES

Can. 1141 states: " A marriage which is ratified and consummated cannot be dissolved by any human power or by any cause other than death". In the light of can. 1061 §1 this means that in the Catholic Church the principle of absolute indissolubility of marriage is bound to three indispensible premises: the baptism of both spouses, the valid celebration of the marriage and finally its consummation. If one of the three

---

[311] On this point, cf. H. Heinemann, *Die Konfessionverschiedene Ehe,* in: HdbkathKR, pp. 796-808, here p. 806.

[312] On the whole of this question, cf. *Die christlich-islamische Ehe,* edited by B. Huber, Frankfurt 1984

[313] Cf. P. Krämer, *Kirchenrecht I,* pp. 124-125

premises is lacking the indissolubility is no longer absolute and the marriage can even be dissolved[314]. This notwithstanding the juridical institution of divorce is completely extraneous to canonical matrimonial law. In fact in this, alongside the seldom practiced separation of the spouses[315] while the marriage bond remains (cans. 1151-1155 and 1692-1696), there are only two forms of dissolution of marriage: the declaration of nullity (cans. 1671-1691) and the dissolution of the bond (cans. 1141-1150 and 1697-1706). The first form by its nature is not a dissolution of the marriage bond but rather the establishment that this was never validly constituted and therefore also that the marriage never really existed; the second, on the other hand, is thus a true and proper breaking of a validly constituted marriage bond, but before this has – albeit for different reasons – been able to acquire the character of full and absolute indissolubility. The canonical procedures to be followed in cases of dissolution of the bond of marriage are by nature substantially administrative and thus partially different from those of the processes for nullity of marriage. It would be useful therefore to present them in a different way.

A) THE CANONICAL PROCEDURES FOR DECLARING THE NULLITY OF MARRIAGE

As we have had the opportunity to underline many times the nullity of a marriage can come from a threefold source, that is to say from a defect of consent, from a diriment impediment and from a lack of form. If all three reasons lead to the same result, the nullity of the marriage, nevertheless these are situated on a different level both under the substantial profile and under the procedural. In fact, whenever from a document the existence of a diriment impediment or a defect of canonical form is established in a certain manner and it is likewise certain that a dispensation was not granted, according to the norms of cans. 1686-1688, it is possible to apply a short canonical procedure, called a documentary process[316]. The latter takes place before the judicial vicar or the judge designated by him without the solemn formalities of the ordinary process. The documentary process therefore has an oral character and while envisioning the intervention of the parties and the defender of the bond it is certainly quicker and if it arrives at a sentence this is always affirmative[317], the right of the defender of the bond remaining firm to appeal to the judge in the second instance, which can confirm the declaration of nullity or send the case back to a tribunal of the first instance, in order that it be dealt with according to the ordinary process. The latter is the canonical procedure to be applied in all the other causes of nullity of marriage, with the exception of those that – by reason of some particular circumstances – can be dealt with by the administrative method and, prescinding from the principle of *duplex*

---

[314] In this regard, cf. H. Flatten, *Nichtigerklärung, Auflösung und Trennung der Ehe*, in: Idem, *Gesammelte Schriften zum kanonischen Eherecht*, edited by H. Müller, Paderborn, 1987, pp. 477-490.

[315] There is no lack of those who in the work of reform have proposed remitting the question to the Conferences of bishops so that this material can be regulated according to the customs of the place, cf. Communicationes 10 (1978), p. 118.

[316] For a deepened analysis of these norms of the Code, cf. A. Bonnet, *Il processo documentale*, in: *I procedimenti speciali nel diritto canonico, op. cit.*, pp. 51-92.

[317] In fact if they do not resort to extremes for a documentary process the judge must with a decree order that the cause be dealt with according to the ordinary process (can. 1617).

sententia conformis, by the Apostolic Signatura, the one ecclesiastical tribunal which enjoys the competence to declare a marriage null in this way [318]. Although this is not the right place to discuss whether the possibility of applying a similar administrative procedure in order to declare a marriage null could in the future be extended also to diocesan tribunals [319], nevertheless the fact itself of its existence allows a greater highlighting of not only the declarative character of the ordinary canonical procedure, but also its peculiarity in relation to the contentious process (can. 1691).

The ordinary process for marriage nullity cases, reserved to a collegiate tribunal of three judges (can. 1425) happens in three phases: the introductory phase or introduction of the cause, the instructing phase or probative instruction and the decisive phase, whose pivot is the sentence [320]. To the introduction of the cause belong the norms relative to the competent forum (cans. 1671-1673), which normally is the diocesan tribunal of the place of celebration of the marriage; the norms relating to the right to impugn the marriage (cans. 1674-1675), which normally is one of the spouses; the norms on the parties capable of being present in judgment, that is the curator (can. 1479) and the advocate (can. 1481), as well as on the defender of the bond (can. 1432) and on the notary (can. 1437). Decisive for the introduction of a marriage cause is keeping in mind that this begins with the presentation of the judicial petition or *libellus,* in written form, requesting the declaration of the nullity of the marriage for a determined heading or *causa petendi* on the basis of a brief description of the facts and the proofs. After the acceptance of the libellus the president of the tribunal (or the presiding judge/ponens) notifies the citation to the parties and to the defender of the bond; fifteen days having elapsed he gives cause for the joinder of issues or the fixation of the doubt with the specific nullity heading and its notification to the parties. Ten days after this notification the presiding judge orders with a decree the instructing or probative phase of the process (cans. 1677 §4). The latter is designed for the acquisition of the useful and licit proofs in order to demonstrate the nullity of the marriage starting from the established nullity heading. In order to fulfil this purpose the principal means of instruction is the interrogation of the parties, the witnesses and the experts. The confessions and the declarations of the parties (cans. 1530-1538), the documentary proofs (cans. 1539-1546) and the testimonial (cans. 1547-1573), as well as possible experts or expert proofs (cans. 1574-1581), must all be evaluated by the judge according to his conscience (can. 1608), unless the law does not establish what the efectiveness of some of the proofs would be, as for example the value of full proof of a public document. The probative instruction complete the judge must arrange for the publication of the acts (can. 1598) and fix a suitable time for the pre-

---

[318] Cf. R.L. Burke, *La procedura amministrativa per la dichiarazione di nullità del matrimonio,* in: *I procedimenti speciali nel diritto canonico,* op. cit., pp. 93-105. It is a question of causes coming from mission countries, where ecclesiastical tribunals are lacking, or of cases of non-observance of the obligation of canonical form (cf. AAS 76, 1984, pp. 745 ff).

[319] On the point, cf. K. Lüdicke, *Der kirchliche Ehenichtigkeitsprozess – Ein processus contentiosus?,* in: ÖAKR 39 (1990), pp. 295-308, above all pp. 304-308.

[320] For a brief summary of the historical evolution of the marriage process, cf. L. Lefebvre, *Evoluzione del processo matrimoniale canonico,* in: *Il processo matrimoniale canonico,* op. cit., pp. 25-38; for a synthetic exposition of the structure of the marriage process, cf. A. Stankiewicz, *Processi matrimoniali,* in: NDDC, pp. 839-843, above all pp. 840-843.

sentation of the pleadings, the observations and the rejoinders (can. 1603). After this the final phase begins of the ordinary matrimonial process or a definition of the cause with the definitive sentence (can. 1607). This last must reply to the doubt agreed upon, declare if the nullity of the marriage stands or does not stand (constat or non constat) and expound in law and in fact the reasons upon which " the dispositive part of the judgement is based" (can. 1611 no 3). The affirmative decision must be transmitted ex officio to the appeal tribunal within twenty days of its publication and the appeals tribunal must confirm it by decree (can. 1682); against a negative decision, on the other hand, the party who believes himself aggrieved (but also the promoter of justice and the defender of the bond) has the right to appeal to the tribunal of the second instance, which will procede in the ordinary manner (cans. 1628-1640). A double conforming decision in favour of the nullity having been obtained, the parties can celebrate new nuptials provided that the executive decision does not have any prohibition appended to it (can. 1684 §1).

B) THE CANONICAL PROCEDURES FOR THE DISSOLUTION OF THE BOND OF MARRIAGE

In the Canon Law in force three types of procedure for the dissolution of the bond of marriage are known, all of an essentially administrative nature and therefore distinct from the judicial processes of marriage nullity by dint of a more pronounced application of the criteria of simplicity, celerity and pastorality: the procedure for the dispensation of a ratified and non-consummated marriage (cans. 1142 and 1697-1706), the process of presumption of death of the spouse (can. 1707) and the procedures for the dissolution of marriages by reason of the *salus animarum*. For the latter type the use of the plural is obligatory because it is a question of four distinct cases, resolved with analogous but not totally identical procedures and namely: the procedure for the dissolution of the bond of marriage in the case in point of the *privilegium paulinum* (cans. 1143-1147), that to be followed in the case in point of the *privilegium fidei* or *petrinum* [321], as well as those relating to the polygamist who is to be baptised (can. 1148) and to the convert who "by reason of captivity or persecution cannot re-establish cohabitation with his or her unbaptised spouse" (can. 1149).

As far as regards the procedure for a dispensation of a ratified and non-consummated marriage it is enough to record the following: 1. the procedural initiative, being aimed towards the request for the grace of a dispensation, is an exclusive right of the spouses; 2. the object of the instruction relates both to the verification of the non-consummation of the marriage (by means of three proofs: physical, *per coarctata tempora* and moral), and to the existence of a just cause (reconciliation impossible, divorce already taken place, spiritual good of the party who has put forward the *petitio*) for requesting the dispensation; 3. the unfolding of the procedure is articulated in two stages: the phase before the diocesan bishop and that before the

---

[321] The norms to be followed in this matter in hand are not contained in the CIC, but have been published by the Congregation for the Doctrine of the Faith, cf.: *Instructio pro solutione matrimonii in favorem Fidei*, in: SC pro Doctrina Fidei, *Documenta inde a Concilio Vaticano Secondo expleto edita (1966-1985)*, Città del Vaticano 1985, pp. 65-71; Idem, *Normae procedurales pro conficiendo processu dissolutionis vinculi matrimonialis in favorem Fidei*, in: EV, Vol. 4, nos. 2730-2774.

Congregation for the Sacraments, which after having completed everything within its competence presents the request for the dispensation to the Supreme Pontiff[322]. With the dispensation, granted in the form of a rescript, the reciprocal rights and duties of the spouses cease, but the possible children always remain legitimate.

The process of the presumed death of a spouse is normally an administrative procedure leading up to a declaration, based of the presumption of death of the spouse who has disappeared or has been absent for a long time, applied when the surviving spouse cannot get access to an authentic ecclesiastical or civil document in order to enter into – according to the norms of can. 1085 §1 – a new marriage[323].

The four canonical procedures for the dissolution of the marriage bond by reason of the *salus animarum* are directed only partially by the new Code and already this fact reveals a certain embarrassment on the part of the ecclesiastical legislator[324]. In particular in the CIC no emphasis is made on the dissolution of a marriage *in favorem fidei,* if not just in a totally indirect way in can. 1150, which states: "In a doubtful matter the privilege of the faith enjoys the favour of the law"[325]. Does this mean that the only possible limitation of the faculty of the competent ecclesiastical authority to dissolve a validly constituted marriage bond is represented by the *ratum et non consummatum* marriage (can. 1141), and what's more only when it has the certainty that this is such? A similar interpretative hypothesis, which implies a prevalence of can. 1150 *(favor fidei)* over can. 1060 *(favor iuris),* seems to be confirmed by the double widening of the field of application, which has had to be applied in recent times to the pauline privilege.

According to its traditional juridical configuration the pauline privilege, called thus because it is based on the First Letter of Saint Paul to the Corinthians (1 Cor 7, 12-17), consists in the possibility of the ecclesiastical authority dissolving the valid marriage bond when one of the two infidel, non-baptised, spouses coverts to the faith. Its application is however subordinate to three conditions: 1. it is a question of a marriage validly contracted between two non-baptised persons; 2. one of the two spouses after the marriage converts and receives baptism; 3. the non-baptised person refuses to continue the common life with the baptised spouse peacefully *(sine contumelia Creatoris).* Moreover, still in the canonical tradition reprised in the CIC of 1917, the possibility does not figure of the latter, that is the baptised spouse, once free from the previous bond, being able to enter into a new marriage with a non-Catholic or

---

[322] For a deepened study of the two phases of the process, cf. O. Buttinelli, *Il procedimento di dispensa dal matrimonio rato e non consumato: la fase davanti al vescovo diocesano,* in: *I procedimenti speciali nel diritto canonico,* op. cit., pp. 107-124 and R. Melli, *Il procedimento di dispensa dal matrimonio rato e non consumato: la fase davanti alla Congregazione,* in: ibid., pp. 125-144.

[323] Cf. R. Melli, *Il processo di morte presunta,* in: *I procedimenti speciali nel diritto canonico,* op. cit., pp. 848-849.

[324] For a brief presentation of the four canonical procedures, cf. R. Puza, *Katholisches Kirchenrecht,* op. cit., pp. 348-352.

[325] After the last edition of 1982 in the schemas for the renewed CIC any reference to the dissolution of a marriage *in favorem Fidei* has disappeared, cf. A. Silvestrelli, *Scioglimento di un matrimonio in favorem Fidei,* in: *I procedimenti speciali nel diritto canonico,* op. cit., pp. 179-204, here p. 190 and 204.

absolutely non-baptised party [326]. Now, this possibility is explicitly recognised by the ecclesiastical legislator in can. 1147 and represents the first debatable widening of the field of application of the pauline privilege.

The second widening is represented by the so-called *privilegium fidei*, according to which valid non-Christian or semi-Christian (between a baptised and a non-baptised person) marriages can be dissolved in favour of the faith even when the conditions for the applicability of the pauline privilege are not fully respected. Even if the faculty to apply a similar privilege belongs only by right to the Pope, nevertheless the actual progressive widening of the casuistry is such as to give rise to some legitimate worries [327]. In point of fact, if in the future it is wished to avoid giving the impression that Canon Law is in some way playing with the sacraments and people it is extremely important and urgent to rethink, in the light of the conciliar teaching on the sacrament of marriage, the theological foundations of this ecclesiastical practice not only in function of the marriages celebrated in the so-called mission countries, but above all in function of a more general and deeper coherence of the whole of canonical matrimonial law [328]. It should then finally be possible to clarify the significance of such a practice also in relation to the delicate problem of the marriages of the baptised who have abandoned the Catholic Church, in order to verify if these do not represent a further example of valid but non-sacramental marriages.

FUNDAMENTAL BIBLIOGRAPHY

Ahlers R.-Gerosa L.-Müller L. (Hrsg.), *Ecclesia a sacramentis. Theologische Erwägungen zum Sakramentenrecht,* Paderborn 1992.

AA.VV., *I procedimenti speciali nel diritto canonico,* Città del Vaticano 1992.

AA.VV., *Il processo matrimoniale canonico,* Città del Vaticano 1988.

Corecco E., *Natura e struttura della "Sacra Potestas" nella dottrina e nel nuovo Codice di diritto canonico,* in: Communio 75 (1984), pp. 25-52.

De Luca L., *The new law on marriage,* in: *Le nouveau Code de Droit Canonique I. Actes du Ve Congres de Droit Canonique tenu à l'Université St Paul d'Ottawa 1986,* pp. 827-851.

Gerosa L., *Diritto ecclesiale e pastorale,* Torino 1991.

Longhitano A. (a cura di), *Il Codice del Vaticano II. Matrimonio canonico tra tradizione e rinnovamento,* Bologna 1985.

---

[326] On this point cf. G. Girotti, *La procedura per lo scioglimento del matrimonio nella fattispecie del "privilegio paolino",* in: *I procedimenti speciali nel diritto canonico,* op. cit., pp. 157-174, here p. 168; on the worries and reservations, arising for the most part from the reforms, opposed to the actual can. 1147, cf. Nuntia 15 (1982), p. 91.

[327] Analogous worries arise from the matters in hand of cans. 1148 and 1149; on this point cf. R. Puza, *Katholisches Kirchenrecht,* op. cit., pp. 349.

[328] For a first theological approach to the question, cf. J. Tomko, *De dissolutione matrimonii in favorem Fidei eiusque fundamento theologico,* in: Periodica 64 (1975), pp. 99-139.

Molano E., *Dimensiones juridicas de los sacramentos,* in: *Sacramentalidad de la Iglesia y sacramentos.* IV Simposio Internacional de teologia de la Universidad de Navarra, edited by P. Rodriguez, Pamplona 1983, pp. 312-322.

Navarrete U., *Structura iuridica matrimonii secundum Concilium Vaticanum II,* Romae 1968.

Prader J., *Das kirchliche Eherecht in der seelsorglichen Praxis,* Bozen 1983.

Schmitz H., *Taufe, Firmung, Eucharistie. Die Sakramente der Initiation und ihre Rechtsfolgen in der Sicht des CIC von 1983,* in: AfkKR 152 (1983), pp. 369-408.

FIFTH CHAPTER: CHARISMS AND FORMS OF ASSOCIATION OF THE FAITHFUL

In the deep conviction that, within the conciliar ecclesiology developed around *communio* as its central idea, *charismata sunt necessaria pro vita Ecclesiae*[1], in the first chapter on the theological foundation of Canon Law their juridical value was amply illustrated and in particular that of the so-called originating charism[2]. The study of the juridical-constitutional role of the latter has allowed the contemporary canonistic both to complete the first steps towards the development in detail of a true and proper general theory of charism in Canon Law, and above all to rethink the theological foundations of the Canon Law concerning the associative phenomenon in the Church[3].

The variety and multiplicity of the new associative ecclesial forms recognised by the Vatican Council II and by other documents of the Magisterium[4], as well as the variety and multiplicity of the traditional forms of ecclesial association religious and secular, impose some preliminary doctrinal clarifications on the study of the normative of the Code on the associations of the faithful (cans. 298-329) and that relating to the institutes of consecrated life and to the societies of apostolic life (cans. 573-746).

1. THEOLOGICAL FOUNDATIONS AND CRITERIA FOR DISTINCTION

1.1 THE CONSTITUTIONAL CHARACTER OF THE VARIOUS FORMS OF "aggregationes fidelium"

A first clarification is concerned with the distinction, never totally adequate in Canon Law, between constitutional right and a right relative to the different forms of ecclesial association. Already for some years or so, the analysis of the debates on the systematic of the new Code of Canon Law, has allowed the formulation of these difficult distinctions in the following manner: while the constitutional right finds its key concept in the

---

[1] W. Bertrams, *De aspectu ecclesiologico sacerdotii et magisterii Ecclesiae: praemissae et conclusiones,* in: Periodica 51 (1970), pp. 515-562, here p. 521.

[2] Cf. especially 1. chapter 3.2 c) and d).

[3] In this regard cf. L. Gerosa, *Carisma e diritto nella Chiesa. Riflessioni canonistiche sul "carisma originario" dei nuovi movimenti ecclesiali,* Milano 1989, especially pp. 205-242; Idem, *Carisma e movimenti ecclesiali: una sfida per la canonistica postconciliare,* in: Periodica 82 (1993), pp. 411-430.

[4] cf. for example AA 19 and PO 8, as well as no. 58 of the EA *Evangelii nuntiandi* of Paul VI (AAS 68, 1976, pp. 5-76) and nos. 21-29-30 of the EA *Christifideles laici* of John Paul II (AAS 81, 1989, pp. 393-521).

conciliar idea of *communio*, the right of association appears to evolve entirely around the idea of *consociatio*[5].

Now, if it is true that this method of distinguishing the canonical constitutional right from that relating to the various *aggregationes fidelium*, and in particular to the right of association, it certainly has the merit of witnessing how living in the *communio* is a necessary condition for salvation, contrarily to the choice of participating in the life of a *consociatio*, however the same distinction does not give enough attention to a series of historical-ecclesiological data and some questions of a doctrinal order.

Among the historical-ecclesiological data is to be pointed out first of all the fact that many ecclesial associations, ancient (as for example the orders and confraternities) or recent (as for example the ecclesial movements), were not born of the purely human will to associate but from the aggregative force acquired by their founder or foundress through the gift of an originating charism. In second place is to be pointed out that, often, such forms of ecclesial life, conforming to the teachings of the Vatican Council II, do not have specific or particular aims, but rather "look to the general end of the Church" (AA 19,1).

Among the theoretical questions on the other hand the following are to be pointed out. First of all the principle of the *communio* while having an extraordinary relevance on the constitutional level directs all sections of Canon Law and therefore also that of the different aggregative forms of the faithful and in particular of associations. Consequently in this perspective the idea of *consociatio* is not to be seen as a different or alternative reality to that indicated by the term *communio*, but as its specific realisation. The pontifical Magisterium confirms it where it speaks of the new ecclesial movements as specific forms of "self-realisation of the Church"[6]. This means that the originating charism, in a certain analogy with the Eucharist celebrated in a given place, can play a decisive role in the constituting of any type of *consociatio*, as a reality of ecclesial communion or *communitas fidelium*.

In second place, the Church being as a *communio* a "unique complex reality, that is constituted of divine and human elements" (LG 8,1), the ecclesial juridical order in all its sections also participates in this "unique complex reality". In other words in every section of the juridical system of the Church there is in force – even with a diversified intensity – a unity of tension between the *ius divinum* and the *ius humanum* or *mere ecclesiasticum*[7] . Consequently, as constitutional canonical law cannot limit

---

[5]   See above all the essay of W. Aymans, *Kirchliches Verfassungsrecht und Vereinigungsrecht in der Kirche*, in: ÖAKR 32 (1981), pp. 79-110. The debate was then widened after the promulgation of the new CIC, cf. for example: H. Schmitz, *Die Personalprälaturen*, in Hd-bkathKR, pp. 526-529; P. Rodriguez, *Iglesias particulares y Prelaturas personales. Consideraciones teológicas a propósito de una nueva institución canónica*, Pamplona 1985.

[6]   The expression, created by Karol Wojtyla when he was still Archbishop of Krakow, is in the substance of its meaning reprised by John Paul II when, in the discourse at Castelgandolfo on the 27 September 1981, he stated that "the Church herself is a movement" and this "multiple movement" is concretely expressed by ecclesial movements; cf. *I Movimenti nella Chiesa. Atti del I Congresso Internazionale* (Roma, 23-27 September 1981), edited by M. Camisasca-M. Vitali, Milano 1982, pp. 9 and 14.

[7]   Cf. P. Krämer, *Katholische Versuche einer theologischen Begründung des Kirchenrechts*, in: *Die Kirche und ihr Recht* (=Theologische Berichte 15), Zürich-Einsiedeln-Köln 1986, pp.

itself to studying the divine aspects of the Constitution of the Church and much less to reduce the same to the hierarchy, so also the Canon Law relating to the various forms of ecclesial association cannot be reduced to the study of the purely human aspects present in every type of *consociatio*, as if the right of association of the faithful were a *ius nativum* based exclusively on natural law. In point of fact, this latter is specified in its contents for all the faithful by baptism and confirmation, and moreover can discover its most radical and specific realisation in the gift of a charism, to be exercised "for the edification of the Church" (AA 3,4).

Keeping in mind both these historical-ecclesiological data and the doctrinal specifications suggested by the conciliar teaching on the Church as *communio* and on the role of charisms in its edification, the distinction between constitutional right and the right of the ecclesial associations, and in particular of the associations of the faithful, could be reformulated in the following terms: in the Church the right of the ecclesiastical associations, and in particular of the associations of the faithful, is the representation in prefixed schemata or juridical formulas – and therefore the functional regulation – of a constitutional element, the Charism [8]. On the other hand the sections of the canonical normative that do not concern either associations or aggregations juridically structure the other two constitutional elements: Word and Sacrament. Both these normatives together have a constitutional character. Under the legislative framework their distinction cannot therefore be formalised in an absolutely rigorous manner. For this reason in the new Code of Canon Law, based on the example of that of 1917, the ecclesiastical legislator prudently avoids speaking either of constitutional right, or of the right of association and places the norms relating to the latter in the large book *De populo Dei* alongside those on the lay faithful, on the hierarchy, and on the members of the institutes of consecrated life and societies of apostolic life.

It would in any case be a mistake to deduce from this new general formulation of the distinction between constitutional and associative that in Canon Law the only constitutional factor capable of giving rise to forms of ecclesial association is the Charism. With this and before this, in fact, the other two primary constitutional elements too, but of an institutional nature (that is the Word and Sacrament) are eminently aggregative factors. Moreover, in the Church from time immemorial the primordial and indispensable aggregating factor is the Eucharist, rightly defined by the Vatican Council II as the *fons et culmen* of that *aggregatio fidelium* which is the Church herself [9]. Consequently, precisely because it is through the eucharistic assembly that the *genuinam verae Ecclesiae naturam* (SC 2) in its divine and human elements are known, it is above all from this that the canonist must draw the criteria in order to distinguish the constitu-

---

11-37, here p. 33.

[8]   This definition was formulated for the first time by E. Corecco, *Istituzione e carisma in riferimento alle strutture associative,* in: Akten VI IKKR, pp. 79-98, here pp. 95-96.

[9]   Cf. LG 11,1: CD 30,6 and also SC 10,1, where the expression is applied to the liturgy in general, whose centre is the *divino Eucharistiae Sacrificio* (SC 2). The most significant text at the level of the associative and educative force of the sacrament of the Eucharist is therefore to be sought in the conciliar Decree on the ministry and life of priests: *Nulla tamen communitas christiana aedificatur nisi radicem cardinemque habeat in Sanctissimae Eucharistiae celebratione, a quia ergo omnis educatio ad spiritum communitatis incipienda est* (PO 6,5).

tional elements from the merely associative in the different forms of communities of the faithful.

1.2 EUCHARIST AND CHARISM AS THE ULTIMATE CRITERIA FOR DISTINCTION BETWEEN THE "INSTITUTIONAL" AND "CHARISMATIC" GROUPINGS IN THE CHURCH

A first verification of how the Eucharist and Charism are both the primordial constitutional elements from which to draw the criteria for the distinction between the different forms of *aggregationes fidelium* is offered by the history of the parish. Although it is not easy to distinguish with precision the trajectory of the historical development of this canonical institution, having seen also the different semantic evolution of the Greek term compared with the corresponding Latin one [10], the thesis which places the rural parish safely between the IV and V Century, and that of the urban parish only towards the XI Century, is however by now commonly accepted. The two models are not entirely comparable.

The former model notwithstanding the multiple differences between a parish Church and a non-baptismal Church arising on private property, is always determinable in its juridical configuration by means of the criteria of organisation of a territory or of a patrimony. The latter model is on the other hand often bound to a personal, family or corporative criterion and does not always posess the same juridical autonomy of the first.

After the Council of Trent, notwithstanding the notable reflourishing of confraternities and religious associations [11], the rural type of parish assumes a foremost role. With the advent of phenomena such as industrialisation, secularisation and the mobility of populations within the same territory, this rigid model has entered into a crisis and the Vatican Council II saw itself compelled to rethink the theological presuppositions of the parish prior to proposing the reform of the juridical structure [12]. The result was the realisation that the parish can assume, and in fact in the history of the Church has assumed, a plurality of juridical configurations, as emerges with clarity also in the juridical flexibility characterising the image of the parish given by the new Code (cans. 515-522), the element of greater prominence of which is certainly having defined it first of all as a *communitas fidelium* (can. 515 §1).

This notion of the parish as a community of the faithful, whose norms in the Code were studied in 2.2 of the last chapter, finds its most complete expression *in communi celebratione Missae dominicalis* (SC 42,2), which is the *centrum et culmen totius vitae communitatis christianae* (CD 30,6). This means that the Parish, among the

---

[10] In this regard cf. T. Mauro, *Parrocchia*, in: EDD, Vol. XXXI (1981), pp. 868-887 and in particular pp. 868-869; A. Longhitano, *La parrocchia: storia, teologia e diritto*, in: AA.VV., *La parrochia e le sue strutture*, Bologna 1987, pp. 5-27 and in particular p. 7, note 2.

[11] Cf. L. Nanni, *L'evoluzione storica della parrocchia*, in: ScCatt 81 (1953), pp. 475-544 and in particular pp. 539-543 where the author gives a detailed analysis of the tridentine dispositions concerning the parish.

[12] Cf. G. Baldanza, *L'incidenza della teologia del Vaticano II sulla riforma della Parrocchia*, in: *Ius Populi Dei, Miscellanea in honorem Raymondi Bigador*, edited by U. Navarrete, Vol. II, Rome 1972, pp. 177-205.

many *coetus fidelium* that the bishop can and must erect in order to be able to preside efficaciously over his own *Populi Dei portio* (SC 45), is the paradigm of ecclesial association born in the celebration of the Eucharist. The Vatican Council II once again and subsequently confirms it when it underlines the missionary dimension asserting that the parish must offer an *exemplum perspicuum apostolatus communitarii* (AA 10,2).

To affirm that the parish is the paradigm of ecclesial associations born from the Eucharist means two things: on the one hand this is not the only form of eucharistic community, and on the other it is also not an ecclesiologically necessary juridical entity, given that the principle *in quibus et ex quibus* of LG 23,1 is not applicable as such within the particular Church. The different eucharistic communities in which in some way a particular Church is structured can therefore assume different juridical forms: the fixed or institutional, of the parish precisely, and the variable of the ecclesial associations of charismatic origin. In the former form the aggregative power of the Sacrament prevails, the Eucharist celebrated in a determined place, in the latter form on the other hand the aggregative power of the originating charism prevails. In both, obviously, the aggregative power of the Word also expresses itself, because "where two or three are gathered in my name I am in the midst of them" (Mt. 18,20), but the eminently charismatic nature of the latter form constitutes a further verification of how not only the Eucharist, but also the Charism represents an ultimate criterion for distinguishing between the various forms of ecclesial association.

According the the *incipit* of the §1 of can. 298, the ecclesial associations of charismatic origin are distinguished in their turn into two major categories, the associations or *consociationes* comprising the faithful of all states of ecclesial life (such as confraternities, associations and ecclesial movements) and associations, called *Instituta* or *Societas* [13], comprising only the faithful who live the consecration to God above all through the evangelical counsels (such as religious orders and the other institutes of consecrated life). These two categories cannot however be reduced to the distinction of Pio-Benedictine origin between the so-called lay associations and religious associations [14].

In fact clerics and religious can also participate in the first type of ecclesiastical associations, as can easily be deduced from cans. 298 §1 and 307 §3. Moreover, the actual latter type of ecclesiastical associations for at least three reasons differ notably from the notion of *religious associations* used by the preceding Code. The first motive consists in the fact that the Religious Institutes are flanked by the so-called Secular Institutes, whose recognition only came about on the 2 February 1947, when with the Apostolic Constitution *Provida Mater Ecclesia* Pope Pius XII promulgated the *Lex*

---

[13] Notwithstanding all of the differences that can be witnessed between the first and the second, it is the same Code that underlines the similarity of the Societies of apostolic life with religious Institutes, where it affirms that these *accedunt* (=draw near) to Institutes of consecrated life (cf. can. 731 §1). And revealing this similarity the ecclesiastical legislator does nothing other than follow in the footsteps of the Vatican Council II (cf. LG 44,1 and PC 1).

[14] This type of classification, where *associations* or *religious societies* and *lay associations* are considered as two categories subsumed under the fuller one of *ecclesiastical associations*, is proposed for example by V. Del Giudice, *Nozioni di Diritto Canonico*, Milano 1953, pp. 123 ff.

fundamentalis that ratified the existence of Secular Institutes, determining the essential norms relative to their nature and their erection in quality of special and qualified associations [15]. Collectively, Religious Institutes and Secular Institutes form the large category of Institutes of Consecrated Life. The second motive consists in the fact that alongside this first category of associative forms of religious faithful, the ecclesiastical legislator distinguishes another, that of the Society of Apostolic Life, according to a more pragmatic than theological logic. In point of fact, the law of Institutes of Consecrated Life is applied to these in great part, even if their members do not practice the evangelical counsels *ut sic*, but simply as demands of their own apostolate. The third and last motive consists finally in the fact that, in spite of the also notable differences existing between them, these three forms or itineraries of sanctification, theses for the perfection of christian life [16], clearly manifest a common characteristic: the consecration of life through the evangelical counsels. This consecration although under the theological framework being a complex and difficult concept to define with exactitude, is realised through the personal choice to practice the evangelical counsels, these being taken singularly, in twos or according to the classical set of three, professed in ways and according to different bonds, all in any case reconductible to the theological reality of only one counsel, "that of full filial dependence on the Father in love, which is the Spirit" [17]. In other words, all of these forms of consecrated life have in common the experience of a charism, by nature eminently prophetic and eschatological, that general and personal of the so-called evangelical counsels seen as a renunciation of the values which it is not reasonable to renounce if not by dint of an opening to the grace of a particular state or form of ecclesial life, practicable in community or in solitude, in secular life or in flight from the world.

This particular form of ecclesial life, outside of the concrete modalities in which it is expressed, constitutes a true and proper state of Christian life, the *status perfectionis*, alongside the matrimonial and clerical [18]. This consists however in a *sequela Christi*

---

[15]   Text of the Constitution in AAS 39 (1947), pp. 114-124. On the quality of "qualified special associations" of secular Institutes see the observations of A. Gutierrez, *Lo stato della vita consacrata nella Chiesa. Valori permanenti e innovazioni*, in AA.VV., *Lo stato giuridico dei consacrati per la professione dei consigli evangelici*, Città del Vaticano 1985, pp. 37-63, here p. 40.

[16]   To these three communitarian forms are added also those of individual consecrated life, like those of the hermitical or anchoritic life (can. 603 §1), the so-called order of virgins (can. 604 §1) and all those new forms, like the fraternity of consecrated widows officially approved in Paris in 1983, and not considered by the CIC; cf. J. Beyer, *Originalità dei carismi di vita consacrata*, in: Periodica 82 (1993), pp. 257-292, above all pp. 266-267.

[17]   J. Beyer, *Dal Concilio al Codice. Il nuovo Codice e le istanze del Concilio Vaticano II*, Bologna 1984, p. 85.

[18]   On how this state has its own autonomy and its own eschatological type priority within the Constitution of the Church (and thus different from that of clerics, stretched to guarantee the unity of the whole the community of the faithful, and that of the laity, stretched to cultural recapitulation of all things in Christ), cf. E. Corecco, *Profili istitutzionali dei Movimenti nella Chiesa*, in: *Movimenti nella Chiesa. Atti del I Congresso Internazionale*, op. cit., pp. 203-234, here p. 218 and H.U. von Balthasar, *Christlicher Stand*, Einsiedeln 1977, pp. 294-314.

that is a different way of reaching the holiness to which all of the baptised are called [19].
It is in this diversity of charismatic origin that there is to be found the theological place
for the distinction between the fundamental associative category of the Institutes of
Consecrated Life and the Societies of Apostolic Life on the one hand and that, also
fundamental, of the associations of the faithful or ecclesial movements on the other.
Indeed, the latter normally are born in the Church starting from the gift of a specific
originating charism, by nature eminently communitarian and missionary, which as
such can involve, albeit according to different modalities, not only lay people married
or not, but also priests and religious, that is to say members of the faithful empowered
either by the sacrament of holy orders or by the charism, personal and general, of the
evangelical counsels.

The specific diversity of the two fundamental types of charism [20], prophetic-
personal that of the evangelical counsels and communitarian-missionary that at the
origin of the associations or ecclesial movements (but often also of the same plurality of forms as consecrated life in which case it is legitimate to speak of a double
charismatic origin!), is under the ecclesiological framework the principal element that
determines the different normative formalisations of the two corresponding sections
of the canonical ordering.

2. THE DIFFERENT FORMS OF ECCLESIAL ASSOCIA-
TIONS OF A PREVALENTLY CHARISMATIC NATURE

2.1 ASSOCIATIONS OF THE FAITHFUL
The new normative of the Code on the associations of the faithful (cans. 298-329)
presents in its entirety a certain value: its being anchored solidly itself in constitutional
right of all the faithful to freely associate for specific charitable or pious purposes, or
simply to help them to grow in their own common Christian vocation. Before elucidat-
ing the general norms, which govern the normative of the Code on the associations in
the Church, it would be worth our while to briefly examine the juridical configurations
and consequences of the constitutional right to associate.

A) THE CONSTITUTIONAL RIGHT OF ALL THE FAITHFUL TO ASSOCIATE FREELY
The foundation of such a right, codified by can. 215 and comprising not only the right
to found associations but also those correlated to it of enlisting in associations as well
as of enjoying a just statutory autonomy, is twofold: natural, in as far as such a right
corresponds to the social nature of man; supernatural, in as far as the mission of the
Church can be efficaciously fulfilled only by a communitarian subject, for whom the
associating proves to be necessary, or at least very useful for the pursuance of such

---

[19]   Cf. LG 40-42 and 44,3.

[20]   The personal character of the charism of the evangelical counsels is underlined by the Vatican Council II in LG 46,2 while the so-called communitarian character of the apostolate
of the laity, explicit and reinforced by the originating charism of the new associative forms
of the faithful, is highlighted in AA 18,2. On the importance of the charism as a visual
point from which to start to understand these two sections of Canon Law, cf. P. Krämer,
Kirchenrecht I. Wort-Sakrament-Charisma, Stuttgart-Berlin-Köln 1992, pp. 153-154.

a mission [21]. In this latter sense such a right wells up first of all from baptism and is reinforced either by the sacrament of confirmation or by the gift of a charism. To have codified this right of all the faithful is certainly a positive innovation. In the CIC/1917 this was not in fact formalised, because the old can. 684 limited itself, in a non constitutional juridical perspective, to praising those faithful who have wanted to become members of associations erected or recommended by the hierarchy. Nonetheless, the typically ecclesial value of this constitutional right of the faithful would have been made more evident if the ecclesiastical legislator of 1983, in dictating the common norms to all associations, had paid greater attention also to the right to their own spirituality, recognised by can. 214 on the reinforcement of the conciliar teaching concerning the diversity of possible paths in the search for holiness, and to that of promoting or sustaining the apostolic activity of the Church even with their own initiatives. In particular if the latter, recognised by can. 216, had been integrated to the former as a basis upon which to establish the common norms for the associations of the faithful, it would have allowed the ecclesiastical legislator a more correct legislative translation of the teaching of the Vatican Council II.

In point of fact, in the Decree on the Apostolate of the Laity the term *incepta apostolica* while not refering to any particular organisative form does not simply mean work [22]. With the term *incepta* the Fathers of the Council wanted to point towards any initiative, personal or communitarian, thanks to which the *missio Ecclesiae melius impleri potest* (AA 24,3).The strict connection between *incepta apostolica* and *missio Ecclesiae* is also intuited by the ecclesiastical legislator precisely in the first of the common norms relative to the associations of the faithful and that is in can. 298 §1 where among the various aggregative forms the initiatives *ad evangelizationis* and *ad ordinem temporalem christiano spiritu animandum* [23] are also pointed out. Now nothing prohibits the canonists from placing the new ecclesial movements, born from an originating charism, precisely in such a category of ecclesial associations which, still according to can. 216, can rightly be called Catholic while not necessarily assuming the juridical statute of association. Certainly, if the ecclesiastical legislator had systematically developed this intuition he would have been able to translate better on the normative level the conciliar teaching on the three fundamental forms of ecclesial association: the associations having a special *mandatum* on the part of the ecclesiastical authority; the associations which, prescinding from the *recognitio* on the part of the authority, are substantially founded on the associative will of the faithful themselves; and finally the so-called *incepta apostolica* that, while not necessarily being associations, by dint of their originating charism possess a greater power of missionary insight [24].

---

[21]   Cf. AA 18,1 and 19,4; PO 8,3; CD 17,2. In this regard cf. also L. Navarro, *Diritto di associazione e associazioni dei fedeli*, Milano 1991, pp. 7-17.

[22]   Cf. W. Schulz, *Der neue Codex und die kirchlichen Vereine*, Paderborn 1986, p. 18, note 45.

[23]   This link proves almost constant in the new Code (cf. X. Ochoa, *Index Verborum ac locutionum CIC*, Roma 1983, voce: *Inceptum*, pp. 202-203). In particular it is worth while to underline how the promotion of these particular associative forms is a task of parish priests, cf. can. 777 no. 5.

[24]   On the character open to further possible completions of this classification, cf. W. Schulz, *Der neue Codex und die kirchlichen Vereine*, op. cit., pp. 36-39.

To the latter form of ecclesial association, even if the possibility is recognised of obtaining a differentiated recognition on the part of the authority, the new Code – guilty of incoherence – does not offer a specific juridical base. This notwithstanding can. 327 invites the lay faithful to keep these types of *consociationes* under greater consideration, because they are more adapted to the inspiration of temporal realities with the Christian spirit.

B) TYPOLOGY OF THE CODE AND GENERAL NORMS

In the common norms of the associations of the faithful (cans. 298-311) the ecclesiastical legislator offers a true and proper typology of the Code, in which alongside ancient distinctions, such as that between associations *erectae* and simply *laudate vel commendatae* (can. 298 §2) or between clerical and lay or mixed associations, new distinctions emerge and take the upper hand, such as those between public (cans. 302 §1; 312-320) and provate associations (cans. 299 §2; 321-326). The latter typological distinction, which is simultaneously the most important in the normative of the Code but also the newest in Canon Law, partially places itself above the more traditional one between erected associations (can. 298 §2) and recognised associations (can. 299 §3). Two facts confirm this.

First of all, the CIC of 1983 appears to make its own not only the principle of permission, according to which an ecclesial association does not exist juridically if it is not erected by the competent authority, but also that of enrolment or recognition, according to which a non erected association can be recognised as existing juridically without however acquiring juridical personality. In fact can. 299 §3 speaks of a *recognitio* as distinct from the *approbatio* of cans. 314 and 322 §2, which on the other hand requires the acquisition of public or private juridical personality.

In second place the juridical configuration of the two categories also allows it to emerge sufficiently clearly that it is a question of a mixture between old and new, as such to legitimise the position of those who define this typology of the Code as a mixed system [25]. If both categories of association must have according to the norms of Canon Law their own proper statute, these distinguish themselves for the following reasons: private associations are constituted from the private agreement of the associated faithful and distinguish themseves in their turn into those that, while being recognised, do not have juridical personality and into those which have a private juridical personality, because their statutes have been approved; public associations on the other hand are those erected by the competent ecclesiastical authority, and thus are constituted into a public juridical person, because they propound the teaching of Christian doctrine in the name of the Church or the increase of public worship, or other purposes whose attainment is by its nature reserved to the ecclesiastical hierarchy. The unity of measure of the publicity of an association of the faithful consists therefore in the lesser or greater possibility given to the members of the same to speak and act in the name of the Church and of her authority for the usefulness of the whole People of God. What is at stake is regrettably once again the lesser or greater closeness of an association to the ecclesiastical authority, almost as if the *nomine Ecclesiae* were to be necessarily inter-

---

[25]   Agreeing with this opinion: J. Beyer, *Dal Concilio al Codice*, op. cit., p. 80; E. Corecco, *Profili istituzionali dei Movimenti nella Chiesa*, in: *I movimenti nella Chiesa*, op. cit., pp. 203-234, here p. 222.

preted as a *nomine hierarchiae*[26]. In point of fact, a little in all the statutory sections, from the admission of members to the administration of goods, from the structure of government to the very extinction of the association in question, private associations – even when they are erected to a juridical person – enjoy a greater autonomy in relation to the ecclesiastical authority and thus depend to a lesser extent on common Canon Law[27].

If the terminological oscillation is one of the reasons why the new normative of the Code on associations ends up leaving the clear impression that in substance we find ourselves facing abstract distinctions[28] without an effective correspondence with an ecclesial reality living and in constant development, the briefest analysis of the typology of the Code lets us easily understand how the ecclesiastical legislator of 1983 not only has not given sufficient attention to their ecclesiological dimension and in particular their charismatic origin, but also has at the same time shown an excessive dependence on the state law on associations.

C) THE TWO-FOLD DEPENDENCE OF *De christifidelium consociationibus* ON THE STATE LAW ON ASSOCIATIONS

The excessive dependence of the ecclesiastical legislator on the state juridical doctrine on associations emerges with particular prominence in two fields: in the introduction into Canon Law of the distinction between public associations and private associations and in the use of the very notion of association.

The distinction between public and private has always been considered as non applicable to the juridical system of the Church by the best Catholic canonical tradition[29]. This could be why it was introduced by the ecclesiastical legislator of 1983 solely as a practical criterion for establishing a certain differentiation between the different ecclesial associative phenomena[30]. In other words, without wishing to match himself against complex theoretical questions, in introducing this distinction the ecclesiastical legislator very simply proposes to render juridically operative a typology or a didactic categorisation by which to distinguish the various degrees of ecclesiality proper to a determined association and determined movements. A legitimate basic

---

[26] In this regard, cf. G. Feliciani, *Diritti e doveri dei fedeli in genere e dei laici in specie. Le associazioni,* in: *Il nuovo Codice di Diritto Canonico,* edited by S. Ferrari, Bologna 1983, pp. 253-273, here p. 270.

[27] On all of this argument, cf. G. Ghirlanda, *Associazioni dei fedeli,* in NDDC, pp. 52-61.

[28] The expression *abstrakte Abstufungen* was introduced in relation to the distinction between public and private associations by H. Schnizer, *Allgemeine Fragen des kirchlichen Vereinsrechts,* in HdbkathKR, pp. 454-469, here p. 459.

[29] Cf. K. Mörsdorf, Lb, Bd. I, p. 23 and P. Fedele, *Discorso generale su l'ordinamento canonico,* Roma 1976, pp. 104-108.

[30] In this regard it has been observed: "In reality the distinction of public and private associations do not intend to compete with complex theoretical and doctrinal questions but intend, much more simply to respond in a perhaps debatable way to a demand of a practical and contingent character. The recognition of the right of association for all the faithful while overcoming the rigid and verticalist preceding discipline requires also stabilising a certain differentiation between the different associative phenomena" (G. Feliciani, *I diritti e doveri dei fedeli,* op. cit., p. 270) The substance of this opinion is shared by H. Schnizer, *Allgemeine Fragen des kirchlichen Vereinsrechts,* op. cit., p. 459.

question nonetheless immediately presents itself: permitted and not conceded that it is possible to free the juridical distinction between public and private from every doctrinal influence, what is the contributory clarification that this gives to the delicate question concerning the determination of the ecclesiality or not of a determined association or of a determined movement? Outwith every good intention the only true criterion used by the legislator to resolve the question of ecclesiality remains substantially that of the first canonical codification: the degree of closeness to the ecclesiastical hierarchy.

In the new Code this criterion is made more elastic only thanks to the correction that the legislator brings to the old system of permission with the simultaneous application of the so-called principle of enrolment. In an ecclesiology governed at all levels by the principle of *communio* this manner of proceding in the determination of the ecclesiality of a group, movement or association, is inadequate for at least two reasons.

First of all the pontifical Magisterium has already fixed other criteria for judging the authenticity of the originating charism of an ecclesiastical association[31], as well as some fundamental principles for the discernment and recognition of the ecclesiality of every type of association[32]. In second place every movement or association is ecclesial first of all in the measure in which it participates in the nature of the Church[33], through listening to the Word and the celebration of the sacraments, through responsible obedience to the gifts of the Spirit and the communitarian life of the whole Church, when by dint of the principle of the *communio* the freedom of the Spirit is always joined together with the bond of authority. This means that in the Church even the so-called private associations if they realise the principle of the communion are always an ecclesial reality, that is a phenomenon in which the Church is realised and consequently, as such, these are never a merely private fact in terms of the juridical science of the state[34]. And this even before the ecclesiastical authority intervenes to control the statutes of associations according to can. 299 §3 or to praise or recommend the association in the sense of can. 299 §2. This is further confirmed by the fact that, if the purpose of a private ecclesial association can be particular and thus not explicitly recontain all the finalities of the Church, such a specific purpose – by dint of the principle of reciprocal immanence of the whole in the part – always implies however. at least *in nuce*, the entire content of Christian life and thus the entire universal experience of the Church, because otherwise the association would not even be ecclesial. This last assertion implies a clarification also on the level of the very notion of association.

Beyond the difficulties encountered by canonical science in the attempt to distinguish with clarity an *associatio* or *consociatio* from the more general notion of *aggregatio*, both the CIC and the contemporary study of Canon Law use the concept

---

[31]   Cf. the directives, *De mutuis relationibus inter episcopos et religiosos*, published on 14 May 1978 by the Congregation for Bishops and the Congregation for Religious and secular institutes, in AAS 70 (1978), pp. 473-506 and the commentary of L. Gerosa, *Carisma e diritto nella Chiesa*, op. cit., pp. 236-242.

[32]   Cf. no. 30 of the EA *Christifideles laici* and the commentary of G. Ghirlanda, *Associazioni dei fedeli*, op. cit., pp. 52-53.

[33]   J. Beyer, *Dal Concilio al Codice*, op. cit., p. 79.

[34]   Cf. E. Corecco, *Istituzione e carisma in riferimento alle strutture associative*, op. cit., p. 96.

of association substantially identical to that developed in detail by the juridical science of the state. If we take as an authoritative point of reference the first evaluation of the totality of the debates which unfolded on the argument at the International Congress in Munich of 1987 [35], the notable progressions made do not yet seem enough to reply in an exhaustive way to the question concerning the true nature of an ecclesial association.

In point of fact, the four constitutive elements of the very essence of a *consociatio* are identified in the following way. The first element is the collectivity of people, not understood however as a *communitas fidelium*, but simply as a *universitas personarum* in which a juridical person can consist. The second element is the free choice of a canonically circumscribed objective, containing in its turn two principal elements: the free and common will to associate oneself (the so-called *Vereinigungswille*), expressed in the act of foundation on the part of the future associates, and the fact that this same will addresses one or two specific aims, all in some way included in the mission of the Church without however coinciding ever with its global mission. The third element is the so-called internal order, determined in its form by the freely chosen purpose. The fourth and last constitutive element of a *consociatio* is the free belonging (*freie Mitgliedschaft*) that juridically categorises it as a phenomenon of freedom.

Now all four of these elements are pointed out, albeit with a slightly different terminology, as essentials in the determination of the notion of association in the juridical science of the state. In point of fact, even the latter speaks of a plurality of subjects and of a will that constitutes in an autonomous way the assembly of the associates, of a common purpose from which is born a juridical bond between the associates of a generally voluntary or free nature [36]. This is nevertheless conscious for a time of the difficulties, sometimes insuperable, that the privatistic doctrine comes across when it wishes to distinguish, on the basis of these elements, an association in the strict sense from any other associative element, and in particular from a consortium [37]. Indeed, the latter is excluded by some from the list of associations given the coercive or necessary nature of the bond existing between its members, by others it is considered as an association obligatory in its constitution in reply to a common need, but not for this less free in its acting. Consequently in the classifications of associations attempted by the juridical doctrine of the state there is a variety so multiple that it witnesses in an unequivocal way to the complexity of the associative phenomenon in general.

Such a complexity is even greater in the Church because at the base of every ecclesial association, precisely because it is ecclesial, there is always a supernatural impulse from the Holy Spirit. It is in the light of this ecclesiological datum that the four essential elements of a *consociatio* have to be reinterpreted, at least so as not to wish to simply indicate with this term a phenomenon of private autonomy, as such without any ecclesiological relevance and thus under the juridical framework structurally identical

---

[35] Cf. the final report held by W. Aymans, *Das konsoziative Element in der Kirche. Gesamtwürdigung*, in: *Akten VI IKKR*, op. cit., pp. 1029-1057.

[36] Cf. A. Auricchio, *Associazione. V. Diritto civile*, in: EDD, Vol. 3 (Milano 1958), pp. 873-878, above all pp. 875-876.

[37] For an analysis of the doctrinal debate surrounding the way in which a consortium is distinguished from other associations cf. G. Ferri, *Consorzio. A) Teoria generale*, in EDD, Vol. IX (Milano 1961) pp. 371-389 and in particular pp. 371-373.

to an association of the law of the state. A similar association can exist in the Church, but this does not certainly represent the model sort of a canonical association and does not exhaust however the significance of the Latin term *consociatio*.

If in the Code of Canon Law the titles mean something, then the term *consociatio* is taken as a general notion (*Oberbegriff*) under which can be found a differentiated collocation of many and different forms of ecclesial association. In particular this should offer a juridical frame of reference not only to those ecclesial associations which by their nature have the statute of a true and proper *associatio*, but also to those new forms of ecclesial associations, for the greater part nowadays the most numerous and pastorally perhaps more efficacious, which present a structural, and in some cases juridical, configuration not able to be encapsulated in the four elements mentioned above as constitutive to the notion of association. Indeed these forms do not present themselves as simple totalities of people but as true and proper communities or fraternities of the faithful which are constituted either as a consequence of an exclusively voluntaristic free choice to associate, or in order to pursue a specific and particular aim. These are communities of the faithful born from the following of an originating charism and thus whoever participates does not do so in the name of a moralistic activism but because he tries out these forms of fraternity as a necessary structure in which to express totally his own Christian personality. According to the Vatican Council II, precisely because born from the gift of a charism[38], these forms of associative life render more immediately operative the fact that every baptised person is called by the Spirit to live in community and as such these render it more ready (LG 12,2) to responsibly assume the general mission of the Church.

2.2 THE INSTITUTES OF CONSECRATED LIFE

Even if it is not easy to avoid every possible confusion, the term consecrated life is not synonymous with religious life[39]. The ecclesiastical legislator of 1983 is conscious of it and employs a first elementary clarification dividing the normative of the Code on the institutes of consecrated life into three titles: 1. norms common to all institutes of consecrated life (cans. 573-606); 2. religious institutes (cans. 607-709); 3. secular institutes (cans. 710-730). To this first section on the institutes of consecrated life is immediately added a second on the societies of apostolic life, almost wishing to underline simultaneously the diversity and the strict relationship with the former. The clarification would have been greater, and juridically more effective, if the ecclesiastical legislator starting from the conciliar teaching on the role of the originating or founding charism and on the theological significance of the consecration to God[40] had given preference in all of this normative of the Code to some preliminary canons on the elements common not only to all the institutes of consecrated life and to the societies of apostolic life, but also to those most exceptional forms of ancient consecrated

---

[38] For a detailed analysis of the conciliar teaching on charisms, cf. G. Rambaldi, *Uso e significato di "carisma" nel Vaticano II. Analasi e confronto di due passi conciliari sui carismi,* in: Gregorianum 66 (1975), pp. 141-162; L. Gerosa, *Carisma e diritto nella Chiesa,* op. cit., pp. 46-57.

[39] In this regard cf. J. Beyer, *Originalità dei carismi di vita consacrata,* op. cit., p. 263.

[40] Cf. above all LG 44; PC 2; CD 33-35.

life, such as those of hermits and virgins, or new consecrated life, such as those of consecrated widows or widowers.

A) TYPOLOGY OF THE CODE AND GENERAL NORMS

The variety of charisms and concrete forms of the *sequela Christi* ill-support any kind of generalisation. Nevertheless, on the basis of tradition and conciliar teaching can. 573 §1 states the following definition: "Life consecrated through profession of the evangelical counsels is a stable form of living, in which the faithful follow Christ more closely under the action of the Holy Spirit, and are totally dedicated to God, who is supremely loved. By an new and special title they are dedicated to seek the perfection of charity in the service of God's Kingdom, for the honour of God, the building up of the Church and the salvation of the world. They are a splendid sign in the Church, as they foretell the heavenly glory". This consecrated life assumes different concrete forms in the various institutes and societies, regulated by their own laws (can. 573 §2), according to the principle of a just autonomy of life (can. 586 §1). In point of fact, such an autonomy is structurally necessary for the protection of fidelity to the originating charism of every institute, a charism whose fundamental elements are contained first of all in the legislative body of the institute itself, that is to say in the fundamental Code or constitutions (containing the rule of life, nature and aim of the institute, the form of government, the proper discipline relating to incorporation and formation of the members, as well as the object and form of the sacred bonds) and other subsequent Codes containing especially applicative norms[41]. The first type of norm, precisely because these express the fundamental structural elements of the charism of the founder or foundress, necessitate a major stability and a greater juridical protection. Such norms must therefore be approved not only by the general chapter but also by the competent ecclesiastical authority. For the applicative norms contained in other Codes on the other hand the approval of the general chapter is sufficient[42].

While being clear that "in itself, the state of consecrated life is neither clerical or lay" (can. 588 §1), the first typological differentiation of the Code is that between clerical and lay institutes. The criterion for distinguishing the two types of institute is not however quantitative as in can. 488 of the CIC/1917, because for the CIC/1983 the institute is clerical which "by reason of the end or purpose intended by the founder, or by reason of lawful tradition, is under the governance of clerics and assumes the exercise of sacred orders" (can. 588 §2). An institute of consecrated life is on the other hand called lay when by dint of its proper nature and character it does not imply the exercise of sacred orders (can. 588 §3). In cases of doubt it is the recognition on the part of the competent ecclesiastical authority that declares the institute in question clerical or lay[43].

The second typological differentiation of the CIC is that between institutes of diocesan right and those of pontifical right. Here too, by reason of its nature, every institute of consecrated life is founded with the intention of serving the whole Church,

---

[41]   Cf. can. 587.

[42]   In this regard, cf. G. Ghirlanda, *Il diritto nella Chiesa mistero di comunione. Compendio di diritto ecclesiale,* Milano 1990, pp. 179-180.

[43]   On the criteria configuring an institute as clerical or not, cf. E. Gambari, *I religiosi nel Codice. Commento ai singoli canoni,* Milano 1986, pp. 59-64.

however this is called of diocesan right if it was founded and erected by the bishop and has not yet received the decree of approval from the Apostolic See; and on the other hand it is called of pontifical right "if it has been erected by the Apostolic See or approved by means of a formal decree from the same" (can. 589). Both can evidently be clerical institutes or lay institutes, religious institutes or secular institutes.

In synthesis, under the canonical framework, the constitutive elements of all these kinds of institutes of consecrated life are: 1. canonical erection of the institute on the part of the competent ecclesiastical authority (cans. 573 §2, 576, 579); 2. the vows or other sacred ties, according to the proper law of the institute relating to the assumption of the evangelical counsels (can. 573 §2). Moreover it should not be forgotten that among all the types of institute of consecrated life canonical equality is in force (can. 606) and that the typology of the code is open to new forms of consecrated life (can. 605), even if their approval is reserved solely to the Apostolic See.

B) RELIGIOUS INSTITUTES, SECULAR INSTITUTES AND SOCIETIES OF APOSTOLIC LIFE

According to the CIC, "a religious institute is a society in which, in accordance with their own law, the members pronounce public vows, either perpetual or temporary, to be renewed when the time elapses, and live a fraternal life"(can. 607 §2). If the public character of the vows distinguishes religious institutes from societies of apostolic life [44], the separation from the world and the common life distinguishes them from secular institutes [45].

Still according to the CIC, "a secular institute is an institute of consecrated life in which Christ's faithful, living in the world, strive for the perfection of charity and endeavour to contribute to the sanctification of the world, especially from within." (can. 710).

To these two fundamental types of institutes of consecrated life are joined the societies of apostolic life [46]. Of the latter can. 731 gives a double definition: those that expressly assume the evangelical counsels as a rule of life, commiting themselves to these with a bond determined by their Constitutions, and those that do not live the evangelical counsels [47]. In fact nowadays the majority of the societies of apostolic life are of the first type and thus are part with full status of the institutes of consecrated life. However, from an ecclesiological and juridical point of view "it would be better not to enter any more into the frame of consecrated life those societies which refuse this aspect of consecrated life through the evangelical counsels, if these do not live and affirm that they absolutely do not want to live such a life. Their rightful place is

---

[44]   Cf. above all cans. 607 §2 and 654 with can. 731 §2.

[45]   Cf. above all cans. 607 §3 and 608 with cans. 710 and 712-714.

[46]   On the significance of the term *accedunt* of can. 731 §1 cf. G. Ghirlanda, *Alcuni punti in vista del Sinodo dei vescovi sulla vita consacrata,* in: Periodica 83 (1994), pp. 67-91, above all p. 83-85.

[47]   On the theological foundations and on the various juridical configurations of the evangelical counsels, cf. H. Böhler, *I consigli evangelici in prospettiva trinitaria. Sintesi dottrinale,* Milano 1993, above all pp. 33-115 and pp. 154-179.

found in this case among the associations of the faithful, just as they are considered by the Code of 1983"[48].

In conclusion, all of these differences of the Code can be thus summarised: religious Institutes comprise the faithful who profess the three evangelical counsels with public vows in common life; secular Institutes comprise those faithful who *in saeculo viventes* (can. 710) profess the evangelical counsels with non public but recognised vows or other sacred bonds comparable to such vows and without expressing them in the practice of canonical common life; Societies of apostolic life comprise the faithful who practice common life and, very often, also the evangelical counsels, however not expressed in vows but by means of a sacred bond which is directly related to incorporation into the society for an apostolic purpose.

FUNDAMENTAL BIBLIOGRAPHY

AA.VV., *Lo stato giuridico dei consacrati per la professione dei consigli evangelici,* Città del Vaticano 1985.

Aymans W., *Kirchliches Verfassungsrecht und Vereinigungsrecht in der Kirche,* in: ÖAKR 32 (1981), pp. 79-110.

Beyer J., *Originalità dei carismi di vita consacrata,* in: Periodica 82 (1993), pp. 257-292.

Corecco E., *Institution and Charism with Reference to Associative Structures,* in: *Corecco E., Canon Law and Communio. Writings on the Constitutional Law of the Church,* edited by G. Borgonovo and A. Cattaneo, Città del Vaticano 1999, pp. 316-340.

Corecco E., *Profili istitutzionali dei Movimenti nella Chiesa,* in: *I Movimenti nella Chiesa. Atti del I Congresso Internazionale* (Roma, 23-27 September 1981), edited by M. Camicasa-M. Vitali, Milano 1982, pp. 203-234.

Gerosa L., *Carisma e diritto nella Chiesa. Riflessioni canonistiche sul "carisma originario" dei nuovi movimenti ecclesiali,* Milano 1989.

Morrisey F. G., *The Right of Association as a Basic Right of the Faithful,* in: *Das konsoziative Element in der Kirche, Akten des VI. Internationalen Kongresses für Kanonistisches Recht (München 14. – 19. September),* hrsg. v. W. Aymans, K.-Th. Geringer, H. Schmitz, St. Ottilien 1989, pp. 7-24.

Navarro L., *Diritto di associazione e associazioni dei fedeli,* Milano 1991.

Schulz W., *Der neue Codex und die kirchlichen Vereine,* Paderborn 1986.

---

[48]   This is the authoritative opinion of J. Beyer, *Originalità dei carismi di vita consacrata,* op. cit., p. 266.

SIXTH CHAPTER: INSTITUTIONAL ORGANS OF THE CHURCH

1. SOME FUNDAMENTAL THEOLOGICAL-JURIDICAL NOTIONS

1.1 SYNODALITY AND JOINT RESPONSIBILITY AS TYPICAL INSTITUTIONAL EXPRESSIONS OF THE ECCLESIAL COMMUNION

A) PRELIMINARY TERMINOLOGICAL DEFINITIONS

Although collegiality and participation are the most diffuse terms in post-conciliar language, as much in the ecclesial environment as in the mass-media interested in the life of the Church, their proper significance and their respective fields of application in the bosom of the Church, both universal and particular, are much more restricted and limited than one would think. In any case it is a question of notions ecclesiologically less adequate in comparison with those of synodality and joint-responsibility in order to express the structural modalities by means of which the logic of the ecclesial communion determines the exercise of the *sacra potestas*. The ultimate reason for this inadequacy of theirs lies in the fact that in both the technical-juridical value of worldly origin prevails, as such incapable of expressing the theological datum underlying the reality of the ecclesial communion, where the relationship of reciprocal immanence between unity and plurality and its modalities of realisation are ultimately knowable only by faith, being historical-institutional reflections of the unity and plurality of the trinitarian mystery [1].

The truth of this assertion concerning the ecclesiological inadequacy of the notions of collegiality and participation is supported by different reasons of a doctrinal order [2]. Here it is enough to record the following.

---

[1] Cf. M. Philipon, *Die Heiligste Dreifaltigkeit und die Kirche*, in: *De Ecclesia. Beträge zur Konstitution über die Kirche des II. Vatikanischen Konzils*, hrsg. von G. Baraúna, Bd. 1, pp. 252-275; E. Zoghby, *Einheit und Mannigfaltigkeit der Kirche*, in: *De Ecclesia*, ibid, pp. 453-473.

[2] For a full illustration of these reasons refer moreover to the fours essays of E. Corecco: *Parlamento ecclesiale o diaconia sinodale?*, in: Communio 1(1972), pp. 32-44; *Sinodalità*, in: *Nuovo Dizionario di Teologia*, a cura di G. Barbaglio-S. Dianich, Alba 1977, pp. 1466-1495; *Sinodalità e partecipazione nell' esercizio della "sacra potestas"*, in: *Esercizio del potere e prassi della consultazione*. Atti dell'VIII Colloquio Internazionale romanistico-canonistico (10-12 maggio 1990), a cura di A. Ciani-G. Duizini, Città del Vaticano 1991, pp. 69-89; *Ontologia della sinodalità*, in: *"Pastor bonus in Populo"*. Figura, ruolo e funzioni del vescovo nella Chiesa, a cura di A. Autiero-O. Carena, Roma 1990, pp. 303-329.

The abstract substantive collegiality, never used as such in the Vatican Council II, is not adequate to comprehend the modalities with which the principle of *communio* determines the exercise of power in the Church, because in a strictly juridical sense only those acts are collegial in which the will of the individual, losing his own autonomous relevance, is integrated into the will of the college as the only responsible subject of the decision taken[3]. Therefore truly collegial acts are few and far between in the Church, also because ecclesial power is founded on the sacrament of orders, conferred exclusively on physical persons. On the other hand, synodality being an intrinsic ontological dimension of the *sacra potestas* and the exercise of the latter constantly directed by the principle of the reciprocal immanence between the personal and synodal element of the ecclesial ministry, all the acts of governance of the Church are simultaneously hierarchical and synodal, even if according to a different degree of intensity. Unlike collegiality, synodality does not thus pose either as an alternative in comparison with the personal dimension of the ecclesial ministry, nor as a restriction of the sphere of exercise of a given ministry, and especially the episcopal. On the contrary, this confers on them a broader extension and authoritativeness, because it develops the ontological relationship existing between all the ecclesial ministries, relationships inseparably linked to the communal structure or of unity in the plurality of the Church. As such, precisely because it is a typical institutional expression of the *communio Ecclesiae et Ecclesiarum,* synodality is in its turn completed not so much by participation but rather by joint responsibility in the ecclesial mission to which all of the faithful are called by dint of their baptism and confirmation.

The term participation, in fact, does not leave itself less open to different interpretations of difficult applications in the ecclesial field. According to the most recent analyses of its semantic evolutions, with this is shown a complex and polyhedric phenomenon which presents different dimensions and meanings according to the viewpoint from which it is considered: juridical, social, economical or political[4]. In the last decade, under the drive of the ever-present need to take part in the formation of political decisions, participation has become quite a myth, so much so as to place its scientific credibility under discussion. In the actual debate it has thus been realised that participation is a typically modern problem, arisen from the separation of the State from society and the correlative emergence of the concept of citizen as distinct from the human person. The latter affirmation could already be sufficient to make us careful not to use the term participation indiscriminately to explain under the canonical framework the different institutional implications, especially on the level of the various organs of government, of the right and duty of every faithful Christian to "promote the growth of the Church" (can. 210) and to express their own opinion (can. 212 §3) as a result. Two other reasons suggest a similar care and prudence: on the one hand the sacramental root, direct (for the minister invested with holy orders) or indirect (for charismatic authority), of every form of ecclesial power, and on the other the specific

---

[3]   In this regard cf. Aymans-Mörsdorf, KanR I, pp. 352-369.

[4]   For a brief exposition of the significant civil principles of this idea and their acceptance in Canon Law, cf. B. Ruethers-G. Kleinherz, *Mitbestimmung*, in: *Staatslexikon*, hrsg. von der Görresgesellschaft, 7. Aufl., Bd.3, Freiburg-Basel-Wien 1985, coll. 1176-1185; A. Savignano, *Partecipazione politica*, in: EDD, vol. 32, (Milano 1982); R. Puza, *Mitverantwortung in der Kirche*, in: *Staatslexikon*, op. cit., Bd.3, pp. 1188-1192.

significance that the notions of representation and of a deliberative and consultative vote assume in the Church, necessarily implicated in every process of participation.

By dint of the first reason, in the Church the other faithful can participate in the power of which a determined member of the faithful is the title-holder if they are also personally invested with the same degree of the sacrament of orders, and offer both their *cooperatio*, on the basis of a different degree of orders in which they are invested (such as the case of priests in relation to the bishop), or the support of their own joint responsibility, on the basis of their baptism and confirmation. In the second and third case it is not a question however of true and proper participation because the latter always implies some sort of pertinence or a certain taking part in the very nature of a power in which it is not the holder[5].

By virtue of the second reason – that is to say the specific significance of voting in an ecclesial assembly – the nature, purpose and the functioning of the different organs of government, as much on the level of the universal Church as within a determined particular Church, have little in common with those of representative institutes or organs – such as Parliament and other closely related structures – created by modern democratic associationism[6] . In point of fact, the concepts of representation and of a deliberative vote, fundamental in the modern parliament, have a different meaning in the Church.

B) REPRESENTATION, DELIBERATIVE VOTE AND CONSULTATIVE VOTE IN THE CHURCH

In the juridical-institutional structure of the Church, governed by the principle of *communio* and therefore in its essence completely knowable only by faith, the latter cannot be represented but only witnessed to. Consequently the members of the different organs of ecclesial government, even when they are elected with representative or democratic criteria, are not parliamentary type representatives but some of the faithful chosen in order to witness to their faith and to help according to their knowledge and competence (can. 212 §2) the believer who – by dint of the sacrament of orders and the *missio canonica* – is invested with the authority of the Christian community in question. Thus even the distinction between the deliberative vote and the consultative vote does not have, in the dynamic that guides the functioning of the various ecclesial councils, the same specific weight that it possesses in a state structure of the parliamentary type. In fact, precisely because power in the Church is by its nature synodal, even when the members of a determined college have a deliberative vote the decision is not ever exclusively a matter of majority: for example, in the Council, an organ with a deliberative vote par excellence, the power of decision is up to the majority only in as

---

[5]   Cf. E. Corecco, *I laici nel nuovo Codice di diritto canonico*, in: La Scuola Cattolica 112 (1984), pp. 194-218, here p. 215.

[6]   On the evolution known by modern parliamentarism, cf. W. Henke, *Parlament, Parlamentarismus*, in: *Evangelisches Staatslexikon*, begr. von H. Kunst-S. Grundmann, hrsg. von R. Herzog-H. Kunst-K. Schlaich-W. Schneemelcher, Bd.2, Stuttgart 1987 (3. neu bearbeitete und erweiterte Auflage), coll.2420-2428; A. Marongiou, *Parlamento (Storia)*, EDD, Vol. 31, Milano 1981, pp. 724-757.

far as this includes the Pope [7]. Analogously in the presbyterate the power of decision is ultimately only up to that person in whom it is invested by virtue of the sacrament, that is the diocesan bishop. By the same standard the canonical institute with a consultative vote cannot be considered a compromise between an authoritarian and a democratic practice. This is not an instrument of exclusion from power because it is an integrating and constitutive part of the communal formation of the judgement – doctrinal and disciplinary – of the ecclesial authority and accordingly possesses its own specific binding force, generated within the structure of communion proper to the Church by the *sensus fidei* given to all of the faithful and from the charisms aroused by the Holy Spirit in the People of God.

c) COLLEGIAL AND NON COLLEGIAL JURIDICAL PERSONS

In the light of the preceding considerations of a doctrinal order another institute of Canon Law is also to be reconsidered: that of collegial and non-collegial juridical persons, certainly important for the study of the organs of government of the Church.

In fact, although the new Code of Canon Law seeks a better determination of the various juridical persons (cans. 113-123), above all through the distinction between corporations or *universitas personarum* and foundations or *universitas rerum* [8], in fact the classical distinction between *collegiales* juridical persons and *non collegiales* remains of great importance in arranging the modalities of the exercise of the power of governance in the Church, even if such a distinction refers only to the *universitas personarum*, that is to say corporations or societies (can. 115 §2). In order to recognise or erect the latter as juridical persons, that is to say as "a body distinct from physical persons, constituted by the public authority of the Church as a subject of rights and duties with a common objective purpose, not identifiable with the ends of the physical persons involved, corresponding to the mission of the Church" [9], the ecclesiastical legislator "requires at least three persons" (can. 115 §2), obviously physical. Once juridical personality has been acquired the *universitas personarum* are called collegial if their activity "is determined by its members participating together in making its decisions, whether by equal right or not, in accordance with the law and the statutes" (can. 115 §2). Being defined as collegial does not depend therefore on the fact that all the members of the juridical person have the right to a deliberative vote, but from the possibility that all of its members in some way (and therefore even if only with a consultative vote) participate in the formative process of the decision. Thus, for example, the members of many associations all have the same right to a deliberative vote, while in the Conferences of bishops such a right belongs *ipso iure* only to diocesan bishops and to those comparable with them, as well as coadjutor bishops (can. 454 §1). To auxiliary bishops and other titular bishops on the other hand belongs normally only a

---

[7] Cf. cans. 338 §1 and 341 §1; on the whole question cf. also L. Gerosa, *Rechtstheologische Grundlagen der Synodalität in der Kirche. Einleitende Erwägungen*, in: *Iuri canonico promovendo,* Festschrift für H. Schmitz zum 65. Geburtstag, hrsg. von W. Aymans-K.Th. Geringer, Regensburg 1994, pp. 35-55.

[8] Cf. can. 115 §1 and the commentary of Aymans-Mörsdorf, KanR I, pp. 307-328, here p. 309.

[9] L. Vela-F.J. Urrutia, *Persona giuridica*, in: NDDC, pp. 795-799, here p. 795.

consulative vote, unless the statutes of the Conference of bishops – based on their own particular traditions – prescribe something different (can. 454 §2).

The corporations or societies whose decisions are not taken by its members, but rather by those to whom their government is entrusted are called non-collegial. The most classical examples of non collegial juridical persons are the diocese, the parish and the diocesan seminary, canonical institutions which in all juridical negotiations are represented by the diocesan bishop (can. 393), the parish priest (can. 532) and the seminary rector (can. 238 §2). This does not mean however that the latter in taking decisions relating to the non-collegial juridical person represented by them are totally autonomous, as appears evident in the case of the diocesan bishop assisted in the exercise of his functions of governance (that is to say legislative, administrative and judiciary) by a series of diocesan councils [10]. Synodality being, as we have seen, a constitutive ontological dimension of the *sacra potestas*, this expresses itself in some way also in the government of non-collegial juridical persons, almost as if to confirm the fact that collegial is a term of canonical significance much more strict than synodal. Lastly it must be remembered that in Canon Law non-collegial corporations or societies are also clearly distinguished from foundations, because in these the emphasis is placed on the totality of persons who compose them and not on the complex of things or goods, both spiritual and material, raised to the dignity of a juridical person (can. 115 §3).

1.2 ECCLESIASTICAL OFFICES

A) THE NEW NOTION OF THE CODE OF ECCLESIASTICAL OFFICE

As we have already had occasion to observe in the 4. chapter (7.2) the ecclesiastical legislator of 1983 has introduced a new notion of the Code of ecclesiastical office. In fact, can. 145 §1, repeating almost to the letter the conciliar text of PO 20,2, states: "An ecclesiastical office is any post which by divine or ecclesiastical disposition is established in a stable manner to further a spiritual purpose". Now, according to this definition of the Code there are four constitutive elements of an ecclesiastical office: 1. The charge or *munus*, that is the one or more obligatory functions in which this consists, and to which are connected obligations and rights; 2. Objective stability, that is to say that character of endurance in the ecclesial juridical structure that guarantees the pre-existence and permanence to the conferral and loss of this respectively; 3. The being of divine disposition (as for example in the case of the office of bishop) or ecclesiastical disposition (as for example in the case of the office of parish priest); 4. The spiritual purpose, that is the being able to be led back – even when implicated in the administration of temporal matters – to the mission of the Church.

Thus defined the new juridical configuration of the ecclesiastical office presents two important differences in comparison with that of the Pio-Benedictine Code. First of all the distinction between office in the strict sense and in the wider sense is definitively dropped, because according to the CIC the ecclesiastical office no longer necessarily implicates a certain participation in the *sacra potestas* in its holder and thus – unless divine law or the Canon Law in force expressly forbids it – this can also be

---

[10] Cf. 2.2 of this chapter.

acquired by the lay faithful, men and women [11]. In the second place, the ecclesiastical office as such no longer normally possesses a juridical personality; the latter does not even belong to the ecclesiastical office of Pope as such, but rather to the Apostolic See in the global sense [12]. This holds also for other important ecclesiastical offices such as that of diocesan bishop and parish priest. Both begin concretely to exist as ecclesiastical offices from the moment in which the competent authority has erected a diocese and a parish, to which definition of a juridical person these necessarily belong [13].

The ecclesiastical offices that do not have a juridical personality and are not necessarily constituted by means of the erection of a juridical person begin their juridical existence with their concrete conferral on the part of the competent authority instituting them [14].

B) CONFERRAL AND LOSS OF AN ECCLESIASTICAL OFFICE

The ecclesiastical office is conferred with an act of an administrative nature called canonical provision. Without the latter the conferral is null (can. 146). This comprises three moments: the designation of the person, the conferral of the title and the taking possession or induction in the ecclesiastical office. Moreover, according to can. 147, the canonical provision of an ecclesiastical office can come about in four ways: 1. By free conferral (can. 157), when the authority competent to do so designates the person on the basis of his free choice; 2. By institution, when the comptetent authority must institute the person suitable on the basis of a presentation (cans. 158-163) by third parties; 3. By confirmation or by admission when the competent authority gives the canonical provision to a person previously elected (cans. 164-179) or postulated (cans. 180-183); 4. By simple election and acceptance, if there is no need of confirmation, as in the case of the Roman Pontiff (can. 332 §1) and diocesan administrator (can. 427 §2).

In any case he who is promoted to an ecclesiastical office must be "in communion with the Church, and be suitable" (can. 149).

The loss of an ecclesiastical office, according to the norms of can. 184 §1, can be automatic (expiry of the time for which it was conferred or reaching the age limits defined by the law) voluntary (in the case of renunciation, according to cans. 187-189), or forced if realised in one of the three following ways: by transferral (cans. 190-191), by removal (cans. 192-193), by deprivation, that is to say as a canonical sanction for a crime committed (can. 196).

---

[11]   Agreeing in this interpretation of can. 145: Aymans-Mörsdorf, KanR I, pp. 445-502, here pp. 445-446; P. Krämer, *Kirchenrecht II. Ortskirche-Gesamtkirche*, Stuttgart-Berlin-Köln 1993, pp. 45-47; G. Ghirlanda, *Il diritto nella Chiesa mistero di comunione. Compendio di diritto ecclesiale*, Roma 1990, pp. 271-274; F.J. Urrutia, *Il libro I: le norme generale*, in: *Il nuovo codice di diritto canonico. Studi*, Torino 1985, pp. 32-59, here pp. 52-59.

[12]   Cf. cans. 361 and 113, as well as the commentary of Aymans-Mörsdorf, KanR I, p. 446.

[13]   Cf. cans. 369 and 515 §1.

[14]   Cf. cans. 145 §2 and 148; on the whole question and in particular the juridical meaning of the verbs *erigere, constituere* and *instituere* in arranging an ecclesiastical office cf. H. Socha, in: MK, can. 148/1-7.

Finally, he loses the ecclesiastical office *ipso iure*: 1. who loses the clerical state, 2. who publicly abandons the Catholic faith or the ecclesial communion, 3. the cleric who has attempted marriage even if only civilly (can. 194 §1).

2. THE INSTITUTIONAL ORGANS, AND IN PARTICULAR OF GOVERNANCE, IN THE ECCLESIAE ET ECCLESIARUM COMMUNION

The structural essence of the mystery of the Church is that of the reciprocal and total immanence of the universal Church in the and from the particular Churches, captured in the formula *in quibus et ex quibus* of LG 23,1. This conciliar formula – as we already briefly anticipated in the conclusion of the first chapter – is opposed on the level of the constitutional law of the Church both to the principle of autocephaly, and to the monist concept of the Church as a single universal diocese. In the former case it is the internal element that is to be affirmed in an exclusive way, by which the universal Church no longer exists really or is reduced to a simple confederation of particular Churches. In the latter case it is the external element that prevails and the particular Churches end up by being absorbed into the universal Church as simple administrative districts of the same. The indispensability of the two elements allows the conciliar formula to gather together in a perfect theological synthesis the constitutional essence of the *communio Ecclesiarum* [15]. This means that the universal Church and the particular Churches are nothing other if not two constitutive dimensions of the one Church of Christ, as John Paul II has affirmed in one of his homilies [16]. This fundamental structure of the mystery of the Church has to be kept in mind both in order to correctly face up to the problem of the relationship between *ius universale* and *ius particulare* [17], and in order to understand the nature, purpose and reciprocal connections of the various institutional organs of the *communio Ecclesiae et Ecclesiarum*. In fact, the latter with great difficulty let themselves be defined by the political categories of centralisation and decentralisation, or by an exclusive recourse to the principle of subsidiarity, of socio-philosophical origin. A confirmation of this is the uncertainty of the same ecclesiastical legislator faced with the systematic positioning of the so-called groupings or families of particular Churches (cans. 431-459), made objects of continual displacements [18]. The final result is still not totally convincing for at least two reasons: first of all it is not understood for what motive the part on the internal structure of a particular Church (can. 460-572) has been detached from the norms on particular Churches and on bishops (cans. 368-430); in second place the full acceptance of the conciliar teaching on reciprocal immanence between the universal Church and particular Churches

---

[15] Cf. W. Aymans, *Die communio Ecclesiarum als Gestaltgesetz der einen Kirche,* in: AfkKR 139 (1970), pp. 69-90.

[16] Cf. John Paul II, *Omelia a Lugano del 12 giugno 1984*, in: *Insegnamenti di Giovanni Paolo II*, Città del Vaticano 1984, Vol. VII/1, pp. 1676-1683.

[17] In this regard cf. E. Corecco, *Ius universale-Ius particulare*, in: *Ius in vita et in missione Ecclesiae*. Acta Symposii internationalis iuris canonici (Città del Vaticano, 19-24 aprile 1993) Città del Vaticano 1994, pp. 551-574.

[18] Cf. Communicationes 12 (1980), pp. 244-246; 14 (1982), p. 124 and pp. 155-156.

should have suggested a division into three sections: one on the universal Church and its organs of government, one on the particular Church and its internal structure, one on the groupings or families of particular Churches.

2.1 THE INSTITUTIONAL ORGANS OF THE UNIVERSAL CHURCH

Also on the level of the juridical configuration of the institutional organs of the Church the CIC has certainly accepted the substance of the conciliar teaching on the *communio Ecclesiae et Ecclesiarum*. Nevertheless we cannot deny a certain embarrassment of the ecclesiastical legislator of 1983 in completely accepting the principle of reciprocal immanence of the universal in the particular. In point of fact, on the one hand it relegates the formula *in quibus et ex quibus* of LG 23,1 to can. 368 at the beginning of the section on particular Churches, while under the systematic framework this should be placed in a preliminary canon at the beginning of the whole part entitled *De Ecclesiae constitutione hierarchica* (cans. 330-572). On the other the same ecclesiastical legislator in the first section, dedicated to the institutional organs having the supreme ecclesial authority, does not insert them in their ecclesiological context and does not give any definition of the universal Church, in contrast to what on the other hand he does for the particular Church, defined in can. 369 repeating to the letter the conciliar definition of CD 11 [19]. The first section of this part of the Code of Canon Law begins therefore immediately with the norms relating to the organs of government of the universal Church, that is to say the Roman Pontiff and the College of Bishops.

A) THE COLLEGE OF BISHOPS AND THE POPE

Can. 330 states: "Just as, by the decree of the Lord, Saint Peter and the rest of the Apostles form one College, so for a like reason the Roman Pontiff, the Successor of Peter, and the Bishops, the successors of the Apostles, are united together in one". This introductory canon of the first section, entitled *De suprema Ecclesiae auctoritate*, not only repeats almost to the letter the conciliar text of LG 22,1, but offers also on the theme of the supreme authority in the Church a somewhat happy synthesis. In fact, in the light of the *Nota explicativa praevia* added to the Dogmatic Constitution on the Church, from the context of this canon it can clearly be deduced that there is a parallelism between Peter and the other Apostles on the one hand, and the Pope and the bishops on the other. Such a parallelism does not imply however either a transmission of equal power from one to the other nor an equality between the Head and the members of the College. From this can be deduced simply an identical relationship of proportionality within the Apostolic College and the College of Bishops, as well as its foundation in divine law through the apostolic succession. In other words, in this canon it clearly emerges how "the nature of the juridical structure of the Church is simultaneously collegial and primatial by will of the Lord himself" [20]. This double

---

[19]   If the first incongruence is spotlighted by E. Corecco (cf. *Aspetti della ricezione del Vaticano II nel Codice di diritto canonico*, in: *Il Vaticano II e la Chiesa*, a cura di G. Alberigo-J.P. Jossua, Brescia 1985, pp. 333-397, here pp. 368-369), the second is revealed by different authors: G. Ghirlanda, *Il diritto nella Chiesa mistero di comunione*, op. cit., p. 497; P. Krämer, *Kirchenrecht II*, op. cit., p. 99.

[20]   G. Ghirlanda, *Il diritto nella Chiesa mistero di comunione*, op. cit., p. 497; cf. also John Paul II, CA *Pastor Bonus*, in AAS 80 (1988), pp. 841-912, above all no.2.

nature of the hierarchical structure of the Church is reflected evidently in the two subjects of the supreme authority of the Church, the College of Bishops and the Pope,
that thus cannot be adequately distinguished. As the majority of canonists sustain [21],
starting from the conciliar teaching surrounding the fact that the Council of Bishops
"does not exist without the Head" it must necessarily be deduced that "the distinction
is not between the Roman Pontiff and the Bishops taken together, but between the
Roman Pontiff himself and the Roman Pontiff along with the Bishops" (NEP 3).

The balance of the introductory canon is however immediately upset by the successive canons for at least three reasons. First of all the ecclesiastical legislator of 1983
deals with the argument in two distinct articles: the first is entitled *De Romano Pontefice* (cans. 331-335) and the second *De Collegio Episcoporum* (cans. 336-341), as if
the two subjects were adequately distinct and separable [22]. In second place in both articles, but also in the remaining sections of the CIC, the ecclesiastical legislator, against
the teaching of the Vatican Council II and the same can. 330 [23], places the Roman
Pontiff before the College of Bishops with surprising rigorousness [24]. In third and last
place in the article dedicated to the College of Bishops, after the most important can.
336, in the five remaining canons the legislator speaks only of the Ecumenical Council
and not however of the functions and the tasks of the College of Bishops [25].

In order to be members of the College of Bishops – according to the norms of
can. 336 which repeats LG 22,1 – two things are necessary: the first of a sacramental
nature, that is to say episcopal consecration, and the second of a non sacramental
nature, that is to say the hierarchical communion with the head and members of the
College. While the former is indelible, the latter is not because it cannot be so (as
in the case of an episcopal ordination outside of the Catholic Church) or it can be
lost (as in the case of an excommunication). In strict connection with can. 330, the
same can. 336 also affirms that the College of Bishops, in which the apostolic body
perennially remains, together with its head and never without this head as a subject
of the full and supreme power of the universal Church. If the choice of the way with
which the latter is exercised is up to the Roman Pontiff, on his initiative or by his
free acceptance of the initiative of other members of the College [26], the function and

---

[21] Among the more notable intervening authors are to be remembered: W. Bertrams, *De
    subiecto supremae potestatis Ecclesiae*, in: Periodica 54 (1965) pp. 173-232; K. Mörsdorf,
    Über die Zuordnung der päpstlichen Primatialgewalt im Lichte des kanonischen Rechtes,
    in: J. Ratzinger-W. Dettloff-R. Heinzmann (Hrsg.), *Wahrheit und Verkündigung*. Festschrift
    für M. Schmaus, Paderborn-Wien 1967, Bd. II. pp. 1435-1445.

[22] Witnessing to this incongruence A. Longhitano, *Il libro II: Il Populo di Dio*, in: *Il nuovo
    codice di diritto canonico. Studi*, op. cit., pp. 60-79, here p. 71.

[23] For example in LG 17,1; 18,2; 19; 20; 21; 23,3 and 24,1 the Vatican Council II attributes
    priority to the College of bishops over the Pope.

[24] Besides cans. 330 and 336 the only text of the CIC in which the College of Bishops is
    quoted before the Apostolic See is can. 755 §1: this second incongruence is revealed by E.
    Corecco, *Aspetti della ricezione del Vaticano II nel Codice di diritto canonico*, op. cit., pp.
    372-373.

[25] For a critical examination of these canons cf. J. Komonchak, *Il Concilio ecumenico nel
    nuovo codice di diritto canonico*, in: Concilium 19 (1983), pp. 160-169.

[26] Cf. can. 337 §2 and §3.

the tasks of the latter are not defined in the CIC. It is necessary however to refer back to the texts of the Vatican Council II, which on the matter explicitly affirms: "This College in so far as it is composed of many members, is the expression of the multifariousness and universality of the People of God; and of the unity of the flock of Christ, in so far as it is assembled under one head" (LG 22,2). From this derives for its members a role of double representation: taken singly in the College these represent their particular Churches, all together with the Head of the College they represent the universal Church[27].

The Head of the College of Bishops is "the Bishop of the Church of Rome, in whom persists the office uniquely committed by the Lord to Peter, the first of the Apostles" (can. 331). In Catholic and ecumenical tradition he is called the Pope, a term also used by the Vatican Council II five times[28]. In the CIC this term does not appear unless in its adjectival form of papal, in expressions such as "Papal Secretariat" (can. 360) or "Papal enclosure" (can. 667 §3). This does not however impede the ecclesiastical legislator from specifying that the Head of the College of Bishops by virtue of his office of "Pastor of the universal Church", and therefore as a "perpetual and visible principle" as well as a "foundation of the unity both of the bishops and of the whole company of the faithful" (LG 23,1), enjoys an "ordinary power" that is "supreme, full, immediate and universal in the Church" (can. 331). These five terms, used in can. 331 in order to define the nature and content of the supreme power that the Pope by divine law is called to exercise in the universal Church, mean : 1. *ordinary*, that such a power is annexed by right to the primatial office[29]; 2. *supreme*, that in the exercise of this power the Roman Pontiff is free, he does not depend on the bishop members of the College and as such "is not judged by anyone" (can. 1404); 3. *full*, that such a power is not purely directive or of vigilance, because there is no essential element lacking in this both in relation to the unity of the faith and in the order of government of the Church, that is to say as far as it relates to the legislative, executive or administrative, judicial function[30]; 4. *immediate*, that such a primatial power can be exercised by the Pope directly, without intervention, on all of the faithful and on all the particular Churches, even if in arrangement with the latter the immediacy of papal authority tend to reinforce and guarantee the proper, ordinary and immediate power of their bishops[31]; 5. *universal*, that the field of action of the power of the Pope is extended to the whole *Ecclesiae et Ecclesiarum*, because only he is the Head of the College of Bishops and therefore also the *caput totius Ecclesiae*[32].

After these canons that juridically delineate the two subjects of the supreme power in the Church, the ecclesiastical legislator of 1983 gives space to the description of the various institutional organs by means of which this power is concretely exercised: the

---

[27] In this regard cf. P. Krämer, *Kirchenrecht II*, op. cit., pp. 106-107.

[28] Cf. LG 22,2 and 23,1; NEP 1 and 4.

[29] Cf. can. 131 §1.

[30] In this regard cf. G. Ghirlanda, *Il diritto nella Chiesa mistero di communione*, op. cit., p. 499.

[31] Cf. can. 333 §1.

[32] Cf. C. Corral, *Romano Pontefice*, in: NDDC, pp. 931-938, above all pp. 934-935; for a deeper study of the juridical expressions of the supreme power of the Pope, cf. J.B. D'Onorio, *Le pape et le gouvernement de l'Église*, Paris 1994, pp. 64-125.

Ecumenical Council (cans. 337-341), dealt with regrettably under the title *De Collegio Episcoporum* as if it were the only way in which the College of Bishops can collegially express its supreme power; the Synod of Bishops (cans. 342-348); the College of Cardinals (cans. 349-359); the Roman Curia (cans. 360-361); the Legates of the Roman Pontiff (cans. 362-367).

B) ECUMENICAL COUNCIL

The first paragraph of can. 337 states: "The College of Bishops exercises its power over the universal Church in solemn form in an Ecumenical Council". From this canon, drawn from the conciliar texts of LG 22,2 and CD 4, two fundamental principles for the understanding of the canonical statute of an Ecumenical Council can clearly be deduced: 1. The College of Bishops and the Ecumenical Council are not identical, the second being only the solemn form with which the first exercises its supreme power in the Church; 2. this supreme power can therefore be exercised by the College of Bishops in an extra-conciliar or non-solemn way too, while remaining collegial in *sensu stricto*[33].

On the basis of the first principle it can be deduced that while the College of Bishops is of divine law, the Ecumenical Council while being rooted in divine law demands a concrete juridical configuration that, as such, is of human ecclesiastical law[34] . And in fact the twenty-one Ecumenical Councils celebrated up until now have from time to time assumed different juridical forms having nonetheless the following two elements in common. First of all it is always a matter of a solemn gathering of all of the bishops of the *Orbis Catholicus*, in which decisions of great importance for the universal Church are taken[35]. In second place these decisions or decrees in order to acquire an obliging force for all of the faithful must be approved by the Pope together with the conciliar Fathers in the voting of the public session and then personally confirmed by the Pope and promulgated by him[36].

As regards the second fundamental principle of can. 337 §1, relating to the collegial extra-conciliar exercise of the supreme power of the College of Bishops, it has to be observed unfortunately that it has not been concretised in any other norm of the CIC. Some forms of this exercise have been historically well known, as in the case of the so-called *Council by letter*, that is to say consultations undertaken by the Pope on the level of the universal Church prior to the proclamation of a dogma[37]. Other forms could be legitimately introduced, given the great number of bishops dispersed throughout the world and the new developments known in the means of communica-

---

[33] Cf. cans. 337 §2 and 341 §2, as well as the commentary of O. Stoffel, MK, can. 337/1 and 3.

[34] In this regard, cf. K. Mörsdorf, Lb. Bd. I, p. 352; P. Krämer, *Kirchenrecht II,* op. cit., pp. 109-113.

[35] Cf. can. 339 §1.

[36] Cf. can. 341 §1 and the commentary of G. Ghirlanda, *Il diritto nella Chiesa mistero di comunione,* op. cit., pp. 510-511.

[37] For example for the proclamation of the dogma of the Immaculate Conception and of the Assumption of Mary into heaven; cf. O. Stoffel, in MK can. 337/3.

tion, eventually applying the principle of representation in a correct way [38]. Precisely on the basis of the elements emerging from the conciliar discussions on this problem, Pope Paul VI on the 15 September 1965 with the MP *Apostolica sollicitudo* [39] instituted the Synod of Bishops.

c) Synod of Bishops

The Synod of Bishops (cans. 342-348) is certainly one of the more important institutional innovations, on the level of the universal Church, introduced from the teaching of the Vatican Council II. According to can. 342 the Synod of Bishops is an assembly of bishops, "selected from different part of the world", who "gather together at specified times to promote the close relationship between the Roman Pontiff and the Bishops", and in order to help "in the defence and development of the faith, as well as "the strengthening of ecclesiastical discipline". It is a question therefore of an institutional organ of the universal Church of a consultative nature [40], in which is expressed – according to the representative principle – the so-called collegial affection of all the bishops, their care for the universal Church and that of the latter for the particular Churches [41]. As such the Synod of Bishops has a permanent character, even if it only exercises its functions intermittently [42]. The difference is therefore clear between a Synod of Bishops and an Ecumenical Council: their compositions, purposes and authority are different. In point of fact in the Synod not only is the whole College of Bishops not gathered but neither is the collegial power in *sensu stricto* exercised, because "even in the case in which it has deliberative power this is delegated by the Roman Pontiff, it is a means for the Pope to exercise his primatial office in a collegial way" [43].

d) The College of Cardinals, the Roman Curia and Legates of the Roman Pontiff

Differently from the episcopate, which is the fullness of the sacrament of orders and as such belongs to the very essence of the constitutional structure of the Church, the cardinalate is an institution of merely ecclesiastical law, emerging in the early Middle Ages and developing itself into a true and proper college only starting from the XII Century, that is to say from when the election of the Pope was attributed to it in an

---

[38] Under the ecclesiological profile it remains legitimate to ask if the disposition introduced by John XXIII, according to which even auxiliary and titular bishops are members by right and have a deliberative vote in an Ecumenical Council, truly respects this principle. cf. MP *Appropinquante Concilio*, in AAS 54 (1962), p. 612.

[39] Cf. AAS 57 (1965), pp. 775-780.

[40] Cf. can. 343.

[41] For a deeper study of the nature and functions of this new institution cf. W. Bertrams, *Struttura del Sinodo dei Vescovi,* in: Civiltà Cattolica 116 (1965), pp. 417-423; G.P. Milano, *Il sinodo dei Vescovi: natura, funzioni, rappresentatività,* in: Actes VII CIDC, Vol. I, pp. 167-182.

[42] Cf. can. 348 on the role of the general permanent Secretariat.

[43] G. Ghirlanda, *Il diritto nella Chiesa mistero di comunione,* op. cit., p. 514; cf. also cans. 333 §2 and especially 334.

exclusive way [44]. In a juridical sense the College of Cardinals, who "are freely selected by the Roman Pontiff" (can. 351 §2), is to be understood according to can. 115 §2, that is to say as a college whose members are all equal, even if according to tradition they are distinguished into cardinal bishops (those to whom the Pope assigns the title of a suburbicarian diocese), cardinal priests (those to whom the Pope assigns the title of a church in the City) and cardinal deacons (those who normally have an appointment in the Roman Curia). This "special College" (can. 349) gathers together in the Consistory [45] and has the function of a "Senate of the Pope" [46]. In this sense, even if the College of Cardinals is not a particular expression of the College of Bishops, through this in some way episcopal collegiality is also still exercised [47]. According to can. 349 the College of Cardinals fulfils three functions: the election of the Pope, in accordance with the norms of a special law; to advise the Pope collegially in the Consistory on questions of major importance; to help the Roman Pontiff individually offering their own labour in the care of the universal Church. On the level of the composition of the College and the exercise of its functions the most important innovations were introduced by Pope Paul VI, that is to say the fact that the patriarchs of the Eastern Church can also be chosen as cardinals [48], as well as the exclusion from the Conclave – and therefore from the election of the new Pope – of all cardinals who have completed their eightieth year of age [49].

The CIC dedicates only two canons to the Roman Curia, specifically cans. 360 and 361. From these, interpreted in the light of the teaching of Pope John Paul II [50], the following definition can easily be deduced: "The Roman Curia is the totality of the dicasteries and organisms which assist the Roman Pontiff in the exercise of his supreme pastoral office for the good and the service of the universal Church and particular Churches, with which the unity of the faith and the communion of the people of God is strengthened and the mission of the Church in the world promoted" [51]. In this not simply bureaucratic-administrative, but eminently pastoral, sense are also to

---

[44] In this regard cf. P. Krämer, *Kirchenrecht II*, op. cit., pp. 116-118; W. Plöchl, *Geschichte des Kirchenrechts*, 5 Bde., Wien-München, 1960-1970, Bd. I, pp. 319-323; Bd. II, pp. 94-99; Bd. III, pp. 128-143.

[45] Cf. can. 353, which distinguishes three forms of Consistory: ordinary, extraordinary and solemn.

[46] Cf. can. 230 of the CIC/1917 and the use Pope Paul VI makes of the term (cf. AAS 61 [1969] p. 436).

[47] Cf. AAS 71 (1979), p. 1449; AAS 72 (1980), p. 646 and the commentary of O. Stoffel in MK can. 351/2.

[48] Cf. Paul VI, MP *Ad purpuratorum Patrum*, in: AAS 57 (1965), p. 295ff. and can. 350 §1.

[49] Cf. Paul VI, CA *Romano Pontifici eligendo*, in: AAS 67 (1975), pp. 609-645. Can. 354 on the other hand speaks only of the renunciation of the office recovered for those who have completed 75 years.

[50] Cf. the CA *Pastor Bonus*, in: AAS 80 (1988), pp. 841-912.

[51] G. Ghirlanda, *Curia romana*, in: NDDC, pp. 326-329, here p. 326.

be understood the functions of the Secretariat of State or Papal Secretariat[52] and the nine Congregations[53] which compose it.

Papal Legates are ecclesiastics, generally endowed with the order of the episcopate, to which the Pope stably gives the office of personally representing him "either to particular Churches in various countries or regions, or at the same time to States and to public Authorities" (can. 362). Among them excell the nuncios, who have the rank of ambassador and *ipso iure* are deans of the diplomatic corps. According to cans. 364 and 365 the Pontifical Legates must not replace diocesan bishops, but rather protect and reinforce their authority, promoting their more effective bond of communion with the Holy See.

2.2 THE INSTITUTIONAL ORGANS OF PARTICULAR CHURCHES

A) PARTICULAR CHURCHES AND DIOCESES

The rediscovery of local Churches[54], that took place within the theological reflection of the last thirty years on the missions, and especially the conciliar lesson on the particular Church[55], is reflected in both of the preliminary canons (cans. 368-374) of the title that the CIC dedicates to particular Churches and the authority constitued in them. In fact, already in can. 368, the first of the whole section, the effort of the ecclesiastical legislator to effect a synthesis between LG 23,1 (containing the definitory formula of the universal Church-particular Church relationship)[56], and CD 11,1, containing on the other hand the definition of Diocese, as the principal institutional form of an *ecclesia particularis* can be perceived[57].

This effort however only partially succeeded, because the CIC, following the Vatican Council II, does not give a legal definition of a particular Church, but only that of a Diocese, thus provoking a certain overlapping of the two ideas, notwithstanding the distinction of can. 368. In point of fact, the following can. 369, repeating CD 11,1 almost to the letter, states: "A diocese is a portion of the People of God, which is en-

---

[52]   For a brief description of its functions cf. O. Corral, *Segretaria di Stato o papale*, in: NDDC, pp. 979-980.

[53]   For an early study of their respective functions cf. O. Corral-G. Pasutto, *Congregazioni della Curia Romana*, in: NDDC, pp. 278-285; P. Krämer, *Kirchenrecht II*, op. cit., pp. 119-124.

[54]   In this regard cf. especially P. Colombo, *La teologia della Chiesa locale*, in: *La Chiesa locale*, a cura di A. Tessarolo, Bologna 1970, pp. 7-38.

[55]   Although the Vatican Council II sometimes uses the term *Chiesa locale* even to indicate Patriarchates and Dioceses, (cf. UR 14,1; LG 23,4; AG 27,1) in fact in order to indicate a portion of the People of God starting not from the territory but from the rite, from theological-spiritual and cultural tradition, as well as the government, it gives preference to the expression *Chiesa particolare*; cf. G. Ghirlanda, *Il diritto nella Chiesa mistero di comunione,* op. cit., pp. 42-43.

[56]   On the constitutional significance of the formula *in quibus et ex quibus*, already fully illustrated in section 3.3 of the first chapter, and on the relationship of reciprocal immanence between the universal Church and the particular Churches, cf. also H. De Lubac, *Les Églises particulières dans l'Église universelle,* Paris 1971.

[57]   With this expression the conciliar Decree *Christus Dominus* always indicates the Diocese or comparable institutions, cf. H. Müller, *Diözesane und quasi-diözesane Teilkirchen*, in: HdbkathKR, pp. 329-335, here p. 330.

trusted to a Bishop to be nurtured by him, with the cooperation of the presbyterium, in such a way that, remaining close to its pastor and gathered by him through the Gospel and the Eucharist in the Holy Spirit, it constitutes a particular Church. In this Church, the one, holy, catholic and apostolic Church of Christ truly exists and functions". According to this definition there are three constitutive elements of the institution "Diocese": the portion of the People of God, the Bishop and the presbyterate. This signifies the following[58]. First of all the Diocese is not, as the Greek etymology of the word would lead us to believe, an administrative district of the universal Church, but rather a *Populo Dei portio*, that is a community of the baptised that profess the Catholic faith itself together with their pastor. In second place the Bishop, as the principle and foundation of the unity or *communio* of this portion of the People of God, makes the same an ecclesial subject in which the territory has only a determinative function, in contrast with the Word and Sacrament which, together with the Charism (even if in a different measure), are the primary elements of the same community. In third and last place, for the proclamation of the Gospel and for the celebration of the Sacraments, and in particular the Eucharist, the Bishop structurally has need of a presbyterate. In fact, the latter is the constitutive element of the particular Church that allows the retracing of an analogy in the same with the constitutional structure of the universal Church.

These three elements of the definition of the Code of Diocese can however be realised also in other juridical figures, different from the Diocese[59]. The criteria with which a particular Church can be given on of these juridical forms, distinct from the Diocese, are only partitially fixed by the ecclesiastical legislator. In fact in can. 372, alongside the territory and the rite, it speaks only vaguely of other similar qualities, in order to resolve a little by little with clarity such a delicate ecclesiological problem, especially if we think of the discussions stirred up around the theological-juridical nature of personal prelatures, in any case not mentioned by can. 368 and placed by the ecclesiastical legislator of 1983 immediately after the normative on the faithful and before those relating to their associations[60]. It is certain that even a territorial prelature, and for greater reason all the other juridical forms of the portions of the People of God comparable with this[61], can be defined as particular Churches only if whoever governs them is a Bishop.

---

[58] Cf. in this regard H. Müller, *Bistum*, in: *Staatslexikon*, op. cit., Bd.I, pp. 821-828.

[59] Cf. E. Corecco, *Chiesa particolare*, in: Digesto (4 Ed.), Torino 1989, pp. 17-20; Idem, *Iglesia particular e Iglesia universal en el surco de la doctrina del Concilio Vaticano II*, in: *Iglesia universal e Iglesias particulares*. IX Simposio internacional de Teologia, Pamplona 1989, pp. 81-99.

[60] From this definitive positioning it is legitimate to deduce that personal prelatures are not comparable to particular Churches, as the Fathers of the Plenary observe, cf. Communicationes 14 (1982), pp. 201-203.

[61] For a brief description of the juridical profiles of these institutions comparable to a territorial prelature, that is to say the territorial abbacy, the apostolic vicariate, the apostolic prelature, the apostolic administration, the military ordinate and the personal particular Church, cf. G. Ghirlanda, *Il diritto nella Chiesa mistero di comunione*, op. cit., pp. 529-530; Idem, *La Chiesa particolare: natura e tipologia*, in: Mon. Eccl. 115 (1990), pp. 551-568.

B) BISHOP AND PRESBYTERATE

The definition of Diocese just illustrated, as has already been revealed, is taken from the conciliar decree *Christus Dominus* and as such is the first that can be found in an official document of the Ecclesiastical Magisterium. If the Fathers of the Vatican Council II felt the necessity of giving a definition of Diocese it was certainly not for ecclesiastical organisation reasons, but due to the fact that the theological and juridical image of the bishop had emerged profoundly renewed from the labours of editing the Dogmatic Constitution on the Church[62].

Indeed, if it is true that the theology of the episcopate developed in detail by the Fathers of the Council is not always perfectly balanced and still suffers from a certain reaction to preceding, strongly papist, ecclesiologies, nevertheless the articles 18-29 of the second chapter of *Lumen gentium* offer a solid basis for understanding the ecclesiastical role and pastoral function of the bishop. This role and this function are inscribed with such a depth in the communitarian structure and the missionary nature of the Church that the *Directorium de pastorali ministerio Episcoporum*[63], published by the *Sacred Congregation for Bishops* on the 22 February 1973, places at the base of the *principia fundamentalia* on the episcopal ministry the axiom according to which the nature and the mission of the Church determine and define the nature and the mission of the episcopate itself. The bishop is therefore the focal point of the particular Church founded *ad imaginem Ecclesiae universalis*, because the office in which he is invested renders possible the reciprocal immanence between the universal Church and particular Churches[64]. This signifies two things. By virtue of the fullness of the sacrament of orders the bishop is a *homo apostolicus*, that is an authentic witness and a master of apostolic tradition in the *portio Populi Dei* entrusted to him; in this sense he guarantees the immanence of the universal Church in the particular Church in which he exercises his *sacra potestas*. In his quality as member of the *corpus Episcoporum* the Bishop is also a *homo catholicus* that is called to have a part in the sollicitude for all the Churches[65]. In this opposite direction he guarantees the immanence of the particular Church in the universal.

The substance of this new ecclesiological image of the Bishop was accepted in the CIC of 1983. In point of fact, can. 375 §2 affirms that "By their episcopal consecration, Bishops receive, together with the office of sanctifying, the offices also of teaching and ruling". In consequence of this can. 379 prescribes for Bishops designate to receive episcopal consecration prior to taking possession of their office and can. 381 explicitly affirms that in the particular Church entrusted to him the Bishop possesses "all the ordinary, proper and immediate power required for the exercise of his

---

[62] For a deepened study of the ecclesiological role of the Bishop cf. L. Gerosa, *L'évêque dans les documents de Vatican II et le nouveau Code du droit canonique*, in: *Visages de l'Église. Cours d'ecclesiologie*, a cura di P. De Laubier, Fribourg 1989, pp. 73-89.

[63] The Latin text of this directory, known also as the *Directorium Ecclesiae imago*, is to be found in: EV, Vol. IV, pp. 1226-1487.

[64] For a fuller explanation of this principle cf. L. Gerosa, *Diritto ecclesiale e pastorale*, Torino 1991, pp. 77-90.

[65] Cf. 2 Cor 11,28.

pastoral office"[66]. Nevertheless, the notion of episcopal power with which the ecclesiastical legislator works is not totally identical to that developed in detail by the Vatican Council II, above all because its synodal element undergoes a partial mutilation[67]. In fact, in the CIC a corporative conception of the presbyterate substantially extraneous to the concept of synodality dominates.

The conciliar notion of presbyterate can be synthesised thus: priests, as the "necessary collaborators and counsellors" (PO 7,1) of their Bishop, with him "form one presbyterate in the Diocese" (PO 8,1). "Called to serve the People of God" these "constitute together with their Bishop one unique presbyterate destined for different offices" (LG 28,2). The particular qualification of *necessarios adiutores et consiliaros* attributed by the Vatican Council II to priests signifies on the one hand that the episcopal ministry is not just personal but essentially synodal and that therefore the Bishop needs the presbyterate in order to fulfil his pastoral task in the particular Church; on the other hand the ministry of the priesthood without any specific link with its Bishop would be crippled. The insistence of the conciliar Fathers on the fact that the priests together with their Bishop form a unique presbyterate in the Diocese means then that this institution is neither a universal college parallel to the College of Bishops, nor a simple corporation the Bishop is faced with, as for example the Cathedral Chapter, because he himself forms part of the presbyterate and is its head. In the conciliar ecclesiology the presbyterate is therefore a fundamental and constitutive institution of the particular Church, hierarchically structured and, precisely because made in this way, capable of witnessing simultaneously to the synodal dimension of episcopal power and the analogous structure of the particular Church with the universal Church[68].

In the CIC, as has already been observed, a corporative conception of the presbyterate predominates instead. In point of fact, on the one hand priests are not considered as necessary cooperators of their own Bishop, but simply as his faithful (*fidi*) collaborators (can. 245 §2). On the other the presbyteral Council, a typical expression institutionally representative of the presbyterate, is defined as the senate of the Bishop (can. 495 §1). For the rest the conciliar doctrine has been accepted. Also in the CIC there are two conditions in order to be a member of the presbyterate: the first is sacramental, that is to say to have received the sacrament of Orders; the second non sacramental, that is to say to have received the charge of an ecclesiastical office. Moreover the members of the presbyterate that are incardinated in the same diocese in which they exercise their office are called ordinary and those that are not incardinated in this extraordinary[69].

---

[66] On how on the level of these three points the lesson of the Vatican Council II has certainly been accepted by the new Code, cf. W. Aymans, *Der Leitungsdienst des Bischofs im Hinblick auf die Teilkirche*, in: AfkKR 153 (1984), pp. 25-55, above all p. 37.

[67] On the whole of the question, cf. L. Gerosa, *Der Bischof: seine Bestellung, seine geistliche Vollmacht und die christliche Verkündigung in Europa. Kirchenrechtliche Erwägungen*, in: ET-Bulletin der Europäischen Gesellschaft für katholische Theologie 3 (1992), pp. 66-94.

[68] For a deeper study of this structure of the Presbyterate cf. O. Saier, *Die hierarchische Struktur des Presbyteriums*, in: AfrKR 136 (1967), pp. 341-391; E. Corecco, *Sacerdozio e presbiterio nel CIC*, in: Servizio Migranti 11 (1983), pp. 354-372.

[69] On this point cf.; P. Krämer, *Kirchenrecht II*, op. cit., pp. 79-81.

The irrenounceable character of the presbyterate and the dynamic of necessary reciprocity between Bishop and priests flourishes indirectly from can. 495 §1, where the constitution is prescribed in an obligatory fashion in every Diocese of the presbyteral Council that, together with the pastoral Council and above all with the diocesan Synod, represents a typical institutional expression of the synodal character of the particular Church.

c) DIOCESAN SYNOD, PASTORAL COUNCIL AND PRESBYTERAL COUNCIL

Alongside the provincial Council[70], the diocesan Synod is the only synodal institution that, while having assumed in the life of the particular Churches different functions according to the frequency with which it is celebrated and depending on the cultural and ecclesial characteristics of the historical moment in which it was called, has endured during the whole history of the Latin Church[71]. Emerging towards the middle of the second century this canonical institution has therefore known a constant juridical evolution up until the Pio-Benedictine codification[72]. According to the norms of the 1917 Code (cans. 356-362) the diocesan Synod is an assembly of clerics and religious of the diocese, presided over by the bishop himself and having as its principal function that of advising the bishop concerning the promulgation of norms or general provisions in the ordering of the government of the particular Church entrusted to his pastoral care. This assembly is not however a true and proper legislative organ and its members express a *votum consultivum* of which the bishop takes heed in his initiatives as the only legislator in the particular Church entrusted to him and in his activity of government of the same.

After the Fathers of the Vatican Council II had on their part expressed the active desire to see this ancient institution of the diocesan Synod assume "renewed vigour, so that the growth of religion and the maintenance of discipline in the various Churches may increasingly be more effectively provided for in accordance with the needs of each time" (CD 36), the Code of Canon Law of 1983 gives to the same a new juridical statute (cans. 460-468).

The most important innovation, introduced by this normative of the Code in the wake of the important synodal experience undergone by different particular Churches in the post-conciliar period, is certainly constituted from the fact that now the lay faithful also are chosen or elected as members with full title of the diocesan Synod (cans. 460 and 463 §1 no.5). The faithful of every state of ecclesial life (laity, clerics, religious) are therefore members of the synodal assembly of a particular Church. In this way the particular Church compared with the diocesan Synod is no longer the recipient of the provisions and pastoral directives decided by the synodal assembly,

---

[70] The importance of this form of Council for the primitive Church is deduced from c. 5 of the Council of Nicea (352), that prescribed its celebration twice a year, cf. W. Plöchl, *Geschichte des Kirchenrechts*, op. cit., Vol. I, pp. 150-152.

[71] Cf. E. Corecco, *Sinodalità*, op. cit., p. 1470.

[72] In this regard, cf. R. Puza, *Diözesansynode und synodale Struktur. Ein Beitrag zur Ekklesiologie des neuen CIC*, in: Theologische Quartalschrift 166 (1986), pp. 40-48 and above all pp. 40-43.

but this is itself a protagonist subject of the same [73]. This clear ecclesiological datum, together with the fact that any problem can be submitted to the free discussion of the members of the diocesan Synod (can. 465), impresses upon the canonical institution of the diocesan Synod a more important pastoral significance than that of the other diocesan councils, even if the Code only determines its purposes in a generic manner: "to lend assistance to the diocesan bishop for the good of the whole diocesan community" (can. 460). This pastoral importance is deduced also from the fact that on the one hand in the individual particular Churches the diocesan Synod is nowadays celebrated only when "the diocesan bishop, after consulting the council of priests, judges that the circumstances suggest it" (can. 461 §1), and on the other in his environment the bishop – without whom there is no synod (cans. 462 §§1 and 2 and 468 §2) – fully expresses his authority as legislator for his own diocese (can. 466) and consequently the activity of the synodal assembly itself leads in some way to the statutisation of general norms and provisions which complete the legislation that determines the particular Church [74]. The pre-eminent place of the diocesan Synod in comparison with the other diocesan councils is therefore unquestionable, so much so that – according to the pastoral directory for bishops – "during the synod .... the priests' council and the pastoral council can be constituted or renewed, and the members of the commissions and offices of the diocesan curia be elected" [75].

Among these institutions, nearer to the new ecclesiological vision of the diocesan Synod, at least on the level of composition and thus as a concrete expression of the communion existing in the particular Church, is the pastoral Council, which basically represents a particular institutional concretisation of the diocesan Synod, at one and the same time greatly stable ("to be convened at least once a year", states can. 514 §2) and with a greater agility under the missionary profile or immediate pastoral efficacy [76]. More expressive of the hierarchical element of the *communio Ecclesiae* is on the other hand the revitalised presbyteral Council, already in use in the early days of the history of the Church and now made known from the positioning of the presbyterate – of which the bishop is head – at the very heart of the constitutional structure of the particular Church. In point of fact, by dint of the fundamental unity of the sacrament

---

[73] Cf. G. Spinelli, *Organismi di partecipazione nella struttura della Chiesa locale*, in: Actes V CIDC, Vol. 2, pp. 627-634, here p. 629; cf. also L. Gerosa, *Les conseils diocésains: structures "synodales" et moments de "co-responsabilité" dans le service pastorale*, in: Actes VII CIDC, Vol. II, pp. 781-794.

[74] Agreeing in this opinion: F. Coccopalmerio, *Il sinodo diocesano*, in: *Raccolta di scritti in onore di P. Fedele*, a cura di G. Barberini, Vol. 1, Perugia 1984, pp. 406-416 and in particular p. 408, as well as P. Valdrini, *Les communautés hiérarchiques et leur organisation*, in: *Droit canonique*, a cura di P. Valdrini, Paris 1989, pp. 186-187. In contrast to what happens with a particular Council (cans. 439-446) the decrees of a diocesan Synod when they are approved by the Bishop do not have any need for their definition of obligatoreity of any subsequent *recognitio* and are communicated to the episcopal Conference only with the aim of information and to favour the growth of the communion (can. 467); cf. the commentary on cans. 466-468 in: *Codice di diritto canonico. Edizione bilingue commentata*, a cura di P. Lombardia-J. Arrieta, Roma 1986, p. 366.

[75] EV, Vol. IV, p. 1411.

[76] Cf. AG 30 and the commentary of F. Coccopalmerio, *Il sinodo diocesano*, op. cit., p.416.

of orders, administered in different degrees, the presbyteral Council by its nature "is a form of institutionalised manifestation of the fraternity existing between the priests" and as such "at the service of the one and the same mission of the Church"[77].

The different ecclesiological value of the two principal diocesan councils, here only briefly emphasised, does not allow placing them as alternatives or opposing them in a concurrent way. A clear confirmation of this first of all is the fact that in the area of their pastoral purposes the ecclesiastical legislator has not succeeded in fixing in a specific way a clear-cut differentiation of their respective competences, as can easily be deduced from the comparison between can. 495 §1 and can. 511. In second place both councils enjoy in principle a consultative vote and even in the seven cases in which the bishop, before making a decision, is obliged by law (cans. 500 and 502) to consult the presbyteral Council it is not easy to perceive the stringent ecclesiological motive by which the lay faithful must be excluded from this consultation[78]. Consequently it is to be recognised that both councils are by nature consultative and in the pastoral field the definitive decision how the ultimate responsibility for the same stays exclusively with the Bishop to whom that determined particular Church has been entrusted. Different on the other hand is the type of approach of the object in question starting from the different specific ecclesial vocations of the greater part of the members of the two councils as well as the different pastoral relationship with Word and Sacrament which determine the two concrete forms of Christian priesthood.

In the logic of the ecclesial communion these differences are in a relationship of interaction and reciprocal integration. For this reason the two organs of government cannot work efficaciously on the pastoral level if not in constant and strict collaboration; nevertheless, from the institutional point of view, an incorporation of the presbyteral Council into the pastoral Council is possible, as for example in the Diocese of Rottenburg-Stuttgart[79]. Such a strict collaboration is not only ecclesiologically unexceptionable but also necessary in order to overcome every temptation of clericalisation of diocesan pastorality.

D) COLLEGE OF CONSULTORS AND CATHEDRAL CHAPTER

Making its own the conciliar invitation of CD 27, the ecclesiastical legislator of 1983 places a new consultative organ alongside the presbyteral Council: the College of Consultors whose members are freely chosen and appointed by the diocesan Bishop "from among the members of the council of priests" (can. 502 §1). This college has a consultative vote relating to the appointment and removal of the financial administrator of the Diocese (can. 494) and in the more important acts of financial administration of the same (can. 1277), but its role becomes decisive both during the sede vacante, a period in which it must govern the particular Church until the appointment of a diocesan Administrator (can. 419), and in the procedure for the designation of the new bishop (can. 377 §3).

---

[77] Synod of Bishops, *Documento Ultimis temporibus (30.XI.1971)*, in: EV, Vol. 4, nos. 1226-1227.

[78] On the whole question cf. H. Schmitz, *Die Konsultationsorgane des Diozesansbischofs*, in: HdbkathKR, pp. 352-364, especially p. 362.

[79] Cf. R. Puza, *Mitverantwortung in der Kirche*, in: *Staatslexikon*, op. cit., pp. 1188-1192, especially p. 1191.

Given the importance the Cathedral Chapter has had historically in Europe, "The Bishops' Conference can determine that the functions of the College of consultors be entrusted to the cathedral Chapter" (can. 502 §3). The latter compared with the other diocesan consultative organisations enjoys a greater autonomy because it is not presided over by the diocesan Bishop but by one of its members (can. 507 §1). However this does not necessarily mean that this old canonical institution is exportable, such as it is (cans. 503-510), also in the new particular Churches, above all as far as relates to the role it plays – in accordance with the Concordats of the Holy See with the German speaking European countries – in the election of the new diocesan bishop. In fact, while being clearly affirmed in can. 377 §1 that "free pontifical appointment" and "pontifical confirmation" represent two different but equivalent ways of proceeding in the choice of bishops in the Catholic Church of the Latin tradition[80], the model represented in this field by the Cathedral Chapter is inadequate under the ecclesiological profile for at least two reasons. First of all the juridical forms in which this has been embodied up until now do not guarantee the full freedom of the Catholic Church versus the State, above all where the members of the chapter are appointed by the state authorities[81], and ends up thus often creating conflicts in the interpretations of the various concordatory norms belonging to them[82]. In second place, where it exists, the cathedral Chapter is no longer, both under the juridical profile and under the pastoral, an organ expressive of the joint responsibility of the diocesan clergy not to mention all of the lay faithful of a particular Church[83]. In the search for new institutional models, as for example that of an electoral Synod for every particular Church[84], it will be necessary to keep the following in mind. The choice of bishops is a process constituted by a double movement: the first finds its apex in the *designatio personae* (the designation of the person upon whom the episcopal ministry should be conferred); the second finds its apex in the *collatio ufficii* (the conferral of the ecclesiastical office on the designated person). The first movement is of an eminently elective nature and therefore embodies first of all the principle of joint responsibility and then that of synodality[85].

---

[80]   Agreeing with this interpretation : R. Potz, *Bischofsernennungen. Stationen, die zum heutigen Zustand geführt haben*, in: *Zur Frage der Bischofsernennungen in der römisch-katholischen Kirche*, hrsg. von G. Greshake, München-Zürich 1991, pp. 17-50, here p. 22; H. Müller, *Aspekte des Codex Iuris Canonici 1983*, in: ZevKR 29 (1984), pp. 527-546, here p. 534.

[81]   Cf. H. Maritz, *Das Bischofswahlrecht in der Schweiz*, St. Ottilien 1977, pp. 47-49; P. Leisching, *Kirche und Staat in den Rechtsordnungen Europas. Ein Überlick*, Freiburg i. Br. 1973, p. 83.

[82]   Typical in this sense is the Coira case: cf. H. Maritz, *Erwägungen zum Churer "Bischofswahlrecht"*, in: *Fides et ius*. Festschrift für G. May, hrsg. von W. Aymans-A. Egler-J. Listl, Regensburg 1991, pp. 491-505.

[83]   Cf. CD 27,2 and PO 7.

[84]   The most convincing models are those developed in this perspective by: E. Corecco, *Note sulla Chiesa particulare e sulle strutture della diocesi di Lugano*, in: Civitas 24 (1968/69), pp. 616-635 and pp. 730-743; H. Schmitz, *Plädoyer für Bischofs- und Pfarrerwahl. Kirchenrechtliche Überlegungen zu ihrer Möglichkeit und Ausformung*, in: TThZ 79 (1970), pp. 230-249.

[85]   Cf. H. Müller, *Der Anteil der Laien an der Bischofswahl*, Amsterdam 1977, p. 242; P. Krämer, *Bischofswahl heute – im Bistum Trier*, in: TThZ 89 (1980), pp. 243-247, here p.

The second movement on the other hand is of an eminently confirmative nature, in order to realise the *communio plena* with the Pope and the other members of the College of bishops. In this sense in this is embodied first of all the principle of synodality in its indispensible unity with the primatial ministry of the successor of Peter[86]. As much the first as the second movement efficaciously concurs with the realisation of the same end in the measure in which it remains structurally open to the action of the Holy Spirit[87]. This means that in the choice of a bishop neither the Pope nor the interested particular Church can be faced with an accomplished fact or an obligatory choice, but – although different one from the other – every *modus procedendi*[88] must guarantee to both subjects a real margin of free choice.

E) DIOCESAN CURIA AND BODIES REPRESENTATIVE OF THE BISHOP

According to the teaching of the Vatican Council II the diocesan Curia (cans. 469-494) must be "so organised that it may be a useful medium for the bishop, not only for diocesan administration, but also for pastoral activity" (CD 27,4). The field of action of the diocesan Curia has thus been greatly extended because this has now to collaborate "in directing pastoral action, in providing for the administration of the diocese, and in exercising judicial power" (can. 469). For this reason in the new Code the new figure of the "Moderator of the Curia" was introduced who "Under the Bishop's authority, is to coordinate activities concerning administrative matters and to ensure that the others who belong to the Curia properly fulfil the offices entrusted to them" (can. 473 §2). If there are no particular reasons for appointing another priest to this important office, it should be assumed by the Vicar General or the Chancellor[89]. While the appointment of a Moderator of the Curia is facultative, that of the Vicar General is obligatory (can. 475), given that the latter is not only the first and most important collaborator of the Bishop but is also invested with ordinary vicarious power (can. 131 §2). He must be a priest (can. 478 §1) and totally dependent on the Bishop, in the sense that the latter appoints him and removes him freely (can. 477 §1) and the office of Vicar General ceases when the Diocese becomes a sede vacante (cans. 417 and 418 §2).

For the exercise of his judicial power the diocesan Bishop must appoint a Judicial Vicar or Officialis, distinct from the Vicar General (can. 1420 §1). The Judicial Vicar is also invested with ordinary vicarious power, but his autonomy in relation to the diocesan Bishop is greater and his charge does not cease even when the see is vacant (can. 1420 §5). For the administration of the goods of the Diocese the Bishop must on the other hand appoint a diocesan Financial Administrator, "expert in financial matters and of truly outstanding integrity" (can. 494 §1). In order to coordinate the diocesan

---

243.

[86] Cf. A. Carrasco Ruoco, *Le primat de l'évêque de Rome. Étude sur la cohérence ecclésiologique et canonique du primat de jurisdiction*, Fribourg 1990, pp. 211-220.

[87] This is the conclusion of the commentary on the biblical image of the choice of the Apostle Matthias (Acts 1,15-26) of: J. Ratzinger, *Zur Gemeinschaft gerufen. Kirche heute verstehen*, Freiburg i Br. 1991, p. 39.

[88] For a detailed analysis of all these different procedures cf. L. Gerosa, *Die Bischofsbestellung in ökumenischer und kirchenrechtlicher Sicht*, in: Catholica 46 (1992), p. 70-86.

[89] In some Curias the role of Moderator has for some time been entrusted to a general Secretary, cf. AAS 69 (1977) pp. 5-18.

and super-parochial pastoral activity the diocesan Bishop appoints for a determined period vicars forane or deans (cans. 553-555), whose office is not bound to that of parish priest of a determined parish (can. 554 §1) and can be regulated by a juridical statute or directory developed by the Council of Priests [90].

F) PARISH AND PARISH PRIEST

Even if the concepts of parish priest and parish are not defined directly by the Fathers of the Council, the principal contents of their definition are easily deducible from the three following conciliar texts: art. 42 of the Constitution *Sacrosanctum Concilium* on the liturgy, where the parish is considered as a *coetus fidelium* with a pre-eminent place among the various communities that the bishop must constitute in his diocese; art. 30 of the Decree *Christus Dominus* on the pastoral office of bishops in the Church, where this is considered as the *determinata pars Diocesis* which is entrusted to a parish priest, as one of the principal collaborators of the Bishop; and finally art. 10 of the Decree *Apostolicam Actuositatem* on the apostolate of the laity, where the parish is pointed out as an *exemplum praecipuum apostolatus communitarii*. The simultaneous and convergent application of the three ecclesiological principles, underlying these conciliar texts [91], allows the identification in the conciliar notion of parish of the three following constitutive elements: the community of the faithful, the guidance of a priest, the relationship of belonging to a particular Church by means of the obedience of the latter to the authority of his bishop. These three constitutive elements make the parish a unitary subject of a mission, identified and restricted as an individual ecclesial community by a fourth non constitutive but exclusively determinative element: the territory, in which this *congregatio fidelium* is established.

In the ecclesiological vision just described, the constitutional positioning of the parish is evidently relativised, insofar as it is only one of the possible juridical forms of the different Eucharistic communities of a particular Church. A similar relativisation of the parish is a dutiful canonical type specification – imposed nevertheless by the conciliar ecclesiology of the *communio* – of a pastoral type demand, already underlined years ago by Karl Rahner, to limit the rigour of the so-called *Pfarrprinzip* of the old Code with a just consideration also of the *Standesprinzip* and of the *Freigruppenprinzip* [92]. This specification also represents a more adequate juridical response to the sociological evolution of the parish, which can certainly still constitute an ecclesial form of the unity of socio-cultural life, but this normally no longer coincides with territorial unity [93].

---

[90]   On the general statute on Vicars forane or Deans, cf. J. Diaz, *Vicario foraneo*, in: NDDC, pp. 1121-1128; for a more detailed study of the organs of the diocesan Curia, cf. H. Müller, *Die Diözesankurie*, in HdbkathKR, pp. 364-376.

[91]   Cf. LG 28,2; SC 42,2; AA 10,2 and the commentary in L. Gerosa, *Diritto ecclesiale e pastorale*, pp. 114-115.

[92]   Cf. K. Rahner, *Friedliche Erwägungen über das Pfarrprinzip*, in: *Schriften zur Theologie*, Vol. II, Zürich-Einsiedeln-Köln 1968, pp. 299-337.

[93]   For an analysis of the sociological evolution of the territorial parish, cf. N. Greinacher, *Sociologia della parrocchia*, in: AA.VV. *La Chiesa locale, Diocesi e parrocchia sotto inchiesta*, Brescia 1973, pp. 133-166 and in particular pp. 133-139.

The conciliar teaching on the parish and the parish priest, summarised briefly here, has been accepted for the most part in the CIC. In point of fact, the first paragraph of can. 515 states: "A parish is a certain community of Christ's faithful stably established within a particular Church, whose pastoral care, under the authority of the diocesan bishop, is entrusted to a parish priest as its proper pastor". There are three consitutive elements of major prominence in the juridical concept of parish here expressed: the *communitas christifidelium*, the *Ecclesia particularis* in which this specific community of the faithful is stably established, and finally the parish priest as its *pastor propius*.

The specific characteristics of the first element, that of the community of the faithful, are highlighted by cans. 516 §2 and 518. Can. 516 §2 shows how the parish is only one of the possible forms of diocesan pastoral organisation. There is here a clear acceptance on the part of the ecclesiastical legislator of the already indicated constitutional relativisation of the parish, adopted by the Vatican Council II and confirmed by the Pastoral Directory for Bishops, in which is rightly compiled an indicative list of the various forms of diocesan pastoral organisation[94]. The ecclesiastical legislator himself however evaluates the parish under another point of view: in comparison with the other forms of Eucharistic communities this represents that juridical form of *aggregatio fidelium* arising precisely from the specific gathering force of the Eucharist, celebrated in a given place or in a given socio-cultural environment. In this sense this is an institutional type Eucharistic community. The expression *stabiliter constituta* of can. 515 §1 should not be interpreted just as underlining the stability of the parish in comparison with the provisory character of the quasi-parish defined in can. 516 §1, but rather as an indication of the juridical specificity of the parish: this is the institutional, fixed and hierarchical form of the Eucharistic community of a particular Church and therefore different from the juridical, variable and of charismatic origin forms of the Eucharistic communites known under the name of associations or ecclesial movements. While in the first form prevails the aggregative and structuring force of the sacrament, the Eucharist celebrated in a given place or in a determined environment, in the latter form the aggregative force of the originating charism prevails[95]. Can. 518 specifies moreover that the parish, while being as a rule defined by territorial criteria, can be fixed also according to personal criteria. The reason for which a community of the faithful can be constituted as a personal parish can be the rite, the language, the nationality. Can 518 does not point it out however in a taxative way given that, as no. 174 of the Pastoral Directory for Bishops teaches, a parish can be instituted with the personal (and not territorial) criterion even on the basis of the sociological homogeneity of those who form part of it (*ex unitate quadam sociali membrorum suorum*) or because objectively requested for the good of souls. The second constitutive element of the notion in the Code of parish, that is the fact that this be a *pars* and not an autonomous entity of the particular Church, is more greatly specified under the ecclesiological aspect by can. 529 §2, which normatively fixes the duty of the parish

---

[94]   Cf. EV, Vol. 4, pp. 1432-1425.

[95]   This interpretation corresponds not only to the semantic evolution of the term *paroikia*, but also to the historical development of this canonical institution; cf. A. Longhitano. *La parrocchia fra storia, teologia e diritto*, in: AA.VV., *La parrocchia e le sue strutture*, Bologna 1987, pp. 5-27.

priest to collaborate *cum proprio Episcopo et cum diocesis presbyterio* so that all of the faithful feel members of the Church and are helped to live according to the principle of the *communio*, recalled by can. 209 §1 as an obligation to which every believer is always bound.

The principle of *communio* also directs the way with which the *mens legislatoris* conceives the function of the third constitutive element of the notion in the Code of parish: the parish priest, as its own special pastor. In point of fact, the new Code not only envisages in can. 517 the possibility that the pastoral care of one or more parishes can be entrusted *in solidum* to various priests, but repeating no. 30 of the conciliar Decree *Christus Dominus* gives a richer ecclesiological content to the figure of the parish priest in comparison with the sterile and formal one of the old can. 451. Both, can. 519, that speaks of the threefold *munus* of the parish priest, and can. 528, which specifies the contents of his educative and sanctifying function, present all these aspects of the function of the parish priest as constitutive particular attributes of that *communitas christifidelium* which is the parish. The latter appears thus as the concrete institutionalisation of the community of faith generated by the proclamation of the Word of God and the celebration of the common Eucharist, presided over by the parish priest in his quality as pastor who takes the place of the Bishop.

The evaluation of the communitarian element of the parish, adopted by the Vatican Council II, is finally juridically concretised by the ecclesiastical legislator of 1983 recognising *ipso iure* the juridical personality of the community of the faithful that is the parish (can. 515 §3). Rather, more that that it witnesses to the fundamental ecclesiological element which is at the very origin of this ecclesial institution, that is the Eucharistic assembly, which is the true *centrum congregationis fidelium paroecialis* (can. 528 §2). The parish is therefore not just a community of the faithful, hierarchically organised around its parish priest as a *pars* of that *portio Populo Dei* which is a particular Church, but the same parish priest is its proper pastor only in as far as he presides in place of the Bishop over the Eucharistic assembly and as such can and must *moderari* (can. 528 §2) the active participation of all the faithful in the liturgy.

2.3 THE INSTITUTIONAL ORGANS OF THE GROUPINGS OF PARTICULAR CHURCHES

"From the earliest ages of the Church, bishops in charge of particular Churches, inspired by a spirit of fraternal charity and by zeal for the universal mission entrusted to the Apostles, have pooled their resources and their aspirations in order to promote both the common good and the good of individual Churches. With this end in view Synods, provincial councils and, finally, plenary councils were established in which the bishops determined on a common programme to be followed in various Churches both for teaching the truths of the faith and for regulating ecclesiastical discipline" (CD 36,1).

Conscious of the riches of this super-diocesan synodal tradition the Fathers of the Vatican Council II hoped that these would "flourish with renewed vigour" (CD 36,2), because "Bishops, as legitimate successors of the Apostles and members of the episcopal college, are bound, by institution and by Christ's command to be solicitous for the whole Church" and must therefore not only "be united among themselves" but also show "care for all the Churches" (CD 6,1).

The substance of this conciliar teaching has been accepted in cans. 431-459 of the CIC. In fact in these, notwithstanding the somewhat precarious systematic arrangement[96], the groupings or families of particular Churches and their respective organs of government are no longer considered simply as institutions at the service of the supreme ecclesiastical authority, but rather as institutional expressions of the *communio Ecclesiarum*, that is to say of the collegial relationship between bishops and the relationship of communion with the different particular Churches.

A) THE ECCLESIASTICAL PROVINCE, METROPOLITAN AND PROVINCIAL COUNCILS

Among the groupings of particular Churches, which by divine providence (LG 23,4) have constituted themselves throughout the centuries, a particular importance belongs to the ancient patriarchal or metropolitan Churches and their ecclesiastical provinces, which "enjoy their own discipline, their own liturgical usage, and their own theological and spiritual patrimony" (LG 23,4) The pastoral importance of the ecclesiastical province, formed by the particular Churches nearest to a determined territory (can. 431 §1), is underlined by the ecclesiastical legislator in a twofold way: first of all declaring that as a rule there should be no exempt Dioceses (can. 431 §2); in second place decreeing by statute that "the ecclesiastical province *ipso iure* has juridical personality" (can. 432 §2). Its organs of government are the Metropolitan and Provincial Councils (can. 432 §1).

The office of Metropolitan is bound to a determined episcopal see (can. 435) and consists in a certain authority of vigilance in the arrangement of the faith and ecclesiastical discipline to be exercised in relationship to the suffragan Dioceses (can. 436 §1). The Provincial Council, on the other hand, "enjoys the power of governance, especially legislative" (can. 445), over all "the different particular Churches in the same province" (can. 440 §1). This is celebrated "every time that, in the judgement of the majority of the diocesan bishops of the province, it is considered opportune" (can. 440 §1). It cannot however be convoked if the metropolitan see is vacant (can. 440 §2).

In the future, for a full re-evaluation of the office of Metropolitan and the pastoral role of the ecclesiastical province – a canonical institution in which the personal element and the synodal of the exercise of the *sacra potestas* are integrated together in an harmonious manner – can. 436 §2 could assume a notable importance stating: "Where the circumstances require it, the Apostolic See can give the Metropolitan special functions and power, to be determined in a particular law". Starting from this norm of the Code we could in fact find new institutional solutions both to the pastoral problems posed by mega-dioceses, which could be tranformed into ecclesiastical provinces in order to avoid for example that the figure of the diocesan Bishop be overshadowed by a plethora of auxiliary bishops, and those posed by the no less anomalous case of the groupings of totally exempt Dioceses[97].

---

[96] This opinion is confirmed both by the already revealed uncertainties of the legislator (cf. above, note 18), and by a careful analysis of the quoted norms, cf. P. Krämer, *Kirchenrecht II,* op. cit., pp. 130-147 and O. Stoffel, in: MK, can. 431/1.

[97] For example in Switzerland there is no ecclesiastical province and the Dioceses are all exempt, cf. O. Stoffel, in MK, 431/5.

B) THE ECCLESIASTICAL REGION, PLENARY COUNCIL, CONFERENCE OF BISHOPS

Alongside the ancient institution of the ecclesiastical province the Vatican Council II introduces a new juridical figure, affirming in CD 40,3 that "whenever it seems expedient", evidently of a pastoral origin, ecclesiastical provinces can be "consolidated into ecclesiastical regions, the organisation of which is to be determined by law" [98]. The advice is accepted by the ecclesiastical legislator of 1983 in can. 433 §1, which envisages in a non-obligatory way the possibility of grouping the nearest ecclesiastical provinces into ecclesiastical regions. The latter, in contrast with provinces, do not enjoy *ipso iure* juridical personality, but can however acquire it (can. 433 §2). Notwithstanding, it is up to the Conference of Bishops of a determined country and territory to propose to the Holy See the erection of an ecclesiastical region, the latter – at least in the normative of the Code in force – does not constitute the ecclesial context of the Conference of Bishops [99]. This given normative, suggested by the desire to avoid the possibility that the various nationalisms would influence the Conferences of Bishops [100], on the one hand weakens the juridical figure of the latter and on the other opens the way to other institutional anomalies [101]. Certainly the ecclesiastical region, such as it is normatively designated by the CIC, is not presided over by anyone and the assembly of its Bishops has no other powers than those granted to it in a special way by the Holy See (can. 434). Under the ecclesiological profile, and above all the practical-pastoral, it cannot be seen however what the difference is between this assembly of bishops of the same region and the Conference of Bishops [102].

The contradictory attitude of the ecclesiastical legislator faced with the new juridical figure of the ecclesiastical region becomes more greatly evident if we think that – according to can. 439 §1 – for a plenary Council we must understand the particular Council that gathers together all the particular Churches of the same Conference of Bishops. Nonetheless, it must be celebrated every time it appears necessary or useful to the same Conference of Bishops, albeit with the approval of the Holy See [103]. Even if the latter specification shows how the plenary Council is more bound to the Holy See than the provincial Council, nevertheless in its convocation and preparation

---

[98] Cf. also CD 41 and 24, as well as no. 42 of the first part of the MP *Ecclesiae Sanctae* (in: AAS 58, 1966, pp. 757-787, here pp. 774-775).

[99] It was still on the other hand in the preparatory schemas, cf. Schema Pop. Dei, cans. 185, 187 and 199; Schema CIC/1980, can. 308; Schema CIC/1982, can. 443 and the commentary of P. Krämer, *Kirchenrecht II*, op. cit., pp. 133-134.

[100] Cf. Communicationes 12 (1980), pp. 246-254; 14 (1982), pp. 187-188; 17 (1985), pp. 97-98; 18 (1986), p. 103 and the commentary of O. Stoffel in: MK. 433/1

[101] In Italy, for example, not only does the concept of ecclesiastical region used in the Statute of the CEI in art. 47 not correspond fully to the notion in the Code, but there are in point of fact 4 ecclesiastical regions (Veneto, Lombardia, Liguria and Lazio) that coincide with an ecclesiastical province; cf. G. Ghirlanda, *Regione ecclesiastica*, in NDDC, pp. 897-898, here p. 898.

[102] On this point cf. J. Listl, *Plenarkonzil und Bischofskonferenz*, in: HdbkathKR, pp. 304-324, here p. 306.

[103] For the provincial Council such approval is not on the other hand normally required, cf. cans. 440 §1 and 439 §2.

the decisive role is played by the Conference of Bishops, which it is in fact substituting in the practical organisation of the pastoral activity concerning a determined grouping of particular Churches.

As a true and proper canonical institution the Conference of Bishops is a conciliar product. Already before the Vatican Council II Conferences of Bishops existed practically everywhere and in some European countries since the XIX Century. The CIC/1917 did not in any case fix the general norms for their constitution and their purpose, even if in cans. 254 §4 and 292 §1 it draws attention to the assemblies of bishops. The first norms of universal law on the Conferences of Bishops are to be found in the MP *Ecclesiae Sanctae* of Paul VI [104], after the Vatican Council II had explicitly affirmed: 1. to hold it to be "to the highest degree helpful if in all parts of the world the bishops of each country or region would meet regularly in one body" (CD 37); 2. that such a body or Conference of Bishops "is a form of assembly in which the bishops of a certain country or region exercise their pastoral office jointly in order to enhance the benificial influence the Church offers to all" (CD 38,1); 3. the decisions of a Conference of Bishops "legitimately taken by at least two thirds of the prelates who have a deliberative vote in the conference", in some cases and once reviewed by the Holy See "have the force of juridical obligation" (CD 38,4). Notwithstanding the fact that the doctrinal debate on the theological and juridical statute of the new canonical institution is not totally closed [105], the substance of the conciliar teaching on the Conference of Bishops has been accepted in cans. 447-459. In these norms of the Code, in some aspects still to be perfected, the Conference of Bishops appears clearly as an institutional expression of the *communio Ecclesiarum*, and more precisely of the synodal dimension of the *sacra potestas* of every Bishop [106]. In point of fact, the ecclesiastical legislator seeks to avoid accurately both the danger of an individualistic exercise of the *sacra potestas* on the part of single bishops which would eliminate the intrinsic synodality of it, and the opposite danger that the Conference of Bishops assumes to such a degree each and every competence as to empty of content the personal element of the *sacra potestas* itself which every individual bishop must exercise especially in his own Diocese [107]. In order to avoid the former danger two limits are attached to the *sacra potestas* of the diocesan bishop in can. 381 §1: on the one hand – *ex iure divino* – the authority of the Pope; and on the other – *ex iure humano* and by dint of the principle of the communion – that of *alii auctoritate ecclesiasticae*, that is to say of the Conference of Bishops in the first place. In order to avoid the latter danger can. 447 speaks explicitly of "some pastoral functions". Consequently "The Bishops'

---

[104] Cf. AAS 58 (1966), pp. 692-694 and pp. 757-785.

[105] In this regard, cf. above all G. Feliciani, *Le Conferenze Episcopali,* Bologna 1974; F.J. Urrutia, *Conferentiae Episcoporum et munus docendi,* in: Periodica 76 (1987), pp. 537-667; *Natura e futuro delle conferenze episcopali. Atti del Colloquio di Salamanca* (3-8 gennaio 1988), a cura di H. Legrand-J. Manzanares-A. Garcia Y Garcia, Bologna 1988.

[106] Cf. W. Aymans, *Wesensverständnis und Zuständigkeiten der Bischofskonferenz im CIC von 1983,* in: AfkKR 152 (1983), pp. 46-61, here pp. 46-48.

[107] This opinion is fully documented by P. Krämer, *Kirchenrecht II,* op. cit., pp. 130-147; on this argument cf. also the section *Gesamtkirche und Teilkirchen,* in: J. Ratzinger, *Wesen und Auftrag der Theologie. Versuche zu ihrer Ortsbestimmung im Disput der Gegenwart,* Einsiedeln-Freiburg 1993, pp. 74-78.

Conference can make general decrees only in the cases where the universal law has so prescribed, or by special mandate of the Apostolic See" (can. 455 §1). Such decrees in order to acquire the force of law must moreover be reviewed by the Holy See (can. 455 §2). Speaking of *recognitio*, and not of *approbatio*[108], the ecclesiastical legislator indirectly underlines how it is a question of decisions and dispositions for which the Conference of Bishops carries full responsibility. Even with the approval of the Holy See it does not however have the constitution of a true and proper *ius pariculare*, because the conciliar principle of the *in quibus et ex quibus* (LG 23,1) is not applicable to the ecclesiastical region and to every other form of grouping of particular Churches. Bishops' Conferences are not intermediary instances, because between the particular and universal dimension of the one Church of Christ *non datur medium*[109]. These too, like particular Councils and Metropolitans, are still an institutional expression – albeit different in form – of the synodal element constitutive of the episcopal *sacra potestas*.

3. BRIEF CONCLUSIVE CONSIDERATIONS

The norms of the Code that regulate the exercise of the power of governance, never in the Church completely distinguishable from judicial and executive powers, embodies only partially the theological principle of reciprocal immanence between the personal and synodal element of *sacra potestas*. On this level the institutional organisations that must be rethought in their nature and restructured in their juridical configuration are different. This work cannot ignore two fundamental principles.

First of all the nature and purpose of these organs can be gathered in their essence only from within a conception of Canon Law as an intrinsic structure of the *communio Ecclesiae et Ecclesiarum*, and therefore in their multiple links with the juridical dimension of the Word of God, Sacrament and Charism, as the primary elements of the constitution of the Church.

In second place the eventual reform of their juridical configuration finds its own natural model-guide in the idea of *ablatio*, applied by Michelangelo to the work of the artist and by Saint Bonaventure to anthropology. Only in this way the reform or *ablatio* of the institutional organs of the Church become the possibility of a new *aggregatio*, because – as Cardinal Josef Ratzinger rightly affirms[110] – "the Church will always have need of new human structures of support, in order to be able to speak and operate in every historical epoch. Such ecclesiastical institutions, with their juridical configurations, far from being something bad, are on the contrary, to a certain degree, simply necessary and indispensible. But these grow old, risk presenting themselves as the most essential thing, and thus distract the gaze from what is truly essential. Because of this these must invariably once again be taken away, like scaffolding become superfluous. Reform is always newly an *ablatio*: a taking away, until the *nobilis forma*

---

[108] The latter is on the other hand required for example by can. 242 §1, for the introduction of a *Ratio institutionis sacerdotalis*, and by can. 1246 §2, for the abolition or transferral of a holy day of obligation.

[109] E. Corecco, *Ius universale-Ius particulare*, op. cit., p. 571.

[110] *Un compagnia in cammino. La Chiesa e il suo ininterrotto rinnovamento,* in: Communio 114 (1990) pp. 91-105, here p. 96.

becomes visible, the face of the Bride and together with this too the face of the Spouse himself, the living Lord".

FUNDAMENTAL BIBLIOGRAPHY

Aymans W., *Der Leitungsdienst des Bischofs im Hinblick auf die Teilkirche*, in: AfkKR 153 (1984), pp. 25-55.

Corecco E., *"Ius Universale" – "Ius Particolare"* in: Corecco E., *Canon Law and Communio. Writings on the Constitutional Law of the Church*, edited by G. Borgonovo and A. Cattaneo, Città del Vaticano 1999, pp. 387-412

Corecco E., *The Particular Church*, in: Corecco E.,*Canon Law and Communio. Writings on the Constitutional Law of the Church*, edited by G. Borgonovo and A. Cattaneo, Città del Vaticano 1999, pp. 307-315.

Gerosa L., *Rechtstheologische Grundlagen der Synodalität in der Kirche. Einleitende Erwägungen*, in: *Iuri canonico promovendo*, Festschrift für H. Schmitz zum 65. Geburtstag, hrsg. von W. Aymans-K.Th. Geringer, Regensburg 1994, pp. 35-55.

Ghirlanda G., *Il diritto nella Chiesa mistero di communione. Compendio di diritto ecclesiale*, Roma 1990.

HdbkathKR = *Handbuch des Katholischen Kirchenrechts*, hrsg. von J. Listl-H. Müller-H. Schmitz, Regensburg 1983.

Krämer P., *Kirchenrecht II. Ortskirche-Gesamtkirche*, Stuttgart-Berlin-Köln 1993.

Valdrini P., *Les communautés hierarchiques et leur organisation*, in: *Droit canonique*, a cura di P. Valdrini, Paris 1989.

INDEX OF BIBLICAL REFERENCES

INDEX OF REFERENCES TO THE CIC 1917

INDEX OF THE DOCUMENTS OF THE VATICAN COUNCIL II

INDEX OF REFERENCES TO THE CIC OF 1983

INDEX OF REFERENCES TO THE CCEO